Global Journalism Education in the 21st [...] empowers journalism educators to str[...] preparing students to "do journalism" [...] in the most effective, professional manner possible.

This volume is a one-stop scholarly yet practical/approachable reference book for educators, trainers, journalists, media activists, policymakers, foundations, non-government organizations, students, and others with a vested interest in quality journalism. It sheds light on the emerging field of comparative journalism education worldwide by building on past research and offering conceptual, theoretical, empirical, and practical insights into where the field has been, where it currently stands, and where it seems to be heading.

Global Journalism Education's findings are based on the combined expertise of many of the world's top journalism education scholars through

- ❏ Descriptive case studies highlighting journalism education and practice-related challenges and innovations in a wide range of countries from six continents;
- ❏ Conceptual chapters examining the past, present, and predicted future of global journalism education and its influence on the profession;
- ❏ Empirical case studies detailing classroom innovations worldwide;
- ❏ A concluding chapter with 10 global journalism education predictions; and
- ❏ An epilogue highlighting final observations regarding the current state of Western journalism education bias, ethnocentrism, and related provincial thinking and efforts to de-Westernize global journalism education and broaden journalists' understanding of the world they live in.

Robyn S. Goodman is Professor of Communication Studies at Alfred University. She teaches a wide array of reporting, global media, media literacy, and gender, minorities, and the media courses. Her research interests include global journalism education, U.S. news coverage of China, and the construction of knowledge. She publishes in a wide variety of academic journals.

Elanie Steyn is Associate Professor and the head of journalism at the Gaylord College of Journalism and Mass Communication, University of Oklahoma. She teaches in media management, women in media leadership and business of media. Her research involves these same topics, and she has recently published on public diplomacy and on engaged research as part of her involvement with the U.S. Department of State's Diplomacy Lab initiative and professional fellows exchange programs.

Global Journalism Education

In the 21st Century:
Challenges and Innovations

Global Journalism Education

In the 21st Century:
Challenges and Innovations

Edited by
Robyn S. Goodman & Elanie Steyn

WJEC
Endorsed by the World Journalism Education Council

Published by Knight Center for Journalism in the Americas,
University of Texas at Austin

First published 2017 by Knight Center for Journalism
in the Americas, University of Texas at Austin

Knight Center for Journalism in the Americas, School of Journalism
1 University Station A1000
University of Texas
Austin, TX 78712
www.knightcenter.utexas.edu
knightcenter@austin.utexas.edu

Paperback
ISBN 13: 978-1-58790-388-5
ISBN 10: 1-58790-388-1
Library of Congress Control Number: 2017934141

Cover design by Chagmion Antoine and Jasmine Brown
Cover art by John Lund, gettyimages®

Printed and bound in the U.S.A. by Regent Press, Berkeley, CA

Disclaimer: The publisher and editors cannot be held responsible for any
errors or consequences that arise from the use of information contained in
this text. The ideas and opinions expressed in this publication are those of the
authors; they are not necessarily those of the publisher, editors, the Knight
Center for Journalism in the Americas, or the WJEC.

To educators and trainers worldwide who teach journalism according to the highest professional standards possible and to the students who carry their torches.

Contents

i

PART 2:
CONTEXTUALIZING GLOBAL JOURNALISM EDUCATION

Tables/Figures/Appendix

Tables

Figures

Appendix

Preface
The Backstory: It Took a Global Village—Origins, Development, and Production

This book's evolution was initiated by, and parallels, two progressions. First, the Association for Education in Journalism and Mass Communication's (AEJMC) efforts to internationalize itself and the field. And second, the development of the World Journalism Education Congress (WJEC)—an unprecedented meeting of journalism education associations and educators/trainers from around the globe to improve journalism education, and therefore journalism, worldwide (Goodman & Hasegawa, 2003).

AEJMC past President Joe Foote (University of Oklahoma) created its International Task Force (ITF) in 2001 in hopes of further coordinating and accelerating its members' exposure to international perspectives. The ITF, headed by Dennis Davis (Penn State) and Kazumi Hasegawa (University of Maryland, Baltimore County), consisted of more than 40 mass communication scholars from North America and abroad. It created the following four committees: strategies (for internationalization), alliances (finding and rallying journalism education associations worldwide), membership (calls to action), and publications (internationalizing AEJMC's research). It also created the following seven world region subcommittees, in which journalism education and practices were examined: Africa, Asia, Central/South America, Eastern Europe, the Middle East, North America, and Western Europe.

The seeds for this book were planted during subcommittee reportbacks, which featured fascinating, updated snapshots of journalism education practices worldwide. The stunning similarities and cultural idiosyncrasies captured everyone's imagination. Extremely limited research on this topic existed at the time, and all hungered to learn more.

The ITF accelerated its globalization efforts during a mid-winter 2002 meeting in London, with representatives from AEJMC,

AEJMC's Association for Schools of Journalism and Mass Communication (ASJMC), and the U.K.'s Association for Journalism Education (AJE). The meeting concluded with a major endorsement for creating the WJEC (Foote, 2011). Soon after, AEJMC embraced the ITF's main recommendation: "to support and be a principal sponsor of" a WJEC conference[1] (Goodman & Hasegawa, 2003, p. 4). Planning meetings occurred in 2004, 2005, and 2006, with representatives from more than a dozen WJEC organizations. And in the summer of 2007, the first WJEC conference (WJEC-1), hosted by the Asian Media Information Centre (AMIC), took place in Singapore.

At WJEC-1, WJEC-endorsed journalism education associations met the day before the conference officially began. The meeting was followed by a three-day academic conference, with more than 450 attendees. Although this organically grown text did not yet have a publisher, it was already being written. At WJEC-1 its growth continued, shepherded along the way by its two original editors, Suellen Tapsall (University of Melbourne Commercial, Australia) and Robyn S. Goodman (Alfred University, U.S.), and their WJEC book steering committee, consisting of the following members/associations from five continents: Tapsall (JEA, Australia, New Zealand); Goodman (AEJMC); Chris Frost (AJE); Sonia Virginia Moreira, Brazilian Society of Interdisciplinary Studies in Communication (Intercom); Guo Ke, Chinese Journalism Education Association; Kaarle Nordenstreng, Global Network for Professional Education in Journalism and Media (JourNet); and Ian Richards (JEA). Tapsall and Goodman, a WJEC executive committee member also serving as WJEC-1's conference chair, also met with chapter authors.

This ITF-inspired text became "the WJEC book"—the WJEC's first major academic publication. Its first iteration featured descriptive case studies and journalism education "hot topics." Its goal: making sense of journalism education worldwide during unprecedented disruptions and placing it in context—past, present, and predicted future. While this original goal remained, some chapter sections changed over the years. For example, when Tapsall left the book project due to per-

---

1   While AEJMC provided early seed money for the first conference, the conferences are subsidized through the host schools/associations' active fundraising and conference registration fees.

sonal and professional reasons and Goodman became editor, some country case study sections were modified and one was added, which highlights each country's approach to academic research and publishing.

From the beginning, this book's editors sought out country chapters written by top scholars from six continents, a goal they achieved. The country chapters were selected based on the availability of such scholars and their willingness/ability to see the project through its final phase. They were also selected to provide a current snapshot of journalism education and related scholarship in a diverse set of Global North and Global South countries. These countries possess small to large economies, extremely authoritarian to relatively free government and media systems, conservative to liberal societies and cultures, and so forth.

In this book's Goodman-led second iteration, country chapters were kept and the hot topics second section was transformed into one offering a more comprehensive understanding of global journalism education as a field. Second-section chapters focus on journalism education and training within and outside academia, internationalizing the field, and assessing journalism education on a global scale.

Goodman also added a third, final section focusing on innovations in the classroom. Both practical and empirical, these chapters introduce readers to often free/inexpensive, accessible new technologies, theories, and teaching approaches that can be used to better train future journalists. This third section was made possible by the text's innovations expert, Amy Schmitz Weiss (San Diego State University). Schmitz Weiss, an award-winning journalism education innovator (see her biography for details), offered us the significant insights and guidance needed to make it as robust, relevant, and cutting-edge as possible. We are grateful for her substantial contributions.

Renowned global journalism education scholar Mark Deuze (University of Amsterdam) kicks off this final section with an analysis of how globalization and new technologies/innovations are dramatically altering journalism and, accordingly, journalism educators' roles. His chapter is followed by five others written by innovative, distinguished journalism education professors. Each is written in a highly accessible fashion in hopes that interested readers can apply what they learn to their own classroom teaching, projects, and/or research.

Much time was spent searching the globe for these third-section chapters, and we did succeed in finding three from the Global South and three from various European countries. That said, three of these chapters did not come to fruition due to a variety of factors. Although we regret not having a more varied mix of international authors demonstrating their classroom innovations—and we hope future such collections will continue seeking them out—we are proud of our resulting vibrant, diverse mix of chapter topics and the hands-on, take-away opportunities they present to journalism educators, and journalists, everywhere.

Two years ago, while researchers were being secured for the new innovations section, Elanie Steyn (University of Oklahoma) signed on as coeditor. Steyn, a global journalism education expert and WJEC officer from South Africa, expertly helped shepherd this project to completion. She did it all: from helping find final authors and editing all chapters to navigating communication, organization, and production requirements. Her impeccable work ethic and unique Global South perspective also proved invaluable, along with bringing Imran Hasnat (University of Oklahoma), from Bangladesh, on board. Hasnat, an exceptionally multitalented international graduate student, helped deal with everything from organizational, design, and technical issues. He also helped keep Global North biases in check.

Last and anything but least, we found a perfect fit with our publisher, the Knight Center for Journalism in the Americas at the University of Texas at Austin. The center, and its distinguished, award-winning journalism innovator and director, Rosental Alves (University of Texas, Austin), are well-known for successfully internationalizing journalism education in the Americas and worldwide. Through innovative ventures and MOOCs, both continue to educate tens of thousands of journalism teachers, trainers, and practitioners from around the globe. The center's nearly 20-year-old, standing-room only International Symposium on Online Journalism's (ISOJ) annual conference, and its especially innovative online journal, #*ISOJ*, also significantly promote journalism education, and journalism, through a global lens.

We are proud that our book is kicking off the Austin Knight Center's official venture into academic publishing and are looking forward to its translation into Spanish. Such an ideal platform was never even imagined in the text's initial idea stage, before the constantly evolving WJEC became a reality—it is now 32-organizations strong and planning is under way for its fifth convention in Paris in 2019 (see wjec.net). And we hope now that this text is widely available, everyone concerned about improving journalism education, and journalism, worldwide will gain the type of inspiration and information from its pages—including content, theories, methods, tools, pedagogy—that will help make such important goals possible.

Robyn S. Goodman
Alfred, New York

References

Foote, J. (2011). WJEC highlights development of journalism around the world. *ASJMC Insights*, 8-10.

Goodman, R., & Hasegawa, K. (2003). AEJMC's road to internationalization: A report of the task force. *International Communication Bulletin*, *38*(1-2), 2-11.

A Note From the Publisher

Rosental C. Alves

It is a great privilege and honor for the Knight Center for Journalism in the Americas at The University of Texas at Austin to be the publisher of *Global Journalism Education in the 21st Century: Challenges and Innovations*—the first project in our new initiative to publish international academic research on journalism.

Since 2002, the Knight Center has helped thousands of journalists, journalism educators, and students with online training and many other programs. The center was created to focus primarily on Latin America and the Caribbean, with the idea of helping journalists with access to training and other programs to assist them in elevating the standards of journalism in their countries.

One of the center's main activities, a pioneer distance learning program in journalism, grew exponentially throughout the Americas and started reaching other continents. Between 2012 and 2016, its massive open online courses (MOOCs) have reached more than 85,000 people in 169 countries! It is the first, and still the only, MOOCs program in the world specializing in journalism.

The Knight Center's main conference, the International Symposium on Online Journalism (ISOJ), started as a national gathering. But it has also become global, attracting journalists, media executives, and scholars from around the world to Austin every year.

ISOJ is a unique conference that creates bridges between academia and the news industry. Its research component has been growing and includes *#ISOJ*, an international journal featuring rigorously blind-reviewed articles by scholars worldwide.

This book is a great way to inaugurate the Knight Center's digital library's new line of publications dedicated to international academic research on journalism. We have already published 13 titles, most of them professional works focused on problems that journalists face in Latin America and the Caribbean. We will now invite researchers from this hemisphere and from around the world to publish in our digital library.

The Knight Center could not have dreamt of a better and more important publication to open our new research initiative. *Global Journalism Education in the 21st Century: Challenges and Innovations* is a strong and unique contribution to the scholarship on an important topic that deserves more attention, especially in these times of globalization and digital revolution.

We are grateful to all the authors, a cadre of some of the best and most active scholars in this field, and we are especially thankful to the book's editors, Dr. Robyn S. Goodman (Alfred University) and Dr. Elanie Steyn (University of Oklahoma). I have been an eyewitness of their tireless work with Dr. Joe Foote supporting the World Journalism Education Council and WJEC congresses and also the years Dr. Goodman and Dr. Steyn have dedicated to this ambitious project.

Now, it is up to the Knight Center to translate *Global Journalism Education in the 21st Century: Challenges and Innovations* into Spanish and to follow this publication with additional research on global journalism and global journalism education. We are dedicated to this pursuit, along with continuing to support journalism educators and trainers on the frontline of journalism education.

Acknowledgements

As mentioned in the preface, it certainly took a global village to bring this book to fruition. Inspired by the editors' AEJMC International Task Force discoveries and nurtured during the World Journalism Education Congress' (WJEC) development, numerous journalism education scholars, colleagues, and family members have generously given their expertise, time, and support to make this book possible.

The editors would like to thank WJEC convener Joe Foote for establishing the task force, guiding the WJEC's creation and development, and supporting this book project from day one. WJEC committee members and volunteers—many drawn from AEJMC's International Communication Division (ICD)—also deserve much credit, along with more than 40 task force members and the WJEC's 32 journalism education associations worldwide for their input and inspiration.

The WJEC's previous conference hosts and their organizations also helped this book become a reality. At WJEC conferences, the editors found many top authors, gathered significant research, and held important book meetings. The hosts not only run WJEC conferences, they also secure funding for them—the WJEC has no budget. Accordingly, the following individuals and organizations deserve our deep gratitude: WJEC-1 Singapore host Indrajit Banerjee (AMIC), WJEC-2 South Africa host Guy Berger (Rhodes University), WJEC-3 Belgium host Nico Drok (The European Journalism Training Association and the Flemish/Dutch Network of Journalism Institutes), and WJEC-4 New Zealand host Verica Rupar (Auckland University of Technology).

Special thanks also go to AEJMC's Executive Director Jennifer McGill, its presidents/elected leadership, and its assessment and accreditation arm, the Association of Schools of Journalism and Mass Communication (ASJMC), for supporting and encouraging the WJEC's development. Goodman also thanks McGill for helping secure her funding for an AMIC conference in Malaysia, which helped her prepare for her role as conference chair of the first WJEC.

The editors are also grateful to Suellen Tapsall, this book's original editor, for getting the text rolling and designing the country chapters' format and the WJEC's book steering committee (see preface for details), which helped nurture the book's early development. And thank you to Amy Schmitz Weiss, our innovations section expert, who juggled an incredibly busy personal and professional workload to give us invaluable feedback. Also especially appreciated are Melinda Robins and April Gacek for their skillful editing help during different stages of the project and anonymous reviewers for their expert analyses, which improved this text's content. And Chagmion Antoine and Jasmine Brown for their book cover design.

The book's authors also deserve much credit for seeing this project through different stages until all parts were finally pulled together. Their dedication to this book and journalism education worldwide is especially noteworthy and appreciated. This brings us to the book's publisher (a perfect fit), Rosental Alves and the Knight Center for Journalism in the Americas at the University of Texas at Austin. Thank you, Rosental, for not only supporting this book project from its humble beginnings to its completion, but also for helping it potentially reach thousands of journalism educators, trainers, practitioners, and students of journalism worldwide. Your impact on our field is legendary, and we could not be prouder to join your efforts to improve international journalism education practice and scholarship.

Goodman also thanks coeditor Elanie Steyn for her hard work and pure dedication to this book project, which was essential in bringing it to a successful conclusion. Her likewise dedication to helping build the WJEC and keeping it running, along with her international journalism education background and experience, made her a perfect partner in this enterprise. Her Global South background, professional approach, and joyful sense of humor made her a true pleasure to work with. Special thanks also go to her colleague, international graduate student Imran Hasnat, who assisted with all aspects of designing, producing, and promoting this book. Hasnat was not only an especially valuable member of the team, but his dry wit, insightful perspectives, and overall humanity helped buoy the team to the finish line.

She also thanks her colleagues who offered important help and advice during important stages of the book's development, especially

Kazumi Hasegawa, Michael Elasmar, Larry Greil, Joseph Straubhaar, Tsan Kuo (TK) Chang, Elizabeth Burch, Eric Freedman and Patricia Fitzpatrick, who was instrumental in helping keep the ship afloat on cloudy days, appreciation also goes out to the late Todd Simon, her Michigan State mentor and dear friend.

In addition, she especially appreciates Alfred University's (AU) administration and staff personal support and financial assistance. Such generous support has helped make possible her WJEC, book, and over-all global journalism education endeavors. After all, such backing has enabled her to attend and contribute to most WJEC planning sessions and all WJEC conferences abroad, to keep up on global education trends, and to work in-person with many of this book's authors. AU individuals and grants that have helped her achieve the above include the following: past and present AU and College of Liberal Arts & Sciences (LAS) administrators, Bill Hall, Rick Stevens, Charley Edmondson, Lou Lichtman, Nancy Furlong, Mary McGee, Dani Gagne, Michael McDonough, and Pamela Schultz; LAS staff professionals, Kaaren Reeder and Pat Sweeney; and AU provost funds, Pamela and Gene Bernstein Funds, and LAS conference and faculty development grants. AU truly cares about journalism education and its faculty achieving its goals. For such gifts, she is truly grateful.

And finally, she thanks her family for putting up with her many absences during vacations, social occasions, and everyday events in order to finish this text. She is especially grateful to her parents, Larry and Sharlene Goodman, for being her biggest cheerleaders and always supporting her academic endeavors. Their dedication is legendary, as is illustrated by their active WJEC attendance: They have attended all four WJEC conferences abroad and are planning to attend the WJEC-5 in Paris in 2019! Sheila Goodman also deserves special acknowledgement for her amazing encouragement and backing throughout the project's ups and downs. And Teri Goodman has also always supported her academic pursuits and offered great design advice. She is grateful to the late Khananiya Kaplan and Sarra Belyakova for their love and support, and turning their living room into a makeshift study whenever she needed it, and to her late stepson, Ilya, for opening up her heart and mind in unexpected ways. And last but not least, Irene

Belyakov-Goodman, who possesses the spirit of a lioness and patience of a saint, deserves vast gratitude for her fierce, unwavering support. This book would not have been possible without her infinite personal care and dedication to the advancement of journalism education, and journalism practice, worldwide.

Steyn is also thankful to the above people and institutions, especially AEJMC and WJEC for helping make this book project a reality and for the many additional career opportunities they have provided. She also wishes to thank Goodman and Hasnat for their patience and dedication to this project over several years and iterations. And she is especially appreciative of her mentors, who have introduced her to the people, qualities, and skills needed to advance professionally and have stuck with her as she continues her professional and personal journey.

Steyn thanks every person who believes in her despite her inability to let a good opportunity go by and who has said (and meant it): "I will go to the end of the journey. With you." You know who you are!

Robyn S. Goodman, Alfred University
Elanie Steyn, University of Oklahoma

Introduction
Global Journalism Education: Accelerating Forward, Coasting, or Losing Ground?

Robyn S. Goodman

"If a nation expects to be ignorant and free, in a state of civilization, it expects what never was and never will be."—THOMAS JEFFERSON

In this current era of great economic, political, technical, and cultural upheaval, journalism educators and trainers worldwide have an unprecedented opportunity to fortify and significantly shape the future of journalism. Will they rise to the occasion, armed with innovative, effective teaching methods backed by research? Or will they squander this unparalleled opportunity? The stakes could not be higher—all global citizens interested in maintaining a democratic society, or aspiring to live in a more open one, have skin in the game. Strong waves of nationalism spreading worldwide—in countries including the United Kingdom, France, the United States, Turkey, and the Philippines—and vigorous assaults against the press' credibility are magnifying the need for truth, fairness, ethics, and logic in governance and civic life. Press owners and advocates, already engaged in a massive struggle to save quality journalism from economic ruin, are being side-swiped by ramped-up attempts by government and other powerful interests to discredit journalism as a whole. The struggle to save journalism's reputation—and thus its effectiveness—is experiencing new urgency during an onslaught of "alternative facts," "fake news," and false equivalency charges. This fallout was dramatically illustrated during the contentious 2016 U.S. presidential race, in which debates were afflicted by a lack of agreed-upon information from which to base positions and policies. And as this book is being published, President Donald J. Trump continues to not only call news coverage he disagrees with "fake news"

1

but also to call respected news outlets like *The New York Times* and CNN "the enemy of the American People!" (Trump, 2017).

As the current "post-truth" phenomenon suggests, the very value of facts, truth, information, and knowledge—the bedrock of journalism and free societies—is under attack. Anti-truth rhetoric during the Brexit controversy and the 2016 U.S. presidential debates are widely credited with intensifying this hazardous trend and popularizing the term "post-truth" to describe it. "Post-truth" became Oxford Dictionaries' 2016 word of the year, defined as "relating to or denoting circumstances in which objective facts are less influential in shaping public opinion than appeals to emotion and personal belief" (Wang, 2016). Such post-truth realities, combined with citizens (especially young people) in democracies questioning whether nondemocratic forms of government—including military rule—may better serve their needs, are setting off serious warning signs for the health of freer societies worldwide (Taub, 2016).

What can journalism educators and trainers do to fight back against such undemocratic trends in an increasingly "less free" (Freedom House, 2016) media and world? Giving future journalists and press advocates the best education possible is a good start. This book discusses how that "best education" is currently conceived and should develop—one of the most debated journalism education issues worldwide. Yet, as for development, there is some agreement among educators. For example, they agree that future journalists must learn how to find and use more varied, nuanced tools to deal with increasingly challenging circumstances. They also need to know how to conduct quality investigative reporting based on verifiable facts during shifting landscapes. They need to do this via all social media, across platforms, and with the community's help. Finally, they need to know how to report in a more transparent fashion and in a way that demonstrates journalism's value to a disillusioned public.

Educators are calling for a united front with industry to help achieve such goals. Jeff Jarvis, director of the Tow-Knight Center for Entrepreneurial Journalism at the City University of New York Graduate School of Journalism, says he is encouraged by the growing economic incentives for journalism academics and industry to work together. He describes the mutually beneficial atmosphere as a new "group hug" type culture (Jarvis, 2013). Educators also find promising the increasing interactions among universities, innovation labs, foundations, training centers, nonprofits, and news entities. For the first time in at least 20 years, academics worldwide seem to agree they have an unprecedented opportunity to proactively shape the field. This new sense of optimism was the focus of the 2013 World Journalism Education Congress (WJEC) in Belgium with its "Renewing Journalism Through Education" theme.

But is this increased collaboration too little, too late? Are educators worldwide building more successful relationships not just among campus entities but also with industry, the public, foundations, nonprofit organizations, appropriate government bodies, etc., in hopes of better nurturing and guiding quality journalism? Does the teaching of liberal arts "ways of knowing" keep pace with the teaching of new technical skills to help future journalists better distinguish fact from fiction? Is there evidence of increased global perspectives and international exchange opportunities to help journalists better understand nation-state and regional biases that threaten the collection and presentation of information and knowledge? And finally, are journalism educators dedicated enough to their field—and do they possess enough chutzpah—to make the necessary changes and create effective innovations? Although only the future will tell, this book points to histories, trends, and circumstances that hint at these answers and many more.

Why this book?

Global Journalism Education in the 21st Century: Challenges and Innovations empowers journalism educators to strengthen the field of journalism by preparing students to "do journalism"—as citizens and/or journalists—in the most effective, professional manner possible. This volume is a one-stop scholarly yet practical/approachable reference for educators, trainers, journalists, media activists, policymakers, foundations, non-government organizations, students, and others with a vested interest in quality journalism. It sheds light on the emerging field of comparative journalism education worldwide by building on past research and offering conceptual, theoretical, empirical, and practical insights into where the field has been, where it currently stands, and where it seems to be heading.

Global Journalism Education's findings are based on the combined expertise of many of the world's top journalism education scholars through

- ❏ Descriptive case studies highlighting journalism education and practice-related challenges and innovations in a wide range of countries from six continents;
- ❏ Conceptual chapters examining the past, present, and predicted future of global journalism education and its influence on the profession;
- ❏ Empirical case studies detailing classroom innovations worldwide;
- ❏ A concluding chapter with 10 global journalism education predictions; and
- ❏ An epilogue highlighting final observations regarding the current state of Western journalism education bias, ethnocentrism, and related provincial thinking and efforts to de-Westernize global journalism education and broaden journalists' understanding of the world they live in.

Since the breadth and scope of global journalism education is so wide-ranging, this volume does not attempt to cover all its challenges and innovations. However, as the field continues to evolve, we hope it will advance scholars' and practitioners' understanding and inspire future research and investigation to further its development.

Global Journalism Education Research: A Brief Overview

Although media systems, societies, political environments, and journalistic cultures vary greatly worldwide, journalists' training needs are quite similar (Gaunt, 1992; Deuze, 2006). After all, as Gaunt (1992) explains, "Whatever the geographic area or sociopolitical context, journalism educators and media professionals have had to come to terms with the same problems" (p. 2). Accordingly, journalists across the globe are being trained, in large part, in similar fashions. As Gaunt (1992) argued in his landmark UNESCO-sponsored text, *Making the*

Newsmakers: International Handbook on Journalism Training, similar training patterns have often arisen from these six shared communicators' needs: an orientation/understanding of one's workplace system and the specialized function of different mass communication fields; a liberal arts and sciences background to better understand how a wide variety of issues—including socioeconomic, political, cultural, and technical ones—affect audiences; basic skills (language, manual dexterity, etc.); technical skills; and the ability to upgrade skills and to learn new ones. Similar training needs and approaches continue to this day, increasingly encouraged by universal trends and ties related to globalization, the Internet and social media, new technologies and innovations, media convergence, community journalism, etc. (Deuze, 2006).

Since educators worldwide tend to train future journalists in similar ways according to universal needs—regardless of often extreme differences in cultural and political realities—scholars continue working on a "global approach to conceptualizing journalism education" (Deuze, 2006, p. 20). After all, the better educators understand global journalism education and training-need trends—past and present—the better chance they have of predicting and guiding the field and most effectively training future journalists. Thus far, the following picture is coming into sharper focus: Journalism education worldwide is becoming increasingly professionalized, formalized, and standardized—and, as a result, increasingly homogeneous (Obijiofor & Hanusch, 2011; Josephi, 2010; Deuze, 2006; De Burgh, 2006; Fröhlich & Holtz-Bacha, 2003; Gaunt, 1992). Accordingly, it is not surprising that most journalism education already takes place in university schools and institutes, mixed systems of both university-level training and stand-alone schools, or appears to be moving toward such setups (Obijiofor & Hanusch, 2011; Deuze, 2006).

While homogeneous educational training trends are clear, there frequently seems to be a disconnect between training systems and actual journalism practice. As Josephi (2010) discovered in her analysis of journalism education in countries with limited media freedom—including Cambodia, Palestine, and Croatia—regardless of similar training, different journalism ecosystems and realities lead to different routines. For instance, she found that journalists worldwide often share democratic universal values. While their education curricula frequently support these, government constraints often hamper their implementation. That said, journalists are encouraged by their training to report more freely when fissures in restrictive systems take place. Accordingly, Josephi argues, journalism education has become an important "potential agent of change" (2010, p. 259).

As for journalism education's often-cited Anglo-American/ Western bias, Deuze (2006), concerned that ongoing standardization may increase Anglo-American influences, argues this topic "begs research" (p. 30). Scholars worldwide (e.g., Wasserman & De Beer, 2009; Breit, Obijiofor, & Fitzgerald, 2013) agree that such provincial biases—an inability or unwillingness to place information within a much-needed global context—threatens the effectiveness of journalism education, the profession, and the validity of knowledge itself. Yet in an increasingly networked, globalized world in which international news is merely a hyperlink away, do such biases continue to hold solid ground? And if so, how can they most effectively be tackled?

As for today's most common global debate in journalism education circles, it focuses on how to best educate students to contribute to society (Obijiofor & Hanusch, 2011). Within such curriculum-related debates, the ideal balance between professional journalism and liberal arts-type classes appears to be hottest—at least in the West (Nordenstreng, 2009). A global increase in university-related journalism training suggests an increasing appreciation for the liberal arts. That said, many educators are concerned with what appears to be a tipping of the scale toward practical/ technical skill courses with a more training-for-industry focus (Mihailidis, 2012). For example, Deuze (2006, p. 30) is troubled by what he calls "the consequences [of] promot[ing] a product-oriented teaching culture instead of a process-focused learning culture." In other words, teaching focused more on preparing students for industry-related jobs rather than developing critical-thinking "supercitizen" skills for changing society in positive ways. He backs this concern with the following quote from Zygmunt Bauman, one of the world's most prominent social theorists: "[t]he way learning is structured determines how individuals learn to think" (2000, p. 123). Such educators are pushing for innovations in journalism education that break down silos and walls, both physically and mentally, in hopes of reimaging journalism education and the ways it can help students better serve society. The innovations section of this book develops and explores such themes.

Global Journalism Education: Laying the Groundwork

As Gaunt (1992) explains, the significance of journalism training, especially during times of upheaval, is clear:

> Journalism training perpetuates or modifies professional journalistic practices and molds the perceptions journalists have of the role and function of the media. Because journalism training influences the selection and processing of the news, it also has an indirect effect on the way in which we view the world around us. In times of crisis . . . those who process the news play a key role in informing mass audiences and shaping public opinion. (p. 1)

Yet relatively few books focus on the field of journalism education from a global perspective. In fact, *Global Journalism Education* seems to be the first in 25 years to provide comparative journalism education case studies from six continents. Like Gaunt's work (1992), it analyzes a diverse set of Global North and Global South countries with small to large economies, authoritarian to free media systems, conservative to liberal societies and cultures, etc., to shed light on global journalism education past, present, and predicted future. In a bricolage fashion, it builds on knowledge gathered from research articles and chapters, reports, websites, and books, including the following three prominent global journalism education comparative texts: Fröhlich and Holtz-Bacha's (2003) *Journalism Education in Europe and North America: An International Comparison*; Terzis' (2009) *European Journalism Education*; and Josephi's (2010) *Journalism Education in Countries with Limited Media Freedom*. While the first two focus on Global North countries, the third focuses mostly on the Global South.

Journalism education systems worldwide are best understood—and later compared—when placed in context. Accordingly, this book begins by emulating such research, which often starts by addressing each region's or country's media systems and journalists' characteristics and professional values, practices, and role perceptions. As Gaunt (1992) found, "Media systems themselves are a result of press law, economic and political variables, cultural and social influences and such basic considerations as demographic distribution, literacy or personal income levels" (p. 13). Since his seminal book, researchers examining media systems have studied such variables and influences (e.g., Hallin & Mancini, 2004; Josephi, 2010; Fröhlich & Holtz-Bacha, 2003). That said, media systems worldwide have proven to be more complicated than originally anticipated due to factors such as cultural differences and country-based idiosyncrasies (e.g., Nordenstreng, 2009; Obijiofor & Hanusch, 2011). Hallin and Mancini's (2004, 2011) landmark work on this topic, while supporting the contributions of such inquiries, warns researchers about the limited value of trying to force media systems into distinct categories. Still, attempts at classifying media systems continue to be seen as helpful when trying to determine their characteristics and potential influence on journalism education systems and vice versa. Once media systems and societies come into sharper focus, so do their journalism education systems and the ability to compare them (Gaunt, 1992; Fröhlich & Holtz-Bacha, 2003; Josephi, 2010; Obijiofor & Hanusch, 2011).

Research examining journalists' professional characteristics, beliefs, values, practices, and role perceptions illustrate how they tend to select and process information within diverse media systems and environments. Their perceived professional roles offer unique insights into the role a country assigns the media—a reflection of its deepest values. These roles are considered such a significant influence on coverage that "in journalism studies, no area of research has flourished more" (Hanitzsch & Maximilians, 2013, p. 1). The Worlds of Journalism Study (worldsofjournalism.org) has found such variables so important that its global volunteer researchers continuously investigate and monitor them. While gathering related data, they recently reported breaking all comparative communication research records by interviewing more than 27,000 journalists in 66 countries. Many educators find journalists' view of their role in society so fundamental to the practice of journalism that they argue curricula should be largely based on such considerations (Deuze, 2006; worldsofjournalism.org).

Educators and trainers influence media systems and journalists' professional beliefs, perceived roles, and resulting coverage (Gaunt, 1992; Fröhlich & Holtz-Bacha, 2003; Weaver & Willnat, 2012). Accordingly, this book analyzes education and training systems worldwide and considers their impact on the media, journalists, and their work. And since journalism education is becoming more universal and homogeneous, it examines this trend as well. For example, organizations such as UNESCO and the World Journalism Education Council (WJEC) actively promote universal standards. UNESCO provides educators in developing countries with universal syllabi and aid based on their stated needs. And WJEC was founded to strengthen journalism education as a global field. To achieve this goal, it adopted the Declaration of Principles at its first conference in Singapore in 2007. This declaration, endorsed by WJEC members worldwide, "identified 11 principles to serve as a standard for journalism education" (wjec.net/about/declaration-of-principles). Two of the key principles follow:

❑ Journalism is a global endeavor; journalism students should learn that despite political and cultural differences, they share important values and professional goals with peers in other nations. Where practical, journalism education provides students with first-hand experience of the way journalism is practiced in other nations.

❑ Journalism educators have an obligation to collaborate with colleagues worldwide to provide assistance and support so that journalism education can gain strength as an academic discipline and play a more effective role in helping journalism to reach its full potential.

Global Journalism Education Structure— Parts, Sections, and Chapters

This book is divided into three main parts. Part 1, *Global Journalism Education Country Case Studies,* covers journalism and education challenges and innovations—past, present, and predicted future. Its 10 descriptive case studies deal with Australia, Chile, China, Egypt, India, Israel, Russia, South Africa, the United Kingdom, and the United States. These countries alone do not represent the full lay of the land for journalism education across all continents and world regions. However, analyzing and comparing them does offer a sense of journalism education history, processes, and happenings in some of the most historically, economically, politically, legally, technologically, socially, and culturally diverse nations.

To write these chapters, we sought top journalism education professors and researchers—from a wide range of countries—well-versed in their nations' journalism education environment. To ensure uniformity and aid country comparisons, each author covered the same aspects of journalism education and practice in their respective countries (see preface for details).

Part 1, Sections I and II, give an overview of each country's media system and how journalists tend to operate within it to help put country-specific journalism education findings in context. Section III focuses on the journalism education lay of the land, with an emphasis on how educators are striving to prepare future journalists to stay ahead of the curve while producing quality journalism in a continuously evolving field. This section also examines changes in the relationships between educators and professionals/industry in different countries, continuing academic challenges and innovations, and future possibilities for growth and change. Last but not least, a special section on journalism research offers insights into how educators worldwide learn about our field and produce research that influences it.

Part 2, *Contextualizing Global Journalism Education,* concentrates on making sense of global journalism education as a field. Beginning with Chapter 11, Guy Berger and Joe Foote examine global journalism education and training within and beyond academic borders. In light of this evolving global journalism education ecosystem, the authors argue that journalism educators must embrace the fray and get more involved in hybrid journalism education for the good of the field.

In Chapter 12, Ian Richards and Charles C. Self examine the evolution of global journalism education as a field and the impact of regional and national journalism education associations in its development. They conclude that such organizations, along with non-government organizations like the WJEC, are helping journalism education get its international act together.

In Chapter 13, Foote and Felix Wao advise journalism educators and trainers worldwide how to examine the quality of their programs. They discuss the advantages and disadvantages of three approaches to quality assurance centered heavily on learning outcomes assessment. They conclude that the most effective type of assessment is multi-faceted.

Part 3, *Global Innovations in Journalism Education*, focuses on innovations in the classroom and beyond. These chapters, both practical and empirical, introduce readers to often free/inexpensive new technologies and methods, theories, and teaching approaches in hopes that they can apply what they learn to their own teaching projects and research.

This section begins with Chapter 14, Mark Deuze's introduction to the new era of journalism and journalism education in an age of constantly evolving technologies and innovations: personal, interactive, liquid, all-encompassing, and constantly changing. His chapter is followed by five others in which experts discuss and demonstrate innovative classroom practices through which they teach journalism skills and concepts.

In Chapter 15, Melissa Wall examines "the ways journalism students respond to a new form of student media: the Pop-Up Newsroom, which operates without a permanent space, editing hierarchy, or traditional timetable." Her findings suggest that students using their own phones and social media platforms and networks produce liquid journalism: "a more fluid, networked form of news."

In Chapter 16, Julie Jones helps educators navigate "going mobile" in their curricula or classes by demonstrating how her students have covered severe weather, sports, and racial conflict and by reflecting on the trials and tribulations mobile reporting classes bring to journalism programs.

In Chapter 17, Wajeehah Aayeshah discusses how Alternate Reality Games (ARG) can be successfully used in classrooms to teach crucial investigative journalism skills. She demonstrates this practice, in detail, via an educational ARG case study featuring a game called *The Seed*.

In Chapter 18, Cindy Royal examines "the reasons for journalists, journalism students, and educators to learn to code and how these skills may begin to be integrated into curriculum." Through specific examples and detailed tables, she also offers educators advice on how to kick-start and sustain such efforts.

In Chapter 19, Oscar Westlund and Seth C. Lewis explain how understanding and describing to students the potential interplay of actors, actants, and audiences in news production can improve journalism education.

In Chapter 20, Foote summarizes this book's findings within a discussion of three major journalism education challenges: striving for recognition and respect within the university, bringing the journalism and mass communication professions closer to the academy, and remaining current in a highly dynamic professional and technological environment. He then closes with 10 predictions about where the future of journalism education is headed.

And in the epilogue, Robyn S. Goodman offers final observations on this book's conclusions regarding the following: the current state of Western journalism education bias, ethnocentrism, and related provincial thinking and efforts to de-Westernize global journalism education and broaden journalists' understanding of the world they live in. She also discusses whether journalism educators worldwide are demonstrating enough passion and ability to help their students become valuable global citizens and/or journalists.

References

Bauman, Z. (2000). *Liquid modernity*. Cambridge: Polity Press.

Breit, R., Obijiofor, L., & Fitzgerald, R.   (2013). Internationalization as de-Westernization of the curriculum: The case of journalism at an Australian university. *Journal of Studies in International Education, 17*(2), 119-135.

De Burgh, H. (Ed.). (2006). *Making journalists: Diverse models, global issues*. London: Routledge.

Deuze, M. (2006). Global journalism education: A conceptual approach. *Journalism Studies, 7*(1), 19-34.

Freedom House. (2016). Freedom in the world 2016, anxious dictators, wavering democracies: Global freedom under pressure. Retrieved from http://freedomhouse.org/report/freedom-world/2016/russia

Fröhlich, R., & Holtz-Bacha, C. (Eds.). (2003). *Journalism education in Europe and North America: An international comparison*. Cresskill, NJ: Hampton Press.

Gaunt, P. (1992). *Making the newsmakers: International handbook on journalism training*. Westport, CT: Greenwood Press.

Hallin, D. C., & Mancini, P. (2004). *Comparing media systems: Three models of media and politics*. Cambridge: Cambridge University Press.

Hallin, D. C., & Mancini, P. (Eds.). (2011). *Comparing media systems beyond the Western world*. Cambridge: Cambridge University Press.

Hanitzsch, T., & Maximilians, L. (2013, July). *Role perceptions and professional values worldwide*. Report presented to the WJEC syndicate group on "Role perceptions and professional values worldwide." Belgium: Mechelen.

Jarvis, J. (2013, July). *New relationships, forms, and business models for journalism*. Paper presented at the WJEC3 conference, Mechelen, Belgium.

Josephi, B. U. (2010). *Journalism education in countries with limited media freedom*. New York, NY: Peter Lang.

Mihailidis, P. (Ed.). (2012). *News literacy: Global perspectives for the newsroom and the classroom*. New York, NY: Peter Lang.

Nordenstreng, K. (2009). Soul-searching at the crossroads of European journalism education. *European Journalism Education*, 511-517.

Obijiofor, L., & Hanusch, F. (2011). *Journalism across cultures: an introduction*. New York, NY: Palgrave Macmillan.

Taub, A. (2016, November 29). How stable are democracies? "Warning signs are flashing red." *The New York Times*. Retrieved from https://www.nytimes.com/2016/11/29/world/americas/western-liberal-democracy.html?_r=0

Terzis, G. (2009). *European journalism education*. Bristol: Intellect Books.

Trump, D. [DonaldTrump]. (2017, February 17). The FAKE NEWS media (failing @nytimes, @CNN, @NBCNews and many more) is not my enemy, it is the enemy of the American people. SICK! [Tweet]. Retrieved from https://twitter.com/realdonaldtrump/status/832708293516632065?lang=en

Wahl-Jorgensen, K., & Hanitzsch, T. (Eds.). (2009). *The handbook of journalism studies*. New York, NY: Routledge.

Wang, A. B. (2016, November 16). "Post-truth" named 2016 word of the year by Oxford Dictionaries. *The Washington Post*. Retrieved from https://www.washingtonpost.com/news/the-fix/wp/2016/11/16/post-truth-named-2016-word-of-the-year-by-oxford-dictionaries/?utm_term=.b02eddff49d0

Wasserman, H., & De Beer, A. S. (2009). Towards de-westernizing journalism studies. *The Handbook of Journalism Studies*, 428-438.

Weaver, D. H., & Willnat, L. (Eds.). (2012). *The global journalist in the 21st century*. New York, NY: Routledge.

PART 1:

Global Journalism Education Country Case Studies

1

Journalism Education in Australia: Educating Journalists for Convergent, Cosmopolitan, and Uncertain News Environments

Penny O'Donnell

n 1919, university-level classes for Australian journalists were first offered at the University of Western Australia with the support of the Australian Journalists' Association (AJA) (Coleman, 1992). Thereafter, journalism diploma programs were introduced to the following universities: Melbourne (1921), Queensland (1921), Sydney (1926), and Western Australia (1928) (Lloyd, 1999; Coleman, 1992) (see Table 1.1 for major journalism associations and journalist-related organizations). For the AJA—a non-manual trade union formed in 1910 and amalgamated into the Media, Entertainment and Arts Alliance (MEAA) in 1992—higher education meant raising the social respectability of journalism. In the early 1900s, journalism was considered a low-status occupation populated by "hard-living" and "barely respectable" bohemians (Coleman, 1992, p. 9). By 1940, however, most of these pioneering programs were discontinued since their experimental and inadequately funded curricula proved unpopular. Another significant disincentive was the prevailing industry belief that "real journ;alists were born not made" (Coleman, 1992, p. 10).

Beginning in 1969, higher education reform set the stage for journalism diploma programs to re-emerge in 10 newly established Colleges of Advanced Education (Stuart, 1996). In 1988, journalism degree programs began proliferating throughout the country, and today 32 of Australia's 40 universities offer them (Tanner, M. O'Donnell, Cullen, & Green, 2013). Even so, Australian journalists and academics continue to disagree, sometimes sharply, over the best preparation for professional journalism (P. O'Donnell, 2014, p. 226). For example, Australian newspapers routinely criticize journalism educators for teaching too much theory and ideology (Green, 2005). And in a recent high-profile incident, the sector's professional association, the Journalism Education and Research Association of Australia (JERAA), was forced to defend academic independence against press criticism of journalism educators "indoctrinating" rather than educating students (Ricketson, 2014).

Journalism in the Media Landscape

A wide range of traditional and digital news media populate Australia's journalism landscape, providing employment to an estimated 22,500 journalists (Department of Employment, 2014). These media also give news consumers much choice and flexibility in how they get their news. The major newspapers moved to digital-first production in 2012 and now have a strong online and mobile media presence. These outlets exist alongside digital-only news sites, such as *The Conversation*, *Crikey*, *The Daily Mail Australia*, *The Guardian Australia*, *Independent Australia*, *Buzzfeed*, *Junkee*, *Birdee*, *Hijacked*, and *City Journal*.

Three decisive socio-historical factors have shaped the role of journalism in Australia's media system: colonialism, demography, and national media policy. First, the British penal colony, established in 1788, initially had an authoritarian press system. The first Australian newspapers, *The Sydney Gazette* (1803-1842) and *The Hobart Town Gazette* (1816-1882), were published "by authority" of the governor. These publications were heavily censored, and, imitating *The London Times'* business model, funded through "saturation" advertising and subscriptions (Lloyd, 1999). The British strictly controlled the flow of information in the six colonial settlements dispersed across Australia's vast continent. Officials believed "unchecked political discussion was unthinkable in a colony where public safety depended on the disunity of the convict population" (Cryle, 1997, p. 26). However, by the mid-1820s, independent newspapers, such as *The Australian* (1824-1848), were circulating without authorization and demanding an end to the penal colony and its cruelties (Cryle, 1997). When anti-press taxes failed to silence these critics, officials turned to more draconian measures, using defamation and sedition laws to prosecute and imprison outspoken editors and to constrain public speech (Lloyd, 1999). Australia has since developed into a strong liberal democracy with a pluralist media system. Yet, there is no constitutional or legal protection for freedom of speech (Nash, 2003). Moreover, stringent defamation laws continue to "chill" reporting on politics and business matters (Kenyon & Marjoribanks, 2008, p. 19).

Second, ever since the Commonwealth of Australia achieved independence in 1901, demographic factors have shaped media development and the journalism landscape. These factors have ranged from intense post-colonial urbanization and low population density to high levels of migration, beginning in the 1950s. The press has a decentralized structure, with the most important daily newspapers circulating in state capitals (Tiffen, 2014). These newspapers cover territory containing over one half of Australia's 24 million people *and* the most lucrative media advertising markets. By contrast, people in the vast, sparsely populated regional and remote parts of the country depend on two national public service broadcasters, the Australian Broadcasting Corporation (ABC, created in 1932) and the multicultural, multilingual Special Broadcasting Service (SBS, created in 1980). The Australian Broadcasting Corporation Act 1983 and the Special Broadcasting Service Act 1991 restrict government interference in the internal operations of these state-owned media and guarantee their editorial independence (Cunningham & Turnbull, 2014). In addition, a not-for-profit community media sector emerged in the mid-1970s, following persistent campaigns by indigenous and migrant communities for access to their own forms of media and opportunities for self-representation. Some 400 community media projects, operated by 22,000 volunteers, now give voice to a plethora of community perspectives. Such perspectives would otherwise go unheard in a national media system plagued by one of the highest concentrations of commercial media ownership in the world (Jolly, 2014).

Third, despite the growing pressures of globalization and convergence, national media policy is trying to keep the media distinctly Australian (Cunningham & Flew, 2000; Jones & Pusey, 2010). Controls on foreign investment in Australia's media, designated a "sensitive sector" of the national economy, aim to protect domestic ownership and control. Mandatory Australian content quotas for commercial television and radio support local media jobs and production of media content that tells Australian stories. Industry guidelines for media portrayal of indigenous people and minority ethnic communities foster social inclusion and tolerance (Australian Communications and Media Authority, 2015). Media diversity, an important public interest policy objective, argues that audience access to a wide variety of news and opinion sources enhances democracy (Department of Communications and the Arts, 2014). In part to foster media diversity, government controls in place since 1987 restrict cross-media ownership to two of the three traditional news platforms (television, radio, and newspapers). The government also limits the audience reach of any one commercial television license to 75% of the population. Finally, it specifies a minimum of five independent radio license holders or "media voices" in each of the state capitals (Department of Communications and the Arts, 2014, p. 5). These rules, administered by the Australian Communications and Media Authority (ACMA), do not apply to online media.

High levels of print media concentration, dominated by News Corp Australia and Fairfax Media, are unintended by-products of media policy. News Corp, the nation's biggest newspaper company, owns seven of the 12 major national and metropolitan daily newspapers. This includes successful tabloids in major capital cities, such as Sydney, Melbourne, Adelaide, Brisbane, Hobart, and Darwin. Fairfax Media owns four of the five other major dailies, while Seven West Media owns the remaining masthead, *The West Australian*, along with Australia's largest commercial television network. News Corp Australia and Fairfax newspapers are, on average, read each week by around 60% and 36% respectively of Australia's newspaper-reading public (Department of Communications and the Arts, 2014, p. 21). For journalists, the ultimate impact of this oligopolistic media ownership pattern is limited employer options. A related problem is that those who take principled stands on issues such as commercial interference in news content risk both dismissal and career loss (Nash, 2003; Aedy, 2013).

Professional Characteristics

Journalism is a medium-sized occupation in Australia. It has experienced strong employment growth over the past decade and has a predicted positive job outlook up until at least 2018 (Department of Employment, 2014). Almost 75% of journalists are employed full time.

They work an average of 40 hours per week and earn an above-average weekly income (approximately U.S. $1,100). The median age of journalists is 39 years (around 14% are less than 24 years old, while around 5% are 65 years or older). The majority of workers in this occupation have a bachelor's degree (48.8%) or higher degree (32.6%) (Department of Employment, 2014).

Information media and telecommunications is the main industry sector employing journalists, with most jobs in the eastern states of New South Wales, Victoria, and Queensland. Sydney is the undisputed "news capital" of Australia. Employment levels have remained steady over the past decade, and job prospects for journalists are considered "average." Job vacancies mainly result from journalists changing jobs or leaving the occupation. Only 2.1% of job vacancies are the result of employment growth (Department of Employment, 2014).

While men (53.4%) outnumber women (46.6%) in this occupation (Department of Employment, 2014), greater gender parity exists today than in the early 1970s. At that time, only one in 10 journalists were female (Henningham, 1998). Men also dominate executive and managerial positions. In the 1990s, only 3% of female journalists were working as editors or news directors, compared to 12% of male journalists (Henningham, 1998).

Monoculturalism in mainstream newsrooms is a long-standing problem because it contrasts sharply with the multiculturalism and multilingualism of the wider society. About 20% of Australia's 24 million people are first-generation immigrants with a native language other than English (Australian Bureau of Statistics, 2012). However, as Jakubowicz (2010) has argued, "Australian news media typically have Anglo-Australian editors and senior staff, directing more junior staff (who may be from non-Anglo backgrounds) in the framing of news stories, choice of sources, and journalistic perspectives." The problem even attracts media commentary, with headlines such as "At the ABC, diversity means British journos" (Cleary, 2015) and "Whitewash? That's not the colour of the SBS charter" (Vatsikopoulos, 2015). Research suggests newsrooms need diversity to ensure social inclusion and improve coverage of immigration and citizenship issues (Jakubowicz, 2010; Deuze, 2005; Forde, 2005).

Cross-national comparative research indicates Australian journalists' perceptions of the function and role of journalism in society imitate those found in other Western democratic countries. An 18-nation study (Hanitzsch et al., 2013) classified Australia with Austria, Germany, Spain, Switzerland, and the United States as "western-oriented journalism cultures" that value "non-involvement, detachment, monitoring the government, as well as providing political and interesting information to motivate the people to participate in civic activity" (p. 281). Interestingly, journalists from Australia and the United States are more committed to an interpretative but factual mode of reporting than those in Austria, Germany, and Spain (Hanitzsch et al., 2013, p. 283). Conversely, when compared to their U.S. counterparts, Australian journalists are less inclined to follow universal ethical rules and are more willing to accept harmful consequences of reporting for the sake of a greater public good (Hanitzsch et al., 2013, p. 285).

According to the latest study of Australia's journalistic workforce (Hanusch, 2013a), the typical Australian journalist today is more likely to be female, older, better educated, more experienced, and with more left-leaning political views than 20 years ago. However, despite growing numbers of women in journalism, gender parity in terms of positions of power or salaries remains elusive. And journalists' ethnic backgrounds have changed little in 20 years, with minority groups still "drastically under-represented" (Hanusch, 2013a, p. 39).

Journalism Education, Professional Training, and Research

There is a high national demand for entry into journalism programs and student interest in journalism careers is impressive. Journalism program enrollments rose by 42% in the 2001-2008 period, compared to an increase of 27% in overall enrollments in higher education programs (Scanlon, 2009). This demand is linked to optimism about employment opportunities for graduates who have information and communication technology skill sets and fascination with the news media (Putnis, Axford, Watson, & Blood, 2002). Research indicates that unrealistic perceptions of the high profile work opportunities, glamor, and wealth supposedly found in journalistic careers are also a factor (Alysen & Oakham, 1996). Many journalism graduates aspire to work in metropolitan daily newspapers. A 2011 survey found 57% of final-year journalism students would look for work "reporting at a newspaper" (Callaghan, 2011). Yet, these newsrooms offer very few entry-level job opportunities (Cokley, Edstrom, McBride, & Ranke, 2011; Cokley, Gilbert, Jovic, & Hanrick, 2015). As a consequence, most of the journalism graduates entering the labor market each year (Hirst, 2010) have to settle for other types of media or non-media work (e.g., niche magazines, public relations).

Teaching and Training Future Newsmakers

Thirty-two of Australia's 40 universities, as well as private colleges, offer journalism degree programs at either undergraduate and/or postgraduate levels (Tanner et al., 2013; see Table 1.2 for major academic journalism programs and non-academic training). In 2008, the most recent year for which detailed figures are available, 4,288 students studied journalism—3,624 undergraduates, 664 postgraduates (Scanlon, 2009).

The most comprehensive recent study of Australian university-based undergraduate journalism programs (Adams & Duffield, 2006) found many divergent pathways to a journalism degree. All 25 programs surveyed were career-oriented and journalism educators recruited from the industry (also known as "journalist-academics") taught in tenure track positions in these programs (Bromley, 2013, p. 5). The exact number of journalism faculty is unknown. However, JERAA reports a stable national membership of 120 journalism educators, including over 60 with doctoral qualifications (P. O'Donnell & Van Heekeren, 2015).

Journalism programs commonly require full-time students to complete 24 units (six credit points per unit) of study over three years and to engage in a three-part structure known as the "bachelor of arts" curriculum model (Adams & Duffield, 2006). This model consists of up to eight university-designated liberal arts units of study, a compulsory journalism major of 8-12 units of study focused on journalism skills and technologies (Nielsen, 2015), and minor options of 4-8 units of study from cognate disciplines. However, educational offerings within this structure vary widely according to the distinct institutional history and disciplinary orientation of each program. For example, journalism programs are found in colleges of Business, Communications and Multimedia, Creative Industries, and Informatics, as well as the more traditional Colleges of Arts, Humanities and Social Sciences (Adams & Duffield, 2006).

Journalism majors also vary in the curricular mix of career skills and knowledge. According to Adams and Duffield (2006), the most common compulsory journalism units of study are news writing, print editing and publishing, and introductory media/journalism studies. Online journalism is a compulsory subject in 14 of the 25 journalism programs they surveyed. Journalism law and/or ethics are also common subjects in this group. Irrespective of the mix, all journalism graduates are expected to know about news values, journalistic ethics, media law, politics, and Australian press history (Adams & Duffield, 2006).

In 2015, a study of 19 Australian journalism programs explored the question of graduate employability, asking whether journalism graduates have the "job-ready" skills and knowledge that news organizations are looking for in new recruits (Nielsen, 2015). It found no consensus across programs on what makes a person job-ready for journalism work. Moreover, it found constant change in journalism platforms and practices made the task of reaching consensus difficult and, therefore, improbable (Nielsen, 2015, pp. 56-59).

Professional education aims to initiate students into the existing knowledge and practices of a specific occupation and provide them with the qualifications necessary to begin work (McGuire, 1992). Building on the scholarship of teaching and learning, Australian journalism educators have adopted five main approaches to professional journalism education (P. O'Donnell, 2002; P. O'Donnell & Van Heekeren, 2015). The first, most common, model focuses on training for entry-level jobs in the news industry and relies on mass communication as the cognate disciplinary field. The J-School, Macleay College, and the Australian College of Journalism, all privately owned journalism education providers, adopt this approach. The second model focuses on problem-solving journalism and develops a journalistic modus operandi based on teamwork and social inclusion. The third model develops reflective practice, or critical reflection about workplace experience, as a core competency (Sheridan Burns, 2002). It focuses on ethical journalistic decision-making in dynamic news environments. The fourth model focuses on the public intellectual role of journalists in connecting news to debates about public policy. It emphasizes investigative reporting skills and journalistic principles, such as the public's right to know (P. O'Donnell, 2002). The final model focuses on the challenge of new technologies. For example, University of Wollongong journalism researchers have been addressing demands for curriculum renewal, involving digital news platforms and user engagement, through a best practice convergent model (M. O'Donnell, Tanner, Cullen, & Green, 2013).

Overall, such curricular diversity represents a healthy field of study. However, it can also be confusing for prospective journalism students, and further research is needed to assess the "fit" between their aspirations and program offerings (Putnis et al., 2002).

Journalism Research

Journalism research in Australia usually receives more criticism than accolades from the broader scholarly community. This is because historically journalism educators, as a group, have struggled to build a conventional academic research culture (Bromley, 2013; Turner, 2011). Turner (2011) claims the quality and quantity of journalism research in Australia is "poor" when compared to the United States or the United Kingdom. Turner (2011) adds this is the case because Australian journalism education maintains "a particularly compliant relationship" to the news industry, is overly nervous about developing critical research perspectives on news media performance, and, as a result, has failed to make the transition from a training discipline to a research field (p. 6). Bromley (2013) confirms the Australian journalism field's lack of maturation but attributes the problem to both internal and external problems, including "a maelstrom of change" (p. 4) in universities since the 1980s, recent government policy mandating increased auditing of research productivity and quality, and resulting pressures on journalism faculty to adopt more "science like" (p. 13) research. Bromley (2013) found Australian journalism faculty members, many of them practitioners, struggle to meet institutionalized research targets.

JERAA is currently leading a change of direction in journalism research, which for the past four decades has evolved in an *ad hoc* manner through annual conferences, collaborative partnerships with industry, and publications. One such publication, *Australian Journalism Review,* is the sector's leading peer-reviewed journal (established in 1978). Other scholarly journals edited by Australian journalism academics include *Asia Pacific Media Educator, eJournalist,* and *Global Media Journal: Australian Edition and Pacific Journalism Review.* In mid-2015, the association decided to take more decisive leadership of journalism's disciplinary development by publishing, for the first time, a Journalism Research Australia National Statement (P. O'Donnell & Van Heekeren, 2015).

According to the statement, "Journalism as an academic research discipline contributes to the body of scholarly knowledge about the contexts, tools, creation, distribution, consumption, impacts and social relations of journalism via journalism studies and journalism practice" (JERAA, 2015). It includes journalism practice as a research paradigm. Since 2011, the Australian Research Council—Australia's main national research-funding body—has accepted quality newspaper portfolios as non-traditional research outputs (NTROs). This has been a seemingly favorable decision for an area of study staffed by many former journalists. Even so, the idea that journalism practice should count as research remains a controversial issue, with little agreement on how to measure the quality and impact of NTROs (Turner, 2011). JERAA's research statement can be seen as a significant attempt to articulate a clear starting point for further debate on this "unconventional particularity" of the Australian journalism research field (P. O'Donnell & Van Heekeren, 2015, p. 15).

There is evidence that many Australian journalism educators tend to have industry-oriented research priorities, preferring to bypass critical, less practical scholarship in favor of research that supports their teaching, contributes to improving professional practice, and, thereby, raises standards of journalism (Bromley, 2013; Richards, 1997). The journalism education sector, in collaboration with industry, has developed various high-impact initiatives designed to provide solutions to community concerns about journalism's shortcomings. Such initiatives include those dealing with improving suicide, mental health, and minority reporting.

The *Reporting Diversity* project (www.reportingdiversity.org.au) offers an extensive suite of journalism education resources, including anti-racist reporting guidelines and protocols, aimed at redressing the problem of media demonization of indigenous Australians and Muslims from the Middle East (Phillips, 2011; Jakubowicz, 2010; McCallum & Posetti, 2008). Likewise, the *Mindframe* project (www.mindframe-media.info), which continues to address the problem of copycat behavior arising from media coverage of suicide, has significantly changed journalists' suicide-reporting practices over the past 10 years. Research has found news reports now use more accurate language, are less sensational, and routinely include links to suicide prevention services (Skehan & Laybutt, 2009).

Furthermore, news criticism and the quest for better journalism are the driving themes in a range of recent monographs on Australian journalism practices and politics. These include the following:

❑ Lawrie Zion and David Craig's *Ethics for digital journalists: Emerging best practices* (2014);

❑ Shelton Gunaratne, Mark Pearson, and Sugarth Senarath's *Mindful journalism and news ethics in the digital era* (2015);

❑ Matthew Ricketson's *Australian journalism today* (2012);

❑ David McKnight's *Rupert Murdoch: An investigation of political power* (2012);

❑ Halim Rane, Jacqui Ewart, and Mohamad Abdalla's *Islam and the Australian news media* (2010);

❑ Louise North's *The gendered newsroom: how journalists experience the changing world of media* (2009); and

❑ Libby Lester's *Giving ground: Media and environmental conflict in Tasmania* (2007).

Professional Connections in Journalism Education

Australian universities are interacting with industry mostly through workplace internship programs, industry reference groups, and the employment of professional journalists as part-time tutors. In addition, there are numerous collaborative activities, such as industry-judged awards for student work, guest lectures, and public seminars on key issues such as press freedom, media coverage of climate change, and workforce futures.

No formal links currently exist between journalism programs

and news organizations (Green & Sykes, 2004). The Australian media industry is notoriously disinterested in journalism education, a problem that has roots in workplace history (Ricketson, 2001). Many news executives, senior journalists, and industry recruiters began their careers in journalism at a time when newsroom entry required a three-year cadetship (before the 1990s boom in university-level journalism programs). As a result, older generations of journalists tend to believe workplace training, or what is euphemistically termed "the school of hard knocks—the university of life" (Ricketson, 2001, p. 95), is the only real way to learn the business. Furthermore, the journalists' union, the MEAA, has always fixed journalists' pay rates and promotion criteria on the basis of professional experience and journalistic achievements rather than educational qualifications. As a result, journalism graduates recruited into newsroom jobs typically earn the same trainee-level wages during their first year as all other qualified or unqualified new recruits and get no particular workplace recognition for their journalism education (Green & Sykes, 2004). In 2004, JERAA tried, without success, to develop a more productive relationship with industry and the union through talks on a national accreditation scheme, similar to what the American Accrediting Council on Education in Journalism and Mass Communications (ACEJMC) has established (Green, 2005). However, key journalism education providers opposed the move, fearing industry oversight of programs would do little to elevate journalism standards while giving media corporations unwarranted power to reshape the curriculum to their needs. As a result, accreditation of journalism programs remains controversial, despite two decades of debate (Green, 2005; Henningham, 1989; Herbert, 2002; Patching, 1996).

At the same time, journalism academics frequently call for stronger professional links with important industry employers, particularly metropolitan newspaper editors (Cullen, 2014; Green, 2005; Oliver, Bethell, Fernandez, Harrison, & Breit, 2011; Ricketson, 2001, 2014). For example, Green (2005) proposed using existing mechanisms, such as industry reference groups, to develop more frequent and effective academy-industry interactions. And Ricketson (2001, 2014) argued a closer working relationship requires industry respect for the independence of journalism programs. Ricketson (2001) also emphasized that journalism programs need to "stand apart from the industry, to study it, question it and offer new and different ways of doing journalism" (p. 98). More recently, Cullen (2014) reported some success in opening up new dialogue between journalism academics and news editors on graduate employability.

Journalism Education's Professional Impact

While employment is only one outcome of university study, journalism academics and graduates alike judge the success and impact of journalism education by the number of graduates who get newsroom jobs each year. The success rate, however, is difficult to quantify. Universities do not track their graduates' employment destinations, so there are no institution-based statistics on journalism graduate outcomes. National longitudinal data on graduate employment trends, collected by Graduate Careers Australia, the leading national authority, does not detail journalism graduate outcomes as a separate category. Therefore, journalism academics rely on informal student and employer feedback to monitor their impact on the industry. One drawback with this kind of anecdotal information, as Putnis et al. (2002) noted, is that it does not necessarily reflect outcomes for the majority of students. After all, it tends to focus on high profile students and job destinations. Research indicates, for example, that only about one percent of graduates will find work at a metropolitan daily newspaper (Alysen, 2007; Cokley et al., 2015). Further, employers are known to be fickle and journalism graduates sometimes compete with graduates in economics, law, sports, politics, or science for specialist beats or publications. Regional newspapers, radio and television, and magazines and other special interest publications are the most reliable source of entry-level job opportunities for journalism graduates (Green & Sykes, 2004).

However, journalism academics have collected survey data on graduate employment destinations from some specific undergraduate journalism programs, such as Charles Sturt University, the University of Technology, Sydney, and the University of Queensland (Green, 2005; P. O'Donnell, 1999; Patching, 1996). These surveys consistently find that about one third of journalism graduates obtain a newsroom job within one year of graduation, while the remaining two thirds find employment either in the public relations and advertising sectors or in non-media industries. The good news is that journalism graduates have excellent employment prospects even outside their chosen occupation. After all, their skill sets and expertise are attractive to a wide range of employers. Further, as Green (2005) notes, journalism graduates can be unusually tenacious. His research has found evidence that unsatisfying first jobs did not always dampen graduates' aspirations, with many showing "dogged determination" (p. 186) to move on and make it in the news media industry.

Much ongoing debate focuses on the imbalance between the supply of journalism graduates and newsroom demand for new recruits (Callaghan, 2011). While some critics blame structural constraints, such as the volatility of ICT-based industries or changing occupational profiles (Putnis et al., 2002), others suggest Australian universities may be "deceiving" prospective students by overstating the chances of careers in journalism when promoting their journalism programs (Cullen & Callaghan, 2010, p. 117). However, journalism graduates are seen to have better overall job prospects than generalist media graduates because their distinct expertise applies to a wide range of occupational roles (Putnis et al., 2002).

Future Possibilities

"Learning outcomes" and "graduate employability" are two catch-phrases shaping the future direction of Australian journalism education, as government moves to guarantee measurable results from journalism education and training. The Tertiary Education Quality Standards Agency, a government regulatory body, now requires all universities to provide evidence of graduate learning outcomes that comply with the Australian Qualifications Framework (AQF). For undergraduates, the AQF specifies three outcomes: familiarity with a broad and coherent body of knowledge, capacity to apply that knowledge in a range of contexts, and readiness for professional practice and/or further learning (AQF Council, 2013, p. 16).

The journalism education sector is proactively responding to these accountability demands. In 2011, with funding from the national Office of Learning and Teaching, it created a trans-disciplinary network of scholars to develop a suite of model learning outcomes for undergraduate journalism programs across the country. This Journalism, Media and Communication (JoMeC) Network, initiated by former JERAA President Anne Dunn, acts as a national forum for debate on learning and teaching issues, including learning standards, curriculum reform, and graduate destinations. At a time of volatility in the news industry and uncertainty about the future of the profession, a key discussion point is curriculum renewal to prepare graduates for work in convergent journalism (Tanner et al., 2013). A 2013 study of convergent journalism curriculum models found Australian journalism academics struggling to find the right balance between education and training in traditional core skills and digital capabilities (M. O'Donnell et al., 2013). This problem is exacerbated by contradictory pressures to produce graduates who are not only job-ready, according to current industry needs, but also prepared to work in this industry given its unknown future.

Journalism Education Issues, Challenges, and Innovations

The lack of research on Australian journalism students is a pressing issue in Australian journalism education (Hanusch, 2013b). It means curriculum renewal takes place without the benefit of systematic data on what motivates young Australians to enroll in a journalism program and/or how they perceive journalism's roles, values, and practices. It also lacks data on why they aspire to enter the profession or where they end up working. This situation is repeated in public debate over the best preparation for journalistic work, which routinely features industry and university stakeholders but ignores journalism students' perspectives—as if the views of these younger, less powerful stakeholders are of no consequence. Also, through media research, more is known about the online news practices of mainstream news organizations and professional journalists (P. O'Donnell, McKnight, & Este, 2012) than about how younger people consume and interact with the digital news environment (Flew, Daniel, Spurgeon, & Swift, 2011, p. 100). Similarly, little is known about whether younger people's online experiences encourage or discourage them from pursuing careers in journalism. Yet, research in the cognate field of youth studies clearly indicates that opportunities for interactivity and participation drive younger people's engagement in the public sphere, with social media use emerging as a driver of new types of "micro-political engagement and everyday political talk" (Vromen, Xenos, & Loader, 2015, p. 95).

When it comes to students, journalism educators' real challenge is both practical and professional. First, in practical terms, a curriculum that positions journalism students as passive learners rather than engaged online users runs the risk of alienating students. Secondly, in professional terms, journalists and academics who fail to directly seek out students' views on the best preparation for journalistic work face the prospect of being left behind to argue over how to adapt to the changing news environment. In the meanwhile, students will simply create their own diverse, new ways of practicing journalism online. This proved to be the case in a fairly recent media controversy sparked by claims published in a national newspaper, alleging that some of Australia's "most prestigious universities" were "indoctrinating students, not educating them" (Markson, 2014). While journalism academics contested the claims by writing op-ed pieces for major online news sites (e.g., *Guardian Australia*, *The Australian*, *The Conversation,* and *Crikey*), journalism students adopted a more critical role and published a range of news stories, opinion pieces, tweets, memes, and comments on alternative news sites, using humor and wit to ridicule suggestions that they had been "brainwashed" and showcase their impressive convergent journalism skills (P. O'Donnell & Hutchinson, 2015).

Intergenerational change in journalism thus appears to be a potential force for innovation in both journalism and journalism education. The prospects of success will look brighter if the journalism academy is able to extend its successful track record in developing research-based, innovative curricular materials aimed at raising professional standards to include convergent journalism practices. These would include news reporting of complex issues such as suicide and mental health or community conflicts arising from cultural diversity issues.

Conclusion: Educating Tomorrow's Journalists—The Big Picture

Journalism educators, when training tomorrow's journalists, must increasingly take into account the influence of global trends on one's society and journalism education alike (Josephi, 2007; Deuze, 2006; Loo,

2006). For example, the internationalization of higher education and the consequent internationalization of journalism student cohorts are factors driving a more cosmopolitan outlook in Australian journalism education. So are the Australian media's growing cultural and linguistic diversity, the emergence of significant non-Western journalism practices, and the expanding global media employment market. The World Journalism Education Council (WJEC) has, since 2007, led global debate on the need to "internationalize" journalism curricula around the world. However, in Australia, as elsewhere, this is proving to be a more difficult curriculum renewal challenge than convergent journalism.

Journalism educators conceptualize global journalism education in different terms (Deuze, 2006). In Australia, the most common approaches focus on the contexts in which journalism is practiced, ranging from Australia's Indigenous and multicultural communities to Australia as part of the international community (McCallum & Posetti, 2008; Josephi, 2007; Loo, 2006). Ongoing concerns about Australian journalism's monoculturalism—and related problems of racist reporting—drive the focus on making journalism education more "multicultural" (McCallum & Posetti, 2008). Indigenous and ethnic minority media guidelines are used in classrooms to improve minority coverage. Yet, such guidelines are inherently global since they require a cross-cultural approach to journalism teaching, which fosters cross-cultural understanding and interactions (Loo, 2006). Also, key curricular renewal strategies include using Web-based learning opportunities and assignments to encourage cosmopolitan outlooks based on "looking at issues and affairs beyond the boundaries of [our] immediate community" (Loo, 2006). Josephi's (2007) framework for reconceptualizing an international approach to journalism education remains the most far-reaching and productive renewal proposal. She argues that the teaching of freedom of expression and journalistic independence must include research and discussion about their normative value in diverse journalistic contexts. Case studies of such concepts could include analysis of China's transitional media system and transnational, pan-Arab news networks, such as Al-Jazeera.

Deuze (2006, p. 31) suggests how we educate students and engage them in meaningful dialogue about the future of journalism influences the ways we do journalism. The Australian experience confirms this view. Journalism education that prioritizes student engagement, curriculum renewal, and collaborative industry-university links is the best preparation for journalistic work.

References

Adams, D. & Duffield, L. (2006). Profiles of journalism education: What students are being offered in Australia. *Proceedings, Journalism Education Association Annual Conference*, Surfers Paradise: Griffith University.

Aedy, R. (2013, April 12). Interview with Fairfax Media CEO, Greg Hywood. In *Media Report* [Radio broadcast]. Sydney, Australia: ABC Radio National.

Alysen, B. (2007). A strategy for vocational education in the news media at a time of industrial change: Bridging the contradiction in journalism education. Retrieved from http://www.aare.edu.au/pages/publications.html

Alysen, B., & Oakham, K. (1996). The Jana Wendt factor: An empirical study of myths and misconceptions among journalism students. *Australian Journalism Review, 18*(1), 39-53.

Australian Bureau of Statistics (2012). Cultural diversity in Australia. Retrieved from http://www.abs.gov.au/

Australian Communications and Media Authority (2015). Industry. Retrieved from http://www.acma.gov.au/Industry

Australian Qualifications Framework Council (2013). Australian Qualifications Framework. 2nd edition. Retrieved from http://www.aqf.edu.au/aqf/in-detail/2nd-ed-jan-2013/

Bromley, M. (2013). Field maturation in journalism: The role of hackademics as a "motley crew." *International Journal of Cultural Studies, 17*(1), 3-19.

Callaghan, R. (2011). Selling the dream: Are we offering employability or making a vocational offer? Proceedings of the *20th Annual Teaching Learning Forum*. Perth: Edith Cowan University. Retrieved from http://otl.curtin.edu.au/tlf/tlf2011/refereed/callaghan.html

Cleary, P. (2015, July 14). At the ABC, diversity means British journos. *The Australian*. Retrieved from http://www.theaustralian.com.au/business/media/at-the-abc-diversity-means-british-journos/story-e6frg996-1226987539084

Cokley, J., Edstrom, M., McBride, J., & Ranke, A. (2011). Moving away from 'big media': Students, jobs and long-tail theory. *Australian Journalism Review, 33*(1), 107-118.

Cokley, J., Gilbert, L., Jovic, L., & Hanrick, P. (2015). Growth of "Long Tail" in Australian journalism supports new engaging approach to audiences.

Continuum: Journal of Media & Cultural Studies, 1-17. Retrieved from http://dx.doi.org/10.1080/10304312.2015.1099152

Coleman, G. (1992). *Wayward sojourn—Pioneer tertiary journalism education in Australia.* MA Thesis. University of Technology, Sydney.

Cryle, D. (1997). *Disreputable profession. Journalists and journalism in colonial Australia.* Rockhampton: Central Queensland University Press.

Cullen, T. (2014). News editors evaluate journalism courses and graduate employability. *Asia Pacific Media Educator, 24*(2), 209-224.

Cullen, T., & Callaghan, R. (2010). Promises, promises: are Australian universities deceiving journalism students? *Australian Journalism Review, 32*(2), 117-129.

Cunningham, S., & Flew, T. (2000). De-westernising Australia's media system and cultural coordinates. In J. Curran & M. J. Park (Eds.), *De-westernizing media studies* (pp. 221-236). London: Routledge.

Cunningham, S., & Turnbull, S. (Eds.), *The media and communications in Australia.* Crows Nest: Aleen & Unwin.

Department of Communications and the Arts (2014). Media control and ownership. Policy Background Paper No. 3. Retrieved from https://www.communications.gov.au/publications/media-control-and-ownership-policy-background-paper-no3

Department of Employment. (2014). Job Outlook—Journalists and other writers. Retrieved from http://joboutlook.gov.au/occupation.aspx?code=2124

Deuze, M. (2005). What is journalism? Professional identity and ideology of journalists reconsidered. *Journalism, 6*(4), 442-464.

Deuze, M. (2006). Global journalism education: A conceptual approach. *Journalism Studies, 7*(1), 19-34.

Flew, T., Daniel, A., Spurgeon, C. L., & Swift, A. G. (2011). Convenience, loyal, and customising users: a survey of the behaviours and intentions of young online news users in Australia. *Australian Journalism Review, 33*(2), 99-112.

Forde, S. (2005). The changing face of the Australian newsroom: Cultural and ethnic diversity among Sydney journalists. *Australian Journalism Review, 27*(2), 119-134.

Green, K. (2005). Journalism education: Towards a better understanding. *Australian Journalism Review, 27*(1), 185-194.

Green, K., & Sykes, J. (2004). Australia needs journalism education accreditation. Retrieved from http://portal.unesco.org/ci/en/

Hanitzsch, T., Hanusch, F., Mellado, C., Anikina, M., Berganza, R., Cangoz, I., Coman, M., Hamada, B., Hernández, M., Karadjov, C., Moreira, S., Mwesige, P., Plaisance, P., Reich, Z., Seethaler, J., Skewes, E., Vardiansyah Noor, D., & Kee Wang Yuen, E. (2011). Mapping journalism cultures across nations: A comparative study of 18 countries. *Journalism Studies, 12*(3), 273-293.

Hanusch, F. (2013a). Journalists in times of change: evidence from a new survey of Australia's journalistic workforce. *Australian Journalism Review*, *35*(1), 29-42.

Hanusch, F. (2013b). Moulding them in the industry's image: journalism education's impact on students' professional views. *Media International Australia, Incorporating Culture & Policy*, 146, 48-59.

Henningham, J. (1989). Why and how journalists should be professionalised. *Australian Journalism Review, 11*, 27-32.

Henningham, J. (1998). Australian journalists. In D. Weaver (Ed.), *The global journalist: News people around the world* (pp. 91-107). Cresskill, NJ.: Hampton Press.

Herbert, J. (2002). Just think of it as peer review: Industry accreditation will protect the future. *Australian Journalism Review, 24*(2), 173-186.

Hirst, M. (2010). Journalism education "Down Under": A tale of two paradigms. *Journalism Studies*, *11*(1), 83-98.

Jakubowicz, A. (2010). Diversity and news in Australia. Retrieved from http://andrewjakubowicz.com/

Jolly, R. (2014). Media of the people: broadcasting community media in Australia. Retrieved from http://www.aph.gov.au/About_Parliament/Parliamentary_Departments/Parliamentary_Library/pubs/rp/rp1314/Media

Jones, P., & Pusey, M. (2010). Political communication and 'media system': the Australian canary. *Media, Culture & Society*, *32*(3), 451-471.

Josephi, B. (2007). Positioning journalism research and journalism education in times of change. *Australian Journalism Review*, *29*(1), 3-12.

Journalism Education & Research Association of Australia. (2015). Journalism Research Australia National Statement. Retrieved from http://jeaa.org.au/research/

Kenyon A., & Marjoribanks, T. (2008). Chilled journalism? Defamation and public speech in U. S. and Australian law and journalism. *New Zealand Sociology, 23*(2), 18-33.

Loo, E. (2006). Contextualising the teaching of journalism. *Asia Pacific Media Educator*, *17*, iii-iv.

Lloyd, C. (1999). British press traditions, colonial governors and the struggle for a 'free' press. In A. Curthoys & J. Schultz (Eds.), *Journalism: Print, politics and popular culture* (pp. 10-19). St Lucia: University of Queensland Press.

Markson, S. (2014, October, 13). Uni degrees in indoctrination. *The Australian*, 29.

McCallum, K., & Posetti, J. (2008). Researching journalism and diversity in Australia: History and policy. Retrieved from http://www.networkinsight.org/events/cprf08.html/group/6

McGuire, C. (1992). Professions education. In M.C. Alkin (Ed.), *Encyclopedia of Educational Research* (pp. 1056-1062). New York, NY: MacMillan.

Nash, C. (2003). Freedom of the press in Australia, democratic Audit of Australia. Retrieved from http://www.safecom.org.au/press-freedom.htm

Nielsen, E. (2015). *Evaluating the next generation of news makers: What employers want and universities provide.* (BA Honors Thesis). Queensland University of Technology, Australia.

O'Donnell, M., Tanner, S., Cullen, T., & Green, K. (2013). Graduate qualities and journalism curriculum renewal: Balancing tertiary expectations and industry needs in a changing environment. Retrieved from http://ro.uow.edu.au/jer/

O'Donnell, P. (1999). The other 66 per cent? Rethinking the labour market for journalism graduates. *Australian Journalism Review, 21*(1), 123-142.

O'Donnell, P. (2002). The odd couple? Academic research and journalism education. *Australian Studies in Journalism,* 10/11, 58-83.

O'Donnell, P. (2014). Journalism education. In B. Griffen-Foley (Ed.), *A companion to the Australian media* (pp. 225-227). North Melbourne: Australian Scholarly Publishing.

O'Donnell, P., & Hutchinson, J. (2015). Pushback journalism: Twitter, user-engagement and journalism students' responses to *The Australian. Australian Journalism Review, 37*(1), 105-120.

O'Donnell, P., & Van Heekeren, M. (2015). JERAA@40: towards a history of the professional association of Australian journalism academics. *Australian Journalism Review, 37*(2), 5-22.

O'Donnell, P., McKnight, D., & Este, J. (2012). *Journalism at the speed of bytes: Australian Newspapers in the 21st century.* Sydney: Media Alliance/Walkley Foundation.

Oliver, B., Bethell, P., Fernandez, J., Harrison, J., & Breit, R. (2011). Benchmarking journalism courses with a focus on graduate employability. In *Proceedings of the AUQF: Demonstrating Quality.* Melbourne: Australian Universities Quality Agency.

Patching, R. (1996). Development of journalism courses in Australia: Some preliminary findings. *Asia Pacific Media Educator, 1,* 153-161.

Phillips, G. (2011). Reporting diversity: The representation of ethnic minorities in Australia's television current affairs programs. *Media International Australia,* 139, 23-31.

Putnis, P., Axford, B., Watson, L., & Blood, W. (2002). *Communication and media studies in Australian universities: An investigation into the growth, status, and future of this field of study.* Canberra: University of Canberra.

Richards, I. (1997). Assessing our history: two decades of *Australian Journalism Review. Australian Journalism Review, 19*(1), 181-186.

Ricketson, M. (2001). All things to everyone: Expectations of tertiary journalism education. *AsiaPacific Media Educator,* 10, 94-98.

Ricketson, M. (2014, October 24). Media students gain critical skills at uni. *The Australian,* 14.

Scanlon, C. (2009, November 23). All those journalism graduates ... all these jobs. *Crikey*. Retrieved from http://www.crikey.com.au/

Sheridan Burns, L. (2002). *Understanding journalism*. London: Sage.

Skehan, J., & Laybutt, A. (2009). A 10-year review: The Australian media and responses to reporting suicide and mental illness. Paper presented to Australian Media Traditions Conference, Sydney, 23-25 November.

Stuart, C. (1996). *Our judges' credentials. Development of journalism education in Australia to 1987*. (PhD Thesis). University of Wollongong, Wollongong.

Tanner, S., O'Donnell, M., Cullen, T., & Green, K. (2013). Graduate qualities and journalism curriculum renewal: Balancing tertiary expectations and industry needs in a changing environment. Retrieved from http://ro.uow.edu.au/jer/

Tiffen, R. (2014). The press. In S. Cunningham & S. Turnbull (Eds.), *The media and communications in Australia* (pp. 95-109). Sydney: Allen & Unwin.

Turner, G. (2011). The ERA and journalism research. *Australian Journalism Review*, *33*(1), 5-7.

Vatsikopoulos, H. (2015, April 29). Whitewash? That's not the colour of the SBS charter. *The Conversation*. Retrieved from http://theconversation.com/whitewash-thats-not-the-colour-of-the-sbs-charter-40837

Vromen, A., Xenos, M. A., & Loader, B. (2015). Young people, social media and connective action: from organisational maintenance to everyday political talk. *Journal of Youth Studies*, *18*(1), 80-100.

Table 1.1

Major Journalism Associations and Journalism-Related Organizations in Australia

Organization	Description	Contact
Australian Centre for Independent Journalism	Activities include investigative journalism, continuing education and research, and debate on areas of concern to journalists.	http://www.uts.edu.au/research-and-teaching/our-research/australian-centre-independent-journalism
Australian Communications and Media Authority (ACMA)	Commonwealth regulatory authority responsible for broadcasting, radio communications, telecommunications, and online content since July 1, 2005.	http://www.acma.gov.au
Australian Indigenous Communication Association	Represents indigenous media, including 150 remote community radio and television facilities, 25 urban and regional radio stations, and a commercial television service.	http://www.aicainc.org.au
Australian Press Council (APC)	Self-regulatory print media body, established in 1976 to help preserve press freedom.	http://www.presscouncil.org.au
Journalism Education and Research Association of Australia (JERAA)	Professional association for Australian and South Pacific journalism educators that aims to improve journalism teaching, research, and professional links.	http://jeaa.org.au
Australian and New Zealand Communication Association (ANZCA)	Professional association for Australian and New Zealand teachers and researchers in the diverse disciplines of communication.	http://www.anzca.net
Media, Entertainment and Arts Alliance (MEAA)	Trade union and professional organization created in 1992 by amalgamation of the Australian Journalists' Association (AJA) and related unions.	http://www.alliance.org.au
Media Watch	A weekly program on national, non-commercial television, set up in 1989, to critique journalist practices.	http://www.abc.net.au/mediawatch/
Walkley Foundation	Responsible for the leading national media industry prizes.	http://www.walkleys.com

Table 1.2

Major Academic Journalism Programs and Non-Academic Training Programs in Australia

Program	Description	Contact
University of Queensland	Australia's first journalism school, set up in 1921, and now preparing graduates for a global information society.	http://www.uq.edu.au/sjc
Deakin University	Provides students with the skills and knowledge needed to become qualified journalists in the broadcast and print media.	http://www.deakin.edu. au/study-at-deakin/find-a-course/journalism
University of Technology, Sydney	A national leader in journalism education for over three decades, graduating many of Australia's acclaimed journalists.	http://www.uts.edu.au/ future-students/communication/study-areas/ journalism
RMIT University	Emphasis on preparing graduates for successful media careers within a constantly changing environment.	http://www.rmit.edu.au/ study-with-us/communi cation-and-digital-media
Queensland University of Technology	Offers a comprehensive program, including cutting-edge online journalism options such as reporting, editing, and production.	https://www.qut.edu. au/study/study-areas/ study-journalism
J-School	The one-year J-School diploma gives students the knowledge and skills to apply for an entry-level position in journalism.	http://www.jschool.com. au

2

Journalism Education in Chile: Navigating Historically Diverse Views and Goals

Silvia Pellegrini

Journalism and journalism professionals in Chile receive mixed reviews; while strongly supported by some, they are strongly criticized by others. Some journalists are seen as national leaders, others as untrustworthy. Nevertheless, journalism is deeply rooted in Chilean history.

Chile's first newspaper, *La Aurora de Chile* (www.auroradechile. cl), was created in 1812, six years before Chile's independence from Spain. Although it lasted only a year, this weekly spread liberal ideas by publishing fragments of speeches taken from both the French and American revolutions. The newspaper's founder, Friar Camilo Henríquez, was arrested during the Spanish Inquisition, probably due to reading prohibited books (Amunátegui, 1889).

Chilean journalism was founded on activism for personal freedoms and against colonial mindsets. In 1872, the first Press Law, based on liberal principles, was enacted (Ossandón & Santa Cruz, 2001). Inspired by this law, many journalists left activism and wrote mainly about philosophical and cultural issues (Santa Cruz, 1988).

Early Chilean journalists were mostly bohemians who learned the trade by working in the media. It was not until 1953 that the first journalism schools were created in response to a need for quality control and ethical standards. While academia brought professional attitudes and standards to the field, the tension between objective newsgathering and political activism never quite disappeared.

In past decades, journalism education has spread throughout the country. But its standards are very dissimilar. For many schools, teaching journalism requires only mastering some basic skills, while others strive to develop a very updated, scholarly curriculum.

This chapter will outline the state of journalism in Chile before focusing on the state of journalism education nationwide. In this manner, it will put journalism education, and its many challenges, in context.

Journalism in the Media Landscape

Chile is an institutionally and economically stable democracy and has one of the least regulated communication markets in Latin America (Mastrini & Becerra, 2011). There are almost no legal impediments for media ownership or for foreign investors in communications. The only exceptions are that the same geographical area cannot have two broadcast TV stations belonging to the same owner. In addition, the government or the National Television Council gives radio and TV stations the right to broadcast for a certain number of years. Chile has one TV network, Televisión Nacional de Chile (TVN), that broadcasts throughout the country. A corporate body independently governs this network, which is funded through advertising only.

Although freedom of speech and the press are constitutionally guaranteed and fully practiced (Freedom House, 2016), critics often point to the media's lower-than-expected performance. Such critics condemn the media's centralization (Dermota, 2002), concentration of ownership (Del Valle, 2006; Muñoz & Jiménez, 2007; Monckeberg, 2009), and acquiescence to corporate communication and entertainment (Santander, 2007; Porath, 2007). They also argue that journalists are too dependent on official and anonymous sources and fail to practice rigorous, in-depth reporting. In addition, newsroom budget cuts and self-restraining practices, dating from Chile's dictatorship years (1973-1989), seem to have further weakened Chilean journalism (Faúndes Merino, 1998). Journalists believe that poor news coverage is the main challenge they currently face (Universidad Alberto Hurtado [UAH], 2011).

The traditional media's investigative reporting allegedly lost some of its previous edge in the 1990s after the country´s democracy was reestablished. Some traditional media outlets ceased digging into issues, an act previously considered an important way to fight against the regime (Faúndes Merino, 2001). In the last few years this tendency has reversed: Journalism is now playing a significant role in improving democratic standards via demanding ethical behavior in political and economic arenas. Significant public and private improvements have also taken place to improve journalistic coverage. For example, a Transparency Law was enacted in 2008 to reinforce press freedom and to secure public access to government documents (www.bcn.cl/leydetransparencia). Additionally, a private center for investigative journalism/online media organization, CIPER, was created in 2007 (www.ciperchile.cl). And two additional online media organizations also compete to reveal news not covered by traditional media: El Mostrador (www.elmostrador.cl) and El Libero (www.ellibero.cl).

Today, the Chilean press' main broadsheet, the iconic *El Mercurio*— established in Valparaiso in 1827—is the world's oldest continuously published Spanish-language daily newspaper (www.gda.com). In 1900, *El Mercurio* also started operations in Santiago "according to modern professional standards and techniques" (Bernedo & Arriagada, 2002). It is owned by Agustín Edwards, the founder's grandson, and it has developed a network of 21 regional newspapers. Chile's other main newspaper, *La Tercera,* a tabloid owned by Copesa, is *El Mercurio's* major competitor.

Television is by far the most popular Chilean mass medium. In Chile there are six broadcast networks (www.CNTV.cl) and 10 cable companies. TV is now facing major changes due to the introduction of digital television and ownership shifts. Past President Sebastián Piñera sold Chilevisión to Time Warner, Andrónico Luksic bought a majority stake in Pontificia Universidad Católica de Chile's (UC) Canal 13, and the Bethia Group bought Megavisión in 2012. Accordingly, television channels previously owned by the state and universities are now owned by private investors. Digital television broadcasting, started in 2014, should be fully established in 2020.

Television, including the public network TVN, is fully funded by advertising. Although news programming is very popular, public educators, politicians, and audiences often criticize its quality. Audience demand for better news led to the creation of CNN Chile in 2008, Chile's first 24-hour news channel, followed that same year by TVN's 24 Horas. Both are pay-cable offerings.

Radio is popular among Chilean news audiences. Some 60% of all age and socioeconomic groups listen to radio. The top news radio station is Radio Cooperativa, followed by Bio-Bio (Iniciative, 2011; Ipsos, 2015). The other significant news radio stations are ADN, Tele13Radio, and DUNA. Most of the nearly 1,000 radio stations are privately owned, while over one third belong to transnational consortiums (Ramírez, 2009). Most of the stations are primarily dedicated to music. Regional radio is well established and plays a significant role in social development, especially in remote areas.

Aside from the traditional media with their own websites, there are several online news media outlets successfully attracting audiences, especially the well informed, such as El Mostrador (created in 2000) and CIPER (created in 2007). Approximately 94% of Chilean Internet users visit news sites. Chileans also lead Latin American visits to business and financial sites, in numbers similar to that in developed countries (ComScore, 2013).

Citizen journalism played a significant role during the Feb. 27, 2010, 8.6-point Chilean earthquake, in which local Chileans helped provide information from often inaccessible areas (Pellegrini, 2010; Puente & Grassau, 2011). Eight months later, 57 news sites existed—12 linked into a citizen journalism network—relying on some 7,000 citizen journalists for coverage of events. Today social media have also taken a significant, popular place in Chilean society. Chileans who use social networks, which reach 90% of the population, are commonly used as sources by the media.

Journalists' attitudes toward new technologies and the Internet seem mixed. For example, a survey of journalists found that although 88.2% said the Internet has improved their work, 69.5% said the Internet has also increased the amount of false information published (Universidad Alberto Hurtado, 2012). That said, employers are more likely to hire beginning journalists who possess new technology skills, even though many journalism schools only have traditional technical abilities.

Professional Characteristics

There is a large number of journalists in Chile: around 12,000 in a country of some 17 million people. Journalists are considered more culturally liberal and critical than average citizens. More than two thirds of journalists are younger than 40 (Mellado, Salinas, Del Valle, & González, 2010), and most of them are based in Santiago. Regional media outlets often cannot find journalism graduates to hire. Since a degree in journalism is not required to work in a newsroom, other professionals, especially lawyers and economists, are sometimes hired as journalists. Nevertheless, journalism graduates hold the majority of newsroom jobs, including media management positions.

Although a Chilean journalism association, Colegio de Periodistas, has existed since 1956, Chilean journalists are not strongly committed to collective action. After the establishment of Colegio de Periodistas around one third of journalists joined the association, but only 16% of them are active members (Mellado, Salinas, & Barría, 2010). Media owners have also created an association, Federación de Medios, to safeguard their interests, especially in terms of government interference and regulation. Similarly, entrepreneurs have founded a council for media ethics (see Table 2.1 for major journalism associations and journalism-related organizations).

Currently, some 20 media outlets generate most media jobs (Délano, Niklander, & Susacasa, 2007). Significant job losses, due to higher newsroom costs and decreasing advertising revenues, are being counterbalanced by hiring young people for media outlets' website platforms. About 88% of journalists believe the Internet has improved journalism insofar as it allows better timing within which to cover news events (25%), better investigative reporting (24%), and better detection of fresh news (21%).

Average journalism salaries have declined compared to salaries in similar professions. Since this decline, the national university admission test scores in journalism have decreased by 20%. The highest paid journalists, the top 10%, earn about six times more than the lowest paid journalists, the bottom 10%. Around 1,200 graduates enter the journalism profession every year. Two years after graduation, some 82% of journalists are employed and earn, on average, around U.S. $1,200 a month (Ministerio de Educación, 2013). After five years, such salaries increase some by 50%. Many journalism students are enrolled in post-graduate studies in Chile or abroad; some of them even choose academia as their future career. Only a few universities offer full-time positions to experienced professionals and/or those with master's or doctoral degrees, although many hire journalists for hourly academic positions.

While traditional media jobs are shrinking, corporate communications and consulting jobs are booming. The average salary for these new jobs is almost double that of traditional media positions, so students are very attracted to them. The government is also hiring journalists for communication and public relations jobs (Torres, 2003), and politicians hire them as communication advisors.

Journalists rate strategic or corporate communications "disguised" as news as the most important ethical issue they encounter. Other major professional problems include a "lack of investigative reporting," "reporting against the clock," "too much competition" and a "loss of interest in covering complex stories" (www.puroperiodismo.cl; UAH, 2011).

As in every pluralistic country, Chilean journalists perceive their role in many different ways (watchdogs, agents for development, political activists, etc.), depending on their personal interests and the editorial view of the media they work for. Even though politically biased journalism has deep roots in the country´s history, a more detached professional role has gained much respect among mainstream journalists.

Journalism Education, Professional Training, and Research

Chilean law rules that journalism can only be taught at universities since a degree (for any profession, not just journalism) is mandatory for a media professional (or any other professional) to enter a field.

Once considered an elite profession that required very high test scores and generated only a few graduates every year, programs have rapidly expanded to meet student demands. Just over two decades ago, only four schools offered journalism studies. Today, 31 of 54 universities (www.cned.cl) provide journalism studies. However, some of them lack the appropriate academic staff to ensure quality. Journalism studies experienced its highest enrollment growth, 367%, in the 1990s, followed by its highest enrollment losses, -14.9%, during 2000-2009. Such figures have stabilized recently, and about 85% of students are expected to find jobs after graduation.

Teaching and Training Future Newsmakers

Although the normal pathway to enter the journalism profession is through academia, there are no legal requirements for the curricula, except that a bachelor's degree (*Licenciatura* in Spanish) requires the equivalent of 130 U.S. credits. There are also no requirements regarding what to teach in a journalism curriculum or how to teach journalism or any other subject. Universities are deeply aware of their academic independence. Accordingly, a lack of requirements, along with almost no official information released on journalism school practices, makes it difficult to trace program trends.

However, studies show there tend to be seven types or groupings of courses in journalism curricula, which offer everything from introductory courses striving to correct high school deficiencies to those teaching specialized research skills. Such studies also reveal that the largest grouping of curricula, 30%-40%, focuses on journalism concepts and skill courses, while the second largest grouping, 27.7%, focuses on general education. The remaining five groupings are: technological skills (14.3%), communication theory (11.1%), research (5.3%), ethics and law (4.5%), and management (3.7%) (Cavallo, 2001; Muñoz & Guzmán, 2005; Fuenzalida, Escobar, Pizarro, Villegas, & Cea, 2004; Délano et al., 2007). A recent study of 10 of the more prestigious Chilean schools of journalism found that around 45% of courses focus on professional skills, including technological and research skills; around 20% on general education; around 15% on communication theory; and the remaining 20% on social sciences, including law, ethics, sociology, and management (Facultad de Comunicaciones UC, 2015).

The academic task of journalism education is interpreted in extremely different ways. Some schools attempt to prepare reporters for entry-level jobs with some liberal arts courses and only a few technology classes, limited by the high cost of setting up appropriate labs. Most schools rely on sociology and mass communications as the basic cognate disciplinary fields. Other schools, in keeping with Chilean journalism tradition, focus on teaching political and critical approaches to society and professional skills. Journalism scholars tend to agree that a balance between liberal arts courses and technology/media-oriented ones is needed in order to best prepare students for careers in journalism. Critical thinking is considered essential for training journalists, so much so that lawyers and economists are often hired to teach students such skills. Following European tradition, almost all schools offer a 10-semester fixed curriculum. Still, there are those that offer nine or even eight semesters (Consejo Nacional de Educación Superior [CNED], 2010). Some schools have created a number of elective courses or elective specialization tracks. Others have added professional training to a two-year general bachelor's degree. Probably due to the high cost of implementing a credit-based, flexible curriculum, only Pontificia Universidad Católica de Chile (UC) allows students to choose courses freely (within certain specifications) from schools within the university. It provides up to 150 "minors" or specialist certificates within its bachelor's degree.

In many schools, curricula have evolved very slowly since the first half of the 20th century (González, 2003) and are extremely behind the recent significant changes in media and journalism environments. In an attempt to quickly update journalism education, most current curricula have included communication theory and technology courses and computer labs. Some others have made huge investments in new technologies. However, less than one fourth of schools have taken on innovative leadership roles in journalism education.

To increase job opportunities, many schools prepare students to work in any medium or content area, as well as in corporate communications and public relations. This approach leads mostly to a focus on reporting and writing skills and is primarily responsible for extended studies. This general focus responds to a trend across Latin America (Federación Latinoamericana de Facultades de Comunicación Social [FELAFACS], 2005). However, recently a few schools have differentiated themselves by proposing management skills as a significant part of their curricula (Délano et al., 2007).

Almost half of Chile's regions do not have journalism schools. More than half of the country's journalism schools are located in Santiago. In 2005, enrollment in journalism programs peaked at 8,363 students. Five years later, in 2010, this number had decreased 25.1% to 6,264 students and, as of 2015, to 5,986 students (Ministerio de Educación, 2015). Both historically and currently, journalism students tend to be female (Cavallo, 2001). As of 2015, 55.7% of journalism students are female versus 44.3% male.

Journalism faculty are scarce and expensive to train. Accordingly, many schools offer teaching programs supported by mostly part-time professionals and only two or three full-timers. In 2004, overall faculty size was estimated at 730 professors: 11.5% full-time, 9% half-time, and 79.5% working professionals teaching one or two courses (Fuenzalida et al., 2004). Most full-time faculty work at older, more traditional universities. And while some have earned master's degrees, very few have earned doctorates.

Journalists do not often pursue postgraduate studies, allegedly due to little economic incentive. Regardless, the number doing so has recently increased. Chilean academic tradition, unlike that in the rest of Latin America, is for students to enter postgraduate studies abroad—especially the stronger students pursuing doctoral degrees. Government competitive scholarships and special loans are available under certain conditions (www.conicyt.cl). Chilean universities only began offering their own doctorate degrees during the past few decades, most of them in scientific areas. A recent survey indicates that only around 1% of Chilean journalism students enter doctoral programs—almost all of whom do so abroad. The only doctoral program in Chile is at UC. Slightly over 9% enter master's degree programs inside and outside Chile (UC, 2009). After earning a bachelor's degree, some 7.6% of journalism students study for an extra diploma, or take additional courses, in a variety of content subjects. Skills-training courses are not very popular, and the media do not encourage them: Some 59.3% of journalists report they have never participated in any training course provided by the media or company in which they work (www.puroperiodismo.cl).

Only two universities, UC and Universidad Adolfo Ibáñez (UAI), have created master´s programs in journalism—each of which is very different. Other schools offer master's degrees in communication studies. UC's program, a joint-venture with *El Mercurio,* focuses on print journalism. It combines theoretical university courses with practical newspaper ones, and it recruits students from all over Latin America through a group called Diarios de las Américas (www.gda.com).

UAI's program begins with its regular undergraduate curriculum and adds three trimesters of journalism-related theoretical courses in the mornings and practical courses in the press, radio, and TV in the afternoons. All students then take a UAI-approved media internship of their choice.

When students select schools, they often consider the institutions' accreditation status, brand image, and media rankings. Two levels of accreditation are available: one for each institution, and one for each program. They are provided by the *Consejo Nacional de Acreditación*, through private agencies, and they are not mandatory. That is unless a program is seeking government grants and scholarships, especially scholarships for studying for master's or doctoral degrees abroad. UC runs the first, and for many years the only, journalism school outside the United States with Accrediting Council on Education in Journalism and Mass Communication (ACEJMC) accreditation. It first earned it over a decade ago. Some other journalism schools are accredited at the Comisión Latinoamericana para Acreditación de Escuelas de Periodismo.

Journalism Research

It is not easy to characterize journalism research within journalism programs, let alone how journalism research compares to research conducted in other academic disciplines.

As in any academic area, the most valued journalism research strives to generate knowledge within the discipline. That said, journalism schools also consider as research the following: in-depth reporting, surveys, and polls or focus groups related to the profession, the media, or different aspects of communication. Some universities have created research centers with either dependent or independent statuses from their schools. These research centers primarily aim to either reinforce brand positioning or serve as consulting agencies in communication issues. They often join strategic associations with researchers and public or private institutions (Dittus, 2010), as well as partnerships on national or international projects. Critics argue that the research centers' involvement with corporate sponsors can eventually weaken their academic value.

In 1967, Chile created a governmental advisory council, Comisión Nacional de Investigación Científica y Tecnológica (CONICYT), which determines scientific research policies and oversees human resources. CONICYT has increasingly given competitive grants to promote high quality research. Its administrative unit, Fondo Nacional de Desarrollo Científico y Tecnológico, also known as FONDECYT (www.fondecyt.

cl), was created in 1981. FONDECYT currently has an annual budget of around U.S. $158 million. The funds are allocated to different disciplines, with the sciences receiving most of them. Journalism, which does not belong to its own designated discipline, splits a small budget with sociology. In 2014, this grouping approved and funded only 23 projects out of 581. Only some 22 journalism, media, or communication-related projects, which underwent a blind review with national and international peers, have been funded during the last decade. The projects' topics and approaches are too broad to determine what type of research is most likely to receive funding. Funding lasts from one to four years, depending on the project's timeline and budget needs.

In 2009 CONICYT created a small grant to support applied studies about pluralism in the press and radio, including research dealing with media agendas and media income. Up to two such studies, quantitative or qualitative, are supported each year for up to approximately U.S. $120,000.

In the 1990s another competitive governmental fund, Fondo de Fomento al Desarrollo Científico y Tecnológico (FONDEF; www.fondef.cl), was created to increase national economic competitiveness through research and development projects in pre-determined fields that could generate positive social and economic achievements. One such field is technology, through which communication projects can qualify. UC's School of Journalism has been granted three FONDEF projects which, compared to FONDECYT projects, have very big budgets. Two of these projects are aimed at modeling the information and communication management processes taking place—in the case of journalism, a multiplatform newsroom. No other school of journalism has won FONDEF funds.

Because of an overall scarcity of journalism funds and highly competitive proposals, winning a FONDECYT or FONDEF grant is considered "the real thing." Faculty members are also sometimes able to gain limited research funding by joining international networks and/or getting private grants, which are rare and small.

Research must lead to publication. Researchers get points in CONICYT and in their universities for publishing in journals. The most valued journals are listed at the ISI Web of Science. However, few of them specialize in journalism, and only a few are in Spanish. Recently ISI publications related to journalism have been rising. Second-tier publications are listed in SciELO, a scientific electronic library. Third-tier and lower publications can be found on indexes such as Latindex and DIALNET. And since access to the best journals is increasingly difficult, some schools have created their own journals, which possess different interests, indexations, quality standards, and circulation rates.

Academic journalism also contributes to knowledge through books in print and online. Significant texts are based on journalistic, in-depth reporting of important social/political/ historical events and movements, such as those taking place during Chile's military regime (1973 to 1989). Some of these books have received international acclaim, but book or book chapter publishing does not gain much credit for researchers. This book publishing trend, although fading, continues today.

The quality of Chilean journalism research, along with its depth and breadth, varies even more than curricula in undergraduate programs. However, survey-based research dealing with a wide variety of professional journalism topics, such as innovative newsgathering methods, far outnumbers theoretically oriented research.

Professional Connections in Journalism Education

Chilean journalism schools usually require internships to provide their students with first-hand experience and professional contacts (see Table 2.2 for a ranking of the top 10 academic journalism programs). Media outlets like to choose their own student interns through open competitions, which is how the best internships are granted. In a recent survey, two thirds of students said they found their internship without their university's help and, often, through personal connections. Only one third of students reported they found their internship with some university assistance (Délano et al., 2007).

Internships are not the only link between the media and universities. Many journalism schools build relationships with the media to develop their own projects, such as youth-oriented newspapers or student-run radio programs. In addition, some media outlets rely on the most prestigious journalism schools for innovative news design and journalistic practices, along with ethical analysis and advice.

Some universities offer diplomas and short in-house courses to media professionals. A new trend among universities is to create think tanks, where professionals discuss innovative topics in the media and other related areas, such as strategic communications, advertising, networking, and social media. Universities also tend to hire professional journalists to teach practical courses or workshops. And journalism programs invite well-known media professionals to give guest lectures and to participate in seminars and roundtables on current events for the university community and public. Recently, especially at private universities, schools of journalism have given some well-known media figures top positions to help attract more journalism students to their programs.

Journalism Education's Professional Impact

The social impact of Chilean journalism schools is driven more by its former students' success and visibility than by its academic achievements. Nevertheless, journalism programs enjoy prestige and respect. Yet although journalism school rankings have further aided public evaluations of programs, with variables such as student-faculty ratios and research grants, the prestige of a program's alumni seems most important to potential students. Journalism graduates have been successful in many fields. For example, several ministries of state, congressmen, and mayors have studied journalism, as have entrepreneurs, filmmakers, and the former president of the national soccer association. Journalists themselves are among the most important opinion leaders in the country. Finally, journalism graduates are gaining increased access to top positions in their field, such as chief newspaper editors or television network CEOs.

It is significant that even though the law does not require a journalism degree to work as a journalist, media organizations prefer to hire employees who do have such degrees. It is also ironic that the public often attributes media mistakes or inaccuracies to someone "not being a journalist" (i.e., not having a journalism degree).

Academics and professionals do work well together, although there is always some tension between their mutual approaches to media tasks and ways of performing news gathering. Occasionally the best schools train working journalists in special in-house programs or prepare international seminars on subjects of media interest. Professionals tend to look down on academics for a lack of experience in the field.

Future Possibilities

Chilean newsrooms and journalism education institutions share the common fear of an unknown future, especially regarding permanent adaptation to new job needs and procedures and audience hyper-fragmentation. Dealing with technology is a must, and many students are skilled at using new technology. The challenge is to determine the most effective way to use these technologies and improve the profession in the process.

Since effective journalism is based on journalists' ability to professionally select the news, find diverse and legitimate sources, critically analyze the information gathered, etc., the teaching of core journalism skills should continue to be an important focus.

Standardizing journalism curricula in different Chilean schools and their overall quality continues to be a challenge. Current journalism trends on college campuses—such as entrepreneurial initiatives among students, including Web projects, consulting agencies, and communication analysis for individuals or organizations—need to be supported with new courses or specialties drawn from journalism and other communication-related fields.

The development of interdisciplinary studies and further postgraduate studies are now almost mandatory if journalism education and the journalism profession in Chile are to have a successful future. Convergence and innovation are significant challenges that need constant exploration.

Journalism Education Issues, Challenges, and Innovations

Chilean university students strongly value gaining specific skills that can maximize their job opportunities. Journalism educators should keep this in mind when considering the newest tendencies in tertiary education, especially those dealing with competency approaches.

However, journalism educators will not adequately support journalism development if they train their students mainly according to current, constantly changing job market needs. Instead, they need to help predict and lead future media practices. Journalism schools can be excellent laboratories for testing synergies, new technologies, changing story-telling styles, and developing innovative newsrooms practices. This "lab" work could take place through new methodologies inside the classrooms, internships, or other academically evaluated activities, which could also be reviewed according to professional standards. Journalism educators should pay special attention to redefining what news is, including subjects related to the audience's daily life and new ways of networking and reporting.

Another issue that needs attention is whether or not journalism education should branch out more into newsgathering and/or communication studies. Although Chilean democracy needs strong in-depth reporting, there are not enough jobs in journalism. That said, the outlook for jobs in corporate communication appears strong, and lately most journalism graduates are hired for such positions. The problem is they are not sufficiently trained for such jobs and the often complex ethical dilemmas involved.

The Chilean media's emphasis on sports and entertainment coverage creates another educational problem. This emphasis not only makes it difficult to shape students' professional behavior, but it also leads their vocational expectations away from professional objective newsgathering. Journalists and editors alike state that journalism education should include values such as a commitment to the truth, critical thinking, and independence rather than journalists conforming to journalistic routines, a lack of autonomy, and the tendency to avoid taking risks (Gronemeyer, 2002).

Journalism education is also facing a challenge in developing new, relevant paths to specialization—a challenge journalism educators will probably have to meet with continuous education, development of alternative qualifications, etc. (Muñoz & Guzmán, 2005).

Journalism education goals in Chile are often difficult to pinpoint due to significant differences between approaches on how to educate journalists and huge differences in available resources. However, some challenges are clear. For example, schools need to hire more doctorates to support academic work and avoid hiring journalism professionals as full-time faculty members if they lack teaching experience or a critical view of professional practices. For future journalism education to be successful, schools must find a way to balance faculty who have professional experience with those who have postgraduate qualifications. Improved hiring procedures are very much needed to ensure critical and creative thinking in every aspect of the curriculum.

Examples of three successful innovations/best practices—which focus on service, academic research, and new technologies—follow. The first example, "Más de Chile" TM, was an innovative newscast jointly produced by academics and local broadcasters in 10 different regions using Web 2.0 tools. This allowed for the exchange of information and quality control through a methodology known as VAP ("Added Journalistic Value" in Spanish; Pellegrini et al., 2009; Pellegrini, Puente, Porath, Mujica, & Grassau, 2011). This experience emerged from a research and development project aimed at offering innovate news coverage, especially in distant regions with inadequate news services. It was broadcast during 2009 through professional cable TV at a significantly lower cost and higher quality than comparable newscasts. The team created diverse news teams and innovative products and procedures, all based on applied journalism research. This experiment has led to new teaching methods and newsroom practices. The program received a grant from the National Television Council, which ensured its continuation throughout 2010, with 15 regions involved. Its basic ideas are still being practiced on a CNN Chile program called Panorama 15.

The second two examples, introduced by UC's School of Journalism, have focused on innovative initiatives to improve research and technology abilities among undergraduate students. The first relates to scientific research abilities that are increasingly relevant in undergraduate studies. As such, the school has established a new academic policy that requires every professor who has a research grant to teach a research seminar on the subject for undergraduate students. This is to induce students to have direct experience with scientific logic and methodology. Courses are offered to a maximum of 12 students to ensure that they get firsthand experience in the subject and personal attention. The second relates to using technology to enhance journalism narratives. These skills are being taught through very short, voluntary seminars, which are also open to professionals. The last two seminars focused on 360° lenses and the possibilities and risks of reporting with drones.

Future innovations should be two-fold: They should be able to both include creative adaptation to external professional changes and to respond to internal academic challenges by reinforcing innovative, solid academic teaching based on research and related to state-of-the-art knowledge/findings.

Conclusion: Educating Tomorrow's Journalists—The Big Picture

If developments in the communication industry continue at the current speed, the challenges to journalism education will continue to grow rapidly. In the free Chilean educational system, general guidelines to university education, let alone journalism education, are difficult to obtain. But overall, prevailing university challenges seem to deal with a combination of epistemological matters and the need to meet market and job requirements. An innovative approach to competencies is needed overall and in journalism education specifically.

For journalism students, convergence and synergy are very significant issues. Most of these graduates will probably work in non-journalistic areas, such as corporate communication or advertising, and/or with content increasingly intertwined across media platforms. Professions outside of journalism should benefit from workers practicing core journalism competencies.

The journalism industry will probably need a smaller number of journalists, newsgathering experts, and analysts with significant new technology skills who can easily move across media platforms. However, this elite force of journalists could help serve democracy and set agendas, and employment potential will continue in communication fields. Accordingly, if education in basic journalism competencies is expanded and epistemological definitions are broadened, journalism students will be educated to take on additional professional roles and functions. As a result, not only will the demand for journalism students increase, but journalism students will also be better prepared for their multiple roles in society.

The need for good writing skills should remain high on the agenda. However, new narrative forms in writing and imaging, intertwined with technological skills, analytical abilities, and certification of data and sources, will be more vital.

Due to the shrinking job market, journalism graduates will need some entrepreneurial abilities, including project development and management skills, along with awareness of related legal, government, and policy matters. Such new skills could increase job opportunities.

Unfortunately, the question of how to increase future journalists' interest in covering news remains unanswered. Ironically, journalism students often lack the strong sense of curiosity they need to successfully cover the world around them.

References

América Economía (2015). Ver Ranking. Retrieved from http://rankings. americaeconomia.com/mba2015/

Amunátegui, M. (1889). *Camilo Henríquez*. Santiago: Imprenta Nacional.

Bernedo, P., & Arriagada, E. (2002). *Los inicios de El Mercurio de Santiago en el epistolario de Agustín Edwards Mac Clure (1899-1905)*. [The beginnings of *El Mercurio* in Santiago according to the letters of Augustin Edwards Mac Clure 1899-1905]. *Historia, 35*, 13-33. Retrieved from http://dx.doi.org/10.4067/S0717-71942002003500003

Cavallo, A. (2001). *Análisis y propuestas para la carrera de periodismo, Universidad Adolfo Ibáñez* [Analysis and proposals for Journalism Studies, Adolfo Ibáñez University]. *Manuscrito interno* [Internal manuscript]. Santiago, Chile.

ComScore (2013). *Informe futuro digital Latinoamérica* [Report on digital future in Latin America]. Retrieved from http://www.iab.cl/informe-futuro-digital-latinoamerica-2013-comscore/

Consejo Nacional de Educación Superior (CNED). (2010). *Índices: Matrícula primer año y total* [Indexes: First year and total enrollment]. Retrieved from http://www.cned.cl/public/Secciones/SeccionIndicesEstadisticas/doc/Estadisticas2010/03_EMMatriculas10.pdf

Del Valle, C. (2006). *Comunicación participativa, estado-nación y democracia. Discurso, tecnología y poder* [Participative communication, nation-state and democracy. Discourse, technology and power]. Temuco: Ediciones Universidad de La Frontera.

Délano, M., Niklander, K., & Susacasa, P. (2007). *Los periodistas recién titulados y el mercado laboral* [Recently graduated journalists and labor market]. *Calidad en la Educación, 27*, 205-234. Retrieved from http://www.cned.cl/public/secciones/secciongeneral/noticias/ppts/CSEConferencia01.pdf

Dermota, K. (2002). *Chile inédito, el periodismo bajo democracia* [Unheard of Chile, journalism under democracy]. Santiago: Ediciones B.

Dittus, R. (2010). *La investigación sobre mass media en Chile: del ideologismo a la construcción de paradigmas* [Mass media research in Chile: From ideologism to paradigm production]. *Estudios de Periodismo*, 8. Retrieved from http://www.periodismoudec.cl/estudiosdeperiodismo/index.php?Itemid=41&id=29&option=com_content&task=view

Facultad de Comunicaciones UC, Chile. (2015). *Estudio interno del proceso de admission* [Internal Report on the Admission Process]. *Subdirección de Asuntos Estudiantiles* [Deputy Direction for Students Affairs], Santiago.

Faúndes Merino, J. J. (1998). *Una perspectiva estratégica y compleja del periodismo latinoamericano* [A strategic and complex perspective of Latin American journalism]. *Diálogos de la Comunicación, Revista Academia de la FELAFACS, 51.* Retrieved from http://www.dialogosfelafacs.net/articulos/pdf/51JuanFaundes.pdf

Faúndes Merino, J. J. (2001). ¿Ocaso del periodismo de investigación en Chile y América Latina? [Decline of research journalism in Chile and Latin America?] *Razón y Palabra*, 22. Retrieved from http://www.razonypalabra.org.mx/anteriores/n22/22_jfaundes.html

Federación Latinoamericana de Facultades de Comunicación Social (FELAFACS) (2005). *Informe I Reunión Técnica de FELAFACS: La formación de los periodistas en las escuelas de comunicación de América Latina: situación actual, demandas labores y necesidades sociales* [First Report. FELAFACS Technical Meeting: Journalists' training at communication schools in Latin America: Present situation, labor demands and social needs]. Córdoba: Universidad Nacional de Río Cuarto.

Freedom House (2016). *Freedom of the press: Table of Global Press Freedom Rankings*. Washington, D.C.: Freedom House. Retrieved from https://freedomhouse.org/report/freedom-press/freedom-press-2016

Fuenzalida, D., Escobar, D., Pizarro, D., Villegas, C., & Cea, J. (2004). *Proyecto Carrera de Periodismo* [Internal Report on a Project for a School of Journalism]. Documento de circulación interna, Valparaiso: Universidad Técnica Federico Santa María (UTFSM).

González, R. G. (2003). *50 años de periodismo universitario en Chile: encuentros, desencuentros y desafíos* [50 years of university journalism in Chile: Agreements, disagreements, and challenges]. *Revista Comunicación y Medios, 14.* Retrieved from http://www.periodismo.uchile.cl/comunicacionymedios/14ggonzalez.html

Gronemeyer, M. E. (2002). *Periodistas chilenos. El reto de formar profesionales autónomos e independientes* [The challenge of training autonomous and independent professionals]. *Cuadernos de Información, 15,* 53-70. Retrieved from http://dialnet.unirioja.es/servlet/articulo;jsessionid=6959F-

5BA2CB9FDF2DC86FCACD9C8EBC2.dialnet01?codigo=2935348

Initiative (2011). *Ipsos Radio Ranking General de Audiencia* [Ipsos Radio General Audience Ranking]. Retrieved from http://www.emol.com/modulos/mediacenter/archivos/InformeRadio_jul%20oct2011.pdf

Ipsos (2015). *Informe Rad*io [Broadcasting Report]. Retrieved from http://www.ipsos.cl/ipsosradioalaire/pagdos.htm

Mastrini, G., & Mellado, M. (2011). Structure, concentration and changes of the media system in the Southern Cone of Latin America. Retrieved from Comunicar-36-Mastrini-Becerra-51-59-english%20(2).pdf

Mellado, C., Salinas, P., & Barría, S. (2010). *Estructura del empleo periodístico y validación profesional de sus prácticas en el mercado laboral chileno* [Structure of journalistic employment and professional validation of its practices in the Chilean labor market]. *Innovar, 20*(36), 91-106. Retrieved from http://www.scielo.org.co/scielo.php?pid=S0121-50512010000100008&script=sci_arttext

Mellado, C., Salinas, P., Del Valle, C., & González, G. (2010). *Estudio comparativo de cuatro regiones: Mercado laboral y perfil del periodista* [A comparative study in four regions: Labor market and profile of the Chilean journalist]. *Cuadernos de Información, 26*(1), 45-64. doi: 10.7764/cdi.26.11

Ministerio de Educación, Chile (2013). *Estadísticas por Carrera* [Career statistics]. Retrieved from http://www.mifuturo.cl/index.php/futuro-laboral/buscador-por-carrera?tecnico=false&cmbareas=5&cmbinstituciones=3

Ministerio de Educación, Chile (2015). *Estadísticas por Carrera* [Career statistics]. Retrieved from http://www.mifuturo.cl/index.php/futuro-laboral/buscador-por-carrera?tecnico=false&cmbareas=5&cmbinstituciones=3

Monckeberg, M. O. (2009). *Los magnates de la prensa: concentración de los medios de comunicación en Chile* [Press tycoons: Concentration of media in Chile]. Santiago, Chile: Debate.

Muñoz, M., & Guzmán, E. (2005). *La especialización del periodismo: un desafío aplicado a los modelos de enseñanza en las universidades chilenas frente a las demandas de la era global, hacia un mejor ejercicio en el siglo XXI* [Journalism specialization: A challenge applied to the teaching models in Chilean universities facing the demands of the global era—towards a better practice in the the XXI century]. (Unpublished thesis, Journalism degree). Universidad de Artes, Ciencias y Comunicación (UNIACC), Santiago, Chile.

Muñoz, J., & Jiménez, C. (2007). *La estructura de los medios de comunicación en Chile* [Structure of media in Chile]. *Razón y Palabra, 60*. Retrieved from http://www.razonypalabra.org.mx/anteriores/n60/varia/jimenes_munoz.html

Ossandón, C., & Santa Cruz, E. (2001). *Entre las alas y el plomo: la gestación de la prensa moderna en Chile* [Between wings and the lead: The gestation of the modern press in Chile]. Santiago, Chile: Lom Ediciones.

Pellegrini, S. (2010). *Análisis conceptual del periodismo ciudadano y propuesta metodológica para analizar su contribución informativa* [A conceptual analysis of citizen journalism and a methodological proposal for analyzing its informative contribution]. *Palabra Clave, 13*(2), 271-290. Retrieved from http://www.redalyc.org/articulo.oa?id=64916989004

Pellegrini, S., Puente, S., Godoy, S., Fernández, F., Julio, P., Martínez, J. E., Soto, J. A., & Grassau, D. (2009). *Ventanas y espejos. Televisión local en red* [Windows and mirrors. Local television in the Internet]. Santiago: *El Mercurio*-Aguilar.

Pellegrini, S., Puente, S., Porath, W., Mujica, C., & Grassau, D. (2011). *Valor agregado periodístico. La apuesta por la calidad de las noticias* [Journalistic added value. Betting for quality in news]. Santiago: Ediciones Universidad Católica de Chile.

Pontificia Universidad Católica de Chile. (2009). *Estudio interno de egresados de Periodismo.* [UC Internal Study on graduate students in Journalism]. Santiago, Chile: Vicerrectoría Académica, Pontificia Universidad Católica de Chile—Empresas UC.

Porath, W. (2007). *Los temas de la discusión pública en las elecciones presidenciales chilenas 2005: relaciones entre las agendas de los medios y las agendas mediatizadas de los candidatos y del gobierno* [Public discussion subjects in Chile's 2005 presidential elections: Relationships between the agendas of mass media and the mediatized agendas of candidates and government]. *América Latina Hoy, 46*, 41-73. Retrieved from http://revistas.usal.es/index.php/1130-2887/article/view/2452/2501

Puente, S., & Grassau, D. (2011). *Periodismo ciudadano, dos términos contradictorios. La experiencia chilena según sus protagonistas* [Citizen journalism: Two contradictory terms. The Chilean experience according to their own players]. *Palabra Clave, 14*(1), 137-155. Retrieved from http://www.redalyc.org/articulo.oa?id=64920732009

Ramírez, J. (2009). *La concentración de la propiedad radial en Chile: las exigencias de nuevos paradigmas entre globalidad y localidad* [Concentration of broadcasting stations in Chile: the demands of new paradigms between global and local]. *Redes.com, 5*, 309-327. Retrieved from http://dialnet.unirioja.es/servlet/articulo?codigo=3674199

Santa Cruz, E. (1988). *Análisis histórico del periodismo chileno* [Historical analysis of Chilean journalism]. Santiago: Nuestra América Ediciones.

Santander, P. (2007). *Medios en Chile (2002-2005). Entre la lucha por el poder y la sumisión al espectáculo* [Media in Chile (2002-2005). Between the struggle for power and submission to the show]. In P. Santander Molina (Ed.), *Los medios en Chile: voces y contextos* [Media in Chile: Voices and contexts], (pp. 11-37). Retrieved from http://www.euv.cl/archivos_pdf/medios.pdf

Torres, G. (2003). *La identidad del periodista y los desafíos gremiales y profesio-nales en la sociedad global y de la información. Informe preliminar para el X Congreso Nacional Extraordinario del Colegio de Periodistas de Chile* [The The identity of the journalist and the professional and labor association challenges in the global and information society. Initial report presented at the X National Extraordinary Congress of the Journalists Professional Association, Chile]. Retrieved from http://www.periodismo.uchile.cl/documentos/

Universidad Alberto Hurtado (UAH). (2011). *Encuesta Estado del Periodismo Nacional 2010, Informe de Resultados* [Survey on the state of national journalism 2010. Report on results]. Retrieved from http://periodismo.uahurtado.cl/wp-content/uploads/2010/10/Resultados-Encuesta-Estado-Nacional-del-Periodismo-2011.pdf

Universidad Alberto Hurtado (UAH). (2012). *Encuesta Estado del Periodismo Nacional 2011, Informe de Resultados* [Survey on the state of national journalism 2011. Report on results]. Retrieved from http://periodismo.uahurtado.cl/wp-content/uploads/2010/10/Resultados-Encuesta-Estado-Nacional-del-Periodismo-2011.pdf

Table 2.1

Major Journalism Associations and Journalism-Related Organzations in Chile

Organization[1]	Description	Websites
America's Newspaper Group (GDA)	Created in 1991, GDA brings together 11 influential newspapers in Latin America, including El Mercurio.	http://www.gda.com
Association for Regional Broadcast Television	Gathers 18 regional TV broadcasters to support and promote local contents.	http://www.anatel.cl
Association of Catholic Broadcasters	Provides networking for its associates and trains their broadcasters for better communication.	http://www.canal13.cl
Association of Chilean Schools of Journalism and Social Communications (ASEPECS)	Chilean branch for FELA-FACS (Latin America Federation of Social Communication Schools).	http://www.periodismo.uchile.cl/asepecs
Chilean Association of Radio Broadcasters (ARCHI)	Created in 1933, a trade association that promotes private radio broadcasting and defends expression and opinion.	http://www.archi.cl
Chilean Press Foundation	Created in 2001 to defend the press and opinion and to improve professional practice through training journalists.	n/a
Journalists Circle	Created in 1907 to improve professional and technical skills and to develop collaboration among associates.	http://circulodeperiodistas.cl
Journalists Professional Association (Colegio de Periodistas)	Created in 1956, a voluntary association that defends journalism rights, press independence and expression, and promotes proper practices in journalism.	http://www.colegiodeperiodistas.cl
Council for Media Ethics	Created in 1990 by the Media Federation, a professional self-regulated council that evaluates the ethical performance of the media, especially upon the public's request.	http://www.consejodeetica.cl
Media Federation	Created in 1991, brings together the ANATEL, ARCHI, and ANP in hopes of improving professional culture and ethics in the media.	http://www.consejodeetica.cl

Table 2.1 (cont.)

Major Journalism Associations and Journalism-Related Organzations in Chile

Organization[1]	Description	Websites
National Association of Women Journalists	Strives to be a meeting point for women journalists and writers.	http://mujeresperiodistas.cl
National Press Association (ANP)	Created in 1951, gathers 55 newspapers and 75 magazines belonging to 41 publishing companies. Aims to improve journalism and its social recognition.	http://anp.cl
National Television Council	Created by law in 1970 to supervise the proper operation of television services and content.	http://www.cntv.cl
Chilean Community Radios – (AN-ARCICH)	Promotes the development of community radio and defends expression and opinion.	http://radioscomunitarias.cl
TV Networks Association (ANA-TEL)	Association of broadcast TV networks, which protects press liberty and associates' rights.	http://www.anatel.cl

1   Organization names were translated for better understanding. For additional information, search websites.

Table 2.2

Ranking of Top 10 Academic Journalism Programs (América Economía, 2015)

Organization	Websites
Pontificia Universidad Católica de Chile (Universidad Católica)	www.uc.cl
Universidad de Chile	www.uch.cl
Universidad Diego Portales	www.udep.cl
Pontificia Universidad Católica de Valparaíso	www.pucv.cl
Universidad de Santiago	www.usach.cl
Universidad Austral de Chile	www.uach.cl
Universidad del Desarrollo	www.udd.cl
Universidad de los Andes	www.uandes.cl
Universidad de la Frontera	www.ufro.cl
Universidad Católica de la Santísima Concepción	www.ucsc.cl

3

Journalism Education in China: Serving Two Masters

Gang (Kevin) Han

I t has been more than 90 years since the establishment of college-level journalism education in China (Ding, 1997; Guo, 2010; Wu, 2006; Yu, Chu, & Guo, 2002). Borrowing from the United States' "Missouri model" at its infancy and then switching to the "Soviet model" since the founding of the People's Republic of China, Chinese journalism education has been characterized by tension between these two approaches (Hao & Xu, 1997) and Chinese media peculiarities. The political atmosphere and social change, along with the Chinese media's "tug of war" between the Chinese Communist Party (hereafter the Party) line and the bottom line, continue to shape Chinese journalism education (He, 2000; Zhao, 1998). This chapter analyzes Chinese journalism education past, present, and future, examining the connection between the media landscape and educational links along the way.

Journalism in the Media Landscape

Journalism education, as part of the larger structure of media practice, is intrinsically linked to socio-political and economic environments (Wu & Weaver, 1998; Yu, Chu, & Guo, 2002). This section focuses on the current media landscape in China, a context in which Chinese journalism education is formed and fashioned.

China, the world's second largest economy, is moving rapidly into the information age with an increasing variety of media outlets. State-run media, ideologically controlled by the Party and owned by the government, coexists with innovative forms of news, market-driven media ventures, and emerging Internet platforms. As Schudson (2000, p. 179) maintains, Chinese journalism features "mixed patterns of ownership and control" with "new blends of state, independent and commercial news media."

In 2013 there were at least 2,000 newspapers, 9,000 magazines, 311 radio stations, and 374 TV stations in China (PR Newswire, 2013). More than 88.03 million households, roughly 94.1% of the population, subscribe to cable or satellite television (PR Newswire, 2013).

Print Media

Newspapers have traditionally been the dominant source of information for the Chinese people. Since the early 1980s, both newspapers and magazines have enjoyed rapid expansion in meeting Chinese needs for diversified information. On one hand, state-run media outlets have introduced more mass-appeal and less politicized content while maintaining their function as the mouthpiece of the Party and government. On the other hand, market-oriented newspapers provide more entertaining and sensational coverage to achieve growing readership, despite being subject to the same level of censorship (PR Newswire, 2013). Regardless of ownership, print media are relying more and more on circulation and advertising than government subsidies to survive market competition.

In recent years, newspapers have started suffering from a shrinking market share due to dwindling credibility and the increasing popularity of Internet-based media. Although the print media are still maintaining their vital position in the Chinese media landscape as one of the exclusive sources of news for online portals and news websites, their overall total advertising revenue dropped by an unprecedented 8% during the first half of 2013 (PR Newswire, 2013).

Television

Accounting for 76% of the total advertising revenue in China and a penetration rate of 97%, television is the core method of news consumption in China (PR Newswire, 2013). All television stations in China are state-run. They were institutionalized in the early 1980s at four hierarchical administrative levels: county, municipal, provincial, and national. China Central Television (CCTV) is the one and only national TV network. It broadcasts 20 channels, some of which include English-language programming. In the early 1990s, the four-level broadcasting system was gradually restructured, allowing local and regional TV stations to be accessible through satellite and cable services.

New Media

Since the mid-1990s, the Internet has become an increasingly important information source for the Chinese, especially urban residents. In 2016, there were an estimated 721 million Internet users, or "netizens," in China (Internetlivestats, 2016). One of the primary uses of the Internet is to retrieve news and information (CNNIC, 2006). Web portals, such as Sina, Baidu, Sohu, NetEase, and Tencent, are among China's largest commercial news websites and the most used news sources for the young and well educated (PR Newswire, 2013).

The huge audience market and the onslaught of venture capitalists in China catalyzed the emergence of news websites in the late 1990s and early 2000s. There are mainly three types of leading news websites (Han, 2007). The first type is market-oriented portals operated by commercial enterprises (e.g., www.sina.com.cn, owned and operated by the leading Internet content provider and portal in China). For this type of portal, news is basically bait to attract target audiences to site visits and advertisements. The second type is websites run by print or electronic media. Their online presence diversifies their communication outlets and helps gain market opportunities and advertisement revenue (e.g., www.people.com.cn, owned and run by *People's Daily*, the mouthpiece of the Party's Central Committee). The third type is websites operated by local governments or local Party propaganda departments (e.g., www.eastday.com in Shanghai and www.qianlong.com in Beijing). They aggregate all available content published by traditional media in order to compete with popular commercial websites like Sina (Han, 2007). Nowadays, traditional mainstream media are becoming more actively involved in social media and mobile platforms, looking for new ways to expand their readership in order to survive competition with Internet-based news portals.

One trend in the aggressive growth of new media is the dramatically rapid adoption of mobile phones across the country. According to China's Ministry of Industry and Information Technology (Netease, 2014), by March 2013 China had about 1.15 billion mobile users. As of June 2014, the mobile phone has become the most favored means of accessing the Web for 83.4% of Chinese Internet users (CNNIC, 2014). Over 100 million of them are registered app store users and around 35 million use mobile payment systems. Smart phone applications have become the primary source of information for mobile users (PR Newswire, 2013).

Social Networking Sites

The government's suppression of access to certain social networking sites, such as Facebook and Twitter, has led to successful Chinese copycat sites. In 2014, China had 275 million registered microbloggers (CNNIC, 2014). Weibo, launched by Sina in August 2009, is the most popular microblogging platform and an extremely important information source for Chinese. Combining the features of Twitter, Facebook, and BBS (Bulletin Board System), Weibo has been the fastest growing social network in the world (Baidu, 2012), with 368 million reported registered users by August 2012 (Xinhua News Agency, 2012, 2013).

Since late 2012, WeChat, an emerging mobile social application from Tencent, has quickly become popular among mobile phone users. WeChat had 438 million active accounts by June 2014, becoming Weibo's major rival, if not substitute (Xinhua News Agency, 2014).

As previously described, mass media in China, especially traditional news media outlets, have been tightly controlled by the Party's propaganda system. The Party, the state, and their agents partially or fully own all types of media outlets in local, regional, and national markets. Described as a "command" system by Lee (1990), the Party exerts rigorous ideological control on mass media on all fronts, from content to page layout. Politics and politicians are deeply involved in the daily operation of Chinese media, including allocating financial or personnel resources and setting agendas. As an agency of political power, the Chinese mass media serve as their owners' mouthpiece to "articulate and support policies" (Guo, 2010, p. 15), create and guide public opinion, spread messages in the interest of the Party and the state, and help maintain the status quo either actively or passively (Han, 2007).

Changes in China's media ecology (Lee, 1990, 1994, 2000), due to market-driven economic reforms since the end of the 1970s, have resulted in some loosened censorship on non-political, mass-appeal media content. After all, such content both pleases the audience and maximizes market share (Han, 2007). The de-politicization, decentralization, and commercialization of local market-driven media have characterized "the gradual, instrumental and uneven nature" of the structural change of Chinese media (Xin, 2006, p. 2). However, serving both political and commercial interests, the dual-functional mass media is unavoidably at the mercy of the tension between the Party's constant ideological control and professionals' desire for autonomy, which reaches beyond mere profit-making. Zhao (1998) argues that the contemporary Chinese mass media are lingering between the Party line and bottom line. And He (2000) adds tension is also being felt within the Party itself via a tug-of-war in which the "Party Press" is converting itself into "Party Publicity Inc." (p. 112).

Professional Characteristics

The Chinese media's role, its "propagandist/commercial model" (Zhao, 1998) amid state-market polarity, censorship, and professionalism, has drawn considerable debate.

Censorship

There is a constant struggle in China between the public's right to access information and the Party's and government's control of media content and information flow. This contradiction is partially reflected through institutionalized censorship embedded in regular news making.

Directors and editors-in-chief, appointed by central or regional propaganda departments, pre-censor the Chinese press. On a daily basis, normal coverage is overseen and must "pass through three to six hands before . . . [its] final release" (Scharping, 2007, p. 104). What cannot appear in the media is usually dictated by the propaganda departments' guidelines and/or other officials' written or phone directives to the head of newsrooms (Scharping, 2007, p. 106). The censored content often deals with unauthorized or false reports, investigative corruption cases involving Party or government officials, "incorrect viewpoints," leadership debates, dissidents, riots, political incidents, or controversial events, issues, or individuals (Scharping, 2007, p. 105).

A "Critical Reading Group" post-censors the press. This group is overseen by propaganda departments, composed of current officials, retired propaganda cadres, and veteran journalists. It monitors media coverage and singles out problematic reports for review. It circulates its reading notes in internal bulletins, which are read by those belonging to "higher Party echelons" (Scharping, 2007, p.106). An unfavorable review in "post-censorship" often means disciplinary actions or other punishment against not only an involved staff reporter(s), but Party-appointed officials in charge of pre-censorship.

During the rapid growth of Internet-based communication platforms in China, the Party and government have extended ideological and bureaucratic control to cyberspace to limit the flow of online content (Han, 2007). For example, Internet Service Providers (ISPs), like publications and media organizations, must be state licensed (Coleman, 1999). Meanwhile, although Web-based media cannot employ their own staff reporters to write about news events, they are allowed to use reports from traditional news media. In this sense, commercial news websites merely serve as one-stop markets, or "distributing centers," for repackaged Party-approved information (Han, 2007). Therefore, commercial news websites, along with other emerging online communication platforms, essentially share the voice of government-run news media or websites (Han, 2007).

The public is acutely aware of government censorship when it comes to online outlets. The "Great Firewall of China" also filters news, politics, health, commerce, and entertainment offerings in foreign and Chinese-language websites based outside China (Zittrain & Edelman, 2003). And it bars political publication of "counterrevolutionary" (anti-government) materials and specific Western news websites that are sometimes critical of China, such as the BBC and *The New York Times* (Harwit & Clark, 2001).

Professionalism

The symbiosis of Party journalism and "paid journalism" (Zhao, 1998) brings up another concern relevant to journalistic professionalism in China. On one hand, Chinese journalists attempt to adhere to professional ethics and standards in the production of news. On the other, some journalists take advantage of media by using it as a publicity tool to seek financial returns.

Pan and Lu (2003) maintain that Chinese journalism "does not operate as an apolitical system" where "media serve the whole society and the journalistic profession controls its work" (p. 224). Journalistic professionalism in China is "truncated and fragmented," and the "contradiction [inherent in] the media as market-supported propaganda organs for the communist regime inhibits the wholesale adoption of such a professional ideology" (Pan & Lu, 2003, p. 224). Chinese journalists do not automatically embrace the prescriptions of universal professionalism. Instead, they are "*making* their profession—expressing and realizing their visions of journalistic professionalism—with their everyday practices" (pp. 224-225). Therefore, "'deconstructing' an ideational system becomes both a result of and means for China's journalists to accomplish their profession" (Pan & Lu, 2003, pp. 224-225). For example, Sun (1994) argues that professionalism cannot be achieved in China unless journalists can figure out how to make both officials and the public happy. Chinese journalists interpret and justify their professional practice as a Party-granted right (Guo, 1999, cited in Pan & Lu, 2003) to fulfill the surveillance function of media, enlighten the public, witness social transition, and to ultimately maintain political stability (Sun, 1994; Pan & Lu, 2003).

While Chinese journalists respect professionalism and generally pursue it, paid news or paid journalism, which ethically challenges professionalism, has unfortunately always existed. Paid journalism is the practice of releasing information in the form of news coverage in return for media organization personal gain or material benefits (China Media Project, 2007). "Over the years, paid journalism has grown from an individual practice to a collective custom" (Zhao, 1998, p. 77) and from "unorganized" to "organized" bribery (p. 88). For the unscrupulous, paid journalism brings in cash via advertising, subscription, sponsorship, etc. In addition, negative stories concerning certain organizations are sometimes published because the reporter or the media outlet does not get paid. Paid journalism "blur[s] the line between advertisement and editorial" (China Media Project, 2007), turning a public utility into a tool for private gain (Zhao, 1998, p. 76).

With regard to journalism education, Yu, Chu, and Guo (2002) argue professionalism is gaining increased attention and promotion because Chinese journalism faculty "find faith in it" and see it as "a legitimate tool to circumvent ideological control" (Guo, 2010, p. 24).

Although professionalism is emphasized in both the profession and education, the gap between journalists' professional ideals and actual practices is expanding, as illustrated by journalists' increasing self-censorship and declining credibility and social status (So & Chan, 2007, p. 157).

Journalism Education, Professional Training, and Research

This section provides an overview of journalism education and research in China. It focuses on the historical to current status of journalism education, educational programs and sequences, types of teaching institutions, curriculum development, education and professional links, and related issues, challenges, innovations, and directions.

Teaching and Training Future Newsmakers

As far as journalism education is concerned, scholars argue that its development in China demonstrates a strong correlation with the evolution of news media and the media industry. Journalism education has also been more sensitive to social transitions in China "than any other field of professional training" (Yu, Chu, & Guo, 2002, p. 63; Du, 2009; Guo, 2010).

Brief history. China's modern journalism education started in the early 20th century. In 1920, the first-ever journalism department was established at St. John's, an Anglican university in Shanghai. In 1923, the first Chinese educator-initiated journalism (newspaper) program was established at Populace University in Beijing. Such programs were then established in 1924 at Yenching University in Beijing, in 1929 at Fudan University in Shanghai, and in the 1930s and 1940s at additional universities (Hao & Xu, 1997).

Scholars suggest that modern Chinese journalism education has evolved through five stages: the 1920s to 1940s, the 1950s, early 1960s, 1966 to 1977 (The Cultural Revolution), and 1978 to the present (post-Cultural Revolution; Ding, 1997).

During the first stage (1920s-1940s), when major programs were institutionalized at universities in Shanghai, Beijing, and Xiamen, Chinese journalism education "modeled [itself] " after its American forerunners and counterparts (Guo, 2011, p. 2), especially by adopting similar curricula from the University of Missouri and Columbia

University (Hao & Xu, 1997; Cai, 2003; Ding, 1997). U.S. journalism professors were hired to train Chinese students as the first group of professional journalists at these institutions. Early Chinese journalism education, with distinctive American roots, also trained the first generation of journalism faculty. These faculty members later became core instructors at prestigious journalism programs, like Fudan University and Renmin University of China, even after the People's Republic of China was founded in 1949 (Guo, 2011). China's first graduate school of journalism, founded in 1943 in Chongqing, also mirrored many aspects of Columbia University's Graduate School of Journalism (Chang, 1989, cited in Hao & Xu, 1997).

During the second stage (early 1950s), after the founding of "new China," colleges and universities underwent a nationwide reshuffling and restructuring. After all, journalism education was being thoroughly revamped to fit the Soviet model. This "shock therapy," seen as a "watershed for journalism education" that "stressed political orientation in all social science sectors" (Guo, 2011, p. 3), soon reorganized journalism programs in China. Marxist-Leninist theories were highlighted in the curricula and veteran communist journalists were appointed as administrators and lecturers (Chu, 1980). To enhance Party journalism and to train "media propagandists," more journalism departments were added to a number of universities across the country (Hao & Xu, 1997).

During the third stage (early 1960s), the restructuring of journalism education slowed its pace. Academic programs incorporated more courses on theory, principles, and culture into the curriculum to better adapt to the Soviet model (Guo, 2011; Hao & Xu, 1997).

Unfortunately, during the fourth stage (beginning in mid-1960s), journalism education stagnated during the most chaotic period of The Cultural Revolution. Actually, journalism education "suffered great setbacks" during this stage (Guo, 2011, p. 4). Faculty and students were forced to leave for the country's rural areas to receive "re-education." And when selected universities and journalism programs were allowed to reopen in the early 1970s, journalism education put "even greater emphasis on the political training of students . . . rather than on traditional journalistic practice" (Hao & Xu, 1997, p. 37).

The current, fifth stage began in the late 1970s at the end of The Cultural Revolution with the adoption of reform and Deng Xiaoping's open-door policy. Since then, rapid economic growth and increasing competition in media markets have produced a great demand for professional journalists who understand advertising and audiences. Market needs thus helped China's journalism education come back to the basics (Chu, 1980), which has helped lead to unprecedented growth (Ding, 1997; Hao & Xu, 1997).

Meanwhile, official recognition of "journalism and communica-tion" as a "first-tier discipline" in social sciences has driven the growth of journalism education in China over the past two decades (Guo, 2011, p. 6). Originally, the state's educational authorities regarded journalism as a second-tier subfield or concentration within the discipline of Chinese language and literature, with a limited budget and share of other edu-cational resources. But, in 1977, strong student enrollment and research output pushed the state to finally acknowledge the legitimacy of the journalism/communication major as an independent, doctorate-grant-ing academic unit in social sciences (Han, 2002). The discipline's higher profile has helped journalism and mass communication departments/units gain a greater say in the state's budgetary allocations. This rec-ognition also provides journalism and communication educators with more professional autonomy. Today, journalism faculty and experts, instead of Chinese language and literature professors, are in charge of evaluating and accrediting journalism programs (Guo, 2011).

Current status. In 1949, there were 460 journalism students enrolled in seven universities and colleges in Shanghai, Beijing, Suzhou, and Guangzhou (Hao & Xu, 1997). In 1977, four-year undergraduate pro-grams in Beijing and Shanghai restarted in the wake of The Cultural Revolution. As of the end of 2013 (CHESICC, 2013), there are more than 1,000 undergraduate programs offered in colleges across the coun-try, including the following:

❑   journalism (307),
❑   broadcast journalism (228),
❑   advertising (350),
❑   communication (55),
❑   editing and publishing (70),

❑ new media (33), and

❑ digital publishing (4).

Undergraduate enrollment is estimated at about 50,000 annually. And about 8,000 faculty members are teaching at these undergraduate institutions—14% full professors, 27.5% associate professors, 38.5% lecturers (i.e., assistant professors), and 22% assistant lecturers (Guo, 2011).

In addition, since 1978 postgraduate programs have also seen rapid expansion (Cai, 2003). The first doctoral students were recruited in 1981 (Guo, 2011). As of March 2006, there are about 60 master's programs in journalism and 63 in communication, and there are about 21 doctoral programs in both journalism and communication in 15 universities (Guo, 2011).

Journalism educational institutions in China can be roughly grouped as follows (Cai, 2003):

❑ Top programs housed in prestigious universities, such as Fudan University and Renmin University of China, whose original journalism departments have been upgraded to full-fledged journalism schools. The Communication University of China (formerly Beijing Institute of Broadcasting) is another such program. The prestige of these top three institutions has much to do with their lavish funding, accomplished faculty, well-designed curriculum, and well-equipped facilities.

❑ Programs set up decades ago at flagship universities, such as Wuhan University, Nanjing University, and Sichuan University, among other four-year research universities across the country.

❑ Recently founded journalism and communication schools at top universities. For example, Peking University restored its journalism education school in 2001, and Tsinghua University established its journalism school in 2002.

❑ Programs established at specialized institutions, such as normal universities and colleges for sports, finance and business, science and technology, and polytechnics.

❑ Part-time extension programs offered by universities or colleges.

❑   Programs established at small private universities in metropolitan areas.

Programs and sequences. Under the umbrella term of "journalism and communication" are different concentrations besides the traditional newspaper major. At the undergraduate level, for example,
there are five typical concentrations or majors: journalism (focusing
on newspapers), radio and TV broadcasting, advertising, editing and
publishing, and communication. Two concentrations, journalism and
communication, now offer both master's and doctoral programs (Guo,
2011). Meanwhile, during the last two decades, sequences or majors
other than traditional print and broadcasting media—such as sports
journalism, photojournalism, public relations, and communication
studies—have expanded (Guo, 2011). More up-to-date sequences or
concentrations, such as Web communication and digital publishing,
have also been introduced into the offerings (Cai, 2003; Ding, 1997).

Curricular development. In keeping with the recognition of journalism and communication as among first-tier disciplines is an assort-
ment of measures in the interest of following "the international trend
of upgrading journalists from craftsmen into professionals" (Hao & Xu,
1997, p. 42). They include a less rigid division of majors, reduction in
mandatory courses in the trade, and an increase of required courses in
liberal arts and sciences. Theory classes on communication and mass
communication that introduce Western concepts are being included in
the curriculum as required courses (Hao & Xu, 1997). In the meantime, the proportion of elective courses is increasing so that students
have more choices in their studies (Wu, 2006, pp. 152-155). Courses not
previously available, such as media management, media economics,
the Internet and communication, advertising and public relations, and
mass communication psychology are now being offered (Cai, 2003).

At the same time, there has been a relentless focus on hands-on
courses. As Hao and Xu (1997, p. 42) mention, professional skills,
emphasized in the traditional model of American journalism education, were an integral part of China's journalism programs in its early
years. Today, hands-on courses still enjoy a prominent place in journalism education. The involvement of students in journalistic practice

is usually carried out through internships in media outlets outside of school. Students can also work with student media, such as college daily or weekly newspapers or university-affiliated radio stations, as part-time reporters or news anchors. At the same time, former journalists are hired and veteran journalists are invited to teach skill-based courses on a regular basis. New skill courses in advertising and public relations are also offered to meet the demands of the quickly growing communication industry.

Books are continuously being updated to match the pace of media and mass communication practices. Over the past two decades, there have been several series of books and teaching materials available in the market, all compiled and published by leading journalism schools and endorsed by the Ministry of Education (Cai, 2003).

Furthermore, many journalism schools and departments invest heavily in cutting-age communication technology and facilities. Computer and multimedia labs, laser typesetting and digital publishing labs, newsgathering equipment, and studio and advertising labs are all contributing to the interactive learning environment of skill-oriented courses.

All curriculum redesigns and innovations have carefully followed the Party's guidance for training future journalists. Required ideology-colored courses, such as the history of China's communist revolution and journalism theory based on the ideas of Marx, Lenin, Mao, and Deng, are kept intact in curriculum updates (Hao & Xu, 1997, p. 43).

Journalism Research

Similar to the evolution of journalism education in China, journalism research in contemporary China, according to Yu (1997), can be viewed in stages (three), which correspond to phases of social transitions in China.

The first stage (1949-1982) coincided with the planned economy era, when the Party officially made and implemented dominant socio-economic development policies. While mass media fully functioned as the Party's propaganda mouthpiece, scholars often cited the speeches and publications of top leaders as universal answers to research questions regarding journalistic practice and persuasive communication. When economic reform was initiated in the late 1970s, a large number of Western communication concepts were introduced to China, which "brought a whole and systematic set of terminologies, theories, methodologies, and hypotheses into Chinese academies" (Hu & Ji, 2013, p.9).

The second stage started under the post-planned economy era (1982-1992; Yu, 1997), in which scholars began assessing basic questions about journalism and mass communication.

In the third, current stage (after 1992), journalism research in China took a scientific turn while also displaying an "infusion of Western theories and concepts" (Pan, Chan, & Lo, 2008, p. 199). This positivist paradigm has been well received by Chinese scholars, who started to pay more attention to the practical implications of the mass media as information carriers and economic contributors (Yu, 1997).

Published and state-funded journalism and mass communication studies in Mainland China between 1993 and 2007 mostly focused on the following topics: general journalism and news media topics, media management and the economy, broadcasting, new communications technology, communication policies, laws and regulations, and mass communication processes and effects (Wang, 2009, p. 45). Wang (2009, p. 47) also found that state-funded projects are mainly guided by, and devoted to, the government's media or communication policies and propaganda strategies regarding public opinion and national image-building.

According to Pan et al. (2008), policy studies and problem-solving research have been journalism research's "most prominent feature[s]" in China (pp. 205-206)

> since systemically there is no intellectual space free of the dominating influence of the [P]arty. . . . [Research] basically involves annotating [P]arty policies, offering actionable proposals to policy-makers or to industry leaders, and elaborating normative arguments to justify such policies or proposals. (p. 203)

Such policies or proposals often deal with reconfiguration of media industries, media organizations, and journalism practices, improving media performance and media organizations' adaptation to the Internet and the digital age.

Despite state-motivated topics, Chinese scholars put considerable emphasis on media modalities and performance (Wang, 2009). Pan et al. (2008) pointed out that scholars "are deeply engaged in actual[ly] changing journalism practices and media institutions" (p. 205) by extensively examining journalists, journalism as a craft, and macro contexts of news production. However, although Chinese researchers have broadly borrowed from political economy, socio-organizational, and cultural-theoretical perspectives, most of their studies "are based on impressionistic observations and [are] atheoretical in nature" (Pan et al., 2008, p. 201). Wang (2009) adds that research studies tend to lack theoretical approaches or frameworks and are not targeting theory building.

With regard to research methods, most published articles in Chinese academic journals are essays and reviews. This occurs despite classic journalism research being introduced from Western countries and increasing attention to the positivist approach. "The basic methods employed remain policy annotations and analytical arguments" (Pan et al., 2008, p. 203). Normalizing academic research by employing quality methodology is thus a challenge to China-based journalism scholars (Chan, 2008).

Professional Connections in Journalism Education

Journalism education is geared toward training future journalists and media professionals (Cai, 2003). The rapid development of media/communication-related organizations (see Table 3.1 for important journalism organizations) and the information economy provides students with ample job opportunities upon graduation. Various types of media outlets, publishing houses, and publicity departments in government or nonprofit organizations/businesses, advertising and public relations firms, and marketing communication institutions all keep journalism and communication students in high demand in the job market (Cai, 2003; Ding, 1997).

Journalism students, especially those from leading schools or from schools in metropolitan areas, are popular in the job market. According to a 2002 survey of Renmin University of China Journalism School alumni, for example, 78.8% of respondents said they landed their first job on their own; 72.8% agreed it was not difficult finding a job since they had a degree in journalism and communication; 93.9% believed they were fully or fairly prepared for their jobs; and 68.2% were fully or relatively satisfied with their current job. In this study, employers also spoke highly of such journalism students' performance (Cai, 2003).

However, the ongoing dramatic expansion of college enrollment in journalism majors nationwide is making the job market more competitive. For example, due to the limited capacity of the restructured electronic media market, it has been hard for media outlets to hire the oversupply of broadcasting journalism graduates (Cai, 2003). Another survey conducted in 2001 by the China Ministry of Education's Journalism Discipline Supervisory Committee (JDSC), a semi-official academic organization, also reports that the job market in China's developed coastal areas has already seen saturation, especially for those who majored in traditional news editing and production (Cai, 2003). Therefore, despite the rapid growth of journalism programs, it has been a continuing challenge for journalism education in China to meet the needs of the ever-changing media market.

Journalism Education's Professional Impact

What and how students should be taught in journalism schools are important issues for journalism educators in China (see Table 3.2 for major academic journalism programs). Answers to such questions are highly interwoven within the social context of how news is produced and how education is viewed (Lu, 2004). Lu (2004) finds, for instance, that Chinese journalism education introduces students to universal views of the ideal function of media in society. However, such education does not directly influence students' perception or understanding of the role of journalism in Chinese society.

How well has journalism education prepared students not only as Party propagandists but, more importantly, as qualified journalists or media professionals? And to what extent does journalism education influence students' intellectual growth? Such questions are difficult to answer.

Future Possibilities

According to Wu (2006, p. 144), the best thing about Chinese journalism education is that it is "quick and cheap." It takes undergraduate students less than two years, in a four-year program, to complete core courses for a journalism major. While this education mode trains crafts-men for news work, it also leaves students with inadequate academic and intellectual preparation for journalism or non-journalism careers.

The conventional focus of journalism education, within China and beyond, is professional training. Courses dealing with professional know-how are in the core curriculum. They are offered in accordance with the needs of professional skills in newsrooms, mainly categorized based on mediums, such as newspapers, magazines, radio, and television.

Today, there seems to be a shift in journalism education from train-ing journalists as generalists to training them as specialists or experts in a particular beat, such as politics, economy/finance/business, sports, and medicine. Meanwhile, when the lines between different mediums blur or even disappear on the Internet, students are expected to become all-weather journalists, who can adapt to ever-changing information communication technologies. Scholars argue that Chinese journalism schools should "cultivate hybrid journalism and communication pro-fessionals" (Wu, 2006, p. 153) and the hybrid professionals need to have a solid foundation in the humanities, communication theories, and information technologies, with a multidisciplinary knowledge base.

To achieve this goal, scholars (e.g., Wu, 2006) advocate a balance between academic and skill training in journalism programs, through expanding courses in communication principles, theory, and technol-ogies, along with curtailing courses teaching traditional journalism skills. As journalism education demarcates itself from the humanities and has arguably become multidisciplinary, journalism programs may also include more courses in statistics and computer programming to respond to new paradigms in news making (e.g., data journalism and Internet-based communication). Educating students as communica-tion professionals, instead of narrowly defined journalists, will better prepare them for an increasingly competitive job market. After all, as traditional media and related jobs decline, the continued growth of advertising, public relations, marketing, and communication fields are offering an unprecedented number of new positions (Han, 2002).

Journalism Education Issues, Challenges, and Innovations

Current issues and challenges. During the past decade, after years of relatively loosened ideological control over the media, the Party and the government have gradually "re-tightened the screws" on the news media (Denyer, 2014). Concurrently, the Party's propaganda authority has been strengthening its control over major journalism schools across the country and indoctrinating the Marxist view of journalism at universities with regenerated enthusiasm. For example, provincial and municipal propaganda departments have been working with universities to jointly administer, or "co-build," major journalism schools. Often in recent years, to ensure everything is in line with Party directives, senior propaganda officials or heads of major news media outlets have been picked to serve as top administrators at leading Chinese journalism schools. This administrational restructuring of journalism schools at the college level is believed to have started at Fudan University in the early 2000s. Similar overhauls are likely to be made at other journalism schools in the future (Ng, 2014; Denyer, 2004). The authorities' tendency to "resort to the old style of . . . [an] ideological grip" continues to threaten the limited academic freedom faculty now enjoy under the supervision of their universities and the Ministry of Education (Ng, 2014).

Ideological control aside, scholars are also concerned about the current non-political components of journalism education in China. Leading journalism educators (Du, 2009) believe China's journalism education is in crisis. First, it has yet to meet the demands of the job market. Second, a number of schools or departments are desperately short of professional-track and/or journalist-turned-academic instructors. Third, faculty members' research needs to advance much quicker in many newly established programs. Fourth, the curricula offered by different journalism schools and programs are essentially the same, lacking unique selling points to differentiate them. And finally, the paltry state-allocated funding for journalism programs is worsening the situation.

Expectations on innovations. Educators and experts believe that China's journalism education needs to be reformed in many ways. According to Du's interview (2009) with faculty members from 23 journalism programs, the following three issues are crucial:

❑ The balance between theory and skill courses—which type of courses should be added more often to the current curriculum: theory and knowledge-based courses or skill-training courses?

❑ The approaches of journalism education—should general communication courses (such as mass communication and society, interpersonal communication, and organizational communication) be incorporated into current journalism core curricula? Many journalism educators believe this is the right direction. Or, conversely, should the core curriculum be streamlined to highlight purely journalism-related courses?

❑ The standardization of Chinese journalism education—should it still borrow ideas and practices from the West, especially the United States, to keep it in line with international standards?

Cai (2003) also describes the major challenges facing journalism education in China, including the need to redesign curricula for different course levels, to make consistent academic quality across different institutions, and to solve the problem of a shortage of qualified faculty and a lack of sufficient investment in teaching facilities—which hampers pedagogical innovation and reform.

Additional strategies for pushing forward Chinese journalism education—on top of revamping curricula, enhancing liberal arts education, and balancing theory and skill courses—include reinforcing education in professional ethics and creating more internship opportunities and interactions between journalism educators and practitioners.

Nevertheless, the ultimate question concerning China's journalism education may still lie in the choice of approaches or models that can successfully fit into the Chinese media system and its socio-political context.

Conclusion: Educating Tomorrow's Journalists—The Big Picture

When reviewing contemporary journalism education in China, scholars generally agree on the nature of its evolution. Guo (2010) maintains that China's journalism education trajectory over the past three decades has been "almost identical to that of the [Chinese] media industry, from totalitarian control to measured self-determination driven by the market" (p. 28). This education trajectory has been characterized by a series of struggles between opposite forces: "political conservatism versus market liberalism, harsh oppression versus tactic resistance, . . . and commonality versus variation" (Guo, 2010, p. 28).

Hao & Xu (1997) note that China's journalism educators now have more leeway in developing new programs and in applying more internationalized standards to update the current curricula. The acceptance and spread of professionalism also suit the market-driven growth of China's media industry. However, an ideological or political red line always exists in journalism education reform in China, regulating implicitly and explicitly what can be changed or accomplished.

Hao and Xu (1997) conclude that China's educators have yet to find a workable model for journalism education—neither the American model nor the Soviet model works. They argue educators thus need to take "a realistic rather than idealistic approach" (p. 43) to tackling journalism education challenges. Scholars seem to agree that the future of China's journalism education depends on whether it can escape the restraints of China's unique social transition. As Guo (2010) argues, "whether reform-minded journalism educators can achieve their desired goals [in educating future journalists] depends on their ability to maneuver around, negotiate with, and ultimately break through the barbed wires of constraints" (p. 29).

References

Baidu. (2012). *Microblogging*. Retrieved from http://baike.baidu.com/view/1567099.htm

Cai, W. (2003). Looking into the training pattern of news communication personnel. *Chinese Journal of International Communication, 1*, 67-73.

Chang, W. H. (1989). *Mass media in China: The history and the future*. Ames, IA: Iowa State University Press.

Chan, J. M. (2008). 中国传播研究的发展困局:为什么与怎么办 [The dilemma of communication research in China: Why and what to do]. Retrieved from http://academic.mediachina.net/article.php?id=5621

CHESICC. (2013). Information database on undergraduate major programs in colleges in China. Retrieved from http://gaokao.chsi.com.cn/zyk/zybk/index.jsp?pageId=1050050301&type=xk

China Media Project. (2007). 有偿新闻 [Paid-for news]. Retrieved from http://cmp.hku.hk/2007/07/05/422/

Chu, J. (1980). China is "back to basics" in journalism education. *Journalism Educator, 1*, 3-7, 12.

CNNIC. (2006). The 18th statistic report on the Internet in China. Retrieved from http://www.cnnic.cn/uploadfiles/doc/2006/7/19/103601.doc

CNNIC. (2014). The 34th statistic report on the Internet in China. Retrieved from http://www.cnnic.cn/hlwfzyj/hlwxzbg/hlwtjbg/201407/t20140721_47437.htm

Coleman, S. (1999). The new media and democratic politics. *New Media & Society, 1*(1), 67-73.

Denyer, B. (2004). Chinese journalists face tighter censorship, Marxist retraining. Retrieved from http://www.washingtonpost.com/world/chinese-journalists-face-tighter-censorship-marxist-re-training/2014/01/10/6cd43f62-6893-11e3-8b5b-a77187b716a3_story.html

Ding, G. (1997). 大学新闻教育的培养目标与课程体系应该怎样确定? [How to formulate training objective and course structure in university journalism]. *Journalistic University*, 70-73.

Du, J. (2009). 新闻传播教育向何处去? —专家意见测量与变革路径分析 [Where should journalism education go?: Analysis of approaches to reform based on interview with experts]. Retrieved from http://www.studa.net/xinwen/090808/11054318-2.html

Guo, K. (2011). Journalism and communication education in China (Mainland): An introduction. Retrieved from http://www.rcgpoc.shisu.edu.cn/picture/article/22/d6/75/99d974884d2d84a8e56c5223fdf5/afa518d9-d959-413e-9240-f8883867f6fd.pdf

Guo, Z. (1999). 舆论监督与西方新闻工作者的专业主义 [Media surveillance and journalistic professionalism in the West]. *Chinese Journal of International Communication, 5*, 32–38.

Guo, Z. (2010). Through barbed wires: Context, content and constraints for journalism education in China. In B. Josephi (Ed.), *Journalism education in countries with limited media freedom* (pp. 15-32). New York, NY: Peter Lang.

Han, G. (2002). Divergence and convergence: A comparative study of programs and curricula of communication and journalism education in China and the U.S. In G. Zhang & Z. Huang (Eds.), *Communication research in China: Reflections and prospects* (pp. 111-124). Shanghai: Fudan University Press.

Han, G. (2007). Mainland China frames Taiwan: How China's news websites covered Taiwan's 2004 presidential election. *Asian Journal of Communication, 17*(1), 40-57.

Hao, X., & Xu, X. (1997). Exploring between two worlds: China's journalism education. *Journalism & Mass Communication Educator*, 35-47.

Harwit, E., & Clark, D. (2001). Shaping the Internet in China: Evolution of political control over network infrastructure and content. *Asian Survey, 41*(3), 377-408.

He, Z. (2000). Chinese Communist Party press in a tug-of-war: A political-economy analysis of the Shenzhen Special Zone Daily. In C. C. Lee (Ed.), *Power, money and media* (pp. 112-151). Evanston, IL: Northwestern University Press.

Hu, Z., & Ji, D. (2013). Retrospection, prospection and the pursuit of an integrated approach for China's communication and journalism studies. *Javnost-The Public, 20*(4), 5-16.

Internetlivestats. (2016). Internet users by country. (2016). Retrieved from http://www.internetlivestats.com/internet-users-by-country/

Lee, C. C. (Ed.) (1990). *Voice of China: The interplay of politics and journalism*. New York, NY: Guilford.

Lee, C. C. (Ed.) (1994). *China's media, media's China*. Boulder, CO: Westview Press.

Lee, C. C. (Ed.) (2000). *Power, money, and media: Communication patterns and bureaucratic control in cultural China*. Evanston, IL: Northwestern University Press.

Lu, Y. (2004). 动机、认知、职业选择—中国新闻教育现状与问题调查报告 [Motivation, perception and choice of occupation: A survey on journalism education in China]. *Journalism University*, (Winter), 3-8.

Netease. (2014). 中国手机用户数量达到11.46亿 [Mobile phone users in China reached 1.146 billion]. Retrieved from http://tech.163.com/13/0424/17/8T8AR9UR00094MOK.html

Ng, T. (2014). *Propaganda officials to head top-tier Chinese journalism schools*. Retrieved from http://www.scmp.com/news/china/article/1385380/propaganda-officials-head-top-tier-chinese-journalism-schools

Pan, Z., & Lu, Y. (2003). Localizing professionalism: Discursive practices in China's media reforms. In C. C. Lee (Ed.), *Chinese media, global contexts* (pp. 215-236). London: Routledge.

Pan, Z., Chan, J. M., & Lo, V. (2008). Journalism research in Greater China. In M. Loffelholz & D. Weaver (Eds.), *Global journalism research: Theories, methods, findings, future* (pp. 197-210). Malden, MA: Blackwell Publishing.

PR Newswire. (2013). Updated white paper from PR Newswire explores China's changing media landscape. Retrieved from http://en.prnasia.com/p/lightnews-0-80-9346.shtml

Schudson, M. (2000). The sociology of news production revisited (again). In J. Curran & M. Gurevitch (Eds.), *Mass media and society* (3rd Ed.) (pp. 175-200). London: Edward Arnold.

Scharping, T. (2007). Administration, censorship and control in the Chinese media: The state of the art. *China Aktuell, 36*(4), 96-120.

So, Y. K., & Chan, M. (2007). Professionalism, politics and market force: Survey studies of Hong Kong journalists 1996-2006. *Asian Journal of Communication, 17*(2), 148-158.

Sun, Y. (1994). What could be thought of and could be done: reflections on "Oriental Time and Space" and "Focused Interviewing". Retrieved from http://www.media-china.com/cmzy/xwpj/taofengxinwenjiang/tf07.htm

Wang, Y. (2009). 初探中国大陆新闻传播研究的回顾与展望 [Review of the journalism and mass communication research for Mainland China: A preliminary analysis]. *Communication and Management Research, 8*(2), 37-78.

Wu, T. (2006). Journalism education in China: A historical perspective. In K. W. Y. Leung, J. Kenny, & P. S. N. Lee (Eds.), *Global trends in communication education and research* (pp. 133-157). New York, NY: Hampton Press.

Wu, W., & Weaver, D. (1998). Making Chinese journalists for the next millennium: The professionalization of Chinese journalism students. *International Communication Gazette, 60*, 513-529.

Xin, X. (2006). Editorial. *Westminster papers in communication and culture 3*(1), 1-10.

Xinhua News Agency. (2014). Tencent reached 12.2 billion profit in the second quarter; *Wechat* gained large increase in number of users. Retrieved from http://news.xinhuanet.com/finance/2014-08/15/c_126875228.htm

Yu, G. (1997). 九十年代以来中国新闻学研究的发展与特点 [The development and characteristics of journalism research on the Mainland China since 1990s]. *Journalism Research, 55*, 272-290.

Yu, X., Chu, L. L., & Guo, Z. (2002). Reform and challenge: An analysis of China's journalism education under social transition. *International Communication Gazette, 64*(1), 63-77.

Zhao, Y. (1998). *Media, market and democracy in China: Between the party line and the bottom line.* Urbana, IL: University of Illinois Press.

Zittrain, J., & Edelman, B. (2003). Empirical analysis of Internet filtering in China. Retrieved from https://orangemail.syr.edu/redirect?http://cyber.law.harvard.edu/filtering/ china/

Table 3.1

Important Journalism Organizations in China

Organization	Description	Contact
All-China Journalists Association (ACJA)	The largest state-controlled, nonprofit national professional organization for journalists and editors.	http://www.zgjx.cn
China Sports Journalists Association	Nonprofit organization for journalists and media professionals specializing in sports.	http://tiyujixie.sport.org.cn
China Forum of Environmental Journalists (CFEJ)	Nonprofit organization for journalists and media professionals specializing in environmental issues.	http://www.cfej.net
Chinese Society for Science and Technology Journalism (CSSTJ)	Nonprofit organization for reporters, editors, and communicators in general – as well as entrepreneurs, government officials, and educators devoted to science and technology communication and the promotion of science and technology.	www.csstj.org.cn
Institute of Journalism and Communication Research in Chinese Academy of Social Sciences	Leading research institute outside of colleges and universities.	http://www.mediaresearch.cn/cate/1600.htm
Chinese Society of Journalism History	A national academic association focusing on research in history of journalism and communication in China and abroad.	http://xwsxh.pku.edu.cn
Communication Association of China (CAC)	Nonprofit national academic association for researchers and scholars in journalism and communication disciplines.	http://www.mediaresearch.cn
China Media Culture Promotion Association (CMCPA)	State-controlled, nonprofit society promoting research in journalism, the publication industry, and the development of cultural undertakings.	http://www.cmcpa.cc/index.html

Table 3.1 (cont.)

Important Journalism Organizations in China

Organization	Description	Contact
China Association of Journalism and Communication Education (CAJCE)	A national association composed of journalism education units in colleges and universities across the country, with a mission of promoting journalism and communication education in China – under the supervision of the Ministry of Education.	n/a
Journalism and Communication Discipline Supervisory Committee (JCDSC)	Semi-official body under the Ministry of Education composed of leading scholars and educators in journalism and communication disciplines from 40 colleges and universities in China.	n/a
Journalism and Communication Discipline Appraisal Group (JCDAG)	Sub-committee under the Academic Degrees Committee of the State Council of China composed of seven members appointed by the State Council, who review and approve the institutionalization of doctoral programs in journalism and communication schools in China's colleges and universities.	n/a

Table 3.2

Major Academic Journalism Programs in China

Program	Description	Contact
Journalism School, Fudan University	The school consists of four departments, with six master's programs and four doctoral programs. The department was upgraded to a school in 1988.	http://www.xwxy.fudan.edu.cn
School of Journalism and Communication, Renmin University of China	The department was upgraded to a school in 1988.	http://jcr.ruc.edu.cn
Chinese Communication University	Formally known as Beijing Institute of Broadcasting, it is the first university in China solely devoted to journalism education and training. Also a training center for TV anchors and broadcasting technicians.	http://by.cuc.edu.cn
School of Journalism and Communication, Wuhan University	One of the best journalism programs in Central China.	http://journal.whu.edu.cn
School of Journalism and Communication, Peking University	Founded in May 2001, it is a pioneer of modern journalism education. Among the first to start journalism courses and to publish an introductory text and magazine on journalism in the early 20th century. Along with Tsinghua University, it has become one of the fastest growing programs at a top university.	http://sjc.pku.edu.cn
School of Journalism and Communication, Tsinghua University	Founded in April 2002, it offers comprehensive, interdisciplinary education. Also one of the fastest growing programs at a top university.	http://www.tsjc.tsinghua.edu.cn
School of Journalism and Information Communication, Huazhong University of Science and Technology	Originated in 1983, formally founded in 1988. A pioneer in running journalism and communication programs in colleges of science and technology.	http://sjic.hust.edu.cn

4

Journalism Education in Egypt: Benchmarking Academic Development and Professional Needs

Rasha Allam and Hussein Amin

Throughout modern history, the media have played a significant role in Egypt's political, economic, and social development. For much of that history, Egypt has led the Arab world in the practice of journalism. The West first introduced modern journalism to Egypt, with Western missionaries bringing the first movable type presses to the Middle East. Napoleon published Egypt's first newspaper after the 1798 French invasion. And in 1828 the first newspaper in the Arab world actually printed in Arabic was published in Egypt.

Traditionally, Egyptian print and broadcast journalism have been leaders in the Arab world. But today that leadership position is being strongly challenged by media organizations like Al Jazeera, Al Arabiya, and transnational media in Arabic—such as France 24, Russia Today, and the BBC. The extraordinary rise of private and quasi-private media organizations in the Gulf have produced strong competitors. There are a multitude of regional and international voices, each struggling to attract and retain viewers, readers, and advertisers.

In addition, the Internet and the changes that modern communication technologies have brought to journalism and to society have drastically altered not only the media landscape, but also the expectations of both national and international audiences and society at large. Increasing demands for public accountability and transparency, rising concerns about the role of media, the changing economics of print and broadcast media industries, and ever-advancing technologies that circumvent traditional governmental control require today's journalists to embrace new skills and methods of reporting to compete and remain relevant.

Journalism schools in Egypt are among the most attractive ones throughout the Arab world. National and private universities provide more than 30 academic journalism and mass communication programs. They vary in their theoretical and practical approaches and the educational tools used to teach and practice journalism. The Ministry of Education also runs four academic programs, and major newspapers provide in-house training centers.

Journalism in the Media Landscape

Media and government power are tied together in Egypt and have been for most of Egypt's modern history. From the time of Ottoman rule of Egypt (1517-1798), when Ottoman representative Mohamed Al issued a decree prohibiting printing without his permission and increasing censorship and control of the press, until today, the government has exercised varying levels of control over the media (Amin & Napoli, 2000).

Egypt's media operate under an authoritarian press system, in which the government controls and supervises most media functions (Amin, 2002a). The first legislation to control the press in Egypt was issued in 1881, providing the government with the power and authority to suspend and confiscate publications in order to maintain public order, morality, and religious observance (Amin, 2002a). During the British occupation from 1882-1952, many Egyptian nationalists used the press as a political tool to keep pressure on the British for more freedoms. Their use of the press is credited with Egypt's successful bid for limited independence in 1922. Although Egypt's 1923 constitution mentioned freedom of the press, it effectively limited this freedom by observing that it was guaranteed only "within the law" (Amin & Napoli, 2000). Today, the country is a presidential republic, operating under the Permanent Constitution of 1971 (Amin & Napoli, 2000).

Two of the three presidents who ruled Egypt after the revolution (excluding the first, Mohamed Naguib, who headed the government from 1952-1954 immediately following the revolution) shaped the development of Egypt's modern mass media. Egypt's second president, Gamal Abdel Nasser, exerted widespread control over the media. Prior to Nasser, political parties managed and controlled the press, while many foreigners owned the publishing houses. In 1960, Nasser, motivated by his understanding of the power of the press to mobilize the public, nationalized the Egyptian press. Political parties surrendered their ownership to what became the only legal political organization, the National Union, which later became the Arab Socialist Union (Napoli & Amin, 1997).

Nasser's successor and Egypt's third president, Anwar Sadat, released Egypt from a state of emergency and gave journalists access to news sources not controlled by the Arab Socialist Union. Sadat also issued a decree establishing the Supreme Press Council and authorizing it to oversee press affairs and grant licenses to journalists and media organizations. Sadat theoretically adopted an open attitude toward the press. However, in practice, he removed censorship while retaining control of the media (Napoli & Amin, 1997).

Former Egyptian president Hosni Mubarak lifted some of the restrictions and official censorship of the press. During his presidency, new projects were initiated, such as Media Production City, a massive studio property located outside Cairo that rents space to satellite channels. Another was Nilesat, a state-of-the-art digital satellite system transmitting across North Africa and the Arab Peninsula. Steps were also taken to privatize and liberalize the media (S. Al Sherif, personal communication, October 2, 2009). The Egyptian press under Mubarak operated in a far more open environment than the two previous regimes and more freely than in the majority of Middle Eastern and North African countries (Napoli & Amin, 1997).

Under the current presidency of Abdel Fatah al-Sisi, the media is experiencing more freedom of expression (Allam, 2015). Now in Egypt there is a great variety of media platforms: national, oppositional, and independent. Egypt is witnessing a greater margin of media freedom under the current president than any previous administration (Allam, 2015).

That said, Egypt's media still operates within an authoritarian press system—the government controls and supervises the media. Journalists must adhere to the country's press codes. These codes call for adherence to cultural principles and national morals. They also forbid content that criticizes Egyptian society's principles and traditions or anything that causes "social confusion." Within Egypt, and in most countries in the Arab world, censorship is easily tolerated and even expected. It is seen as a form of social responsibility. National media policies reinforce cultural and national traditions and values. Criticism of state leadership, the military, and/or that harms Egypt's reputation is not welcomed. Egyptian journalists may not offend Islam or other religions or religious beliefs. It is forbidden to publish or broadcast any material likely to cause disputes among different religious groups, create social confusion, or criticize Arab and Egyptian society principles and traditions. This perhaps explains why most Arab journalists exercise self-censorship and do not conduct investigative reporting that may cause conflict (Amin, 2002b).

Another obstacle that Egypt and most Arab governments have created to limit press freedom is their insistence on licenses for newspaper publishers. The Egyptian government has complete control over the authorization, renewal or non-renewal, and revocation of licenses. In addition to licenses, the government uses advertising revenue to further control the press. In other words, the government oversees the flow of advertisements into national newspapers. Advertisements represent major income for newspapers, and the government uses this leverage to reward and maintain good behavior.

Furthermore, the government restricts publication of reports that could fracture the state's social order. However, today such rules have been relaxed to allow criticism of security officers, religious leaders, and prominent members of government and the business community (H. Ragab, personal communication, January 13, 2009), resulting in several high-profile prosecutions for corruption and criminal behavior.

The government has also loosened its grip on the media, such as national newspapers, including *Al-Ahram*, *Al-Akhbar*, and *Al-Gomhoraiah*. And over the last decade it has allowed new private newspapers, such as dailies *Al-Masry Al-Youm, Al-Osboa, Al-Dostour*, and business newspaper *Alam Al-Youm*.

The market is rich with private newspapers as well. Although their circulation and influence were initially low in comparison to the power and authority of the ruling party and the National Democratic Party newspapers, they attempt to present balanced and objective journalism (H. Ragab, personal communication, January 13, 2009). Among the main players in the current market are *Al-Masry Al-Youm*, *Elyoum7*, and *Al-Shorouk*.

Professional Characteristics

In 1960, television started in Egypt. Its system included three channels and was considered one of the most extensive and effective television systems among all the developing countries of Asia and Africa, particularly the Arab world. The first content to be broadcast in Egyptian television was verses from the Holy Koran, followed by a Nasser speech. It was quite clear from the beginning that the medium would be used as a government propaganda tool (Napoli & Amin, 1997). As of 2011, more than 95% of households in Egypt had access to television (Trading Economics, 2015).

The Egyptian Radio and Television Union (ERTU) runs all domestic broadcast media. ERTU is a government arm, affiliated with the Ministry of Information (see Table 4.1 for major journalism associations and journalism-related organizations). It was formed and operates under Law 13 of 1979, last modified by Law 223 of 1989.

Egypt's radio and television cultural products are by far the most popular in the Arab world, particularly in a culture that gets most of its entertainment at home. The Egyptian culture is still considered the most influential Arabic culture in the region (Tutton, 2011). For example, the Egyptian movie industry has dominated the Arab industry, as Egyptian movies are watched everywhere (Biagi, 2009). Moreover, Egyptian TV programs continue to be distributed throughout the region because of the Egyptian dialect, which is easy for those in Arab countries to understand (Rugh, 2004). Television is an important medium in Egypt since the illiteracy rate is 30%, which makes many citizens especially dependent on it (Unicef, 2015, p. 108). During the last few decades, Egyptian television has decentralized. It now broadcasts several local channels that are required to serve their own constituencies.

The government is struggling with a growing reliance on transnational broadcasts rather than government-controlled terrestrial broadcasting for both news and entertainment. In addition, the government is faced with the impact of new media technologies and social networking amid calls for dealing with election fraud and economic, health care, and educational crises. While pressure on journalists and media organizations continues, the government is trying to balance competing demands for media control with the desire to foster a competitive, vibrant media environment that will retain its leadership position in the region. Today, newspapers, broadcasts, and magazines report on corruption scandals, allegations of police torture, and other stories that would have been unimaginable just a decade ago. Yet journalists, editors, bloggers, and media organizations who push the boundaries of this more liberal attitude toward the press face possible government sanctions.

Freedom of the press in Egypt faces political, social, economic, and technological challenges. Furthermore, journalists face many additional problems and challenges, such as low salaries and a lack of adequate legal protection (Hafiz, 1993). Low salaries make journalists more vulnerable to conflict of interest compromises and outright corruption. The status of journalism as a profession is further reduced by perceptions that most journalists are merely government mouthpieces; the accuracy of information, including news from the opposition press, is highly suspect. Commitment to an informational press versus an opinionated press is weak. Political, legal, and administrative constraints continue to inhibit press freedom. Journalists have reported their concern that the government is using new surveillance technologies to monitor their activities. In his 1993 study, Hafiz found that most journalists are monitored and are aware of this fact, thus increasing self-censorship.

In March 2004, Mubarak announced a ban on imprisonment of journalists in Egypt. This call generated some hope for improvement in press freedom. But despite this ban, imprisonment of editors, journalists, and bloggers has continued, albeit on a less frequent basis. According to the Committee to Protect Journalists (2009), Internet traffic in Egypt passes through servers controlled by the state, which allows the state to monitor content, potential fraud, theft, and security violations. However, under the al-Sisi administration, bloggers and social media activists have reached a very high ceiling in terms of freedom of expression.

Journalism Education, Professional Training, and Research

As mentioned above, Egypt has over 30 academic journalism and mass communication programs in national and private universities, four Ministry of education academic programs, and major newspaper in-house training centers—some of them quite large, such as the Al Ahram Regional Press Institute (see Table 4.2 for top schools and departments of journalism and mass communication). There are also government training centers for the Higher Press Council, the Press Syndicate, and the Middle East News Agency, the state's national news agency. ERTU, the governing body of Egyptian broadcasting, hosts an additional training center. There is some disagreement, however, as to whether these programs are of sufficient quality to supply the Egyptian media market with journalists able to operate effectively in today's media environment. Egypt also has IPSOS, a global marketing research company and major research center, which calculates viewership ratings.

Teaching and Training Future Newsmakers

Academic programs in journalism and mass communication began in Egypt in the 1930s at The American University in Cairo (AUC). Five years later, Cairo University (CU) established an institution for editing, translation, and journalism. CU's Faculty of Mass Communication is considered one of the most important communication institutions in the Arab World. Moreover, AUC's Department of Journalism and Mass Communication attracts elite students due to its strong, well-rounded, internationally accredited program. Al Azhar University's Department of Communication was converted into a School of Mass Communication with three departments: Journalism, Radio and Television, and Advertising and Public Relations (H. Ragab, personal communication, January 13, 2009).

Most of Egypt's departments of journalism and mass communication offer the same curricula, with the exception of AUC. Its program is one of the few in the region grounded in the liberal arts. Its English-language program integrates theory with practical training in three majors: Multi-media Journalism, Communication and Media Arts, and Integrated Marketing Communication. It emphasizes critical thinking, ethics, lifelong learning, effective citizenship, and professional skills. National, regional, and transnational media organizations heavily recruit its graduates. The program is, however, relatively small and draws its students primarily from the region's academic and socio-economic elite. The curricula for the rest of the schools, especially the rural programs, are derived primarily from CU's Faculty of Mass Communication curriculum. This curriculum focuses on theory, with many courses offered in development communication.

Journalism education is very much centralized. With the exception of a relatively small number of AUC students, those not working in the main program at CU are considered peripheral. Almost none of them have adequate academic and/or practical experience. AUC and CU are also the only universities that have student-produced weekly newspapers.

Egypt has a very well-developed system of public and private universities, at least 15 of which offer a range of journalism-related courses. CU is one of the more prestigious public universities, with a total of some 550 communications studies students enrolled in the Faculty of Mass Communication at bachelor's, master's, and doctoral levels. These students are taught in three departments—journalism, broadcasting (radio and television), and public relations and advertising. And additional students pursue distance-based programs. Ain Shams University (ASU), like CU, is another public university offering communications specializations.

AUC, one of the more established private universities, offers three mass communication majors through its Journalism and Mass Communication Department (within the School of Global Affairs and Public Policy). These majors are Communication and Media Arts (CMA), Integrated Marketing Communication (IMC), and Multimedia Journalism (MMJ). It also offers master's programs in Journalism and Mass Communication and Television and Digital Journalism. Other leading private universities offering journalism programs include the Modern Science and Arts University (MSA), Ahram Canadian University (ACU), and the Modern University for Technology and Information (MTI), all of which offer three journalism majors similar to the universities listed above.

While a large number of books exist in Arabic, some media and communication institutions use English books for some specialized subjects. They also use English books to broaden the range of views and perspectives available to students. CU provides a full program of media studies in English.

Many challenges face the development of the state universities' journalism and mass communication programs, such as far too high student-faculty ratios (Abdel-Rahman, AlMageed, & Kamel, 1992). Most of the Media and Communication programs seek accreditation from The National Authority for Quality Assurance and Accreditation of Education (NAQAAE). Programs at state universities in Cairo and rural programs often suffer from a lack of adequate technology and library resources, a problem that continues to increase with advances in media technologies. Also, few programs provide training for those interested in pursuing careers in online journalism and graphic communications. And most national universities cannot afford to update their programs with expensive technologies (El Gody, 2009).

Regional and rural journalism programs face additional difficulties in areas such as funding, personnel, and facilities. Rural journalism programs also suffer from a lack of quality instructors. Lately, interest has shifted toward production, as most students in rural departments are likely to work for the Egyptian mass media. The introduction of small television studios, photography labs, and computer labs is essential to their training. The high number of students admitted is far too many compared to the number of faculty, resulting in little personal attention. Rural university libraries are extremely limited in their number and quality of books, reference materials, and journals. Many local programs in the countryside integrate little practical training into their programs; the shortage of financial resources and trained production staff is a barrier to hands-on training. There is a need for rural programs to devise mission statements and strategic, long-range plans that provide vision and direction for the future. They must identify needs and resources to achieve their mission and goals.

Most of the national journalism and mass communication programs in Egypt are still in the early stages of development. They suffer from both internal and external political problems, especially regarding their relationship with the political sphere and the state. Many programs lack grounding in objectivity and critical thinking. Instead, they support the state's propaganda goals and graduate cadres of poorly prepared journalists. The journalists serve as mouthpieces for state achievements rather than guardians of the public interest. Likewise, in the classroom censorship and denial of freedom of expression are not uncommon.

The establishment of private universities has enhanced the quality of journalism and mass communication programs in the country and increased competition among them. Development of journalism and mass communication programs in the Modern Science and Arts University (MSA), Misr International University (MIU), ACU, and 6th of October University has provided some balance with national program offerings. In addition, the Akhbar El-Yom Academy, International Academy for Media and Engineering Sciences (IAMES), International Media Institute (IMI), MTI, and Canadian International College (S. Kilini, personal communication, January 13, 2010) are forming a new prototype of media education in Egypt, based on hands-on training and production-oriented programs. Most of these programs are in English and have ties with European and/or U.S. universities. Many of them are popular programs and attract a good number of students, although registration fees are considered high by Egyptian standards. The curricula are usually kept up-to-date with national, regional, and international trends in journalism and journalism education, matching peer offerings in European, Canadian, and U.S. universities.

One of the main problems facing the development of these programs is that they have yet to obtain accreditation from the Supreme Council for National Universities (SCNU), which evaluates programs based on curricula and CU's model. Egypt recently launched an initiative to provide national accreditation of academic programs using a model that aligns more closely with international accrediting agencies. Egypt's NAQAAE, an independent authority reporting to Egypt's prime minister, is responsible for evaluating more than 50,000 institutes of higher education (including pre-university and technical education). The authority, led by educational experts, university professors, and entrepreneurs, awards accreditation to programs developing best practices in teaching, research, and faculty development (NAQAAE, 2015).

Egyptian public universities offer graduates appointments as instructors, which begin their career paths. These instructors must work on their master's degrees. Once they earn them, they must earn a doctoral degree to be promoted to a lecturer, the equivalent of an assistant professor. They then become part of the faculty and continue through the promotion process to earn the rank of associate and full professor. Private universities' tenure process is conducted by CU's tenure and promotion committee. That is except for AUC's tenure process, which follows American tenure standards.

Journalism Research

Scholarly research on journalism and mass communication, along with teaching, is not well developed in Egypt. There are few publications in Arabic or other venues for scholars to meet and discuss developments in the field. Most scholarly research is distributed in university publications, where most faculty compete fiercely to publish their work. Some Egyptian scholars, mostly Western educated, publish their work in English-speaking international journals—not in Arabic or in national journals. This creates numerous barriers for researchers, particularly those with limited English and at national universities with limited budgets for travel and attending conferences.

From the early stages of the development of media research in Egypt, the focus has been on historical research. One of the first books that described and analyzed the Egyptian press, written by Qasstaki Elias A'tarah AlHalabi, is titled *History and Development of Egyptian Newspapers*. This book, published and printed by Progress in 1928 (Rachty, 1979), is still one of the most important reference books in Egyptian press history. It offers an overview of the Egyptian press since its introduction in the 17th century (during the French expedition in 1789-1801) up to the 1920s.

Another important reference source is an eight-part series of articles, titled *The Art of the Newspaper Article in Egypt*, written by Abd Al Latif Hamza. It deals with the development of the Egyptian press and the impact of Egyptian writers and editors on the press. It details the life stories of the most influential journalists in Egypt, such as Sheikh Mohammed Abdou, Adeeb Ishaq, and Abdalah Al Nadeem.

In addition to this historical research, scholars have examined areas such as the legal and philosophical aspects of the media (Rachty, 1979). Since the establishment in 1954 of CU's Department of Journalism's Faculty of Art and Literature, research in mass media has expanded and improved. As of 2006, this program has research centers in public opinion, documentation, and production, as well as women and the media (Amin, 2006).

In the late 1950s, Egyptian radio started publishing a quarterly journal, *Broadcasting Art,* including different kinds of articles dealing with the role of radio in national development and how to produce a radio program. When television was introduced in Egypt in 1960, *Broadcasting Art* began to include articles that dealt with both radio and television. Since the state owns, controls, and operates radio and television, most of the content of *Broadcasting Art* was about the impact of electronic media on Egyptian culture. Specifically, it examined the effects of radio and television on Egyptian social life, and it promoted state officials' political decisions and wisdom. Most of the articles were subjective and descriptive. The publication also translated foreign articles into Arabic, particularly those in engineering and other fields dealing with new communication technologies and different broadcasting services.

Today, *Broadcasting Art* often publishes reports from ERTU's Center of Audience Research. These reports deal with audience viewing and listening habits, audience profiles, opinions, and trends. Also, it often publishes reports that discuss Egyptian broadcasting services' Arabic language preservation and Islamic content concerns.

Another journal, with a limited circulation among Egyptian researchers, is the *Quarterly Review of Communication Research.* The journal is published by the Arab States' Broadcasting Union (ASBU), established in 1968. CU's Faculty of Communication and Al Alzhar University both publish journals of faculty research. However, CU also publishes three main Arabic journals focusing on journalism and communication: the *Journal of Communication Research*, the *Journal of Public Opinion Research*, and the *Journal of Journalism Research* (S. Al Sherif, personal communication, January 22, 2010).

The AUC faculty also generates a substantial amount of research. The majority is in English and published in international publications and conference proceedings. AUC also hosts *Arab Media and Society*, formerly *Transnational Broadcasting Studies* (TBS), a highly regarded English-language online journal established in 1998. It features articles by scholars and media professionals from around the world.

One of the most critical challenges facing journalism research in Egypt is its culture of secrecy, as there is no "access to information" law. But the new parliament is expected to approve such a law soon. This makes it difficult for researchers to gain access to information held by the state, as well as public and private organizations and institutions. There is little transparent sharing of information or public reporting of activity. Legislative prohibitions and bureaucratic impediments have so far made it exceedingly difficult to conduct research based on any information that authorities deem threatening to national security.

Journals must become more selective and weed out articles merely intended to enhance government propaganda. In order to promote a diverse range of ideas and representation when it comes to journalism research, it is important that journalism leaders (educators, researchers, and practitioners) organize conferences that bring Western researchers, and those from the rest of the world, to Egypt.

Professional Connections in Journalism Education

Although the relationship between most academic programs and industry is minimal, it has been growing in recent years. Many journalism programs have developed internships as either optional or required components of their curricula. The large number of journalism students is a barrier to the widespread adoption of this learning model, which is not offered in all schools. AUC is the first program to include a required supervised internship. AUC's program includes reflection activities, student reporting, and a supervisor's evaluation, all aimed at increasing the effectiveness of the learning experience.

CU's Faculty of Communication leads all programs in the number of conferences and workshops offered throughout the year. Most of the other national programs have an annual conference. AUC's Department of Journalism and Mass Communication hosted the International Association for Media and Communication Research (IAMCR) in 2006, as well as the Arab-US Association for Communication Education (AUSACE) in 1998, 2004, and 2009. The latter is the only regional association of communication educators in the Middle East and North Africa, and it accepts papers published in both English and Arabic.

Communications research in Egypt is also hampered by restrictions on survey and audience research. Government regulations state that (Napoli & Amin, 1997):

> No entity in the government, public or private sector shall be allowed to conduct any surveys except after obtaining a written decision from the Central Agency for Public Mobilization and Statistics (CAPMAS). The decision should include approval on the procedure, determine the purpose of the research survey, and set the dates and methods in which it will be conducted and the results published. (p. 157)

While researchers and industry professionals apply, and often are granted permission, for such research, these restrictions have created a barrier to conduct academic and industry research, including research on audience viewing habits and ratings.

Market research. However, market research is available, and those conducting it in Egypt include the following:

❏ The Central Agency for Population Mobilization and Statistics, Egypt's official statistical agency. It collects, processes, analyzes, and disseminates all statistical data.

❏ The ERTU, which has a center conducting research on all nationally owned radio and television stations in most of the constituencies.

❏ Taylor Nelson Sofres (TNS) and IPSOS are among the leading private market research companies in Egypt. They, and others, conduct audience-related research on national and private radio and television stations involving ratings, advertising, and other issues.

Journalism Education's Professional Impact

The value of a country's journalism profession is based on the availability of quality academic programs, professional skills, and ethics training. However, the impact of journalism education is felt far beyond the confines of the classroom due to the crucial role the media play in helping develop and maintain a civil society, a democratic government, and effective governance. In order for the media to effectively function in such roles, colleges, universities, and training centers must deliver journalists with the skills, abilities, knowledge, and professional standards necessary to operate effectively in today's media landscape.

Egypt's universities are now hosting journalism programs with more academic freedom, especially in private universities. These programs are providing graduates with updated skills and greater access to a market that is relatively more open than before, especially in television journalism. Coverage of political party activities is more common today, as is criticism of government performance, which is frequently featured on satellite television channels. Protocol news, news that pays attention to government officials' activities, is not as extensive as it was 10 years ago. And talk shows that critique the news are still popular among Egyptian audiences. While some university journalism departments, such as AUC, have succeeded in publicizing Egyptian journalism education in the Arab region, much promotion is still need.

Future Possibilities

In spite of the problems facing journalism and mass communication education in Egypt, the country still has some of the most well-developed, relevant, and successful programs in the region. It also hosts some of the most influential and prolific scholars in the Middle East and North Africa. Egyptian academics and graduates have been at the forefront of most of the major developments in industry and continue to yield influence in regional policy-making, advertising, public relations, broadcasting, radio, and print.

Economic pressures will continue to present challenges for universities, especially national universities, to invest adequately in infrastructure, research, and faculty development. Failure to invest in technology and 21st century skills is a significant challenge. If not addressed, it will result in graduates no longer relevant to the journalism profession. The number of students in journalism programs continues to grow, albeit at a reduced rate. And national universities must absorb this growth. There is little indication that student-faculty ratios will decrease in the near future, although the continuing growth of private universities should partially offset the demand on national programs. Increased competition among universities for the best students will hopefully result in improved teaching methods and curricula, as well as a requirement for NAQAAE accreditation.

Since Egypt's January 25th (2011) revolution, censorship has been decreasing. There is also a new spirit of openness in broadcast programming and print that should reduce the threat to journalists. However, the new government is still struggling to understand many of the issues and challenges related to new media technologies and social networks, which are still feared since they helped overthrow the previous government.

There is a strong need to develop national and regional professional associations to broaden access to scholarly research, including pedagogical research, and to publish in Arabic. The government needs to reduce barriers to academic and industry research and to revise press laws to expand press freedom. In addition, Egypt needs to develop a code of ethics for journalism and mass communication professionals and industry to encourage adherence to ethical standards. Currently, there is only one code of ethics for the print media, which is neither enforced nor updated. And social media, blogging, and mobile media should continue to find their way into journalism curricula, which will teach future journalists how to help establish converging media platforms in newsrooms.

Journalism Education Issues, Challenges, and Innovations

There is a tremendous need to close the gap between academia and industry by constantly upgrading journalism programs in accordance with the evolving needs of industry and society. Programs should be challenged to emphasize performance characteristics the industry values: strong writing skills, broad-based knowledge, a well-rounded personality, ethical behavior, and diligent work habits. In addition, journalism program curricula need to continuously evolve with the changing media landscape. Today this means increased emphasis on multi-platform skills and cross-disciplinary programs that draw on print, broadcast, interactive and social media, and multimedia platforms. The increased emphasis on communication and media technologies will require additional resources for equipment, software, and facilities, as well as faculty and staff with the requisite knowledge and experience to effectively teach such technologies.

Journalism programs across the country need to raise admission standards to select higher quality students. They also need to work with secondary schools to improve English-language abilities, decrease over-reliance on memorization and rote learning, and increase exposure to critical thinking. Ethics training must become a required component of all journalism programs, and faculties should be encouraged to publish case studies for use in their programs and in programs throughout the region. In addition, programs, particularly those in public universities, need to guarantee freedom of expression in the classroom. Students need to be encouraged to question and critically examine issues of interest without fear of repercussion or sanctions.

Few programs support or require student internships with print and broadcast media organizations. Most do not have industry and alumni advisory boards, nor do they seek out research or funding opportunities. Close ties with media organizations in the region could provide important input into curriculum development, opportunities for hands-on skills training for students, employment for graduates, and increasing academic relevance and influence.

Additional challenges facing journalism programs in Egypt are recruitment, retention, and evaluation of qualified and effective faculty instructors. Many programs do not routinely conduct student evaluations of teachers and do not have resources to invest in faculty professional development. Most programs do not conduct systematic assessment of learning outcomes, and few programs have resources to regularly send their faculty to professional conferences abroad.

Also, the lack of adequate instructional facilities hampers many programs. The top challenges of many journalism programs include an insufficient number of smart and well-equipped classrooms, electronic newsrooms, digital audio and video facilities, computer labs, and Internet connections.

Journalism programs should explore opportunities to leverage scarce resources and expertise by seeking linkages with quality programs worldwide. Currently, Egyptian journalism programs have ties with Canadian programs, like the University of Ottawa, University of Windsor, and Cape Breton University; and programs in the United Kingdom, like the University of Wales and Middlesex University. Similar ties with outstanding journalism programs in the United States, Europe, Africa, and Asia should also be encouraged.

Conclusion: Educating Tomorrow's Journalists—The Big Picture

Training tomorrow's journalists in Egypt is going to be affected by the status of democratization and the political environment in the country. The forces of globalization and the growth of information and communication technologies and social networking could have a massive impact on the training of journalists, opening up the media environment for all voices and paving the way for a more democratic agenda. Yet technology alone is not going to establish excellent training programs. All journalism programs must modernize their instructional methods, curricula, and facilities to provide graduates with an education that is relevant for tomorrow's media landscape. Training and professional faculty development should be a priority, which will require support from colleges and universities, the private sector, the Press Syndicate, and the government. Linkages with prestigious universities in the West could also help leverage scarce financial, technical, and instructional resources. Such linkages could also help build capacity for research, its promotion, and publication.

With the relaxation of censorship and increased freedom created by new technologies, journalism programs will need to focus on responsible journalism and journalism ethics. With increasing calls for democratization and accountability, journalists need to be trained regarding media roles and responsibilities. Finally, journalists need to work together, with the support of journalism programs, to strengthen their professional organizations, such as the Press Syndicate. Such organizations need to protect and defend the rights of journalists, increase calls for more openness and sharing of information, and create a code of professional ethics to which members are held accountable. Although traditional university training of journalists should not be abandoned, it needs to be updated and modified to meet the needs of the rapidly changing, converging media landscape.

References

Abdel Rahman, A., Abed AlMageed, L., & Kamel, N. (1992) *AlQa'em be Iletissal fi AlSahafa al Maissrieh* [Communicator in the Egyptian Press]. Cairo: School of Mass Communication Press.

Allam, R. (2015, March 17). *Masr Al-Mostaqbal* [Egypt: the future]. Al-Masry Al-Youm Newspaper.

Amin, H. (1996). Broadcasting in the Arab World and the Middle East. In A. Wells (Ed.), *World broadcasting: A comparative view* (pp. 121-144). New Jersey, NJ: Ablex.

Amin, H. (2002a). Egypt, status of media. In D. Johnston (Ed.), *Encyclopedia of international media and communications* (p. 116). Elsevier: Academic Press.

Amin, H. (2002b). Freedom as a value in Arab media. Perceptions and attitudes among journalists. *Political Communication*, *19*(2), 125-136.

Amin, H. (2006, March). *Media Reform.* Keynote Speaker, Al Ahram Press Institute. Cairo, Egypt.

Amin, H., & Napoli, J. (2000). Media and power in Egypt. In J. Curran & M. J. Park (Eds.), *De-Westernizing media studies* (pp. 178-188). London: Routledge.

Baigi, S. (2009). *Media/impact: An introduction to mass media.* Belmont, CA: Wadsworth Publishing.

Central Agency for Public Mobilization and Statistics. (2015, December 13). Retrieved from http://www.capmas.gov.eg/Pages/StaticPages.aspx?page_id=23

Committee to Protect Journalists (2009, November 30). Bloggers held in Egypt without charge. Retrieved from https://cpj.org/2009/07/bloggers-held-in-egypt-without-charge.php

El Gody, A. (1999, March). "Journalism for the 21st Century." Paper presented to the Fourth AUSACE Research Conference. Beirut: The Lebanese American University.

Hafiz, S. E. (1993). *Ahzan Horiat Al Sahafah* [Sorrow of press freedom]. Cairo: *Markaz Al Ahram Lel Targamah Wa Al Nasher* [Al Ahram Center for Translation and Publication].

Napoli, J., & Amin, H. (1997). Press freedom in Egypt. In F. Eribo & W. Jong-Ebot (Eds.), *Communication and press freedom in Africa* (pp. 185-210). New Jersey, NJ: Africa World Press.

National Authority for Quality Assurance and Accreditation of Education. (December 2015). Retrieved from http://naqaae.org.eg/

Rachty, G. (1979). *Al Nozon Al Iza'aih fi Al Mogtama'at Al Ishtrakayeh* [Broadcasting systems in social communities]. Dar Al Fikr Al Arabi Cairo Egypt.

Rugh, A. W. (2004). Arab mass media: Newspaper, radio, and television in Arab politics. Westport, CT: Greenwood Publishing Group.

Trading Economics. (2015). Households with television (%) in Egypt. Retrieved from http://www.tradingeconomics.com/egypt/households-with-television-percent-wb-data.html

Tutton, M. (2011, February 12). Egypt's cultural influence pervades Arab world. *CNN.* Retrieved from http://www.cnn.com/2011/WORLD/meast/02/12/egypt.culture.influence.film/

Unicef. (2015). Children in Egypt. A statistical digest. 2015. Retrieved from http://www.unicef.org/egypt/UNICEF_2015_Children_in_Egypt_Statistical_Digest(1).pdf

Table 4.1

Major Journalism Associations and Journalism-Related Organizations in Egypt

Organization	Description	Contact
Al Ahram Regional Press Institute	The institute is associated with Egypt's largest newspaper, the state-owned *Al Ahram*. It provides training for journalists from Egypt and the region on current journalism trends, journalism graphics, and journalism laws and regulations.	http://ahrij. ahram.org.eg
The Egyptian Radio and Television Union (ERTU)	This state-owned union is the governing body of broadcasting in Egypt. It was established in 1970 with four distinct sectors: Radio, Television, Engineering, and Finance. Each has a chairman who reports directly to the ERTU's chairman, who reports to the Minister of Information. It has introduced Nile Television Networks, offering a specialized network of thematic television channels.	http://ertu.org
The Egyptian Press Syndicate	Founded in 1941, it plays an important part in the development of the press in Egypt and the preservation and the protection of Egyptian journalists and freedom of the press.	http://www.ejs. org.eg
Middle East News Agency (MENA)	Established in 1955-56 as the first regional news agency in the region. MENA was nationalized in the 1960s and was brought under the control of the Ministry of Information. Its main goal is to collect and distribute news in the region and in the world.	http://www. mena.org.eg
Higher Council of the Press	Established by President Anwar Sadat in 1975 to protect the press after the introduction of the multi-party system. This first council lasted only two years. It was reintroduced in 1981. It is an independent body of the Shura Council, a parliamentary advisory body whose members are appointed by the president, which deals with all press affairs and preserves press freedom. It is also the only body responsible for issuing newspaper licenses.	www.scp.gov.eg

Table 4.2

Top Schools and Departments of Journalism and Mass Communication in Egypt

Schools and Departments	Contact
Department of Journalism and Mass Communication, the American University	http://www.aucegypt.edu/academics/dept/jrmc/Pages/default.aspx
Kamal Adham Center for Television and Digital Journalism	http://www1.aucegypt.edu/academic/cej
School of Mass Communication, Cairo University	http://masscomm.cu.edu.eg
School of Mass Communication, Modern Sciences and Arts University	http://www.msa.eun.eg/index_mcom.htm
School of Mass Communication, Misr International University	http://www.miuegypt.edu.eg
The International Academy for Engineering and Media Science	http://www.iams.edu.eg
Ahram Canadian University	http://www.acu.edu.eg
Canadian International College	http://www.cic-cairo.com/cic
Akhbar El-Yom Academy	http://www.university-directory.eu/Egypt/Akhbar-El-Yom-Academy.html
School of Mass Communication, Modern University for Technology and Information	http://www.mti.edu.eg/app/page.aspx?pageID=33

5

Journalism Education in India: Maze or Mosaic?

Mira K. Desai

India, a 5,000 year-old civilization, has been a democracy for more than 65 years. It is a sovereign, socialist, secular republic of 29 states and seven territories with 22 officially recognized languages. It is geographically, geologically, climatically, culturally, and linguistically diverse, a land of contradictions united by a complex national policy framework. The private sector launched the press, film, radio, and transnational television industries, whereas government initiatives launched television and the Internet. The Indian media mosaic, with its varied ownership and wide-ranging linguistic and distribution markets, is representative of its diverse society.

Print media in India has remained primarily privately owned, with government ownership and circulation limited to about 2%. India's newspaper market had a daily circulation of 330 million in 2011 (World Association of Newspapers, 2011). Circulation has gone up by 288% from 2004 to 2014 (Government of India, 2014).

India has 99,660 registered publications, 850 government-licensed television channels (413 hosting news and current affairs, 437 hosting entertainment programming), and public service broadcasters Doordarshan and All India Radio (AIR, http://prasarbharati.gov.in/). It has private FM stations and radio stations operated by academic institutions and non-government/civil society organizations. India, with a 462 million Internet user base, has the second most Internet users worldwide. China, at 721 million, has the largest, and the United States, at 286 million, is currently in third place (Internetlivestats, 2016).

Journalism education in India began in pre-independent India, with its roots in university language departments. Linguistic purity and journalistic responsibility drove the early years of journalism education, which newspaper owners largely ignored. Post-independence and post-emergency[1] business interests surpassed journalism rigor. And in the post-1990s, many news organizations started journalism schools.

Today, there are multiple players in journalism education. They range from public universities and media houses running journalism schools to journalism associations partnering with businesses and non-profits (see Table 5.1 for journalism/journalism educator associations). Indian journalism education is viewed as a subset of mass communication education. There are about 700 universities in India with programs of varied scale, scope, and nomenclature. India has two state universities devoted exclusively to journalism and mass communication education and a national university that houses a School of Journalism and teaches new media studies. In addition, there are hundreds of colleges at each of these universities, which also offer undergraduate and sometimes post-graduate programs in journalism and mass communication.

Journalism in the Media Landscape

For centuries, politics, not economics, has driven India's press. But post-2000, politics *and* economics drive the news media (Desai, 2012). The history of India's news media is well documented (Menon, 1930; Rau, 1974; Hassan, 1980; Raghavan, 1994; Ravindran, 1997; Vilanilam, 2005; Desai, 2012; Tere, 2012). It can be categorized into five parts: pre-independence India (1780 to 1947), post-independence until emergency (1977), post-emergency (1978 to 1990), post-globalization (post-1991), and post-television news channels (post-2000). There are also hundreds, if not thousands, of geographical and linguistic histories of the news media across India (Ravindranath, 2005; Vilanilam, 2005). Much such information remains to be researched and documented.

Between 1977 and 1999, Indian daily circulations increased some 500% (Jeffery, 2000). According to the Newspaper Association of India (NAI), India's combined circulation of mostly small and medium regional language newspapers is 11 times greater than all Indian similarly sized English-language newspapers. After 1992, India's television landscape, dominated by state-controlled TV stations, was "invaded" by numerous indigenous and transnational television channels (ZEE TV, in October 1992, kicked off the era of private television broadcasting in India).

In 1995, television news channels were launched. In 2004, TRAI

(Telecom Regulatory Authority of India) started expressing concerns about cross-media ownership and a lack of diversity (www.trai.gov. in). Media houses had entered into content-sharing arrangements and content management across media platforms. Journalists increasingly became managers and corporate executives at media outlets, and media owners' control over editorial content increased further than during post-emergency times.

Until the 1980s, Indian newspapers were treated as modest, small-profit businesses. But everything changed in the late 1990s, when public relations departments were established in newspaper offices. Newsrooms were now concerned with making significant profits, and "paid news" and "private treaties," bribes for positive coverage, flourished (Radhakrishnan, 2010). The Indian government, which sees paid news coverage as a serious threat to democracy, continues to fight this practice. For example, in 2009, India's Election Commission charged electoral candidates for purchasing paid news during general elections. Although many such candidates were found guilty and punished, this unauthorized activity continues. In 2010, the Election Commission distributed guidelines and mechanisms to curb paid news (Press Council of India, 2010). And in May 2013, the Ministry of Information and Broadcasting issued its 47th report investigating paid news.

Scholars have severely criticized India's television news channels for inadequately covering disasters and tragedies, creating news rather than covering it, and generating media-initiated investigations (media trials; Agrawal, 2005; Sultana, 2008; Thussu, 2007; Cottle & Rai, 2008; Gupta, 2009). For example, TV news coverage of the November 2008 Mumbai terrorist attacks was condemned for inadvertently providing security information to terrorists. And in the December 2012 New Delhi gang-rape case, after a young woman died of her injuries, media coverage took on an activist role by creating awareness about violence against women. Finally, during the 2014 general elections, TV channels began overtly endorsing candidates and taking sides on issues.

The Indian press continues to produce multiple editions and local supplements, to survive circulation wars, and to participate in electronic news media ownership. The government has also made it easier for newspapers to access foreign investments (TRAI, 2008). Most newspapers, including Indian-language newspapers, have started online editions easily accessible through mobile phone apps (Thakur, 2009). And such innovations continue. For example, in 2011, the South Indian multimedia Eenadu Group launched a mobile newspaper. And in 2015, the Rajsthan Patrika Group started *Catch News*, a multimedia digital platform news outlet.

A 2015 Federation of Indian Chambers of Commerce and Industries (FICCI) and international consulting corporation KPMG report stated that rising literacy, growing disposable income, brand consciousness, and strong commercial development in larger cities have contributed to increased regional print media circulation. It also stated that online reading behavior studies have found only 35.4% of the total Indian population use the Internet and visit newspaper websites, and only about 10% of daily Web users turn to newspaper sites every day. It added that regional newspapers are conversing with readers in their local languages, leading to a much higher growth rate in revenues compared to India's English-language dailies.

Since 2015, newspapers, news magazines, TV news, and social media have been flourishing in India. The Indian television news market is crowded with diverse languages, coverage, and presentation styles. Online newspapers are a reality, and the mainstream media is actively using social media. Alternative media exist, but their scope and scale remain largely unknown due to a lack of research. Mainstream news media tend to focus far more on speed than on accuracy and social responsibility. And news sites provide information and perspectives on Indian current affairs (such as twocircles.net, indiatogether.org, infochangeindia.org, and kafila.org).

Professional Characteristics

Although much has been written over the years about journalism standards and professionalism in India (Menon, 1930; Kamath, 1997), scholars debate progress made (Jagannathan, 2005). For example, the World Press Freedom Index ranked India 136th out of 180 nations worldwide in 2015 (up from 140th in 2013), which still indicates significant struggles for an independent media environment. And although specialists are replacing generalists and many more women are entering Indian newsrooms (Jagannathan, 2005), there are still significantly fewer women in newsrooms than men (Balasubramanya, 2006), and newsroom staff still hold biases against lower castes (Rajpurohit, 2014). Also, the Press Council of India (PCI) argues that although "undue favors" (Sanjay, 2006a, p. 24) are highly unethical (it lists 30 of them), such practices continue. For example, in exchange for positive coverage, decision makers often provide journalists, their agencies, and owners with special government accommodations, travel, nominations to committees, jobs for relatives, and/or even company shares. In addition, there is more pressure on Indian journalists today than ever before as market forces (through owner-managed media companies) expect journalists to "broker news," to help bring politicians and corporate interests together and to "suitably" report on their projects/interactions (Gupta, 2009; Rao, 2009; Desai, 2012; Secretariat, 2013). And, as illustrated in the "Radia tape"[2] and other such controversies, present-day journalists are departing from pre-independence, anti-establishment roles and embracing economic, political ones.

Indian journalists continue to struggle with a wide variety of pressures, including personal security. In 2011, the Indian Journalists Union (IJU), regularly advocating the need for protecting journalists, reported that 47 journalists have been killed in India since 1992. One such high-profile case involved the murder of Special Investigations Editor Jyothirmoy Dey, who was killed in Mumbai in 2011 after reporting on the oil industry-related mafia (Chandavarkar & Srivastava, 2011). And in 2012, media organizations protested police manhandling of press staff, which was reported by news magazine *India Today* (Rahman, 2012). Free speech hub thehoot.org has also documented attacks against free speech and media personnel. A special law is now being called for to get professional organizations to give journalists the same type of protections as other civil servants. Additional pressure arises from journalists' desire for privacy versus their need for security and their vulnerability to political and corporate lobbying and state and local vested-interest groups.

But despite the pressures and problems facing the journalism profession, local journalists still tend to enjoy respectability. More and more students aspire to become media professionals, leading to increasing enrollment figures in media schools. And aspiring journalists tend to prefer working for the electronic rather than print media. The advent of electronic media has brought glamour and increased salaries to professional journalists, and the dot-com boom has provided them with alternative career paths.

The Indian government tries to protect journalists through "wage boards," a mechanism that ascertains newspaper employee salaries. After the Working Journalists Act in 1955 was issued, six wage boards were created under the Ministry of Labor and Employment to protect print journalists' salaries and working conditions (Ministry of Labor & Employment, n.d.). But by 1993, a media contract system was introduced. This system reduces journalists' bargaining power and stops them from unionizing and negotiating their working conditions. Interestingly, wage boards do not apply to the electronic media (ABP Pvt. Ltd. & Anr. V. Union of India & Ors., 2011). Currently, newspaper owners and the government are fighting a legal battle over this contract system. Journalists' unions argue that journalists, especially newcomers, are exploited by this system, treated like temporary, disposable employees (Tambat, 2012; Choudhary, 2014).

As for formal journalism education, recent studies about newspaper newsrooms and television news personnel—while an important beginning—suggest unclear, inconsistent, and limited overall findings. On one hand, Balasubramanya's (2006) study, a survey of 835 journalists from 11 different language publications in over 14 Indian states, found that only 35% of respondents had formal journalism education. That said, the author added, "as a country of diverse socio-cultural values, it would be difficult to present a complete profile of journalists in a massive country like India" (Balasubramanya, 2006, p.48). On the other hand, Gupta's (2009) study of 100 electronic journalists, conducted in Mumbai, found that the majority, 65%-68%, were formally trained at some 20 different journalism schools and had prior print media experience. Regardless, the media industry acknowledges a shortage of trained personnel across media outlets, especially in print. And there is also a definite concern regarding the quality of journalism schools (FICCI-KPMG, 2013).

Overall, journalists in India often lack formal qualifications, and newsrooms do not adequately represent social and economic realities. In March 2013, the PCI decided to set up a committee to determine "minimum qualifications" for journalists. The idea, rejected by media professionals, may gain more ground in years to come. Historically, journalism was a profession of passion to promote public welfare. It now often seems more like a profession geared toward acquiring bribes and securing political positions. Although journalists in India are supposed to be detached watchdogs and information facilitators for the masses, "they often act more like, and even become, lobbyists, PR professionals, etc." (Sharma, 2010).

Journalism Education, Professional Training, and Research

The Centre for Media Studies (CMS-UKIERI, 2015) states there are 300 institutions offering journalism and mass communication programs in India, compared to just over 25 in the early 1980s (Belavadi, 2002). Throughout Indian journalism education history, language has played an important role. Journalism education has traditionally been based within language departments and has focused more on the purity of language than on job skills. U.S.-trained scholars initiated most journalism education programs, and their approach to journalism education was Western, not local. This Western orientation continues, along with a lack of standard curricula across India. Often curricula depend completely upon teachers' decisions rather than on variables such as institutional needs, the relevance of content, and student expectations. There is no monitoring and assessment specifically for journalism programs: The National Accreditation and Assessment Council (NAAC) focuses only on the overall quality of education for institutions.

Teaching and Training Future Newsmakers

In India, journalism education is mostly referred to as "mass communication" or "media" education, and it is viewed as a subset of mass communication. It was born of, and is nurtured by, government investments. Indian scholars repeatedly argue that the Indian media industry has not until recently made a significant investment in journalism education (Eapen, 1982; Agrawal, 2006). Ever since the post-1990s, since the advent of television news channels and new media, electronic and broadcast journalism have actively participated in media education.

Journalism/media education became visible in the 1960s, post-independent India, when various traditional universities started diploma/degree programs. A 1961 UNESCO report found that six Indian universities, most in Southern India, offered journalism courses (United Nations Educational Scientific and Cultural Organization, 1961). In 1982, India hosted the Asian Games in New Delhi, prompting the start of color television transmissions. Next came a rise in private TV-set ownership, along with the "UGC's (University Grants Commission's) vocationalization of education mandate" (Yadav, 2003, p. 13). As a result, media and journalism became recognized as a viable career option.

In 1981, some 25 universities taught journalism and mass communication. Today, there are some 70. Most such university programs offer diploma or postgraduate programs. In addition, the National Institute of Rural Development (NIRD) and about a dozen other agricultural universities offer agricultural communication courses for print and broadcast media throughout India.

Undergraduate programs in mass communication began initially in the South and later traveled northwest. As Eapen (2007) explained, the bachelor's degree was supposed to be a how-to type, with additional studies needed to recognize the economic, socio-political, and cultural environment in which the media system exists. This implied a distinction between "skill" and "knowledge" applications. In 2000, the University of Mumbai, in Western India, started a bachelor's degree in mass media with two specializations: journalism and advertising. By 2011, colleges offering undergraduate programs grew to around 80. In 2012, five colleges affiliated with the University of Mumbai started offering master's degrees, suggesting an increasing demand for journalism/media education.

The UGC is a statutory body responsible for providing professional standards in Indian universities, colleges, and research institutions. In 1977, it recognized "journalism" as a subject of academic inquiry via a panel on "journalism and communication" (AMIC, 2002, p. 5). In 2001, the UGC recommended a model curriculum, program execution specifications, and uniform "journalism and mass communication" terminology. It also described journalism "as a part of a larger discipline of mass communication" (UGC, 2001, p. 8). But most universities did not make any changes, and scholars debated whether "uniformity was a good thing" (Sanjay, 2006b, p. 31). In July 2014, the UGC required public universities to standardize their terminology, including giving their degrees "arts" versus "science" designations in order to retain their validity. This process did not impact private institutions offering journalism programs.

Indira Gandhi National Open University, established in 1985, started its School of Journalism and New Media Studies (SOJNMS) in 2007—offering a mixture of on-campus and distance learning programs. Also, as mentioned above, two state universities exclusively focus on journalism and mass communication education: Makhanlal Chaturvedi National University of Journalism (MCNUJ) in Madhya Pradesh, established in 1990, and Shri Kushabhau Thakre Patrakarita Avam Jansanchar Vishwavidyalaya in Chattisgarh, established in 2005. (The Rajasthan-based Haridev Joshi University of Journalism and Mass Communication, established in 2012, no longer exists—it was merged into Rajasthan University's Journalism Department.)

Private sector involvement with journalism education can be placed into four categories: private universities/institutes, media houses/agencies, practitioners/professional bodies offering educational endeavors, and individuals offering piece-meal programs. Private universities, such as Symbiosis Institute/University and Manipal Academy of Higher Education, and trusts, like Bharatiya Vidya Bhawan, run institutes across India. They offer diploma and degree programs in journalism and allied subjects.

In addition, institutes offer many vocational journalism programs. They include the American College of Journalism Bombay (now Mumbai), the Rajendra Prasad Institute of Communication and Management, the K.C. College of Journalism, and Horniman College of Journalism.

Across India, professional bodies, such as press academies and press clubs, offer vocational programs in journalism for full-time students and working journalists. No consolidated databases or agencies/professional bodies track the nature and scope of these programs.

Private enterprises generate resources from student fees without any regulatory body to control or monitor their finances. Critics argue that while private institutions can proactively meet market needs and job demands, their often high fees make them too expensive for students from average economic backgrounds. And their policies, regarding enrollment, recruitment, curriculum reform, and evaluation appear arbitrary when compared to traditional universities' policies.

Many media groups have in-house training schools for their employees. In some cases, they are even open to the general public. Although Eenadu Group owner Ramoji Rao "sent his own son abroad to study journalism, in the early 1990s he used his newspaper, *Eenadu*, to start his own school of journalism and paid students stipends for working at his publication" (Ravindranath, 2005, p. 102). Today, the Eenadu Group has an electronic media presence and owns media production facilities and an amusement park, Ramoji Film City, in Hyderabad. Many newspaper establishments now have their own training institutes, such as *The Times of India's* Times Centre for Media Studies, *The Hindu's* The Asian College of Journalism, and *The Pioneer's* Pioneer Media School. In 2009, the Times School of Journalism was re-established in Mumbai, and the Express Institute of Media Studies launched its eight-month program in Delhi.

There are numerous collaborative programs in India, many of which start small and keep building. For example, in 1979, the University of Pune's (now Savitribai Pule Pune University) Ranade Institute started offering a part-time certificate program in collaboration with the Pune Shramik Patrakar Sangh (the journalists' trade union in Pune). In 1986, it upgraded its offering to a Diploma in Journalism (in Marathi, a regional language). In 2003, it added a part-time post-graduate Diploma in Journalism (in English), and it eventually added, also in English, a master's program in journalism and mass communication (Barve, 2007).

In the 1960s, journalism education nonprofits, like the Press Institute of India (PII) and the Indian Institute of Mass Communication (IIMC), began appearing. By 2013, some 306 IIMC students earned post-graduate diplomas from its six campuses, located in New Delhi, Jammu, Dhenkanal, Aizwal, Amravati, and Kottayam. During the past few years, newer forms of nonprofit journalism education have popped up. Examples include Journalism Mentor in Mumbai, International Media Institute of India (IMII) in New Delhi, and Indian Institute of Journalism and New Media (IIJNM) in Bangalore. IIJNM was founded in 2001 by the BS&G Foundation, a nonprofit trust dedicated to promoting democratic values and institutions in India.

Although the Indian Constitution recognizes 22 official languages, 1,700 languages are spoken throughout India. Journalism education is offered, mostly in English, within professional or vocational programs. There are also language departments within public universities that offer journalism degrees. Language is also class/caste/region-linked in India. Many languages are dying off and coming alive at the same time due to new technologies.

Journalism Research

Due to private media ownership, print media research is mostly concerned with bottom-line issues, such as circulation, marketing, and sales promotion. And most market research is subscription-based and expensive, carried out for circulation figures. Only about 10 to 15 universities in India offer doctoral programs in journalism, and U.K.-trained Indian researchers often find it difficult to contribute to skill-based journalism programs in the country (due to cultural and resource-based differences, etc.) (Murthy, 2011).

Academic journalism research is mandatory for public universities teaching journalism (see Table 5.2 for well-known journalism education programs). But this research, with a limited scope and resources, is conducted more for practical reasons—to meet requirements and earn a degree—than academic ones. This is not surprising since the journalism industry seems more interested in good stories than research abilities. And when academic research is conducted in Indian languages, it often remains undistributed for various reasons, including a lack of resources, bi-lingual proficiency, and ability to contextualize research for global audiences.

Most Indian academic journalism research focuses on journalists' perceptions, opinions, and backgrounds (through sociological surveys); the nature and language of news (through content analysis); and critical, theoretical analysis of news production practices. Journalists also write books in Indian languages and in English focusing on their firsthand personal experiences and mostly non-academic media analysis or social commentary.

The government's Publications Division publishes in 10 (of 22) official languages. Its Research and Reference Division publishes two reference books annually: *India: A Reference Manual* and *Mass Media in India*. Although academic journals do exist, their quality and stability are cause for concern. This researcher could not find a long-running Indian journalistic research journal, and no Indian consolidated media journal listings exist. However, there are several long-running, media-related publications, including the following: IIMC's *Communicator* (in English), *Sanchar Madhyam* (in Hindi), PII's *Vidura* (in English), *Grassroots* (in Hindi and Telugu), and *Media Mimansa* (in Hindi and English). In addition, the University of Calcutta supports the Indian edition of *Global Media*, an online journal. And in 2010, the Centre for Communication Studies, Orissa, launched the biannual *Media Watch*.

Many journalism programs also produce student-run newspapers and newsletters. And many educational institutions host blogs, such as Jamia Millia Islamia (Jamia) in New Delhi (The Indian Medialogue, 2015). Unfortunately, no national databases exist that categorize/count such efforts.

As in many "third world" countries, India's journalism research suffers from a lack of skills, motivation, research resources and focus, and a common language (Eapen, 2000). Murthy (2011) also cites flawed recruitment practices. And since many private institutes follow a "placement centric" training approach, research remains a low priority.

While the UGC supports limited research primarily for those in academia, the Indian Council for Social Science Research provides grants to practicing journalists. There are also websites, like thehoot.org, that critique journalistic coverage and rely on readers' support to do so. The Mudra Institute of Communication, Ahmedabad (MICA), a leading private school teaching mainly advertising and management, eventually started a sister branch—the Mudra Institute of Communication Research (MICORE). MICORE critiqued the quality of journalism schools on its website (when it was live), saying, "though there are various schools of journalism in the country, there is a distinct lack of rigorous, systematic research in this field" (www.mica.ac.in). In 2007,

MICORE merged with MICA, indicating private media schools' difficulty running academic research institutes in India not focused on market research.

Professional Connections in Journalism Education

Historically, newspaper management has remained indifferent to university training programs (Hassan, 1980). And although today the Indian media industry "expects media education curricula to meet . . . industry demands," it is not optimistic about the "suitability of [academic] training for long-term career goals" (AMIC, 2002, p. 40). Even though traditional public university journalism programs naturally situate themselves within university system academic molds, there are "frequent debates about . . . [their] relevance, curriculum, quality of teachers, infrastructure and critical responses by media practitioners" (Sanjay, 2006a, p.28). Academia's emphasis on theory, and general lack of practical journalism training and facilities, continues to alienate the professional media from university training. Although various researchers have criticized university programs for such practices, they still continue (Belavadi, 2002; Aram, 2005; Sanjay, 2006a). While it is common for academics to conduct journalism research, it is uncommon for former or present journalists to do so. That is, unless they are enrolled as doctoral students.

Although the news industry gives low priority to the academic training and education of future newsmakers, most academic programs expect their students to be prepared for potential journalism employment. Accordingly, they require short internships in media organizations. Since the industry is not very helpful with such placements, academics find placements through personal connections. However, with many media houses opening their own schools, it is becoming increasingly difficult for university academics to find such internships. As a partial result, the gap between industry and academia continues to widen (Barve, 2007).

While it is difficult to find practitioners with doctoral degrees to work full time at media schools, it is equally difficult to find academic institutions with faculty possessing media experience (Belavadi, 2002; Pereira, 2003; Rangnathan, 2006). Although most communication

schools recruit retired professionals, such individuals often have difficulty teaching newer practices (Pereira, 2003).

Regardless of educators' backgrounds, most journalism schools
depend, in part, on practicing journalists visiting classrooms. But the
continuity and sustainability of such efforts depends on interpersonal
networks, not institutional arrangements. To partially solve this problem, many practicing journalists have become full-time journalism
educators. They have also helped solve the problem of limited Indian
journalism books by publishing new ones.

Although there are many journalism associations in India, there
are not many Indian journalism/media educator associations. The first
Indian Association of Education in Journalism was formed in 1956 in
Calcutta at Punjab University (CMS-UKIERI, 2015). Today most associations for journalism educators exist mainly via email, Facebook, and
WhatsApp groups. While there have been multiple efforts to create a
truly national association of media educators, no such organization exists.

Journalism Education's Professional Impact

Since Indian journalism coverage is highly localized, traditional
universities offer journalism programs in vernacular languages to help
future journalists prepare for small and medium news organizations.
But while the Indian-language media have expanded in terms of reach
and circulation, this has not been the case for journalists working at vernacular newspapers. In addition, English-language newspapers often
do not hire mass communication graduates. As Aram (2005) explains,

> Vernacular media cannot afford to pay (rather do not pay)
> much. And most media that pay well are English, and only
> they prefer university specialization. But given the paucity
> of English knowledge among post-colonial students, the
> media go in for English literature graduates rather than
> mass communication graduates. (p. 85)

Finally, industry acceptance of journalism education is a faraway
dream (FICCI-KPMG, 2013). Benerjee (2009, p. 170), referencing Asia
at large, notes, "this situation [has] encouraged students to study overseas because they [have] found that the standard of teaching, research,

and scholarship in their own countries is too weak to give them sufficient credibility in their academic and professional pursuits." Accordingly, students studying overseas often promote the continuance of
Western dominance in journalism education and research in India
rather than researching local realities. As a result, journalism education
at home and abroad is not as influential as it could be.

Future Possibilities

Indian journalism education and the journalism profession are
continuing to gain attention and to grow. In 2010, the University of
Mumbai titled its national conference "Journalism in India: From Mission to Profession—1947 to 2010." Today, traditional print journalism
often shares platforms with broadcast and new media. Privatization
and globalization are adding many new private players to the education
scene, players not always willing to conform to state mandates. Public
university mandates are controlling fees so poorer students can afford
their education (Hassan, 1980; Yadav, 2003; Ranganathan, 2006). And
there is an increased interest in research and analysis about journalism/
media education itself (AMIC, 2002; Lal, 2002; Belavadi, 2002; Gupta,
2002; Yadav, 2003; Aram, 2005; Sanjay, 2006a; Desai, 2008; Maheshwari, 2009; Desai, 2012; CMS-UKIERI, 2015).

Journalists seem to be getting trained more in technology and skills
rather than in critical-thinking and content. Unlike their forefathers in
pre-independent India, today's news organizations often treat journalists as laborers rather than intellectuals contributing to national goals.
This has impacted the nature of the journalism profession. New journalists are being forced to make a decision to pursue money and power
or to serve society.

Journalism Education Issues, Challenges, and Innovations

Nomenclature and scope. Major challenges facing journalism education academics include figuring out whether journalism programs
can retain enough independence in communication departments,
whether they should be more vocational or academic, and/or whether
they should belong to the humanities or social sciences. Journalism programs today are located within a wide variety of departments, from

home science (home economics) to the humanities (Desai, 2008).

Curricular aspects. Another major challenge deals with specialization. While a one-year diploma program covers traditional journalism classes, the job environment demands specialization. At the same time, programs focused on specialties, such as electronic media or advertising, limit job opportunities and narrow understanding among students. In a diverse country like India, approaches to any program curricula, especially in journalism, is a challenge and concern. After all, journalism training has to not only build skills, but also sensitivity toward societal ills, such as poverty, malnutrition, and gender inequality.

Journalism education in India began as postgraduate programs. Public universities, like Pune and Nagpur, still offer one-year programs after bachelor's degrees (Barve, 2007). Many scholars have critically examined the content and design of such programs and their courses (Solomonraj, 2006; Ranganathan, 2006; Maheshwari, 2009; Murthy, 2011; CMS-UKIERI, 2015). They often conclude that such programs' curricular, pedagogic, and structural factors result in students who "neither become skilled journalists nor good researchers" (Belavadi, 2002).

A lack of updated technical facilities is another significant problem. Public universities find it difficult to keep up with technical advancements in the media industry due to limited funding and operational, bureaucratic issues. Even though the UGC distributes funds to universities to help upgrade their technical abilities, this funding is often inadequate and inconsistent. Private institutions may have the technical infrastructure but might not be interested in following UGC's guidelines to collect "reasonable" fees from prospective students.

Media houses now entering the media education sector often care more about business concerns than the quality of future journalists. As a result, private journalism education either commodifies social issues or pays no attention to them. Either way, journalism education impacts the quality of future journalists.

Representation. While private institutes charge higher fees and have better resources, the quest for increased profits often reduces investments in training resources. Furthermore, the high price tag of such programs leads to more affluent students being trained as journalists and less diversity in the newsroom (Akhileshwari, 2004; Vij, 2004; Balasubramanya, 2006; Ranganathan, 2006; Sanjay, 2006a; Rajpurohit, 2014). The representation of different castes, classes, and genders among journalists is a critical challenge for newsrooms. The Centre for Social and Development Studies survey of 37 Delhi-based media organizations found: "Hindu Jamia Milia Islamia upper-caste men hold nearly 71 percent of top jobs in the national media. Women, non-upper castes, and Muslims are grossly under-represented" (Sanjay, 2006c, p.29).

Innovations. Innovations include newer journalistic practices and cutting-edge, specialized training programs. The Asian College of Journalism and Jamia programs are treated with respect for their industry-linked pedagogical innovation. Jamia offers programs such as a master's of arts in media governance. Mumbai University and the Ali Yavar Jung National Institute for the Hearing Handicapped offer a media and disability communication program. Punjab University offers a diploma in Agricultural Journalism and Mass Communication, and institutions like Journalism Mentor offer short-term courses in citizen journalism.

In addition, Maharashtra Patrakar Sangh, Yashwantrao Chavan Maharashtra Open University, and the University of Pune offer programs in collaboration with journalism associations, attempting to bridge academia and industry. Several past and present journalists are practicing innovation, such as former journalist Shubhranshu Choudhary, who created CGNet Swara, a unique mobile phone and online news service in the tribal state of Chattisgarh. It provides news in four languages, including Gondi, the local tribal dialect (CGNet, 2015). And renowned rural journalist Palgummi Sainath has started documenting the "everyday lives of everyday people" (People's Archive of Rural India, 2015). The community radio movement in India has also shown innovative local news practices. The critical challenge is to institutionalize and sustain such innovations, which demand human, technical, and infrastructure investments.

Conclusion: Educating Tomorrow's Journalists—The Big Picture

Many media houses over the last few years have started journalism training institutes, and many more public universities have expanded their programs. Still, a great divide exists between academics and journalism professionals. India's many languages further complicate this divide. In addition, privatization of education in general, and elitist journalism education in particular, hamper attempts for social equality. Market pressures accentuate the need for speed over standards. With multiple players, languages, and contexts, Indian journalism and journalism education operate within a maze of processes and a mosaic of practices.

As social inequality deepens in India, journalism ethical codes demand that journalists more accurately portray social realities. Media education will need to respond to such issues with journalistic competence and sensitivity, appropriate technology, and knowledge from a wide array of academic fields, including sociology, politics, economics, gender studies, and globalization. Journalism educators, as well as future journalists, will need to continue pushing themselves to be as locally relevant and globally aware as possible in order for journalism to live up to its greatest potential.

References

ABP Pvt. Ltd. & Anr. V. Union of India & Ors., No. 246. 2011.

Agrawal, B. C. (2005). Reporting news or creating news: The every day dilemma. *Journal of Communication Studies*, 54-59.

Agrawal, B. C. (2006, September) *Citizen's media movement and education in India: A country report*. Paper presented at the International Confernence on the media and democracy in the knowledge society, Seoul.

Akhileshwari, R. (2004). Language media versus English Media. *Vidura, 41*(3), 33-36.

AMIC. (2002). *Communication education and media needs in India: A study*. Singapore: Asian Media Information and Communication Centre of India.

Aram, A. I. (2005). Where go communication studies and media education? *Journal of Communication Studies, 4*(4), 83-102.

Balasubramanya, A. S. (2006). Journalists in India—A profile findings of a national survey. *Vidura, 43*(3), 45-49.

Barve, U. (2007, July). *Cross cultural journalism teaching: Case of an Indian university*. Paper presented at the 16th AMIC conference and First World Journalism Education Congress, Singapore.

Belavadi, V. (2002, July 16). *What ails media education in India?—A teacher's perspective*. Retrieved from http://www.thehoot.org

Benerjee, I. (2009). Asian media studies: The struggle for international legitimacy. In D. Thussu (Ed.), *Internationalizing media studies* (pp. 165-174). London: Routledge.

CGNet. (2015). Gondi Reports. Retrieved from cgnetswara.org

Choudhary, V. (2014, February 7). *SC upholds Majithia wage board recommen-dations*. Retrieved from http://www.livemint.com/Consumer/PMBDN-jXi6e2ovpvss2SQoN/SC-upholds-validity-of-Majithia-wage-board.html

CMS-UKIERI. (2015, August 7). Vision for media and communication educa-tion in India. *Vision for media and communication education in India*. New Delhi: CMS Academy.

Cottle, S., & Rai, M. (2008). Television news in India. Mediating democracy and difference. *International Communication Gazette*, 70-76.

Chandavarkar, R., & Srivastava, S. (2011, June 13).Oil mafia killed J. Dey, Suspects Cops. *India Times*. Retrieved from http://articles.economic-times.indiatimes.com/2011-06-13/news/29653399_1_oil-mafia-yashwant-sonawane-tankers

Desai, M. K. (2012, July). *Indian media/communication educators: Territories and traumas*. Paper presented at the 21st AMIC Annual Conference, Malaysia.

Desai, M. (2008). Reviewing communication/media education in India: Many players, diverse directions but lost focus...?! *Journal of Global Media, 1*(2), 118-131.

Eapen, K. E. (1982). Education for communication: Indian scenario. *Media Asia*, 99-104.

Eapen, K. E. (2000, July). *Problems of research in some third world countries*. Paper presented at the 22nd IAMCR conference, Singapore.

Eapen, K.E. (2007, July 15). Journalism Education. *The Hindu*. Retrieved from http://www.TheHindu.com/Todays-Paper/TP-Openpage/Journal-ism-Education/Article2275985.ece

Election Commission of India. (2010). Measures to check paid news during elections i.e. advertising in the garb of news in media. Retrieved from http://eci.nic.in/eci_main/recent//PAIDNEWS.pdf

FICCI-KPMG. (2011). *Hitting the high notes, FICCI-KPMG Indian media and entertainment industry report*. Mumbai: KPMG India.

FICCI-KPMG. (2013). *Power of a billion. Realising the Indian dream FIC-CI-KPMG Indian media and entertainment industry report*. Mumbai: KPMG India.

FICCI-KPMG. (2015). *#Shootingforthe stars Indian Media and Entertainment Report 2015*. Mumbai: FICCI-KPMG. Retrieved from www.kpmg.com/ in Government of India (2014). Press in India 2013-14. 58th Annual Report of The Registrar of Newspapers of India. Retrieved from http://rni.nic.in/pin1314.pdf

Gupta, G. (2009). *Perceptions andopinions of television news personnel about role of news media*. Department of Extension Education, SNDT Women's University, Mumbai. Unpublished Master Dissertation.

Gupta, V. (2002, September 16). *Take journalism graduates more seriously.*

Retrieved from http://thehoot.org

Hassan, M. S. (1980). Two hundred years of Indian Press: Case of lopsided growth. *Media Asia*, 218-228.

Indian Journalists Union. (2011). Retrieved from http://www.indianjournalistsunion.org/press/18.pdf

Internetlivestats. (2016). Internet users by country (2016). Retrieved from http://www.internetlivestats.com/internet-users-by-country/

Jagannathan, N. S. (2005). Changed character of Indian media. *Vidura, 42*(1), 7-10.

Jeffery, R. (2000). *India's newspaper revolution: Capitalism, politics and the Indian language press.* New Delhi: Oxford University Press.

Jyothi, K. (2003, January 26). *Is there an online journalism in India?* Retrieved from thehoot.org

Lal, M. (2002, July 8). *How useful are journalism courses?* Retrieved from http://thehoot.org

Kamath, M. V. (1997). *Professional journalism.* New Delhi: Vikas Publishing.

Maheshwari, P. (2009, July 27). *Mixed media: What ails journalism education in India.* Retrieved from http://www.exchange4media.com

Menon, E. P. (1930). *Journalism as a profession.* Tellicherry: The Vidya Vilasam Press. Retrieved from https://archive.org/details/journalismasapro035287mbp

Ministry of Labor & Employment. (n.d.). Wage board for working journalists. Retrieved from http://labour.gov.in/content/division/majithia-wageboard.php

Murthy, C. S. (2011). Dilemma of course content and curriculum in Indian journalism education: Theory, practice and research. *Asia Pacific Media Educator* (21), 24-42.

People's Archive of Rural India. (2015). Retrieved from https://ruralindiaonline.org

Pereira, M. (2003, August). *The changing face of professional media education- A note.* Paper presented at the AMIC Symbiosis Seminar, Pune.

Press Council of India. (2010). Report on paid news. Retrieved from presscouncil.nic.in/OldWebsite/CouncilReport.pdf

Radhakrishnan, R. K. (2010). Media in the era of paid news: A perspective. *Vidura, 2*(2), 6-9.

Rahman, M. (2012, December 21). Blowing up in Bombay. *India Today.* Retrieved from http://indiatoday.intoday.in/story/bombay-police-go-berserk-with-city-journalists/1/308216.html

Rajpurohit, S. (2014, March 27). *Dalit students and journalists—from classroom to newsroom.* Retrieved from kafila.org: http://kafila.org/2014/03/27/dalit-students-and-journalists-from-classroom-to-newsroom-shivnarayan-rajpurohit/

Raghavan, G. N. (1994). *The press in India: A new history*. Delhi: Gyan Books.

Rangnathan, M. (2006). A statutory body for media education. *Vidura, 43*(4), 31-32.

Rao, S. (2009). Glocalization of Indian journalism. *Journalism Studies, 10*(4), 474-488.

Rau, M. (1974). *The press*. New Delhi: National Book Trust.

Ravindran, R. K. (1997). *Press in the Indian constitution*. New Delhi: Indian Publishersand Distributors.

Ravindranath, P. K. (2005). *Indian regional journalism*. New Delhi: Authorspress.

Sanjay, B. P. (2006a). News media teaching in India. In U. Sahay (Ed.), *Making news* (pp. 28-37). New Delhi: Oxford University Press.

Sanjay, B. P. (2006b). The dynamics of news content in mass media. In U. Sahay (Ed.), *Making news* (pp. 12-27). New Delhi: Oxford University Press.

Sanjay, B. P. (2006c) Limited diversity in media newsrooms, *Vidura, 43*(4), 27-30.

Secretariat, L. S. (May 2013). Standing Committee Report on Information Technology- Issues realted to paid news. New Delhi: Ministry of Information and Broadcasting.

Sharma, K. (2010, November 30). *Journalism after Radiagate—Second Take*. Retrieved from http://www.thehoot.org

Shrivastava, K. M. (2000, July). Indian media: Complex and diverse. Paper presented at the International Association of Media and Communication Research conference, Singapore.

Solomonraj, S. (2006, February 10-12). Professional education in mass media at the undergraduate level: A Mumbai University experience. Mumbai: Tata Institute of Social Sciences.

Sultana, N. (2008, March 8). *Where is the news?* Retrieved from http://indian-television.com/special/y2k8

Tambat, S. V. (2012). *Review of the press in India (2008-2012)*. New Delhi: The Press Council of India.

Tere, N. S. (2012). Commentry - Increasing journalism education in India: Concern for quality. *Asia Pacific Media Educator, 22*(1), 127-133.

Thakur, K. (2009, November 13). *Marathi newspapers on Internet*. Retrieved from http://mediascenceindia.blogspot.com

The Indian Medialogue. (2015). Home. Retrieved from http://indianmedia-logue.com

Thussu, D. K. (2005). Adapting to globalization: The changing contours of journalism in India. In H. Burgh (Ed.), *Making journalists: Diverse models, global issues* (pp. 127-141). New York, NY: Routledge.

Thussu, D. K. (2007). The 'Murdochization' of news? The case of STAR TV in India. *Media, Culture and Society, 29*(4), 593-611.

TRAI. (2008). *Consultation Paper on cross-media ownership.* New Delhi: Tele-communication Regulatory Authority of India.

UGC. (2001). *Model curriculum in journalism and mass communication.* New Delhi: University Grants Commission.

UNESCO. (2007). *Model curricula for journalism education for developing countries and emerging democracies.* Paris: UNESCO.

United Nations Educational, Scientific and Cultural Organization. (1961). Seminar on journalism training methods in South and East Asia. Retrieved from http://unesdoc.unesco.org/images/0014/001473/147390eb.pdf

Vij, S. (2004, June 24). *Caste in the newsroom?* Retrieved from http://thehoot.org/

Vilanilam, J. V. (2005). *Mass Communication in India- A sociological perspective.* New Delhi: Sage.

World Association of Newspapers. (2011). Retrieved from http://www.wan-ifra.org

Yadav, J. S. (2003). At the cross road. *Vidura, 40*(4), 13-15.

Endnotes

1   "Emergency" took place from 1975 to 1977 when Prime Minister Indira Gandhi declared a suspension of fundamental rights, imposed censorship on the press, and silenced prominent political leaders. Hundreds of journalists were arrested. Ramachandra Guha documented Emergency in his book *India after Gandhi: The history of the world's largest democracy,* HarperCollins, 2007. Another book discussing this period is *The Emergency: A Personal History* by Coomi Kapoor, Penguin Viking, 2015.

2   In 2010, *Open* magazine brought the Nira Radia tape controversies to light, exposing relationships among politicians, corporate lobbyists, and senior journalists. India's Income Tax Department taped conversations among a corporate lobbyist, named Nira Radia, and three reputed journalists, who refuted misconduct allegations.

Table 5.1

Journalism/Journalism Education Associations in India

Organization	Degree	Website
National Union of Journalists (India)	Founded in 1972, it claims presence in five zones across India.	http://www.nujindia.com
Indian Federation of Working Journalists (IFWJ)	Founded in New Delhi on Oct. 28, 1950, it is independent India's first trade union of media persons. It has over 30,000 primary and associate members working for electronic media, news agencies, and 1,260 journals in 17 languages in 35 states and Union Territories.	http://ifwj.in
The Indian Journalists Union (IJU)	In October, 1950, leading and militant journalists met in New Delhi to set up this first all-India organization of working journalists. Members include 23,000 journalists and affiliate unions across India.	http://www.ijuindia.org http://www.indianjour nalistsunion.org
The Journalist Association of India (JAI)	A platform for any Indian who aspires to make his presence known in the field of Journalism/ Mass Communication through academic programs.	http://www.journalistsin dia.com
All India Freelance Journalists Association (AFJA)	Created in 2009, its formation is still under way.	http://www.common wealthjournalists.com
All-India Newspaper Editors' Conference	Started in 1940, it is an organization of editors of Indian newspapers and periodicals.	50-51 Theatre Communication Buildings, Connaught Place, New Delhi
Commonwealth Journalists Association (CJA)	Founded in 1978 by a group of journalists after a conference of Commonwealth nongovernmental organizations at Dalhousie University, Nova Scotia, Canada.	http://commonwealth journalists.org
The Andhra Pradesh Union of Working Journalists (APUWJ)	With a membership of about 8,000 working journalists, it is the biggest union of working journalists in the country.	http://www.apuwj.org
The Network of Women in Media, India (NWMI)	Formed in January of 2002 from the National Workshop on Women in Journalism, it brings together more than 100 female journalists from 16 centers across the country.	http://www.nwmindia. org
Association of Communication Teachers of Tamil Nadu and Pondicherry	A professional forum of communication teachers in Tamil Nadu and Pondicherry. Its objective is to uphold high professional standards in journalism and communication education throughout the state.	Department of Journalism and Communication University of Madras Chepauk Campus Chennai 600005

Table 5.2

Well-known Journalism Education Programs in India

Organization	Degrees	Websites
Jamia Millia Islamia Central University, Anwar Jamal Kidwai Mass Communication Research Center	Doctoral and master's degrees, including a master's in convergent journalism, and diploma programs. Started a diploma in broadcast technology in 2011.	http://www.ajkmcrc.org http://jmi.ac.in
Asian College of Journalism	Post-graduate diploma in journalism, master's in journalism from Cardiff University.	http://www.asianmedia.org
Indian Institute of Mass Communication (with centers across India)	Post-graduate diplomas in journalism (Radio, TV) in Hindi, English, and Oriya, and in advertising and public relations.	http://www.iimc.nic.in
Xavier Institute of Communications	Diploma programs in Integrated Communication Program, C4D, journalism and mass communication, public relations and corporate communication, advertising and marketing communication, Marathi Mass Communication.	http://www.xaviercomm.org
Yashwantrao Chavan Maharashtra Open University	Diploma in agro journalism, distance learning.	http://ycmou.digitaluniversity.ac
Indian Institute of Journalism & New Media Opp. BGS International Residential School	PG Diploma and Diploma in print journalism, broadcast journalism, and Multimedia.	http://iijnm.org
Press Academy of Andhra Pradesh	Mid-career training of journalists in English and Telugu	http://www.pressacademy.ap.gov.in/

6

Journalism Education in Israel: Between East and West, Tradition and Modernity, Practice and Theory

Yehiel Limor

n 2013, Israel's press marked the 150th anniversary of the publication of the country's first Hebrew newspaper, *Ha'Levanon*. Two of the three owner-editors of this slim monthly had no experience whatsoever in journalism, and this short-lived publication survived for less than a year. Only the third had some experience writing for the periodical press abroad.

An unsystematic hiring of journalists without formal training, academic or professional, has continued over succeeding generations (Caspi & Limor, 1999). And yet, the press has nurtured the growth of numerous political leaders—who left journalism and joined the political arena (among them Israel's third president, Zalman Shazar). The press has even given rise to recipients of the country's highest and most prestigious national award, the Israel Prize (awarded mainly to scientists). Although in the 1960s Tel Aviv University made a short, unsuccessful attempt to establish journalism studies in Israel, the country's first institutionalized academic journalism education program was not established until the early 1990s. Throughout journalism history the academic world and the media have always been, and continue to be, often at loggerheads—expressing mutual contempt, alienation, and mistrust. Yet during the last 20 years the first signs of change in journalistic training, both professional and academic, have become evident. In a slow and gradual process, employee recruitment has finally begun to include graduates of academic institutions.

Journalism in the Media Landscape

Peri (2012) claims that the Israeli media system might have converged toward the liberal model had war and the culture of national security not pushed it into a different direction. However, in retrospect, over the past more than 65 years, one can adopt this diagnosis only in a limited manner: applying it to periods of hostilities and emergency. In more peaceful times, the Israeli media is independent, free of any government pressure, and even aggressive with the government and the political elite. Such aggressiveness was recently referenced in articles published by leading journalists in both leading left-wing and right-wing newspapers. For example, while the elitist, left-wing daily *Ha'aretz* argued that "fear of the biting, brutal media hovers above the heads of the decision-makers" (Verter, 2015, p. 3), the right-wing *Makor Rishon* argued that "one of the bad traits that characterize politicians is fear of the media" (Segal, 2015, p. 3).

Since the establishment of the State of Israel in 1948, local journalists have enjoyed considerable freedom, which has expanded during the years to almost complete freedom. In its 2015 annual country report on Israel, Freedom House stated that "press freedom is generally respected [in Israel]." This depiction is relevant to the Israeli media within its 1967 borders but not to the Palestinian media in the occupied territories in the West Bank.

The birth of Israel as a democratic state ostensibly guarantees freedom of the press after many decades of tight official supervision. The Ottoman authorities, who ruled the country from the 16th century until the end of World War I, allowed only licensed newspapers, imposed meticulous censorship and prison sentences on editors convicted of publishing articles harmful to national interests, and closed down newspapers. Thereafter, the British Mandatory authorities (1918 to 1948) practiced stringent control and censorship. The British did not hesitate to suspend or shut down newspapers "to avoid improper and outrageous news" (Canaan, 1969, p. 31).

Although freedom of the press has been part of Israeli culture and has been guaranteed in Supreme Court decisions, it is still not anchored in legislation to this day. The British Mandate left Israel with several legal legacies capable of restricting the press, such as the 1933 Press Ordinance. This ordinance not only requires a license for publication of a newspaper, it even gives the Minister of the Interior the authority to close papers suspected of disrupting public order. In 1953 the Israeli High Court of Justice laid the initial foundations of support for freedom of the press by severely restricting the Minister of the Interior's authority to shut down newspapers (High Court of Justice 73/53). In succeeding years, Israel's Supreme Court reinforced de facto freedom of the press by upholding the right of journalists to not reveal their sources of information. Conversely, legislative proposals aimed at restricting the press failed without exerting any adverse effect on freedom of the press.

Since its establishment in 1963, the Israel Press Council has fulfilled an important role in protecting freedom of the press (see Table 6.1 for major journalism associations and journalism-related organizations). Time after time, the council, whose members include public representatives, publishers, editors, and journalists' unions, has succeeded in blocking legislative initiatives likely to diminish freedom of the press. In general, these measures were thwarted after the press council agreed to include new sections in its code of ethics guaranteeing self-restraint as substitutes for external supervision.

Today's Israeli press has been clearly influenced by traditions. During the 19th and early 20th centuries, the first Israeli journalists, arriving from Eastern and Western Europe, were affected by Western European press norms and the writing styles of Jewish periodicals published in Poland and Russia. Also, Israeli journalists sent to the United States as correspondents returned home with a clear preference for American reporting styles and procedures. The modern Israeli press is largely a result of such Israeli-American encounters and conflicts.

Today Israel offers its nearly eight million citizens a varied and highly professional media landscape including the following:

❑ three nationwide television channels, one public (Channel 1 and two commercial (Channel 2 and Channel 10);
❑ one multichannel cable network (Hot);
❑ one multichannel satellite television network (Yes);
❑ 16 commercial regional radio stations;
❑ 50 local educational radio stations;

❑   15 daily nationwide morning newspapers;

❑   some 350 local and regional newspapers; and

❑   hundreds of periodicals (weeklies, by-weeklies, monthlies, etc.).

Evening papers gradually disappeared from the Israeli media land-scape in the late 1970s, when the two nationwide afternoon/evening papers, *Ma'ariv* and *Yediot Aharonot*, began transforming into morning papers to increase circulation (Limor & Mann, 1997).

The Israeli press maintains high professional standards. Even Israeli tabloids tend to be of a much higher quality than their Western counterparts, displaying meticulous attention to wide-ranging content and sections such as literature and art, investigative reporting, eco-nomic affairs, and political commentary.

Regardless, Israeli public confidence in the media has been steadily declining during the past several years: from 51% in 2011 to 47% in 2013 and 29.7% in 2014 (Herman, Lebel, Be'eri, Cohen, & Heller, 2015).

The partisan, highly self-censored, ultra-Orthodox press exhibits perhaps the most blatant and outspoken rejection of conventional free press norms (Levi, 1989; Michelson, 1990). The ultra-Orthodox pirate radio stations, which flourished in the 1990s, follow similar practices (Limor & Naveh, 2006).

Professional Characteristics

Israeli journalism's professional characteristics can be analyzed on two levels: that of the press, a macro level, and of journalists, a micro level.

On the macro level, three major periods can be discerned. The first took place during the first two decades after the establishment of Israel, in which the media and press adopted thought and behavioral patterns compatible with the developmental media model. Many of the news-papers were political party organs whose operation was guided more by ideology than professional principles. The second period took place during the 1970s and 1980s, in which, as noted by Tsfati and Meyers (2011, p. 445), "Israeli journalism changed in various significant ways due to shifts and crises in Israeli society [that] contributed to the devel-opment of critical political reporting." During these years, most of the party newspapers folded. The third period, from the 1990s on, is marked by many changes, especially the tendency for media to turn into ratings-driven infotainment suppliers like much of the Western media.

On the micro level, various studies enable researchers to trace some of the professional characteristics of Israeli journalists and their sense of professional autonomy. These include the following:

❏ A conviction that "they have a lot of control over the work they do" (The Worlds of Journalism Study, 2011).

❏ Their feeling that "they are allowed to take part in decisions that affect their work and that the ownership, pressure from advertisers, or economic considerations only slightly influence the 'day-to-day job'" (The Worlds of Journalism Study, 2011).

❏ Over two thirds have an academic education, while only 6.5% study in a school of journalism (Tsfati & Meyers, 2011).

❏ About one third earn less than the average wage in Israel (Tsfati & Meyers, 2011).

❏ Some 87% said they agreed with the statement: "I feel that my superiors allow me to freely function" (Tsfati & Meyers, 2011).

The National Union of Journalists was, for decades, a powerful body. Its power as a trade union was derived from its status as the representative organization in negotiations over wage agreements, all of which are collective in the national media (Caspi & Limor, 1999). Changes in hiring patterns and a gradual shift from collective work agreements to individual contracts weakened the union's status, and it gradually turned into members' clubs primarily concerned with cultural and social activities.

One of the significant characteristics of Israeli journalism is the existence of a code of ethics that was drawn up by the Israel Press Council, "perceived as the supreme body of the media establishment in Israel" (Caspi & Limor, 1999, p. 19). The national journalist unions are members of the Israel Press Council, thus supporting and promoting its code of ethics. The council maintains ethics tribunals, which "try" media outlets and journalists accused of deviating from accepted professional ethics. Each tribunal is comprised of three representatives: a journalist, publisher, and member of the public, who serves as chairman. The tribunals have no actual authority and do not carry out punitive measures. They cannot impose fines or expel anyone from the profession, and their power stems only from their moral authority. The tribunals' decisions are published in the media, and all newspapers and journalists are wary of such publicity, which could harm their credibility and be detrimental to their professional standing.

Journalism Education, Professional Training, and Research

Even though there were many newspapers printed for the Jewish community in Palestine prior to the establishment of Israel, there were no frameworks for the professional or academic training of journalists and other media specialists. In the following years, appropriate attention was not paid to the orderly training of professional journalists. And journalism did not receive much academic attention until the establishment in 1970 of the first degree in communication and media studies, a master's degree at the Hebrew University in Jerusalem, and the establishment in the early 1990s of bachelor's degrees in communication at many universities and colleges (see Table 6.2 for top academic journalism programs and non-academic training programs). Numerous articles in academic journals also brought attention to journalism education.

Teaching and Training Future Newsmakers

In the early 1960s, soon after its founding, Tel Aviv University attempted to establish a department of journalism. The department was soon shut down for several reasons. First, the university had difficulty developing a proper academic and professional curriculum, as well as hiring lecturers with both academic standing and professional knowledge in the field. (Two U.S. journalism professors returned to America after realizing what was promised, especially financial resources and proper facilities, would not materialize.) Second, personal rivalries within the university were detrimental to the developing department. And third, the university and the Tel Aviv journalists' union disagreed over the department's approach. For example, union representatives were opposed to the department's American-style curriculum, preferring one based on local realities. And the university leadership, unlike the unions, wanted journalism studies to be a supplement to regular academic courses instead of a degree program (Nevo-Blobstein & Limor, 2016).

In late 1964, the Hebrew University of Jerusalem, the oldest and largest Israeli university at the time, appointed a special committee to discuss the establishment of an instructional and research body specializing in communication and journalism. Based on its recommendations, The Communication Institute was set up, headed by sociologist and communication researcher Elihu Katz. Professor Katz aspired to have the new institute address three major aspects of the communication field: (a) academic research and theory, (b) practical research relevant to journalists and cultural policymakers, and (c) professional training of journalists (Adoni & First, 2006). The plans included cooperation with the public Israel Broadcasting Authority, which had two arms—television, Channel One (the only TV channel broadcasting during those years); and radio, the Kol Israel, the largest nationwide radio station. (Broadcast media were mostly based in Jerusalem, whereas most newspapers were, and are, located in Tel Aviv.)

Ironically, The Communication Institute at Hebrew University, first to award media studies certificates and later graduate degrees, concentrated primarily on theory. It offered no substantive professional training beyond a few rather short and eclectic workshops in journalism. From the early 1990s, departments of communication and media studies were opened, one after the other, in Israeli universities and colleges. However, none of these academic institutions created a department of journalism or departments of radio or television.

Abandonment of professional study programs reflects a dispute that had been raging for some time in the academic world. It focused on whether communication studies should be theoretical and research-oriented or aim at training young cadres for the professional work force. This clash of opinions has continued for more than two decades and has yet to be decided. One result is that even today there are no departments of journalism (or radio and television) in any university or college in Israel. The vacuum left by all universities and colleges has been filled by private enterprises, mostly run by journalists, who provide semi-professional courses to train journalists and other media personnel.

In the early 1990s, communication studies in Israel underwent a dramatic change. Within a few years, undergraduate studies in communication were available at most universities in Israel and at many colleges. However, these programs were theoretical without any intention of providing adequate professional training. Some colleges offered compulsory basic courses in journalism or a limited number of elective workshops. But since most students in communication departments were interested in advertising and public relations, journalism courses remained only a marginal part of the curriculum. While many journalism teachers are retired journalists, some are active journalists who consider teaching "moonlighting" (Lahav, 2008). At the same time, Israel opened its first and only private school of journalism, Koteret. Each year it trained dozens of young professionals, many of whom were hired by the local media.

But in the 1990s, most media personnel found their way to the profession by chance. Journalism training itself took place primarily on the job: Journalists learned the secrets of their profession as they worked, without any systematic prior training.

The early 2000s displayed the first palpable signs of change. Some colleges intensified journalism studies in their communication departments and, within a few years, graduates were being offered press jobs. Tel Aviv University, which had previously offered only theoretical studies in communication, adopted Koteret. However, Israel's only professional school of journalism did not become an integral part of academic studies.

As journalism studies were, and are, still considered relatively insignificant at universities and most colleges, students can only choose from a handful of practical courses covering topics such as newsgathering, reporting, and editing. Only two institutions, Sapir Academic College and Ariel University, offer a "journalism track" that provides professional training based on six-to-eight semester workshops as part of the academic curriculum. The two programs, developed by the same dean and thus closely resembling each other, consist of a series of courses, including the following: field reporting, investigative reporting, news editing, magazine editing and writing, Internet journalism, practical local newspaper work, and writing and editing for magazines.

Many Israeli journalists still begin their careers during their compulsory military service working for the Israel Defense Forces (IDF) media: on the radio station Galei Zahal, the weekly magazine *Bamahane,* and other military publications. The military media serve as the major seedbed from which Israeli media professionals emerge. Their compulsory military service—three years for men and two for women—grants young soldiers valuable professional experience. Military media "graduates" are snatched up by their civilian counterparts. After all, these young recruits are trained, hungry for success, and less expensive. Such recruitment has increased over the years for two main reasons. First, as former military media recruits rise in the ranks of the civilian media, they prefer to hire people with the same type of professional background and experience. Second, as the civilian media's financial woes increase, military media recruits, hungry to enter the "real media world" and willing to work for lower salaries, are needed more than ever.

Journalism Research

During the last two decades, Professor Katz, Israel's founding father of communication studies, has promoted intensive research activities in the field. Israeli scholars participate in almost every major international media, communication, and journalism conference. And every year they publish many books and articles, several in leading academic journals. An increasing number of Israeli professors are interested in journalism research. Such scholars have focused on a wide variety of research topics, including the following:

- ❑ journalism's future (Katz, 1992; Nossek, 2009),
- ❑ coverage of minorities (Avraham, 2002),
- ❑ journalists' sources (Reich, 2009),
- ❑ journalists' perspectives (Tsfati, Meyers, & Peri, 2006),
- ❑ the Israeli media (Caspi & Limor, 1999; Limor, 2003; Soffer, 2015),
- ❑ journalists' rhetoric (Roeh, 1982),
- ❑ literary supplements in newspapers (Neiger & Roeh, 2003),
- ❑ online journalism (Caspi, 2011),
- ❑ journalism and war (Wolfsfeld, 2001),
- ❑ military censorship (Nossek & Limor, 2011),

❏ relations between the media and the army (Limor & Nossek, 2006; Limor & Leshem, 2015),

❏ journalism education (Nevo-Blobstein & Limor, 2016),

❏ journalism history (Elyada, 2015; Soffer, 2004),

❏ media and terror (Weimann, 2006),

❏ journalism ethics (Limor, 2001; Limor & Gabel, 2002; Berkowitz, Limor, & Singer, 2004), and

❏ Israeli journalists (Meyers & Cohen, 2009).

Today there are two scholarly Hebrew journals devoted to mass communication, media, and journalism. The first, *Kesher*, founded in 1987 by Tel Aviv University's journalism studies program (which closed down a few years later), is still published by the university's Rosenfeld Journalism and Media Research Institute. This biannual journal is mainly devoted to the history of Jewish media in Israel and abroad. However, many of its articles deal with the media in general.

The second journal, *Misgarot Media,* was launched in 2007 by the Israeli Communication Association (ISCA), the professional association for Israeli researchers and teachers in communication and media studies. This biannual journal was founded in collaboration with the Second Authority for Television and Radio, which sponsored the publication. In 2014 the Second Authority, the regulatory body of commercial TV and radio stations in Israel, decided to stop subsidizing the publication. As a result, in 2015 it began appearing online only.

Two previous attempts to launch academic journals in Hebrew were short-lived. The first, *Dvarim Ahadim*, published by the Van-Leer Institute in Jerusalem, survived for only about a year. The second, *Patuah*, published by Bar-Ilan University, only produced five issues. In both cases the journals died mainly due to diminishing financial resources. Until 1999 the Tel Aviv Journalists Association had published—for over 50 years—its *Sefer Hashanah shel Ha'itonaim*. Journalists wrote most of the articles, which dealt with professional subjects. However, at times the volumes included semi-academic articles, ones written by journalists dealing with core professional issues such as journalism ethics, professional training, and relationships between journalists and their sources. In the absence of academic journals in the field, this was the only publication in which one could read articles and research dealing with journalism and journalists.

The major reason for the small number of academic media journals in Hebrew lies in the academic promotion process in Israel. Promotion depends on publication in international refereed journals, with clear priority given to major journals. As a result, Israeli academics send their studies to top journals, especially those published in English. They often publish in such leading journals, including the *Journal of Communication*, *Journalism & Mass Communication Quarterly*, *Political Communication*, *Journalism*, *Journalism Studies*, and *Media, Culture & Society*. They also often publish in English-language journals devoted to Israel, such as *Israel Studies* and *Israel Affairs*. Many articles dealing with the media are also published in Hebrew academic sociological and historical journals, such as *Megamot*, *Soziologiah Yisraelit*, and *Cathedra*, a journal devoted to the history of Israel.

Professional Connections in Journalism Education

As previously noted, there are no established frameworks for training journalists in Israel, neither on the academic nor professional level (except the small Koteret school mentioned above). This vacuum is filled irregularly, and often randomly, by three organizations that sometimes organize refresher courses for journalists:

❏ The National Union of Israeli Journalists, the oldest journalists' union in Israel. Its most prominent activity is its annually held conference in the resort city of Eilat, on the shores of the Red Sea. The conference provides formal and informal meetings for journalists and members of the media and for discussion of diverse issues related to the profession.

❏ The Organization of Israeli Journalists. Among its declared objectives, on its website, is "to organize professional events, refresher courses, and study tours whose objective is to improve journalistic capabilities and discuss important issues." Among the activities at these convocations include examining the influence of digital media on the future of journalism and relations between journalists and sources. And courses are available for radio and TV broadcasters and foreign language enthusiasts. Other activities include organizing study tours to the Israel State Archives.

❏   The Israel Press Council. Its refresher courses for journalists are especially devoted to ethical issues. It also initiates or participates in conferences dealing with diverse topics touching on freedom of the press and journalism as a profession.

Journalism Education's Professional Impact

Unfortunately, the impact of journalism education in Israel during the 21st century's second decade is minimal, practically nonexistent. There are three major reasons for this state of affairs. First, the mutual alienation, even hostility, between the academic establishment and professional journalists has contributed to a situation in which academic media studies are held in low esteem. Although this situation has improved over the years, it still mostly holds true today. Accordingly, most media and press employees lack formal academic education in their fields.

Second, the lack of structured academic frameworks recognized by both academic and professional communities result in academic media studies graduates possessing little practical experience. This is why experienced military media graduates are often preferred in the job market. Furthermore, since most graduates of academic media and communication studies programs have little or no practical professional experience, they have no real advantage over graduates from different programs. For example, it is preferable to hire a graduate with a bachelor's degree in economics and train him as an economic correspondent than to hire a graduate of journalism studies with no knowledge of economics.

And third, the economic crisis that plagues journalism in Israel, as elsewhere, is a good reason to prefer young, less expensive personnel. Those with no academic education can be hired for less.

Future Possibilities

The future of professional media, journalism studies, and academic training in Israel appears quite gloomy. Economic crises faced by traditional media, particularly print newspapers, and many digital media outlets indicate a problematic trend: media closures, the firing of many journalists, and the reduction of salaries for those remaining.

Low salaries and a cloudy future could result in a continued decline in the number of students wanting to work in the media and to study it. After all, why learn a profession that has little demand or an unclear future?

Journalism Education Issues, Challenges, and Innovations

The new age of journalism places several challenges before the media and academia.

First, how do we best educate future journalists when those in the Israeli academy are still stuck in silos? And who is to lead and guide today's multifaceted, academic-based journalism education: print journalists and editors, their electronic media counterparts, and/or young academic digital natives?

Second, how do we persuade student journalists to uphold journalistic codes of ethics? For example, traditionally the "deadline" generally left journalists with enough time to gather their facts, to check and countercheck them, and to prepare their final reports. This timely task, the very core of journalistic practice, is the first test of journalism ethics. However, in the modern age of the Internet and social networks, there is no longer "a deadline." Most information is published immediately. How does one maintain a code of ethics, the drive to get the story right, in an age of cruel competition to be first? And how does one educate young journalists to foster ethical practices at the price of losing exclusiveness to one's competitors?

Third, how can we teach journalists to remain loyal to their profession? Journalism's unsure future might continue leading young people to use it as a potential jumping-off point for careers in public relations and advertising. True, the "revolving door" is not a new phenomenon and has been around for a long time. However, it is becoming more widespread in Israel. How can one focus on professional, fair, ethical journalism while distracted by his next job search at the same time?

Finally, how can educators instill in the future generation of journalists the sense that journalism is a mission, one that must be safeguarded and fostered? In the new age, in which economic considerations and cynicism go hand-in-hand, journalists and academics face a double educational challenge: to educate the public "how to consume" media and to raise a cadre of journalists who will see their profession as a vocation and a public mission.

These challenges are even more pronounced because there is no real dialogue between the professional and academic communities. Without dialogue, cooperation, and mutual understanding, it is doubtful the academy will be able to "produce" and train the skilled workers necessary for the media industry, journalism in particular.

Conclusion: Educating Tomorrow's Journalist—The Big Picture

For decades, most—if not all—Israeli journalists received no formal or informal education in journalism or media studies. This picture started to gradually change in the 1990s due to the opening of departments of communication and media studies in many universities and colleges.

But today there is a sharp decline in the number of students registering for communication and media studies programs in Israeli universities and colleges. This situation reflects the sad reality of the media industry in Israel, similar to that in many other countries: newspaper shutdowns, great reductions in staff, lower wages, and narrower employment opportunities (preference given to young, less expensive employees).

Although it is difficult to predict where journalism as a profession is headed in Israel, academia, which for decades has been unable to meet the challenges of educating and training journalists, will likely find it even more difficult to do so in the foreseeable future.

References

Adoni, H., & First, A. (2006). *Communications research and instruction: Built-in dilemmas and changing solutions*. Jerusalem: Magnes Press.

Avraham, E. (2002). Social-political environment, journalism practice and coverage of minorities: The case of the marginal cities in Israel. *Media, Culture & Society, 24*(1), 69-86.

Berkowitz, D., Limor, Y., & Singer, J. (2004). A cross-cultural look at serving the public interest: American and Israeli journalists consider ethical scenarios. *Journalism, 5*(2), 159-181.

Canaan, H. (1969). *The war of the press: The struggle of the Hebrew press against the British regime*. Jerusalem: The Zionist Library.

Caspi, D. (2011). A revised look at online journalism in Israel: Entrenching the old hegemony. *Israel Affairs, 17*(3), 341-363.

Caspi, D., & Limor, Y. (1999). *The in/outsiders: The mass media in Israel*. Cresskill, N.J.: Hampton Press.

Elyada, O. (2015). *Yellow world: The birth of Hebrew popular press in Palestine from Hazevi to Haor 1994-1914*. Tel Aviv: Tel Aviv University.

Freedom House (2015). Freedom of the Press: Israel. Retrieved from https://freedomhouse.org/report/freedom-press/2015/israel#.VZBlrxuqpBc

Herman, T., Lebel, Y., Be'eri, G., Cohen, H., & Heller, E. (2015). *Israeli Democracy Index 2014*. Retrieved from http://bit.ly/1AlDnEH

Katz, E. (1992). The end of journalism? Notes on watching the war. *Journal of Communication, 42*(3), 5-13.

Lahav, H. (2008). If you can't earn enough—Teach. *Journalism Practice, 2*(3), 463-475.

Levi, A. (1989). *The Ultra-Orthodox*. Jerusalem: Keter.

Limor, Y. (2001). The evolution of a conscience: The emergence and development of journalistic ethics in Israel. *Kesher 30*, 66-76.

Limor, Y. (2003). The media in Israel. In E. Yaar & Z. Shavit. (Eds.), *Trends in Israeli society* (pp. 1017-1103). Tel Aviv: Open University of Israel.

Limor, Y., & Mann, R. (1997). *Journalism: Reporting, writing and editing*. Tel Aviv: Open University of Israel.

Limor, Y., & Naveh, H. (2006). *Pirate radio in Israel*. Haifa: Pardess.

Limor, Y., & Leshem, B. (2015). The relations between the Army and the media in Israel. *Kesher, 47*, 76-87.

Limor, Y., & Nossek, H. (2006). The Army and the media in the 21st century: Towards a new model of relationships. *Israel Affairs, 12*(3), 484-510.

Limor, Y., & Gabel, I. (2002). Five versions of one code of ethics: The case of the Israel Broadcasting Authority. *Journal of Mass Media Ethics, 17*(2), 136-154.

Meyers, O., & Cohen, J. (2009). A self-portrait of Israeli journalists: Characteristics, values and attitudes. *Media Frames, 4*, 107-134.

Michelson, M. (1990). The Ultra-Orthodox press in Israel. *Kesher, 8*, 12-21.

Neiger, M., & Roeh, I. (2003). The secular Holy Scriptures: The role of the Holy Day literary supplement in the Israeli press and culture. *Journalism, 4*(4), 477–489.

Nevo-Blobstein, A., & Limor, Y. (2016). The rise and fall of journalism studies in Israeli academia. *Kesher, 48* (forthcoming).

Nossek, H. (2009). On the future of journalism as a professional practice and the case of journalism in Israel. *Journalism, 10*(3), 358-361.

Nossek, H., & Limor, Y. (2011). The Israeli paradox: Military censorship as guardian of freedom of the press. In S. Maret. (Ed.), *Government secrecy* (pp. 103-130). Bingley: Emerald.

Peri, Y. (2012). The impact of national security on the development of media systems: The case of Israel. In D. Hallin & P. Mancini. (Eds.), *Comparing media systems beyond the Western world* (pp. 11-25). New York, NY: Cambridge University Press.

Reich, Z. (2009). *Sourcing the news: Key issues in journalism—An innovative study of the Israeli press*. Cresskill, N.J.: Hampton Press.

Roeh, I. (1982). The rhetoric of news in the Israel radio: Some implications of language and style for newstelling. Bochum: Brockmeyer.

Segal, H. (2015, July 3). *Makor Rishon, Musaf Yoman* [They are the state], 3.

Soffer, O. (2004). Paper territory—Early Hebrew journalism and its political roles. *Journalism History, 30*, 31-39.

Soffer, O. (2015). *Mass communication in Israel*. New York, NY: Berghahn.

The Worlds of Journalism Study (2011). Retrieved from www.worlds of journalism.org.

Tsfati, Y., & Meyers, O. (2011). Journalists in Israel. In: D. Weaver & L. Willnat. (Eds.), *The global journalist in the 21ˢᵗ century* (pp. 443-457). New York, NY: Routledge.

Tsfati, Y., Meyers, O., & Peri, Y. (2006). What is good journalism? Comparing Israeli public and journalists' perspectives. *Journalism, 7*(2), 152–173.

Verter, Y. (2015, July 3). Come on, step on the gas. *Ha'aretz*, 3.

Weimann, G. (2006). *Terror on the Internet: The new arena, the new challenges*. Washington, D.C.: United States Institute of Peace Press.

Wolfsfeld, G. (2001). The news media and the second intifada: Some initial lessons. *Harvard International Journal of Press, 6*(4), 113-118.

Table 6.1

Major Journalism Associations and Journalism-Related Organizations in Israel

Organization	Description	Contact
Israel Press Council (IPC)	Self-regulatory body of the media, established in 1963 to help preserve freedom of the press. Created the Code of Professional Ethics.	http://www.moaza.co.il
Israel's Media Watch (Ha'Agudah L'Zechut Ha'Tzibur Lada'at)	A right-wing media watch organization.	http://www.imw.org.il
Keshev (The Center for the Protection of Democracy in Israel)	A left-wing media watch organization.	http://www.keshev.org.il
The National Union of Israeli Journalists	The first national union of Israeli journalists.	Access via the Tel Aviv or Jerusalem Associations: http://www.jat.co.il; http://www.jaj.org.il
The Association of Israeli Journalists (Irgun Ha'Itonaim B'Israel)	A second national union of Israeli journalists.	http://itonaim.org.il
Journalists Association–Tel Aviv	The professional union of the journalists in the city of Tel Aviv.	http://www.jat.co.il
Journalists Association–Jerusalem	The professional union of the journalists in the city of Jerusalem.	http://www.jaj.org.il
Journalists Association–Haifa	The professional union of the journalists in the city of Haifa (and the northern areas of the country).	http://www.haifapress.org.il
The Second Authority for Television and Radio	The regulatory authority responsible for two commercial nationwide TV channels and local radio stations.	http://www.rashut2.org.il
The Council for Cable TV and Satellite Broadcasting	The regulatory body responsible for cable TV and satellite broadcasting.	http://www.moc.gov.il
Israel Communication Association (ISCA)	Professional association for Israeli researchers and teachers in the diverse disciplines of communication.	http://www.isracom.org

Table 6.2

Top Academic Journalism Programs and Non-Academic Training Programs in Israel

Organization	Description	Contact
Ariel University, Ariel	School of Communication: Print and online Journalism Track (elective), and Radio Track (elective). Various compulsory workshops in each track.	http://www.ariel.ac.il/com munication
Sapir Academic College, Shaar Hanegev	School of Communication: Print and online Journalism Track (elective), Radio Track (elective), and TV Journalism (elective). Various compulsory workshops in each track.	http://colman.ac.il
Academic College of Management, Rishon Letzion	School of Communication: Journalism, Radio, and TV Track workshops (most elective).	http://colman.ac.il
The Interdisciplinary Center, Herzelia	School of Communication: Basic journalism workshops (no journalism track).	http://portal.idc.ac.il
Netanya Academic College, Netanya	Department of Communication: Basic journalistic skills (compulsory workshop).	http://www.netanya.ac.il
Kineret Accademic College, Kineret	Department of Communication: Basic journalistic skills (compulsory workshop).	http://www.kinneret.ac.il
Yizrael Valley Academic College, Afula	Department of Communication: Basic journalistic skills (compulsory workshop).	http://www.yvc.ac.il
Tel Aviv University, Tel Aviv	Department Of Communication: Basic journalistic skills (elective workshop).	http://socsci.tau.ac.il
Jordan Valley Academic College	Department of Communication: Basic journalistic skills (compulsory workshop).	http://www.kinneret.ac.il
The Hebrew University, Jerusalem	Department of Communication and Journalism: Basic journalistic skills (elective workshop).	http://communication.mscc. huji.ac.il
Haifa University, Haifa	Department of Communication: Basic journalistic skills (elective workshop).	http://hevra.haifa.ac.il
Bar-Ilan University, Ramat-Gan	Department of Communication: Basic journalistic skills (elective workshop).	http://communication.biu. ac.il
Koteret, School of Journalism, Tel Aviv University, Tel Aviv	Diploma Studies in journalism (one or two-year track).	http://www.koteret.tau.ac.il

7

Journalism Education in Russia: How the Academy and Media Collide, Cooperate, and Coexist

Maria Lukina and Elena Vartanova

This chapter examines the concept, structure, and basic principles for journalism education in Russia. In the context of the changing media environment, socio-demographic characteristics of the press corps, and peculiarities of professional journalism culture, the authors discuss how future journalists are trained and how educational institutions are associated with media and professional organizations.

From a historical viewpoint, Russian journalism education has been rooted in Russia's post-revolutionary history. Before *perestroika* and liberal reforms, it was considered a part of the ideological foundation of the Soviet media system. Today, journalism education in Russia is aimed at meeting national traditions and international standards. Journalists in Russia are primarily trained in state or private universities, although there are media and nongovernmental organizations that offer mid-career and short-term courses. Universities offer programs similar to the European two-level system with bachelor's and master's degrees, as well as doctoral degrees, and syllabi are created in accordance with world educational practices, the UNESCO model curriculum, the Tartu Declaration, and labor market requirements.

The renovations in journalism education in modern Russia are framed by the driving forces of educational reforms linked with the Bologna process and associated with curriculum reconfiguration, innovations in education programming, and international opportunities for teachers and students. Transformations in the media industry, newsroom reconstructions, new patterns of content production and distribution, and interactions with audiences also shape such renovations.

Journalism in the Media Landscape

The media environment shapes journalism education, forming both its strengths and weaknesses. The Russian media landscape has radically changed since the dissolution of the Soviet Union. A segmented market that brought tangible changes to media structures, journalism practices, audience demands, and patterns of media consumption replaced the Communist press system, established in 1917.

According to official statistics annually published by the Federal Agency for Press and Mass Communications (FAPMC, 2015, p. 18), the Russian print market consists of about 62,000 print editions, including 25,781 newspapers (42%) and 31,714 magazines (51%). As in other parts of the world, the Russian newspaper market is experiencing a decline in advertising revenues and circulation. During the first quarter of 2015, press advertising revenues fell 40% (FAPMC, 2015, p. 6). General subscriptions of newspapers and magazines dropped to 20.2% in the second half of 2014, and in the first half of 2015 they fell even further. National newspapers are suffering the highest losses, but local press markets are holding steady with the help of state donations or investments from local businesses. However, such contributions rob the local press of political and economic freedom.

The magazine sector is also experiencing hard times. Many magazines are leaving print behind, migrating to the Internet, and actively using mobile modes of content distribution and social media platforms for communicating with audiences (FAPMC, 2015, pp. 58-61). There is a developing trend, beside the recent boom of entertainment glossies, for cheaper local publications containing practical information for everyday life related to food, health, shopping, gardens, housing, and travel. Some of these outlets develop blog platforms, while others use user-generated content or practice crowdfunding (FAPMC, 2015, pp. 63-64).

Television plays a key role in Russia's media. It consists of a diverse system of on-air, cable and Web broadband, analogue and digital, central and regional, free and paid, general and special interest, mass and niche, state and private channels. In 2013, more than 40 channels were within reach for a single urban household (FAPMC, 2014a, p. 55). These accessible channels are divided into three main groups: federal (national) channels of general interest, Pervyj Kanal, Russiya-1, and NTV; main network channels, STS, TNT, and REN TV; and channels focused on special topics, like culture, sports, music, and children. A growing fragmentation of the national television audience is seen in the decrease of audience share among the above-mentioned top three national channels: Pervyj Kanal, Russiya 1, and NTV. However, while the share of less popular national channels remains steady (TNT, STS, and 5 Kanal), the share of local channels has increased (FAPMC, 2014a, p. 63).

Television and its federal channels, with signals covering almost the entire country, is the main source of information for Russians regardless of their place of residence, social status, or level of education. This picture has not changed in recent years: tastes and preferences are stable, despite the fragmentation and deepening differences among social groups within the audience. Entertainment is the dominant feature of Russian television. Movies, soap operas, situation comedies, and talk shows prevail and dominate two thirds of broadcasting time on mainstream channels, while news programs on average share only 7% of airtime and political programs even less (FAPMC, 2014a, p. 68).

Radio ownership, as in other media sectors, is either state or private. But, the two main players are state-owned channels with news and music content—Radio Rossii and Mayak. Their main competitors are music stations focused on different types of music, including Western, jazz, rock, pop, and Russian pop. Most of these competitors use FM frequencies, limiting their distribution to local communities or small towns (Radio Broadcasting in Russia, 2014, p. 58). Several radio stations offer talk-radio format. The most popular, Echo Moskvy, claims editorial independence despite its affiliation with Gazprom Media, owned by Russia's biggest natural gas giant.

TV and radio broadcasting in Russia are moving toward a digital platform. A national program titled "Developments of Digital TV and Radio 2009-2015" supports digital TV and radio penetration into local markets, overseas, and distant territories with very limited populations. By the end of 2013, the construction of the first digital multiplex, packaging 10 television and radio channels and broadcasting via a single transmitter, was completed (FAPMC, 2014b, p. 9). And the second multiplex, with the next 10 television channels, is on its way.

As is the case worldwide, the Internet is the fastest-growing media sector. Russia's Internet-related economy is growing by 20%-30% each year (FAPMC, 2014c, p. 83). In 2012, Russia possessed the fourth strongest online advertising market in Europe (FAPMC, 2014c, p. 75). New online platforms are affecting traditional media practices and forcing platform integration, convergent solutions, interaction with audiences, and alternative agenda setting. Although TV remains the main source of news for most Russians, the Internet and new media are rapidly becoming the second most popular choice. In addition, social networks are becoming popular news sources and distribution platforms for all media sectors (FAPMC, 2014d).

Professional Characteristics

Russia's media model differs from those described by Hallin and Mancini (2012) in a key crucial dimension—a strong relationship among media, journalists, and the state—and should be described as a hybrid of both state and commercialized models (Vartanova, 2012, p. 141).

There is no exact data on the number of journalists in Russia. However, in recent years, the Russian Union of Journalists has estimated about 150,000 journalists employed in the media industry (Anikina, Dobek-Ostrowska, & Nygren, 2013, p. 21). Several large-scale surveys have described the professional characteristics of post-Soviet journalists and their communities (Kolesnik, Shiryaeva, & Svitich, 1995; Pasti, 2004, 2009; Anikina et al., 2013; Anikina, 2014; Vartanova & Lukina, 2014).

For example, while journalism was a mostly masculine profession during Soviet times, nowadays journalism is becoming a "predominantly female profession" (Anikina et al., 2013, p. 72). In the 51-plus age group there are fewer females (47%) and more males (53%), in the 36-to-50 age group about 60% females and 40% males, and in the under-35 age group about 70% females and 29% males (Anikina et al., 2013, p. 71). This predominantly female environment is evident not only in the gender breakdown of media professionals, but also in the gender breakdown among journalism students (Anikina et al., 2013, p. 72).

The Worlds of Journalism Survey describes Russian journalists as "young professionals" since their professional experience is often less than 10 years (Anikina et al., 2013, p. 25). But despite their youth, these young professionals are well educated: Some 95% of them have high school or university degrees. Overall, media representatives without a specialized education in journalism and mass communication make up only a small part of the journalistic community (Anikina, 2014, pp. 240-241).

As for the role of journalists in society, those who entered journalism during Soviet times were often described as "propagandists" and "organizers" due to a close media alliance with local authorities, economic groups, or political factions (Juskevits, 2004). Later, professional corps produced another role for journalists, journalists as entertainers—a role often willingly adopted by the younger generation (Juskevits, 2004, p. 194). However, recent studies demonstrate that currently most journalists are reluctant to pursue this entertainment role, and many rank it last place out of all professional duties (Anikina, 2014, pp. 244-245).

Today, Russian journalists have adapted principles typical of Western journalistic culture as their main professional standards, such as objectivity, impartiality, and autonomy (Anikina, 2014, p. 244). Though the Press Freedom Index ranks the Russian Federation at a low 152 out of 180 countries (Reporters without Borders, 2015), Russian journalists rank freedom and independence as one of their most important values (Anikina, 2014, p. 244). Professional obligations "to be a neutral reporter," "provide information objectively," "stand free of special interests," and "bring forward various opinions" take first place in Russian journalists' rankings of their professional duties (Anikina, 2014, p. 244). That said, journalists usually link job dissatisfaction to pressures coming from the state, press owners, and businesses (Shiryaeva & Svitich, 2006, pp. 285-288).

Professionally, journalists in Russia are organized in different forms of alliances similar to those in other countries: professional unions and guilds, human rights foundations, and legal support institutions.

Journalism Education, Professional Training, and Research

Journalism education appeared in Russia after the 1917 October Revolution, with a number of special schools for journalists recruited from the working class. In 1921, the first Institut Zhurnalistiki (Institute of Journalism) was established in Moscow. Similar institutions were founded in St. Petersburg and other cities to train reporters, while chief editors and newspaper directors were expected to be trained separately at Communist party schools (Shiryaeva & Svitich, 1997).

After World War II, Russian journalism education was reorganized and appeared in the framework of state universities as programs within philological departments. For this reason, journalism programs traditionally include Russian and foreign languages, literature, and philological studies. Highly qualified academics began teaching fundamental courses, which enhanced professional training courses and predetermined journalism education peculiarities for years to come.

As journalism evolved into a large profession, most of these journalism programs were enlarged and grew into separate journalism departments: about 23 throughout the former U.S.S.R, including universities in republics of Central Asia, the Caucasus, and the Baltic countries. Until the early 1990s and perestroika, the system of journalism education based on "the Soviet theory and practice of journalism . . . socialized through party membership" (Juskevits, 2002) was completely ideological and state controlled. Furthermore, there still existed Communist schools, especially for training top media managers.

Perestroika and liberal reforms in post-Soviet Russia have transformed journalism education into a much more liberal venture. An increased number of courses in liberal arts topics, the accreditation of private institutions, international cooperation with journalism educational institutions worldwide, and an alignment with Western theory and discourse have helped bring such transformations about. In 2010, this reform was further stimulated by the implementation of the European Bologna system, which forced academia to review old programs and shape them according to Tartu Declaration and UNESCO curricula models. Today, journalism education in Russia is available in higher education, media institutions, and nongovernmental organizations. However, university journalism programs, which combine broad academic education with practical training, are the main educators for future journalists. Out of 134 Russian universities where journalists are being trained, 105 are state, 29 private. Geographically, they are usually concentrated in business and media centers.

Journalists are also being trained in several media outlets (Kommersant, TASS, etc.), which provide short-term, mid-career, and refresher courses for staff and freelancers. They are mostly related to multimedia and social networking. Public and nongovernmental organizations, such as the Union of Journalists and the Guild of Press Publishers, also play an active role in professional education (see Table 7.1 for journalism associations and journalism-related organizations).

Teaching and Training Future Newsmakers

Russia's concept of contemporary journalism university education is based on clear perceptions of the role of media in a democratic society, development trends in media toward digitalization, and the social role of the journalism profession.

The basic principles of journalism education in Russian universities are (a) fundamental studies based on philology (literature/languages/humanities) and social sciences, (b) a balanced combination of theory and practice, (c) professional training in classes and during internships, and (d) teaching modern information technologies (Shiryaeva & Svitich, 2007, p. 129; see Table 7.2 for a list of academic and non-academic journalism programs).

To open an educational program in journalism, both state and private universities must get a license and pass an accreditation procedure. The Russian Ministry of Education is responsible for accreditation, and experts from leading universities in the field review programs.

As in all other spheres of education, Russian journalism schools construct their programs and syllabi within state education frameworks and standards. In 2010-2011 third generation standards came into force. They were created in accordance with world educational practices: two levels of studies, bachelor's and master's tracks, and an opportunity to continue training in post-graduate studies for further academic or professional careers. Journalism education in Russia, which now meets international standards, is similar to the European system, with four years for a bachelor's degree and two years for a master's degree.

Syllabi requirements include obligatory and elective courses, which, in local institutions, maintain a local flavor. Russian academic institutions can now construct their own curricula and allow students to build personal educational tracks as well. The significant growth in electives is an important indicator of academic freedom. For example, the number of elective courses in bachelor's degrees has grown from 12% in the 1980s to about 50% in 2010 (Federal State Educational Standard of Higher Education in Journalism, 2010).

Most Russian universities organize their courses via a module structure. (A module is a group of related-study disciplines that achieve a particular competence goal.) For example, the curriculum for a bachelor's degree program contains modules forming general knowledge in the humanities, liberal arts, and social sciences, which include courses in history, philosophy, sociology, psychology, law, ethics, politics, and economics. And when it comes to journalism, another module is added devoted to it. This journalism module focuses on a deeper understanding of the media and its influence on society, which includes attention to media law, ethics, history, and practical training, such as internships.

While many courses focus on the impact of journalism on society, practical training opportunities focus on teaching the work of journalists: news gathering, writing and storytelling, text structures and formats, content producing, and editing. Special attention is paid to information accuracy and fact-checking, to distinguishing news from opinion, to balancing information, etc.

Elective modules focus on various media types (press, television, radio, online), media convergence, the Internet, and new media. In the past, students' most popular specializations were the press and television. But today, preferences have moved toward the Internet and new media. Taking into account media convergence trends, many journalism schools have updated technical equipment and pay more and more attention to the technological culture of future professionals (Vartanova & Lukina, 2014, p. 228). Journalism education leaders, such as Moscow and St. Petersburg state universities, and several institutions in the Urals and Siberia, provide training in convergent newsrooms. Some institutions pay more attention to specific types of journalistic work: editorial management, media design, and photojournalism. Others focus on spheres of coverage: politics, international relations, economics, culture, sports, etc.

Journalism curricula usually contain a practical module carried out both in classrooms and in the field. School media production—newspapers, TV and radio programs, and multimedia projects—are usually required in all journalism schools. Internships are normally held during the summer and last three-to-five weeks of a semester.

In-house assessment also takes place at the end of a semester, module, or discipline. It includes group discussions, tests, exams, essays, and term papers. The final in-house assessment consists of a qualification paper and final exam. The qualification paper is either theory oriented or focused on a graduate's own professional work or media projects. The final graduate examination usually consists of two parts. The first is a presentation of a professional portfolio, composed throughout one's studies. The second is a demonstrated ability to critically evaluate media practices and to speak about theoretical topics, the history of journalism, professional technologies, and media genres and formats. After students successfully complete a journalism program, they are expected to be competent in various types of professional activities. The activities are usually derived from employer surveys. For example, graduates with bachelor's degrees in journalism, besides gaining competence in general education, should be able to

❏ participate in media production using multiple digital technologies;

❏ gather, select, and check information using different sources;

❏   produce authentic journalistic texts for traditional or multimedia platforms using modern formats and technology;

❏ participate in concept development and editorial planning of a particular medium or local media project, plan and organize his own work, and evaluate results in a critical way; and

❏ work with different social groups, including social networking.

Journalism Research

An understanding of how academic media and journalism research is conducted in Russia would be incomplete without reflection on changes in theoretical frameworks. Media studies in socialist countries traditionally have been rooted in the Soviet media's normative theory, which justified heavy ideological control. After the dissolution of the Soviet system, theories imported from the West became the most important factor in changing Eastern European media studies (Vartanova, 2009, p. 120). In the mid-1980s, libertarian and social responsibility theories became very popular (Mickiewicz, 1988; McNair, 1989; McNair, 1991; Nordenstreng & Paasilinna, 2002). Russian scholars have enthusiastically used the concept of *glasnost* to challenge previous theories and support media transformations based on Western ideals of free and open societies (Zassoursky, 1997; Vartanova & Zassoursky, 1998; Nordenstreng, Vartanova, & Zassoursky, 2002).

Another popular concept, dealing with public debate and originally developed by Jurgen Habermas, has become an important concept for Russian media studies (Habermas, 1989). In a nutshell, academics from Moscow, St. Petersburg, and Yekaterinburg universities began viewing media as a dialogue between the state and citizens that would result in better governance. Recently, researchers have expanded on the related idea of public interest and have made it a basic tenant of journalism (Vartanova, 2009, p. 127).

Karl Poppers' "open society" concept (Popper, 1945), in relation to media studies, was a starting point for extremely productive cooperation between Russian and Western media scholars. This concept has fit well into the general context of liberalization of journalism as a profession and the liberation of journalists from previous ideological pressures. Russian media scholars are particularly interested in related issues. They include open access to information, media accountability to the public before the state, new levels of media freedom and responsibility, media diversity, participatory media's societal impact, and relationships among media, state, and private businesses (Zassoursky & Vartanova, 1998; Vartanova, 2009, p. 129).

However, early dreams of unrestricted press freedom and a borderless, open society have been chased away by an evolving ownership system controlled by oligarchs, influenced by commercialization, and manipulated by political elites. A related theory has focused on the emergence of media-political capital as a corruptive force. It argues that the media is not only a business, but an entity that integrates with dominant political elites and wields political influence while falling short of professional media ethical practices and standards (Becker, 2004; Zassoursky, 2002).

In the early 2000s, Russian scholars began to apply Western approaches to empirical data in terms of concepts and research methods.

Academics started looking at issues like media economics, management, and marketing, and they began countering political economy critics by moving into practical research. As a result, Russian media studies have deepened. For example, they now use sociological research instruments to conceptualize change in media habits and behavior and to predict new trends (Resnyanskaya & Fomicheva, 1999). And scholars now come to newsrooms and interview journalists and media managers to study post-Soviet journalism cultures and media law practices (Juskevits, 2002; Richter, 2002; Pasti, 2004).

The Internet has also opened up a new area for Russian scholars, research investigating new media practices explored through a number of theoretical concepts and media mapping tools (Lukina, 2010). However, since Russian journalism schools originated in the humanities, popular subjects for research have always been languages and literature. Such research, often based on historiography, semiotics, and linguistic analysis, focuses mostly on media and literature texts. Russian researchers are also actively collaborating in international projects on journalism cultures, studying professional competences, and designing curriculum models.

Media studies today are carried out in university journalism departments, which edit and publish books, research monographs, and journals. Such scientific periodicals include Moscow State University's journalism department's *Vestnik of MSU: serija jurnalistika* and the online *Medi@lmanakh* and *Mediascope.* There are several other academic periodicals, including St. Petersburg's *Mass media: 21 vek* and Voronez University's *Akcenty.* Russian media and journalism researchers also have the opportunity to publish their papers in journals in related fields (philology, history, liberal arts, etc.) included in the Russian Index of Scientific Citation (RINC). While publishing in Russian academic journals is popular, publishing abroad helps significantly with promotion and is an important measure for academic position re-appointments, which take place every five years.

Professional Connections in Journalism Education

Journalism education institutions are associated with professional media organizations in different ways. First, all journalism high schools include in their curriculum extracurricular activities and internships in media organizations. Internships comprise nearly one fifth of high school students' studies. They not only help students gain and master professional skills, but they also help students demonstrate the ability to work in a particular media outlet. A successful internship is usually the first step toward finding a job. Because the Russian media industry is rapidly developing, job placement is not yet a problem. This fact is illustrated by Moscow State University's journalism bachelor's degree graduates' job placement stats. Of its 393 graduates interviewed in a 2014 survey, 53% found jobs in media organizations, 28% in public relations, advertising agencies, or similar businesses, and 19% in non-media fields. Figure 7.1 gives additional details on these graduates' media-related job placements.

The Moscow State University survey also found that of these 2014 graduates, 70% worked full time, 15% part time, and 9% as freelancers.

Second, practicing journalists and media managers take part in the teaching process. Russia's federal standards in journalism education recommend that schools of journalism include professionals in the educational process via lectures, master classes, workshops, and grading. Media industry leaders and prominent journalists are engaged in school councils and contribute professional expertise for curricula and

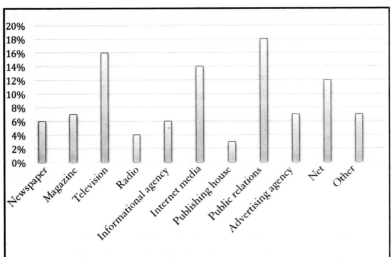

Figure 7.1 Bachelor's degree graduates' job placements by media type (Department of Journalism in Moscow State University, 2014)

the classroom. For example, such members of the Expert Council at Moscow State University evaluate the results of academic studies, provide expertise on programs and syllabi, take part in the teaching process on a regular basis, and participate in the selection of educators.

Journalism Education's Professional Impact

The efficiency of journalism education in Russia is evaluated in different ways. One is state control over the quality of education. Every six years educational institutions must pass an accreditation procedure. The Ministry of Education and Sciences' accreditation agency examines whether an institution meets educational standards using complex testing, syllabi reviews, and a critical analysis of final assessments. Education law requires transparency for all stakeholders in the educational process, and journalism schools in turn must present online all programs, assessments, and schedules. Thus, experts usually start their examination reviewing a school's website. Experts also analyze the level of teachers' and students' satisfaction with the educational process, labor market demands, and employers' assessment of graduates' skills and qualities (Vartanova & Lukina, 2014, pp. 224-226).

Journalism educational institutions are deeply concerned with their impact on professional training. Special attention is paid to examining the final competences a student should possess by the end of his studies. Roundtables and discussions are set up with employers to gain insight into the latest requirements for professional skills. In addition, professionally run panels, seminars, and teacher trainings are held regularly on university campuses.

Professional organizations, associations, and various journalism and publishing guilds take an active part in discussions on the quality of journalism training. Such discussions also regularly take place during journalism conventions, press festivals, and within the pages of special media professional magazines, such as *Zhournalist* and *Zhournalistika i Mediarynok*.

Journalism Education Issues, Challenges, and Innovations

Currently, journalism education abruptly finds itself at the crossroads of different key trends in global media development. The process of digitalization raises the question of students' technological literacy. Journalism departments debate the number of skills needed and the optimal level of technical competence that should be required. In today's convergent newsrooms, journalists need to have all the skills of multimedia journalists and to be innovative. This prompts journalism education to adjust to technological progress and to introduce new courses that address all students, regardless of medium specialization. Recent surveys reveal a vast number of journalism institutions adding IT courses to their syllabi and reshaping programs to increase their focus on tech-savvy skills (Vartanova & Lukina, 2014, pp. 221-224).

Due to constantly evolving media realities, Russian journalism educators are more interested than ever in collaborating with the media industry. This could help new education courses and models to serve industry needs and solve anticipated job placement problems for newer media careers. Most media outlets are open to working with academia, providing master classes, and participating in in-house media production. Though some media outlets try to teach newcomers in their own classes, others hire employees with journalism degrees and then train them to work according to their own corporate standards.

Perhaps the most important question facing Russian journalism education today is what higher educational institutions should teach and how they should do so. For example, classical university education traditions, founded in literature and philology courses, interfere with the media industry's demand for practical-oriented, tech-savvy graduates. Although media researchers and practitioners actively discuss the need for new, mandatory digital media competences (Van Der Haak, Parks, & Castells, 2012), education administrators in several local universities do not rank highly such competencies. Instead, such administrators stress writing and editing skills most (Vartanova & Lukina, 2014, pp. 229-230).

Challenges are also connected with the ongoing reform of education. After a jump to the European Bologna process and transition to the two-level educational system, many schools may now not be able to gain accreditation for a master's-level degree program. Only institutions that meet adequate intellectual, infrastructural, and human resource requirements will earn master's-level accreditation. For many schools that means not only a reduction of college entrants, but a related decrease in teaching staff.

There are also continuing debates on the line that separates bachelor's and master's programs. The main development in Russian journalism education is the emergence of new master's degree programs focusing on online media, multimedia journalism, management of convergent newsrooms, etc. And more Russian universities are also showing interest in launching joint-degree programs with foreign schools.

Conclusion: Educating Tomorrow's Journalists — The Big Picture

Future Russian newsmakers are being educated by two main players. Most are being trained within the higher educational system, earning bachelor's and master's degrees. The rest are being trained in news organizations and mid-career centers, mostly affiliated with big media companies and focused on students with professional backgrounds.

In addition, journalism education reform in modern Russia is framed by two driving forces: revolutionary media changes and educational reforms. Such revolutionary media changes include reconfiguration of the media industry, reconstruction of newsrooms, new patterns of content production, and interaction with audiences. Both academia and industry courses are trying to stay on top of current media trends. While academia's course offerings are often not as cutting-edge/practical as industry's, academia's emphasis on journalism's societal impact and research are essential for preparing future journalists. As for higher education reform, it encourages academia to address international standards for curriculum development, gives institutions more freedom in program development regarding local media market needs, and creates opportunities for faculty and student international exchanges.

Hopefully, education reform efforts will help meet the challenges of diverse media markets, help media professionals cope with both quality standards and financial concerns, and help fulfill journalism educators' most important goal: to produce graduates willing and able to meet journalism's public service obligations.

References

Anikina, M. (2014). Journalism as a profession in the first decades of the 21ˢᵗ century: The Russian context. *World of Media. Yearbook of Russian media and journalism studies,* 2014, 233-254.

Anikina, M., Dobek-Ostrovska, B., & Nygren, G. (2013). *Journalists in three media systems: Polish, Russian and Swedish journalists about values and ideals, daily practice and the future* Moscow: Journalism Faculty, Moscow State University. Retrieved from http://www.journalisminchange.com/ Files/content/book.pdf

Becker, J. (2004). Lessons from Russia: A Neo-authoritarian media system. *European Journal of Communication, 19*(2), 139-63.

Federal Agency for Press and Mass Communications. (2014a). *Televidenije v Rossii. Sosnojanije, tendencii I perspektivy razvitija.* [Television in Russia. Status, trends and development perspectives.] Moscow: FAPMC. Retrieved from http://fapmc.ru/rospechat/activities/reports/2014/television-in-russia.html

Federal Agency for Press and Mass Communications. (2014b). *Radioveshanije v Rossii. Sosnojanije, tendencii I perspektivy razvitija.* [Radio broadcasting in Russia. Status, trends and development perspectives.] Moscow: FAPMC. Retrieved from http://fampc.ru/rospechat/activities/reports//2015/radio/ main/custom/00/0/file.pdf

Federal Agency for Press and Mass Communications. (2014c). *Internet v Rossii. Sosnojanije, tendencii I perspektivy razvitija* [Internet in Russia. Status, trends and development perspectives.] Moscow: FAPMC. Retrieved from http://fampc.ru/rospechat/activities/reports//2015/inet/main/custom/00/0/ file.pdf

Federal Agency for Press and Mass Communications. (2015). Rossijskaja periodicheskaya pechat. Sosnojanije, tendencii I perspektivy razvitija. [Russian periodical press. Status, trends and development perspectives.] Moscow: FAPMC. Retrieved from http://fapmc.ru/rospechat/activities/ reports/2015/pechat.html

Federal State Educational Standard of Higher Education in Journalism (2010). Moscow: Ministry of Education.

Habermas, J. (1989). *The structural transformation of the public sphere.* Cambridge: Polity.

Hallin, D. C., & Mancini, P. (Eds.), (2012). *Comparing media systems beyond the Western world.* Cambridge: Cambridge University Press.

Juskevits, S. (2001). *Professional roles of contemporary Russian journalists: A case study of St. Petersburg media.* Retrieved from http://tampub.uta.fi/bitstream/handle/10024/76288/lisuri00006.pdf?sequence=1

Juskevits, S. (2002). *Professional roles of Russian journalists at the end of the 1990s:*

A case study of the St Petersburg media. Retrieved from http://tampub.uta. fi/bitstream/handle/10024/76288/lisuri00006.pdf?sequence=1

Kolesnik, S., Svitich, L., & Shiryaeva, A. (1995). Rossiiskii i Amerikanskii Zhurnalisty [Russian and American journalists]. *Vestnik Moskovskogo Universiteta, Seria 10. Zhurnalistika*, 1-2, 20-27.

Lukina, M. (Ed.), (2010). *Internet-Media: theory and practice*. Moscow: Aspekt Press.

McNair, B. (1989). Glasnost, restructuring and the Soviet media. *Media, Culture and Society, 11*(3), 327-349.

McNair, B. (1991). *Glasnost, Perestroika and the Soviet media*. London: Routledge.

Mickiewicz, E. (1988). *Split signals: Television and politics in the Soviet Union*. New York, NY: Oxford University Press.

Nordenstreng, K., & Paasilinna, R. (2002). Epilogue, In K. Nordenstreng, E. Vartanova, & Y. Zassoursky. (Eds.), *Russian media challenge* (pp. 189-198). Helsinki: Aleksanteri Institute.

Nordenstreng, K., Vartanova, E., & Zassoursky, Y. (2002). (Eds.), *Russian media challenge*. Helsinki: Kikimora Publications.

Pasti, S. (2004). *Rossijskij zurnalist v kontekste peremen. Media Sankt-Peterburga*. [Russian journalist in the context of changes]. Tampere: Tampere University Press.

Pasti, S. (2009). *Samochuvstvie zhurnalista v professii: konets 2008*. [Being a journalist in the profession: the end of 2008], In P. Gutiontov (Ed.), *Formula doveria. Materialy Mezhdunarodnogo kongressa zhurnalistov*. [Formula of trust. Theses of International Congress of Journalists.] (pp. 69-77). Moscow: Russian Union of Journalists.

Popper, K. (1945). *The open society and its enemies*. London: Routledge.

Reporters without Borders. (2014). Press Freedom Index. Retrieved from http://en.rsf.org

Resnyanskaya, L., & Fomicheva, I. (1999). *Gazeta dlya vsei Rossii*. [Newspaper for the whole Russia]. Moscow: Moscow University Press.

Richter, A. (2002). *Pravovyje osnovy zhurnalistiki* [Legal basics of journalism]. Moscow: Moscow University Press. Shiryaeva, A., & Svitich, L. (1997). *Zhurnalistskoe obrazovanie: vzgljad sociologa* [Journalism education: a sociologist approach]. Moscow: IKAR.

Shiryaeva, A., & Svitich, L. (2006). *Rossijskij zhurnalist i zhurnalistskoje obrazovanij. Sociologicheskije issledovanije*. [Russian journalist and journalism education: sociological research]. Moscow: VK.

Shiryaeva, A., & Svitich, L. (2007). *Innovacionnye podhody k proektirovaniju osnovnyh obrazovatel'nyh programm po napravleniju podgotovki vysshego professional'nogo obrazovanija "zhurnalistika"* [Innovative approach to the designing of journalism education programs]. Moscow: Moscow University Press.

Tartu Declaration. (June 26, 2006). Retrieved from http://www.ejta.eu/index. php/website/projects

UNESCO. (2007). *Model curricula for journalism education for developing countries & emerging democracies*. Paris: UNESCO.

Van Der Haak, B., Parks, M., & Castells, M. (2012). The future of journalism: Networked journalism. *International Journal of Communication, 6,* 2923-2938. Retrieved from http://ijoc.org/index.php/ijoc/article/view-File/1750/832

Vartanova E. (2012). The Russian media model in the context of post-Soviet dynamics. In D. C. Hallin & P. Mancini (Eds.), *Comparing media systems beyond the Western world* (pp. 119-142). Cambridge: Cambridge University Press.

Vartanova, E. (2009). *Mass media theory. Current issues*. Moscow: MediaMir.

Vartanova, E., & Lukina, M. (2014). New competences for the future journalists: Russian journalism education executives evaluate industrial demand *World of Media. Yearbook of Russian Media and Journalism Studies*, pp. 209-233.

Vartanova, E., & Zassoursky, Y. (Eds.), (1998). *Media, communications and the open society*. Moscow: IKAR.

Zassoursky, Y. (1997). *Media in transition and politics in Russia. In J.* Servaes & R. Lee (Eds.), *Media and politics in transition (pp. 213-221)*. Leuven: Acco.

Zassoursky, Y. (2002). *Zhurnalistika i obshchestvo: balansiruya mezhdu gosudarstvom, biznesom i obshchestvennoi sferoi.* [Journalism and society: balance between the state, business and public sphere]. In Y. Zassoursky. (Ed.), *Sredstva massovoi informatsii postsovetskoi Rossii. [Mass media in post-soviet Russia]* (pp. 195-231). Moscow: Aspekt Press.

Zassoursky, Y., & Vartanova, E. (Eds.), (1998). *Changing media and communications*. Moscow: IKAR.

Table 7.1

Journalism Associations and Journalism-Related Organizations in Russia

Organization	Description	Contact
Union of Journalists	Public professional organization uniting all journalist unions of Russian Federation.	http://www.ruj.ru
Mediasoyuz	Independent organization uniting all mass media sectors throughout Russia.	http://www.mediasoyuz.ru
Glasnost Defense Foundation	Nongovernment organization lobbying against restrictions on freedom of expression.	http://www.gdf.ru
Reporters Without Borders	International organization fighting for press freedom on a daily basis since founded in 1985.	http://en.rsf.org
The Federal Service for Supervision of Communications, Information Technology, and Mass Media	Federal executive authority of the Russian Federation controlling and supervising mass media and telecommunications, overseeing personal data processing, issuing radio licenses, and monitoring Internet media.	http://eng.rkn.gov.ru
Guild of Press Publishers (GIPP)	GIPP aims to create favorable facilities for print businesses.	http://www.gipp.ru
Association of Independent Regional Publishers (AIRP)	AIRP coordinates efforts on protection of freedom of speech, exchanging experience, and protecting corporate interests.	http://www.anri.org.ru
National Association of TV and Radio Broadcasters (NAT)	NAT protects rights and interests of TV and radio companies, provides their legal guarantees, and coordinates activities.	http://www.nat.ru
Media Rights Defense Centre	Nonprofit organization protecting rights of mass media and legal protection of journalists.	http://www.mmdc.ru
UMS in Journalism for Russian Universities	Professional public association for Russian universities responsible for improving curricula and journalism education and the academic expertise of advanced journalism education.	http://www.journ.msu.ru/umo

Table 7.2

Top Academic and Non-Academic Journalism Programs in Russia

Name	Contact
Journalism Department, Lomonosov Moscow State University	http://www.journ.msu.ru
High School of Journalism and Mass Communication, St. Petersburg State University	http://jf.spbu.ru
Journalism Department, the Urals State University	http://journ.igni.urfu.ru
Journalism Department, Voronezh State University	http://www.jour.vsu.ru
Department of Philology, Journalism and Intercultural Communications, South Federal State University, Rostov-Na-Donu	http://www.philology.sfedu.ru
Department of Journalism, Tomsk State University	http://www.newsman.tsu.ru
Chair of Journalism and Mass Communication, Peoples' Friendship University of Russia	http://www.rudn.ru/en
Journalism Department, South Urals University, Chelyabinsk	http://fj.susu.ac.ru
Department of Journalism and Sociology, Kazan State University	http://ksu.ru/f13
TV and Radio Journalism Department, University of Humanities, Yekaterinburg	http://www.gu-ural.ru
Academy of Media Industry, Moscow	http://www.ipk.ru
Russian Educational Center for Local TV Journalists, Niznij Novgorod	http://praktika.nnov.ru
Institute for Press Development – Siberia	http://www.sibirp.ru
Regional Press Institute	http://pdi.spb.ru
Journalism Academy at "Kommersant"	http://www.kommersant.ru/academy

8

Journalism Education in South Africa: Taking on Challenges for the Future

Arnold S. de Beer, Sandra Pitcher, and Nicola Jones[1]

South Africa's mediascape and system of journalism teaching changed irrevocably when the African National Congress (ANC) came to power in 1994 to form the country's first democratic majority government. As Searle and McKenna (2013) put it, "the reconstruction of domestic, social, and economic relations [had] to eradicate and redress the inequitable patterns of ownership, wealth, and social and economic practices that were shaped by segregation and apartheid" (p. 103). It also affected journalism education in many ways. This chapter briefly outlines the challenges confronting journalism education as a consequence of these changes. It demonstrates how South African journalism education has developed and interacted with the media and broader society over the last two decades. First, it examines South Africa's journalism landscape, as well as past and present ideological underpinnings of both the news media system and journalism education. It then discusses the current challenges to journalism education within a political system still in a state of flux, along with the uneasy relationship between the country's government and its journalism profession. It highlights both the strengths and shortcomings of journalism education today. With a look toward the future, it explores how some innovations could be adopted to improve journalism education in the current context of a rapidly evolving social media and technological environment.

---

1   With earlier contributions by Gabriël Botma, Pieter J. Fourie, Johannes D. Froneman, Lizette Rabe, and Herman Wasserman.

Journalism in the Media Landscape

South Africa's historical past and social context have shaped its current media system. When the country's first newspapers were founded in the 1800s, South Africa mimicked the colonial British system of journalistic practice. This tradition continued when radio was introduced in 1936 and again with the advent of television in 1975. In addition, South Africa's public broadcaster followed the structure of the British Broadcasting Corporation (BBC; Wigston, 2007). Consequently, journalism education and skills training largely mimicked the British and American tradition. However, unlike the BBC, which Hallin and Mancini (2004) describe as operating under a "professional model" (that is, independent of government), South Africa's broadcast media are more closely aligned with Hallin and Mancini's vision of a "government model" media system, where the South African Broadcasting Corporation (SABC) has to report to parliament.

An authoritarian climate of apartheid rule prevailed until the 1990s with wide-ranging restrictions placed on the media (Hachten & Giffard, 1984), attempting to control the beliefs of all South Africans. The SABC's television channels and radio stations reflected the government's racial segregation policies. Languages indigenous to South Africa were only allowed on separate channels reserved for black audiences in South Africa's separated *homelands* (apartheid-style, self-governed black areas; Teer-Tomaselli & Tomaselli, 2001).

Following the unbanning of the ANC in 1990, there have been significant changes to South Africa's media landscape. These changes have reoriented it within what Christians, Glasser, McQuail, Nordenstreng, and White (2009) would describe as a more pluralist democracy. As a result, South Africa's media have become largely self-regulated. Since the mid-1990s, they have slowly shifted from an authoritarian system to one that could, in theory, be deemed reflective of McQuail's (2010) social responsibility model—but with emerging developmental tendencies (Botma, 2011; De Beer, Beckett, Malila, & Wasserman, 2016).

At the same time, the state eased its monopoly over broadcasting and sold several of its regional radio stations to privately owned "Black Economic Empowerment" firms. It also granted licenses to launch South Africa's only non-SABC, free-to-air television channel, e-tv, and numerous community radio stations (Wigston, 2007).

Due to the global expansion of South African companies like Multichoice, a pay-media Internet and satellite television provider, the country has made vast strides in the international market, especially in the development of media systems in other African countries and elsewhere. So much so that Media24, which started with only the Afrikaans daily *Die Burger* in 1915, is now the world's eighth largest media conglomerate—the biggest outside the United States and China (Rabe, 2015). International investors, particularly from Ireland, China, and India, have also entered the local market. However, they are not always as successful as the Irish take-over of a section of the South African print media (BDLive, 2013).

A marked difference in the pre- and post-1994 South African journalism landscape is the attempt to diversify print/electronic newsrooms and open up economic and journalism education opportunities for South Africa's previously repressed black population. There has been a surge in the growth of black language newspapers, such as *Isolzwe,* as well as English and Afrikaans tabloids, such as the *Daily Sun* and *Son*. These newspapers specifically target the blue-collar, black working class (Wasserman, 2010b). While not being able to compete with the growing tabloid press in terms of audience growth, established traditional newspapers, such as the *Sunday Times,* have made some efforts to reach black, largely lower-income audiences. They have also tried to make their newsrooms much more demographically representative (Daniels, 2013).

Since 2010, state actions have moved the media freedom scale back in the direction of authoritarianism. Most international press freedom listings (e.g., Freedomhouse.org) have placed South Africa between 40th and 45th on the world's media "freedom scale" of about 130 countries, landing it among the weaker electoral democracies. Furthermore, there have been numerous cases in recent times (Harber, 2014) indicating that independent, critical media is under siege. Print newsrooms especially are facing a combination of financial difficulty and pressure from the ruling party, its allies, and state institutions, which are subsidizing friendly media and becoming increasingly hostile to those asking hard questions.

South African President Jacob Zuma has sued print journalists and publishing houses for printing information he believes has damaged his dignity and reputation (Swart, 2008). Moreover, he has effectively secured the SABC as a public broadcaster for the purposes of the ANC-led government. He has done so by deploying loyal supporters to powerful positions and censoring news or reports that show the government, or Zuma, in a bad light (Reid, 2013).

The ruling ANC is also attempting to pass the Protection of Information Bill. This potential law could criminalize journalists for exposing information that the government deems "confidential," even if such information serves the public interest—such as exposing corruption. Additionally, many commentators have also begun to question the autonomy of South Africa's press as more journalists and editors state their allegiance to particular political parties, most commonly the ruling ANC (Du Preez, 2015; Thamm, 2015).

The government's reaction to print media criticism, often viewed as "unpatriotic," could eventually undermine the country's journalism education. That is if journalism lecturers are also told to "toe the line," as is the case elsewhere in Africa (Malila, 2014).

Professional Characteristics

In 1994, the official end of apartheid introduced a number of changes to newsroom culture and professional characteristics, especially in line with racial and gender transformation. Daniels (2013) found that, on average, 61% of journalists in South Africa are black, with an almost even overall split between men and women. Two years later De Beer et al. (2016) found that 62% of journalists are women and 38% men.

Journalists interviewed for Daniels' (2013) study say that transformation policies to increase the number of black journalists are working, and journalists are generally satisfied with the current climate of employment and work conditions in national newsrooms.

Pitcher and Jones (2014) have provisionally found that journalists only consider it "somewhat important" to act as political watchdogs. Instead, many journalists argue that it is more important to report news that attracts the largest number of readers and to provide news readers would find interesting. This result appears to mirror the government's current criticism of the media: that they are only interested in sensational reporting (Cronin, 2010).

However, De Beer et al. (2016) found in their study of 2,200 journalists that South African journalists (N = 371) balance their approach to watchdog journalism with reporting that supports the country's developmental needs. In addition, while they do not tend to see themselves as government adversaries, respondents scored low on seeing their role as either supporting government or conveying a positive image of political leadership. In line with developmental theory, South African journalists consider it important to educate the audience, let people express their views, and promote tolerance and cultural diversity (see Figure 8.1). In the process, they consider journalism ethics to have the most important influence on their work (see Figure 8.2).

On the issue of journalism education, the De Beer, Beckett, Malila and Wasserman (2016) study found that some 75% of South African journalists in their sample completed a journalism degree or degree that combined journalism and other media or communication subjects, which counteracts critics' arguments that journalism education

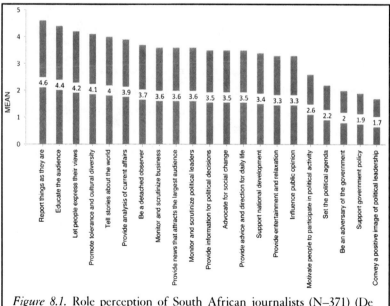

Figure 8.1. Role perception of South African journalists (N–371) (De Beer et al., 2016)

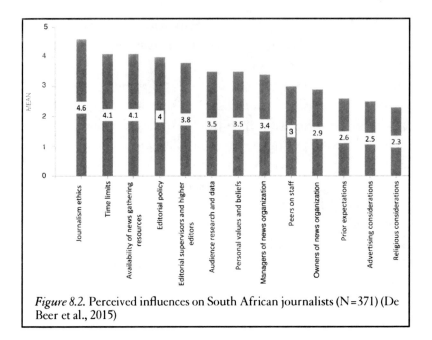

Figure 8.2. Perceived influences on South African journalists (N=371) (De Beer et al., 2015)

is of little value to the practice of journalism. In addition, many media organizations tightening their belts have not tried to retain senior journalists, often retrenched on a rather large scale. A result is the "juniorization" of newsrooms. This has played a role in altering newsroom ideologies pertaining to what journalistic professionalism entails.

Financial constraints have left media organization owners attempting to regenerate their profit margins. Editors have again begun to favor journalists who have large reader followings, especially on social media, and journalists with tertiary-level training (journalism training after high school) (De Beer et al., 2016).

Ultimately, the gravitation away from a watchdog approach in print media is exacerbated by the impact of social media platforms and the concurrent move to an increasingly new media audience, which often acts as both recipient and sender. The current political situation and the financial difficulties that exist in the South African media compound this situation. In addition, public debates about social responsibility and the need for advocacy journalism have created a litany of uncertainty as to what journalism in the "new" South Africa should stand for and what the professional characteristics of journalists should be.

Journalism Education, Professional Training, and Research

South African journalism education still has Anglo-American roots. However, since the 1990s strong calls have been made to "Africanise" the journalism curriculum by developing material that takes more notice of indigenous knowledge systems (Fourie, 2008; Dube, 2010). Additionally, South African journalism training is often still at odds with the needs of the media industry, emphasizing the divorce between ivory-tower research and real-life challenges. This section highlights an approach that could decrease the gap between what is required in the country's high-paced, rapidly evolving journalism profession and the theoretically driven underpinnings of academia in a multicultural, developing democracy (Wasserman, 2010b).

Teaching and Training Future Newsmakers

South Africa has arguably the oldest university-based journalism education system in Africa, beginning in 1959 at Potchefstroom University (now North-West University). The 1970s saw the introduction of a journalism program at Rhodes University and communication (including journalism) programs at the University of South Africa (Unisa), Rand Afrikaans University (now the University of Johannesburg), and the University of the Orange Free State (now University of the Free State). Similar programs were also introduced at previously black-only universities, such as Fort Hare, Zululand, and Bophuthatswana (now part of North-West University). The following three decades expanded journalism education to most of the country's technikons (former educational institutions with career-oriented training, now universities of technology), notably the former Pretoria Technikon (now the Tshwane University of Technology). The universities of technology are more geared to providing skills-based training programs as opposed to academic university degrees with a greater emphasis on theoretical education. The academic universities also support journalism majors with additional majors and minors from the arts and social sciences, such as languages, sociology, political science, and history. On the other hand, the universities of technology tend to focus more on beat-related journalism minors, such as finance, sports, and court reporting.

Of the country's three top research universities—the University of Cape Town, the University of the Witwatersrand (Wits), and the University of Natal (now KwaZulu-Natal)—only Wits offers a journalism program in a separate department alongside media studies. The other two have programs emphasizing a cultural and/or media studies approach, not a journalistic one. This is the result of the traditional view, also found in the United Kingdom and the United States, that journalism should be considered a skill or trade, not a scientific discipline (De Beer & Tomaselli, 2000; Banda et al., 2007).

Changes in both the state and media landscape in South Africa following apartheid have also affected discourse about journalism education. Two aspects have been particularly influential in this regard: transformation and private-public partnerships (Banda et al., 2007). The global "theory versus practice" debate has definitely influenced these discussions. It is encouraging in the South African context that in spite of this perceived "theory versus practice" divide, there is lively and continuing debate on the issue. There is broad agreement, for example, on the need for journalism education to include the cultivation of an informed and critical mindset, as well as the honing of skills in university journalism courses (Motloung, 2007).

Although the market-driven imperatives of corporate media remain, some media and cultural studies scholars, as well as journalism educators, continue to problematize journalism education curricula's relationship to the market. There is an awareness of the impact of problematic neo-liberal political systems in a developing country and an overreliance on Western influence on journalism education. There is also an awareness of the impact of a lack of resources, capacity, and infrastructure on journalism education (Wasserman, 2005).

For journalism education to continue to demonstrate its relevance in both its profile and practice, it needs to ensure continuous innovation in the world of new media. There is wide agreement that future South African newsmakers need to be conversant with new technologies, which, among other things, will help them gather, process, and distribute information. Beyond understanding these technologies, journalists also need to understand the ethical implications of using them (Banda et al., 2007). Although this is problematic in terms of resources and access to new media in many parts of the country, most journalism schools are aware that they need to broaden their range of educational and training sections and, perhaps, their range of students. For example, apart from longstanding journalism undergraduate and graduate degrees up to the doctoral and post-doctoral level, more and more mid-career courses are offered to professional journalists seeking to upgrade their qualifications and to obtain new skills (Jones & Pitcher, 2010).

In terms of political and social transformation, the emerging journalism education discourse is also defining an academic identity for journalism education as "extricating itself from dependency on Western-orientated models of journalism education and training" (Banda et al., 2007, p. 156). South African journalism educators, therefore, (Dube, 2010)

> do not take de-Westernisation to mean a complete removal of Western philosophies and epistemologies from the journalism curricula. Nor do they view Africanisation as adopting black people's cultural values and norms [only, but rather] that Africa's diversity in terms of culture, languages, and norms should inform the Africanisation process. (p. 1)

Academics and journalists alike often argue that the media have a critical role to play in fostering their own maturation. In a higher education context, journalism is located at the nexus of intellectual knowledge and vocational training—demands that are frequently reduced to a crude dichotomy of theory versus practice (Prinsloo, 2010). This dichotomy is especially evident when examining various training institutes around the country. A divide is evident between the number of private colleges offering journalism training and traditional universities with more holistic bachelor and graduate degrees in media and journalism studies. This contrast could be considered one of the greatest dilemmas facing South African journalism education today.

Universities tend to create an environment that teaches both vocational and critical skills. They often incorporate aspects of other disciplines to ensure that students acquire a broad understanding of the socio-political environment within which journalism and media studies is situated. Private colleges, on the other hand, are less concerned with this approach and concentrate on teaching students only the skills necessary in a professional newsroom. In addition, they tend to offer more desirable services to students, including small classes and a constantly tutored environment, made possible by higher fees and quicker student turnover. Editors, however, claim that universities offering a broad liberal arts approach, coupled with specialized journalism training, create the best candidates to train in a real-world journalism environment since they generally possess a more balanced experience and theoretical background (De Beer & Steyn, 2002; Motloung, 2007).

As mentioned earlier, South Africa has also seen a marked increase in the number of community radio stations and tabloid-sized community newspapers. This challenges media educators to incorporate these entities into their curricula, helping future journalists engage critically from a development-communication perspective. The current emphasis on tabloid-style journalism is a move away from traditionally Western-centric broadsheet journalism (Banda et al., 2007).

Hochheimer's (2001) call for the teaching of a "journalism of meaning," whereby journalism curricula need to be embedded in students' own historical, cultural, and social experiences, does not reach outside the walls of South Africa's university education. In recent years a more functionalist approach has become especially apparent in a plethora of private institutions that offer a number of diplomas and short certificate courses concentrating on journalism practice and training. Such vocational schools adopt a more practical approach in their material and equip students with skills that facilitate practical market-related journalism techniques, thus deviating from the media studies approach that some of the more traditional research universities have adopted.

Only the future will tell whether professional journalism education, be it at universities or universities of technology, will "largely become driven by industrial and commercial imperatives, rather than the more civic-minded and critical approach" (Banda et al., 2007, p. 165). It is also difficult to predict what influence the present adversarial relationship between the ANC government and the print media will have on journalism education. There is some concern that journalism educators have done little until now to address the government's eminent threat of curtailing freedom of information.

Journalism Research[2]

Journalism research in South Africa tends to focus on the state and quality of contemporary journalism, such as the representation of race in the media (Wasserman, 2010a; Motsaathebe, 2011). In addition, issues such as journalism ethics, regulation, and self-regulation in a democracy are increasingly topics of investigation. This is a response to government threats against the media and the expectation that the media should "get its house in order" (Wasserman & De Beer, 2004). In a very limited way, journalism research acts as a precautionary measure against increased government threats of censorship by constantly highlighting negative government sentiment.

As mentioned earlier, there is also research interest in the Africanization of journalism and the need to find indigenous epistemologies to guide journalism education, research, practice, and regulation (Fourie, 2008; Dube, 2010; Motsaathebe, 2011).

While some South African researchers' publications can be compared with the best in the world (Fourie, 2008), only a very small number of journalism researchers have made their mark in Western, international, peer-reviewed journals and books. This is partly due to South Africa's educational subsidy system, which only acknowledges research output in journals listed in the World of Science (ISI: Humanities and Social Science) and IBSS (International Bibliography of the Social Sciences) lists. Book chapters (and even textbooks themselves) attract little state research subsidies.

While historically most journalism research in South Africa was either descriptive or quantitative in nature (De Beer, 2000, 2008), there has recently been an increased focus on critical media studies, discourse, and semiotic studies (e.g., Botma, 2010; Fourie, 1991; Wasserman, 2010a).

Given the relatively small number of active journalism, media studies, and communication studies researchers in South Africa, the country has a rather strong presence in national and international peer-reviewed journals. These include the following:

❑ *African Journalism Studies (AJS,* previously *Ecquid Novi: African Journalism Studies)* (ISI listed),

---

2 The authors wish to thank Pieter J. Fourie, University of South Africa, as a large part of this section is based on his earlier contribution to this chapter.

❑ *Communicatio: South African Journal for Communication Theory and Research,*

❑ *Critical Arts: A Journal of Cultural Studies* (ISI listed),

❑ *Communicare: Journal for Communication Sciences in Southern Africa,*

❑ *Communitas: Journal for Community Communication,*

❑ *Global Media Journal-Africa,* and

❑ *Rhodes Journalism Review* (not blind-reviewed).[3]

Generally, the media industry does not seem to be interested in academic research projects focused on journalism. It seems to remain aloof about academic research, and university researchers normally have to apply for funding through the National Research Foundation. An exception to the rule was the landmark journalism skills audit by De Beer and Steyn (2002), funded by the South African National Editors' Forum (Sanef).

The state and quality of contemporary South African journalism are often the basis of research for master's and doctoral studies, the results of which seldom, if ever, make it into the media or its agenda. Moreover, few journalists choose to write for journalism-based research journals or even subscribe to academic journals that focus on their profession (De Beer, et al., 2016).

Professional Connections in Journalism Education

Most journalism educators agree that journalism education and training cannot be taught in an academic vacuum and that industry links are crucial. Most university programs, as already mentioned, attempt to dovetail *conceptual education* and *practical training* to produce capable entry-level journalists. Tertiary institutions increasingly have to balance the need for theoretical depth in education with the industry's need for highly skilled junior journalists who can operate effectively in a converging, multimedia newsroom.

Over the years, two elements in particular have caused reason for

3   These research journals are also associated with some of the main university departments of communication, journalism, media, and cultural studies at institutions, including the University of Cape Town, University of KwaZulu-Natal, University of South Africa, University of Johannesburg, University of the Free State, Stellenbosch University, and Rhodes University.

concern in the interaction between journalism academia and journalism practice: namely limited resources and an oversupply of communication students seeking work in the field of journalism.

Many tertiary institutions lack the resources to maintain a properly functioning multimedia classroom environment for practical education and training. Only a handful of the institutions with a journalism focus are able to emphasize experiential learning. The few that do so usually prescribe internships that range from undergraduate work placement requirements (about 160 hours) to optional short-course, four-week programs.

Universities of technology and private colleges tend to have the necessary infrastructure to allow a compulsory internship, ranging from six months to a year. These internships are usually evaluated by the host company. As part of the curriculum, some institutions also have regular guest lecturers from industry to help bridge the gap between theory and practice. The journalism school at Rhodes University is well-known for the substantial financial support it receives from the South African media industry and other financial organizations, especially U.S. and European donors.

Journalism Education's Professional Impact

The impact of journalism education in South Africa reaches much further than simply the field of journalism. Due to the broad nature of many "journalism" programs, as well as a downsizing of the number of journalists employed, thousands of graduates with media and communication majors seek jobs every year—a perceived oversupply. As a result, many of these students gain employment in government and private sectors. They work as press liaison officers in the field of marketing and corporate communication or in public relations, social media, or marketing departments. A recent study of 2014 graduates in four-year degree programs at the University of KwaZulu-Natal's Pietermaritzburg campus found that out of 16 journalism graduates, three gained employment as journalists, six in social media and marketing, and five continued to pursue master's degrees. In addition, one student obtained a government position and another became a rugby coach (Jones, 2015). Although the population for this study is small, such post-graduation breakdowns seem representative of employment for journalism and communication graduates across the country. Students tend to consider their degrees "beneficial" if they gain employment of any kind. And many professional journalists are returning to universities to pursue graduate degrees for career enhancement, as well as to broaden their employment possibilities (Jones, 2015).

Future Possibilities

When contemplating future directions for journalism education in South Africa, journalism educators, like their worldwide counterparts, need to respond to the realities of their immediate environment. In doing so, two issues are paramount.

First, editors increasingly require journalists who can operate in ever-changing newsroom environments without much additional training. However, as mentioned earlier, university departments often lack the necessary infrastructure and resources to prepare journalists for this task. Some departments have overcome this challenge by using affordable mobile technologies instead of expensive infrastructure when training students in newsgathering. Stassen (2010) promotes this approach and posits that, in addition to mobile literacy, social media literacy is now an essential element of journalism and, subsequently, journalism education. South African educators therefore attempt to integrate these aspects into their teaching about newsgathering, news checking, and news dissemination.

Second, journalism educators need to be concerned with the vast number of citizens lacking both sufficient high school education and knowledge due to the country's apartheid past. A stronger knowledge base is needed, "one that includes a nuanced understanding of the global economy and the interests it serves, as well as of the histories from which we, and other southern countries, emerge" (Prinsloo, 2010, p. 197). In order to put this knowledge into context, it is important for South African educators to use examples of journalistic best practices at home and in other African countries rather than Western countries. In addition, journalists need to speak and write in indigenous languages in order to reflect post-apartheid industry needs and demands.

Journalism Education Issues, Challenges, and Innovations

Over the last two decades, South African journalists and educators have not only had to reorient their professional practices and identities in relation to a shifting political landscape, but have also had to adapt to rapid technological changes in global media. These developments are sometimes seen as threats to traditional journalism. They are also accompanied by questions about the future of journalism, especially in a country where most new media technologies, apart from mobile phones, are still only affordable (and therefore accessible) to a small percentage of the population.

As previously discussed, academics and journalism professionals are often divided on how journalism education should be practiced, despite the various opportunities for collaboration that South African journalism associations and organizations offer (see Table 8.1 for a list of major media organizations). However, Goodman's (2007, 2014) World Journalism Education Congress (WJEC) reports have highlighted a conscious effort by academics to embrace the realities of the journalism profession. "[In] the new digital age future journalists [. . .] need to be highly adaptable and media literate, technology savvy, and able to conduct complex searches via a wide array of data bases" (Goodman, 2007, p. 12). Yet, part of the difficulty many South African universities have implementing this idea is limited access to new media technology. Oates (2008, p. 164) reinforces this point by highlighting that Internet access "is overwhelmingly the privilege of the wealthiest citizens in the most advanced democracies." Many students entering universities do not have new media literacy knowledge due to inadequate secondary school education. As a result, educators are often forced to forgo innovative, hands-on teaching and to focus instead on new media literacy. Although this gap is closing, particularly from a mobile communication perspective, inequality in new media accessibility has significant implications.

Educators are, however, employing innovative schemes to bridge such divides by creating easier transitions from rural secondary schools (with often heavy indigenous populations) to higher education. For instance, some universities have adopted indigenous language programs that encourage educators and students to learn and interact in some of the country's most widely spoken African languages, including isiZulu.

Such innovations are reshaping how journalism schools train students to deal with an ever-changing society, let alone the journalism profession.

Conclusion: Educating Tomorrow's Journalists—The Big Picture

South Africa's current uncertain political climate (Thornton, 2014), together with a steady decrease in print circulation (Moodie, 2015) and threats to journalistic independence (Harber, 2014; Du Preez, 2015), are encouraging journalism educators to combine African experiences with rapidly changing social media and technological developments. Of further importance, educators must be cognizant of the economic realities of the journalism profession so they can create a curriculum that is both relevant for a new generation of journalists and the changing media environment (see Table 8.2 for a list of journalism education and training institutions). Moreover, educators need to introduce measures to combat the lack of media literacy, global and general knowledge lacking in the majority of first-year university students (De Beer & Steyn, 2002). They must also emphasize the need for multi-linguicism in both a South African and an African context. While journalism educators will have to remain responsive to these new challenges, they are also faced with imparting critical knowledge and critical thinking skills to combat threats to media freedom. Budding journalists also need to be aware of the challenges that lie ahead as they enter the profession. As Harber (2014) points out, in South Africa individuals have always needed to assert their agency in newsrooms to protect journalism from the ravages of interfering owners, shareholders, and government officials. In light of this reality, perhaps the most important challenge for South African journalism education is that of fostering individual critical thought.

References

Banda, F., Bukes-Amiss, C. M., Bosch, T., Mano, W., McLean, P., & Stengel, L. (2007). Contextualizing journalism education and training in Southern Africa. *Ecquid Novi: African Journalism Studies, 28*(1-2), 156-175.

BDlive (2013, June 18). Irish parent approves Independent News & Media SA sale. *Business Day.* Retrieved from http://www.bdlive.co.za/national/media/2013/06/17/irish-parent-approves-independent-news-media-sa-sale

Botma, G. J. (2010). Lightning strikes twice: The 2007 Rugby World Cup and memories of a South African rainbow nation. *Communicatio: South African Journal for Communication Theory and Research*, *36*(1), 1-20.

Botma, G. (2011). Going back to the crossroads: Visions of a democratic media future at the dawn of the new South Africa. *Ecquid Novi: African Journalism Studies*, *32*(2), 75-89.

Christians, C. G., Glasser, T. L., McQuail, D., Nordenstreng, K., & White, R. A. (2009). *Normative theories of the media: Journalism in democratic societies*. Chicago, IL: University of Illinois Press.

Cronin, J. (2010). Liberals or the Left—who are the real defenders of our constitution? *Umsebenzi Online, 9*(20). Retrieved from http://www.sacp.org. za/main.php?include=pubs/umsebenzi/2010/vol9-20.html

Daniels, G. (2013). State of the newsroom 2013: Disruptions and transition. Retrieved from http://www.journalism.co.za

De Beer, A. S. (Ed.) (2000). Focus on media and racism. Special edition of *Ecquid Novi, 21*(2), 153-278.

De Beer, A. S. (2008). South African journalism research. Challenging paradigmatic schism and finding a foothold in an era of globalization. In M. Loffelholz, D. Weaver, & A. Schwarz (Eds.), *Global journalism research. Theories, methods, findings, future* (pp. 185-196). Malden, MA: Wiley Publishers.

De Beer, A. S., Beckett, S., Malila, V., & Wasserman, H. (2016). Binary opposites—can South African journalists be both watchdogs and developmental journalists? *Journal of African Media Studies, 8*(1), 35-53.

De Beer, A. S., & Steyn, E. (2002). Sanef's 2002 South African National Journalism Skills Audit. *Ecquid Novi: African Journalism Studies*, *23*(1), 11-86.

De Beer, A. S., & Tomaselli, K. (2000). South African journalism and mass communication scholarship: Negotiating ideological schisms. *Journalism Studies, 1*(1), 9-35.

Du Preez, M. (2015, January 15) A letter to Karima Brown. *Daily Maverick*. Retrieved from http://www.dailymaverick.co.za/opinionista/2015-01-15-a-letter-to-karima-brown/#.VOWHOjhWHIU

Dube, B. (2010, July). Africanising journalism curricula: the perceptions of southern African journalism scholars. Paper presented at the World Journalism Education Conference. Rhodes University, South Africa.

Fourie, P. J. (1991). *Media, mites, metafore en die kommunikasie van apartheid* [Media, myths, metaphors and the communication of apartheid]. *Communicatio: South African Journal for Communication Theory and Research, 17*(1), 2-7.

Fourie, P. J. (2008). Ubuntuism as a framework for South African media practice and performance. Can it work? *Communicatio: South African Journal for Communication Theory and Research, 34*(1), 53-79.

Goodman, R. (2007). The World Journalism Education Congress' syndicate reports: Practical tips for improving journalism education today. *International Communication Bulletin, 42*(3-4), 48-58.

Goodman, R. (2014). World Journalism Education Congress explores methods for renewing journalism through education. Retrieved from http://www.wjec.be/2014/05/insights-wjec3-article

Hachten, W. A., & Giffard, C. A. (1984). *The press and apartheid: Repression and propaganda in South Africa.* Madison, WI: Wisconsin University Press.

Hallin, D., & Mancini, P. (2004). *Comparing media systems: Three models of media and politics.* London: Cambridge University Press.

Harber, A. (2014). Space for independent, critical media is under siege. Retrieved from http://www.bizcommunity.com/Article/196/466/121082.html

Hochheimer, J. L. (2001). Journalism education in Africa: From critical pedagogical theory to meaning-based practice. *Critical Arts, 15*(1&2), 97-116.

Jones, N. (2015). *The University of KwaZulu-Natal's Media and Cultural Studies Postgraduate students' employment trends 2013 and 2014* (Unpublished manuscript). Department of Media and Cultural Studies, University of KwaZulu-Natal, Pietermaritzburg, South Africa.

Jones, N., & Pitcher, S. (2010). Traditions, conventions and ethics: online dilemmas in South African journalism. In N. Hyde-Clarke (Ed.), *The citizen of communication* (pp. 97-114). Claremont: Juta.

Malila, V. (2014). ANC's critique of the media. Understanding media diversity in 20 years of democracy. *Rhodes Journalism Review, 34,* 13-16.

McQuail, D. (2010). *McQuail's mass communication theory.* London: Sage.

Moodie, G. (2015). ABC circulation 10-year comparison: how the mighty have fallen. Retrieved from http://www.biznews.com/grubstreet/knowledge/2015/02/19/abc-circulation-10-year-comparison-mighty-fallen/

Motloung, M. (2007, October 16). The best journalism schools in SA. *The Mail & Guardian.* Retrieved from http://mg.co.za/article/2007-10-16-the-best-journalism-schools-in-sa

Motsaathebe, G. (2011). Journalism education and practice in South Africa and the discourse of the African Renaissance. *Communicatio: South African Journal for Communication Theory and Research, 37*(3), 381-397.

Oates, S. (2008). *Introduction to media and politics.* London: Sage.

Pitcher, S., & Jones, N. (2014) *Measuring journalists' expectations in the newsroom.* (Unpublished manuscript). Department of Media and Cultural Studies, University of KwaZulu-Natal, Pietermaritzburg, South Africa.

Prinsloo, J. (2010). Journalism education in South Africa: Shifts and dilemmas. *Communicatio: South African Journal for Communication Theory and Research, 36*(2), 185-199.

Rabe, L. (Ed.). (2015). *'n Konstante revolusie: Naspers, Media24 en oorgange* [A constant revolution: Napsers, Media24 and Transition]. Cape Town: Tafelberg.

Reid, J. (2013, October 22). No big debate: the SABC, censorship and more censorship on Media Freedom Day. *The Daily Maverick*. Retrieved from http://www.dailymaverick.co.za/opinionista/2013-10-22-no-big-debate-the-sabc-censorship-and-more-censorship-on-media-freedom-day/#.VOWDeThWHIU

Searle, R., & McKenna, S. (2013). Teaching excellence in a transforming South Africa. In A. Skelton (Ed.), *International perspectives on teaching excellence in higher education: Improving knowledge and practice* (pp. 103-117). London: Routledge.

Skelton, A. (Ed.). (2013). *International perspectives on teaching excellence in higher education: Improving knowledge and practice*. London: Routledge.

Stassen, W. (2010). Your news in 140 characters: exploring the role of social media in journalism. *Global Media Journal—Africa Edition, 4*(1), 116-131.

Swart, W. (2008, December 18). Zuma sues for R7m over Zapiro cartoon. *The Times*. Retrieved from http://www.thetimes.co.za/News/Article.aspx?id=906946

Teer-Tomaselli, R., & Tomaselli, K. (2001). Transformation, nation-building and the South African Media, 1993-1999. In K. Tomaselli & H. Dunn (Eds.), *Media, democracy, and renewal in Southern Africa* (pp. 123-150). Colorado Springs, CO: International Academic.

Thamm, M. (2015, January 13). True colours shining through: Should journalists be draping themselves in party political colours? *Daily Maverick*. Retrieved from http://www.dailymaverick.co.za/opinionista/2015-01-13-true-colours-shining-through-should-journalists-be-draping-themselves-in-party-political-colours/#.VOWIDDhWHIU

University of KwaZulu-Natal. (2011). *University of KwaZulu-Natal*. Retrieved from http://celcat.ukzn.ac.za/ccattimetable/2011/PMB/LANs/rindex.xhtml

Thornton, G. (2014). Critical skills shortages, rising crime, political instability and poor government service delivery continue to dampen SA business growth. *Grant Thornton*. Retrieved from http://www.gt.co.za/news/2014/03/critical-skills-shortages-rising-crime-political-instability-and-poor-government-service-delivery-continue-to-dampen-sa-business-growth/

Wasserman, H. (2005). Journalism education as transformative praxis. *Ecquid Novi, 26*(2),159-174.

Wasserman, H. (2010a). *Tabloid journalism in South Africa*. Bloomington, IN: Indiana University Press.

Wasserman, H. (2010b). Political journalism in South Africa as a developing democracy—understanding media freedom and responsibility in the relationship between government and the media. *Communicatio: South African Journal for Communication Theory and Research, 36*(2), 240-251.

Wasserman, H., & De Beer, A. S. (2004, April). *A fragile affair: an overview of the relationship between the media and state in post-apartheid South Africa.* Paper presented at Ethics 2000 Colloquium "Media, Ethics and Politics," University of Missouri, Missouri.

Wasserman, H., & De Beer, A. S. (2012). A fragile affair: The relationship between the mainstream media and government in post-apartheid South Africa. *Journal of Media Ethics, 20*(2-3), 192-208.

Wigston, D. (2007). History of South African media. In P. Fourie (Ed.), *Media studies: Media history, media and society.* (pp. 4-58). Cape Town: Juta.

Table 8.1

Major Media Organizations in South Africa

Organization	Description	Websites
Broadcasting Complaints Commission of South Africa (BCCSA)	An independent body to regulate South Africa's broadcast industry.	http://www.bccsa.co.za
Freedom of Expression Institute (FXI)	A not-for-profit, nongovernmental organization that protects and fosters the right to freedom of expression.	http://fxi.org.za/home
Institute for Media Analysis in South Africa (iMASA)	An academic research and publication organization based in Stellenbosch, South Africa, involved in national and international media research and publication projects.	http://www.imasa.org
The Independent Communications Authority of South Africa (ICASA)	The regulator for the South African communications, broadcasting, and postal services sector.	www.icasa.org.za
Media Development and Diversity Agency (MDDA)	A government organization set up to assist historically disadvantaged communities and persons not adequately served by the media to gain access to the media.	http://www.mdda.org.za
Media Institute of Southern Africa (MISA)	An organization that promotes independence, pluralism, and diversity of views and opinions, media sustainability, competency, and professionalism in the Southern African region.	http://www.misa.org
ProJourn Professional Journalists' Association	Defends the rights of working journalists in their professional work and in their reflection of the voices of the public whom they serve.	http://projourn.yolasite.com
Campaign: South Africa's first post-apartheid freedom of expression and access to information movement (Right-2Know)	A coalition of organizations and people who promote the free flow of information.	http://www.r2k.org.za
South African Communication Association (SACOMM)	A professional association that represents academics from around Southern Africa working in communications and related fields.	http://www.sacomm.org.za
The Southern African Freelancers' Association (SAFREA)	Home to hundreds of media professionals, including writers, editors, photographers, designers, and videographers.	http://www.safrea.co.za

Table 8.1 (cont.)

Major Media Organizations in South Africa

Organization	Description	Website
South African National Editors' Forum (SANEF)	A nonprofit organization whose members are editors, senior journalists, and journalism trainers from all areas of the South African media. It acts as a spokesperson for its members in dealings with government.	http://www.sanef.org.za
SASJA The South African Science Journalists' Association	An association of science media professionals and a registered nonprofit organization.	http://sasja.org
South African Press Council	An independent mechanism to the behavior of the press.	http://www.press-council.org.za
Journalism South Africa	Facebook page.	https://www.facebook.com/groups/25601192554
SA Journos from the '70s, '80s, and '90s – and beyond	Facebook page.	https://www.facebook.com/
Professional Journalists' Association	Facebook page.	https://www.facebook.com/groups/72213329417
Klaaswaarzegger Nou	Facebook page on journalism research and related topics in Afrikaans.	https://www.facebook.com/groups/Klaas-WaarzeggerNou

Table 8.2

Major Journalism Education and Training Institutions in South Africa

Organization	Websites
Cape Peninsula University of Technology	http://www.cput.ac.za/
CityVarsity	http://www.cityvarsity.co.za
Damelin	http://www.damelin.co.za/
Durban University of Technology	http://www.dut.ac.za/
Free State University	http://www.humanities.ufs.ac.za
Monash University South Africa	http://www.monash.ac.za/
Nelson Mandela Metropolitan University	http://www.nmmu.ac.za
North-West University	http://www.nwu.ac.za
Rhodes University	http://www.ru.ac.za/jms
Stellenbosch University	http://www.sun.ac.za/journalism
Tshwane University of Technology	http://www.tut.ac.za/
Unisa: University of South Africa	http://www.unisa.ac.za
University of Cape Town	http://www.uct.ac.za
University of Fort Hare	http://www.ufh.ac.za/
University of Johannesburg	http://www.uj.ac.za/
University of KwaZulu-Natal	http://www.mecs.ukzn.ac.za
University of Pretoria	http://www.up.ac.za
University of Witwatersrand	http://www.wits.ac.za
Varsity College	http://www.varsitycollege.co.za

9

The United Kingdom Juggles Training and Education: Squeezed Between the Newsroom and Classroom

Chris Frost

The United Kingdom is a relatively small country with a population of about 60 million. It has a strong tradition of news consumption encouraging a strongly competitive media industry. As a country, its physically small size has enabled the early growth of national newspapers and magazines that have helped define its style of journalism. Broadcasting started in the 1920s, with TV launching in the mid-1930s—continuing after World War II through The British Broadcasting Corporation (BBC). Journalism training was carried out on the job in newspapers through the first two thirds of the 20th century. It only moved into universities and colleges of "further education"—colleges structured to provide those leaving school at 16 with limited qualifications via a variety of trade courses—in the 1970s and 1980s. First came postgraduate diplomas and then, from the early 1990s, came undergraduate programs. These programs quickly grew, and now more than 70 universities and 20 colleges of further education run programs in journalism of various types.

Staff teaching journalism, particularly the more practical elements, are usually recruited from the industry. Since few such teachers have graduate school qualifications, they have found it difficult to start their research careers. On the contrary, many teachers conducting research are not former journalists and are hired because of their knowledge and research background in media. This has led to an undesirable split between practitioners and scholars.

Journalism in the Media Landscape

Journalism started in the United Kingdom shortly after the introduction of printing with polemic broadsheets circulating among the growing middle classes based in local business and launched by entrepreneurs. By the start of the 20th century, newspaper circulations were high as the working class and the growing middle class developed reading skills. Journalism was considered an important part of political and social life, underpinning a media system as advanced as anywhere in the world.

Journalism in the United Kingdom is a mature industry based on the Western, liberal tradition. It has a newspaper history that reaches back to the invention of printing in Europe. Today it has 12 daily national newspapers and 12 Sunday newspapers with circulation figures varying from just over 171,000 for *The Guardian,* a quality paper aimed at educated professionals, to 1.8 million for *The Sun,* an infamous tabloid (Press Gazette, 2015). These circulation figures confirm significant declines in circulation over the past 20 years.

The magazine industry in the United Kingdom is also strong, probably stronger than newspapers at the present in terms of circulation. While some magazines are losing circulation and switching to online publication only, the teenage girl market is a good example, others are gaining circulation. However, it is clear that Web editions are becoming more important for all publications, and several big magazines have closed or ended their print editions in the past year (Press Gazette, 2013).

The United Kingdom converted completely to digital broadcasting in 2012, offering free access to about 70 video and 20 audio channels. In addition, there are a number of subscription channels through cable, internet, video-on-demand, and satellite. The BBC, the main public service broadcaster, is funded by a license fee of £145.50 annually (U.S. $244.20) paid by all households that own a TV set. The BBC transmits six TV channels and seven radio channels, plus a number of specialist channels for music, Asian audiences, Welsh speakers, and children. All other TV channels, such as ITV and Channel 4, are commercially funded by sponsorship, subscription, or advertising. Many are specialist (cooking, lifestyle, shopping, etc.), while others offer reruns and movies. Although BSkyB, which trades as Sky, is the United Kingdom's major satellite channel, it also offers several of its general entertainment channels on Freeview (terrestrial digital broadcasting).

Virtually the whole country has access to broadband—at least 20 Mb with much of it moving to fiber optic and speeds of up to 100 Mb—with only remote, sparsely populated rural areas having to rely on dial-up. Consequently, Internet channels are a major source of news for many people, and virtually all newspapers, magazines, and broadcast channels have an associated news website. In addition, smart phones are widely used, and many people access news on them along with TV or movies.

The United Kingdom takes press freedom seriously and believes that journalism exists to hold the powerful to account and to inform the public about what is happening in their communities. Campaigning for press freedom started early in the development of journalism. While the authorities heavily controlled the first newspapers, press freedom became widespread in the United Kingdom from the mid-19th century, with parliament allowing full reporting of its debates and the abolition of restrictive newspaper taxes. Although press freedom is not guaranteed under a constitution or specific statute, the Human Rights Act of 1998 guarantees freedom of expression and, by extension, media freedom. However, a number of statute limitations exist in the United Kingdom, including those on defamation, the reporting of crime, and restrictions applied to court coverage to ensure the presumption of innocence and fair trials. International treaties on copyright also apply, as do European regulations on data protection, freedom of information, and counter terrorism.

The United Kingdom has recently gone through a particularly difficult period facing not just a collapse of circulation and advertising but a serious scandal in which journalists bribed police officers and hacked phones of the newsworthy. The scandal started at the *News of the World,* a tabloid Sunday paper owned by Rupert Murdoch's former News International media conglomerate, now News UK. A report issued by the Information Commissioner's Office in 1996 had already found that most national newspapers had been employing private detectives to access mobile phones and other private information, such as bank accounts and health records. But since such activities were believed to impact only a small number of celebrities, the public accepted News International's assurances that these were the work of one rogue reporter, who was subsequently jailed for phone hacking. However, with the exposure of many more such events involving the families of murder victims and others in vulnerable positions, the public's anger exploded. Murdoch closed the *News of the World* and restructured his holdings. The government set up a public inquiry in July 2011, The Leveson Inquiry, to examine the "culture, practices and ethics of the press" (GOV.UK, 2011). The inquiry recommended a new press regulation body and other changes in the working practices of journalists, police officers, and politicians.

Professional Characteristics

Few journalists in the United Kingdom consider journalism to be a "profession" rather than a trade. While wanting to be professional, journalists in the United Kingdom see journalism as an occupation or craft (see Table 9.1 for a list of journalism associations and organizations). Accordingly, they often dismiss training and education as unnecessary. This partly comes from the fear such training would become a compulsory precursor to the registration or licensing of journalists by the state, something that has consistently been rejected in the United Kingdom. British journalists generally prefer the more romantic idea of being seen as a raffish maverick answerable to no one (Cole, 1998):

> It is a peculiar aspect of the hack's [journalist's] character that he (it almost always is 'he') feels the need to reduce an activity requiring very great skill to accomplish well to something so easy it can be achieved to maximum effect when roaring drunk. (p. 65)

Although it is doubtful many such journalists still exist, British anti-intellectualism, combined with a fear of state control through license registration, have strongly inhibited universities' attempts to develop journalism education (see Table 9.2 for a sample of university journalism programs).

The Office of National Statistics estimates that the number of journalists in the United Kingdom, as of August 2015, is 64,000 (depending on one's definition of "journalist"; Office for National Statistics, n.d.). This seems a relatively high number when compared with many other countries. For example, the U.S. Department of Labor estimates there were 54,400 reporters, correspondents, and broadcast news analysts working in the United States as of 2014 (United States Department of Labor, 2015). The United Kingdom figure includes not only reporters and correspondents but also editors and content managers. The number of traditional journalism jobs in newspapers has been falling over the past 10 years, and many have been replaced by editorial content management jobs on social media websites.

A journalist in the United Kingdom is typically in his late twenties or early thirties, a college graduate, and has been in the job for approximately four years. He typically earns £23,254 annually (U.S. $39,489; Office for National Statistics, 2015). In comparison, the median wage of reporters in the United States as of 2014 is U.S. $37,200 (Office for National Statistics, 2015). Most U.K. university journalism programs now report their student intake to be about 65%-70% female. British journalists believe that journalism has a social role, that journalists are here to "inform society about itself and make public that which would otherwise be private" (Harcup, 2004, p. 2) and "capture the beginnings of the truth" (Randall, 2000, p. 1). However, few of them are naive enough to believe this is their only role. The BBC's mission statement, which follows, probably comes closer to the everyday working lives of most journalists (print, broadcast, or online): Journalism's role is to "enrich people's lives with programmes and services that inform, educate and entertain" (BBC, 2016).

Journalism Education, Professional Training, and Research

Systematic, formal journalistic training and education outside the workplace was established in the United Kingdom only around 35 years ago. Although in the 19th century such training was non-existent in the workplace, some thought was given to its development. In 1890, one of the first books about journalism was published, titled *Newspaper Reporting: In Olden Times and To-day*. It shined light on reporting in the early days of newspapers, before the motor car (Pendleton, 1890):

> One of the most detestable of reporting experiences is to attend a similar political meeting far away and be obliged

to get back the same night. It is head-aching, eye-straining work for the reporter to transcribe his shorthand notes, for instance, in the guard's van of a fish train jolting over forty miles of railway, especially when he is expected at the office soon after midnight with his copy 'written up' ready to hand to the printers. (p. 188)

Shorthand was an important skill for such early reporters, and today's trainers and newspaper editors still consider it so. It therefore has a surprisingly strong place in British university courses, often to the bemusement of academics from other disciplines and many journalism academics abroad.

Teaching and Training Future Newsmakers

While journalists in the 19th century took their work seriously, no particular skills were required of them other than a reasonable general education and shorthand. Technology was limited to the telegraph and a horse-drawn coach, and much reporting focused on verbatim coverage of speeches or debates. Neither journalism ethics (Frost, 2011, p. 2) nor formal training or education for journalists was a consideration at that time.

In 1919, London University started a diploma in journalism with courses in practical journalism, English composition, and electives in politics, economics, literature, history, and modern languages. Carr and Stevens (1931, pp. 10-11) were much impressed with the curriculum: "The lecture courses are comprehensive and that in practical journalism is one of great utility to the journalistic beginner." However, the London University journalism curriculum did not survive World War II (Bundock, 1957).

In 1950, Lord Kemsley, a publisher, argued it was time to take a more serious approach to journalistic training. He launched the Kemsley Editorial Plan, an ambitious training program that developed talent within his newspaper group. Elsewhere, journalists often learned shorthand in night classes at local colleges, working as a secretary on the side for shorthand tuition. They also studied media law and politics. But practical journalism skills were usually taught on the job, either in Kemsley-like newspaper programs or the more common apprenticeships run by his competitors. In such apprenticeships, newspapers trained young people (typically men), who were tied to employment contracts and low wages for up to three years.

The first industry-wide move toward recognizing the need for training came after the 1947-49 Royal Commission, which recommended the improvement of "methods of recruitment, education and training for the profession" (1949, p. 178). Many journalism employers, trade unions, and editors took on this call, overseeing training at newspapers and helping to start the National Council for the Training of Journalists (NCTJ). At this stage, journalism training courses were usually only a few weeks long and sometimes only one day a week for a year for journalism workplace trainees. In the 1980s, the Thatcher government's withdrawal of all direct government funding for industry training led to employers reducing their in-house training and to universities and further education colleges increasing their pre-job journalism courses.

Broadcasting stations had until this time exclusively recruited trained journalists who had worked for newspapers. Now they turned more often to recruits with university post-graduate diplomas, which took a year maximum to earn. That said, they still recruited some industry-trained broadcast journalism students who took advantage of the growth of independent commercial radio channels (and trained in-house), which launched one-year, post-graduate certificate programs. The Broadcast Journalism Training Council (Esser, 2003, p. 220) was formed to accredit such courses.

The new pre-job university journalism courses changed the nature of recruitment in the industry, with employers starting to recruit university graduates with already attained, significant professional skills. This began making in-house training a rarity, although there have been moves to reintroduce on-the-job training with "modern apprenticeships:" programs with limited government funding that one or two newspapers have taken up.

The first journalism undergraduate programs were launched in the United Kingdom in 1991. Three universities were in on this new approach: The University of Central Lancashire, City University, and the London College of Printing. Today, more than 60 institutions offer in excess of 600 varieties of undergraduate journalism programs (UCAS, 2015). Some 155 of them are single honors journalism programs (where students only study modules the journalism department designed or chose to support journalism), while there are a number of combined honors programs (where students double major in two or more subjects). Honors programs in the United Kingdom are three-year undergraduate programs (basically a bachelor's degree). Students who complete and pass a thesis or major project at the end of this program graduate with an honor's degree. However, students may graduate with an ordinary bachelor's degree if they fail the dissertation or project module. There are also dozens of postgraduate courses, most of them training-oriented, designed to teach practical journalism skills to graduates of traditional degree programs.

The arrival of undergraduate programs allowed the expansion of the curriculum, which now included courses in topics such as media law, media history, communications, politics, journalism ethics, human rights, international relations, media regulation, and press freedom. In the past, the one-year university curriculum focused on practical skills. Students spent much of their time learning to write news reports from exercise briefs, and, toward the end of their courses, gathering information for stories. However, law and politics were usually taught in a lecture-style fashion. And, although there was little discussion of ethics, ethical situations were introduced when they arose in practical sessions.

One-year postgraduate programs in journalism were, until recently, popular with graduates who want to train as journalists. Most postgraduate journalism programs in the United Kingdom are essentially "conversion" programs designed to train those with a degree in one subject to learn another. For example, those who had studied history could learn how to be a journalist. There is virtually no demand from employers for master's degrees in the United Kingdom. Accordingly, it is normal for students attending graduate school programs to exit them after six months, once they have earned a postgraduate diploma. If, however, they decide to complete the dissertation module, they can earn a master's degree. Significant reductions in higher education funding, introduced in 2012 by the U.K. government, have put such programs at risk. Academics fear as undergraduate debt increases, applications for postgraduate programs will continue to decrease. The increased undergraduate fee of £9,000 a year (U.S. $15,108), up from £3,000 (U.S. $5,034) in 2011, means that a likely university undergraduate degree debt will approach about £60,000 (U.S. $100,721), including living costs. Undergraduate student debt limits enthusiasm for assuming more debt in postgraduate programs.

While the new undergraduate programs were popular with young people (Hanna & Sanders, 2007, p. 404), employers initially met them with much suspicion. However, the NCTJ's and Broadcast Journalists Training Council's (BJTC) accreditation processes, with their industry involvement, have calmed fears that the new courses would be too theoretical. Now most entrants to journalism in the United Kingdom are graduates, many of them from journalism undergraduate or postgraduate courses. However, some have no journalism background at all. Although the introduction of undergraduate programs allowed an expansion into contextual journalism studies, most journalism courses sought to retain the practical elements of the older training courses. This was partly due to the teaching staff's usually strong industry base and partly to gain and retain NCTJ or BJTC accreditation.

Accreditation is extremely useful for universities in terms of marketing, as editors have told more serious, career-oriented students that accredited courses work best. To be awarded accreditation, universities have to show that their teaching staffs are former journalists and that suitable journalism resources and sufficient practical experience are built into the program, including work placement opportunities. And the NCTJ still insists that programs preparing their students for the National Qualification in Journalism in addition to their degrees should teach shorthand.

University study in U.K. institutions is split into modules in line with the principles of the Bologna process, a European-wide system of degree classification. This is implemented in the United Kingdom with bachelor's degrees being awarded on completion of 360 ECTS credits (120 credits a year). Universities typically split programs into six modules a year to give 18 modules of study over three years. Some Scottish programs are four years in length but usually these lead to a master's degree. Unlike many other countries, U.K. journalism students do not take general liberal arts modules unless specifically designed or chosen by the journalism department. Most journalism undergraduate programs in the United Kingdom split their studies into modules as follows: one third for practical modules; one third for contextual modules, such as media history, media studies, or communications theory; and one third to support modules like media law, ethics, politics, and academic research.

Most programs start the practical modules in their first year with basic news writing and reporting. Their work in this area is then typically developed in the second year, with the addition of some work on production methods for various media. And it is usually finalized in year three with a major project.

A fairly typical final project involves a real-time, simulated working environment (Frost, 2002; Davies, 2014; Heathman & Mathews, 2014). Many courses use simulated newspapers or virtual newsrooms to allow students to develop and criticize their professional skills in a non-threatening environment. Such types of projects are essential as "courses without significant practical elements are not supported by the industry and are therefore not so popular with students" (Frost, 2002, p. 3). Such projects also allow for the relatively easy introduction of new requirements, such as those dealing with social media and mobile technology, without the need to rewrite syllabi and seek university approval every year. Most courses in the United Kingdom also require that students take part in a work placement of up to four weeks with a newspaper or broadcast station.

The integration of professional skills into bachelor's degree programs ensures that graduates will be well prepared for the newsroom. So does the National Certificate Examination, which many newspapers still offer via the NCTJ.

Journalism Research

Most university journalism educators enter academia with practical experience only. Only a few have teaching experience and practical experience. Most new lecturers typically have only an undergraduate degree, although some will have a postgraduate diploma. Institutions normally expect new lecturers in journalism to study for a postgraduate certificate in higher education after they start their first teaching job and then to register for a doctoral degree once they have their diploma. While postgraduate qualifications are not yet compulsory in order to teach in a university, most universities now require new entrants to pursue them. That said, they are likely to become a compulsory requirement over the next few years. Unlike the U.S. tenure system, most U.K. faculty are hired on a permanent basis either full or part-time. Some start work in the academy as visiting lecturers but such contracts are limited by law to two years before staff must be employed on a permanent contract. Journalism lecturers with doctoral degrees are rare. Conflict has developed between journalism lecturers without journalism experience working their way through the academy via academic research and those who have worked as journalists before teaching in the academy (Harcup, 2011, p. 37).

The recent growth in the academic approach to journalism education, caused in part by the development of undergraduate programs, has led to growth in journalism research. Those involved in journalism teaching are now more active in research. There has been a considerable expansion in U.K.-based journalism research over the past 20 years, which is illustrated by a rapid growth in journals that focus on journalism. That said, many established journalism teachers are finding it difficult to get involved in research. Several reasons have been identified for this phenomenon (Errigo & Franklin, 2004; Harcup, 2011; Greenberg, 2007). For example, fear, time, and a lack of training are factors. Such teachers fear that "any topic a mere hackademic generates will be knocked back with scornful disdain, some of which might also be offered by other hackademics" (Errigo & Franklin, 2004, p. 44). In addition, newly appointed journalism teachers struggling to develop new courses and university demands lack time to develop active research agendas. According to one such academic: "My [student] contact hours are about 22 a week, sometimes more if cover is needed, leaving me with very little time to research" (Harcup, 2011, p. 44). The growth of research, no matter how tenuous, has also led to a growth in the number of books about journalism produced over the last 15 years. At the end of the 1980s, there were only a handful of current U.K. books used in journalism courses. Now British academics publish scores of books about journalism each year.

Most new academy hires have limited academic research experience. For most, academic research is a new challenge they take on after getting their first teaching jobs, and many work to gain their master's or doctoral degrees while teaching full time. The research they conduct along the way is used as a springboard to develop their academic research portfolio. Those who do not initially take on research often become more involved in teaching, academic administration, or management. They seek promotions through this route, as such teachers find it nearly impossible to take on the extra burden of research later in their careers. This is a problem for U.K. academics, as many become trapped in a system that prevents them from becoming active researchers. As a result, resentment and competition sometimes builds between those who become active researchers and those that are unable to do so. Those who do manage to build a research and scholarship portfolio are able to seek promotion through the academic route first as a "reader" and then as a "professor," the pinnacle for research-active U.K. scholars.

For all these reasons, journalism research in the United Kingdom is far more limited than it should be. The U.K.'s Association for Journalism Education takes this situation extremely seriously. One of its key roles is to offer research training to members and to develop an understanding of the need for, and importance of, research. It has provided funding for several of the papers cited in this chapter and runs the journal *Journalism Education*. This journal joins several others that have been started over the past 15 years, which offer academics a number of international publishing outlets. Research is growing as the number of academics and their experience grow. Research using qualitative methods is most popular, especially research on ethics, journalism practice, and journalism education.

U.K. academics have their research measured every five years by the Research Excellence Framework (REF), which reviews each university's top researchers' four best projects in each discipline. Journalism submits in a sub-panel with researchers in film studies, media studies, and cultural studies. REF accolades attract income and heighten reputations.

Professional Connections in Journalism Education

Accrediting bodies are important in the United Kingdom, setting standards of journalism education for universities and providing reassurance for students. The NCTJ was the first such body. It is now a registered charity, which has severed its former direct links to employers and trade unions. The NCTJ accredits programs in both adult education (community colleges) and higher education (universities), identifying basic standards and curriculum for journalism courses. Students studying NCTJ-accredited courses are able to take the NCTJ's preliminary exams in journalism practice, media law, public administration, and shorthand. Many editors still identify these as effective industry benchmarks. Once students graduate and are offered jobs at local newspapers, their courses are registered with the NCTJ. Around 18 months later, they can then take the NCTJ's final exams. Successful candidates receive the National Certificate, which can help them get jobs.

Although the BJTC traditionally accredits broadcast courses, it is now looking at multimedia courses. The NCTJ is also trying to introduce a more multimedia-based approach and is accrediting more programs that include a multimedia approach than a simply broadcast one. The BJTC accreditation process concentrates on identifying basic standards of teaching, important resources, and admission profiles, accrediting programs that match its standards. A few other accreditation bodies exist, such as Skillset. Skillset, government initiated to benchmark courses in media and the performing arts, identifies leading deliverers of journalism programs as Media Academies. Finally, The National Union of Journalists, which helped form the NCTJ and BJTC, has been involved in journalism training and education from shortly after World War II. Its representatives still sit on various committees within these bodies and carry out their own professional training.

Journalism Education's Professional Impact

The journalism academy continues to be career-oriented. Jobs are still the main focus of students, their parents, the government, the industry, and university faculty and staff. New government funding regulations require universities to gather and record employment rates. However, in a recession-hit industry, the number of journalism jobs continue to decline. Although now there is some evidence of economic recovery, some institutions have stuck by earlier decisions to reduce the numbers of students in their programs or to close them altogether. However, other universities are building their programs since journalism students are still getting jobs, albeit less traditional. There is regular debate as to whether it is ethical to accept so many students when few traditional journalism jobs still exist. But since many students still want to study journalism, universities continue taking them in.

Future Possibilities

The constantly changing nature of today's journalism industry offers a real challenge to journalism education in the United Kingdom. However, it is a challenge most journalism education institutions seem confident to meet. Most programs' vocational nature and close links with industry, even though they are often at odds with more research/scholarship-oriented callings, are helping them keep students up-to-date and introducing them to changes as they happen. For example, convergence, social networking, Twitter, and other digital innovations are being quickly incorporated into the curriculum.

The United Kingdom is likely to go through its biggest ever changes in journalism education over the next few years. The Murdoch scandal and the Leveson Inquiry have put journalism practices and ethics under the spotlight at the same time government funding for higher education has been severely cut. Journalism in the United Kingdom is bound to change, and journalism education will change with it. The need to address ethical concerns more seriously and to reassure students they are being taught what they will need to know might not result in a wildly different approach to education. But it should result in a more rigorous approach, one strongly supported by an industry and public who now expect much more from journalists.

Journalism Education Issues, Challenges, and Innovations

The big issue for British journalism education continues to be the on-going debate about journalism degrees. Education is split in higher education institutions into undergraduate degrees and postgraduate diplomas, which consist of conversion training courses. Such postgraduate programs, however, are often seen as the flagship programs that leading U.K. schools build their reputations on. However, the rise of undergraduate programs over the past 20 years has confirmed journalism as a solid undergraduate career. Such undergraduate programs have also proven popular with students to the detriment of postgraduate courses. The 2011/12 increase in undergraduate fees suggests that postgraduate programs will suffer even further depredations over the next five years, with 2015/16 being a key academic year as students graduate with higher-than-ever levels of debt.

The industry and, to a lesser extent, the accrediting bodies, heavily influenced by industry, still seek a return to the days when training was carried out on the job. However, since industry is not prepared to pay for such training, it relies on recruiting students graduating from universities or further education colleges. The NCTJ has concentrated largely on postgraduate, further education, and private courses lately, while pulling away from undergraduate programs. It will probably continue to do so unless undergraduate programs start delivering much more vocational than contextual study, thus risking their internal university accreditation. Balancing university requirements to provide a well-rounded, liberal arts education against the industry requirement for an especially vocational, training-oriented curriculum is a constant struggle for undergraduate programs (Hanna & Sanders, 2010).

Conclusion: Educating Tomorrow's Journalists—The Big Picture

As is the case everywhere else, Britain struggles with trying to make money out of journalism in the age of the Internet. While newspaper sales are falling and advertising is migrating to the Internet or direct sales, funding for traditional media is disappearing. The United Kingdom's strong public service broadcasting ethos is currently under attack by a government that would prefer to reduce public service broadcasting's funding and influence. However, consumer magazines remain buoyant, and there is still a market for journalism that is properly packaged. The challenges education faces to support an industry in crisis are clear, and educators seem determined to rise to them.

References

BBC. (2016). Mission and values. Retrieved from http://www.bbc.co.uk/about-thebbc/insidethebbc/whoweare/mission_and_values/

Bundock, C. (1957). *The National Union of Journalists A jubilee history 1907-1957*. Oxford: OUP.

Carr, C. F., & Stevens, F. E. (1931). *Modern journalism: A complete guide to the newspaper craft*. London: Isaac Pitman.

Cole, P. (1998). Instinct, savvy and ratlike cunning: Training local journalists. In B. Franklin & D. Murphy (Eds.), *Making the local news* (pp. 65-79). London: Routledge.

Davies, K. (2014). Tracking Onslow—Taking journalism out of the classroom and the newsroom. *Journalism Education*, 3(1), 88-101.

Errigo, J., & Franklin, B. (2004). Surviving in the Hackademy. *British Journalism Review*, 5(2), 43-48.

Esser, F. (2003). Journalism training in Great Britain: 'A system rich in tradition but currently in transition'. In R. Fröhlich & C. Holtz-Bacha (Eds.). *Journalism education in Europe and North America. An international comparison* (pp. 333-365). New Jersey, NJ: Hampton Press.

Frost, C. (2002). A study of a vocational group learning project. *Journal of Further and Higher Education*, 26(4), 327-337.

Frost, C. (2011). *Journalism ethics and regulation*. London: Pearson.

GOV.UK. (2011, July 20). PM Announces panel for judge-led inquiry and publishes terms of reference. Retrieved from https://www.gov.uk/government/news/pm-announces-panel-for-judge-led-inquiry-and-publishes-terms-of-reference

Greenberg, S. (2007). Theory and practice in journalism education. *Journal of Media Practice*, 8(3), 289-303.

Hanna, M., & Sanders, K. (2007) Journalism education in Britain: Who are the students and what do they want? *Journalism Practice*, 1(3), 404-420.

Hanna, M., & Sanders, K. (2010). Should editors prefer postgraduates? A comparison of United Kingdom undergraduate and postgraduate journalism students. In R. Franklin & D. Mensing (Eds.) *Journalism education, training and employment* (pp. 177-192). London: Routledge.

Harcup, T. (2004). *Journalism principles and practice*. London: Sage.

Harcup, T. (2011). Hackademics at the Chalkface. *Journalism Practice*, 5(1), 34-50.

Heathman, K., & Mathews, J. (2014). Workplace not workshop: student reflections on the introduction of a work-based approach to the final year. *Journalism Education*, 3(1), 8-46.

Office for National Statistics. (2015). Retrieved from http://www.statistics.gov.uk/statbase/Product.asp?vlnk=1951

Pendleton, J. (1890). *Newspaper reporting: In olden times and today*. London: Elliot Stock.

Press Gazette. (August 15, 2013). MAG ABCs: Full circulation round-up for the first half of 2013. Retrieved from http://www.pressgazette.co.uk/magazine-abcs-full-circulation-round-first-half-2013

Press Gazette (July 10, 2015). Press Gazette retrieved from http://www.pressgazette.co.uk/national-newspaper-abcs-june-2015-most-tabloids-suffer-double-digit-declines-sun-reclaims-sunday-top

Randall, D. (2000). *The universal journalist*. London: Pluto Press.

Royal Commission on the Press. (1947-49). London: HMSO.

The Guardian. (2014, July 11). ABCs: National daily newspaper circulation June 2014. Retrieved from http://www.theguardian.com/media/table/2014/jul/11/abcs-national-newspapers

United States Department of Labor. (2015). Reporters, correspondents, and broadcast news analysts. Retrieved from http://www.bls.gov/ooh/media-and-communication/reporters-correspondents-and-broadcast-news-analysts.htm)

UCAS. (2015). UCAS. Retrieved from https://www.ucas.com/

Table 9.1

Major Media Institutions in the United Kingdom

Organization	Description	Websites
Association for Journalism Education (AJE)	Organization of journalism educators in higher education campaigning for better journalism education and research.	www.ajeuk.org
British Broadcasting Corporation (BBC)	Public service broadcaster	www.BBC.co.uk
National Union of Journalists (NUJ)	Trade union representing journalists in the United Kingdom and Ireland.	www.nuj.org.uk
The Office of Communication (Ofcom)	A regulatory body for the broadcast industry set up under a statute to control access to the broadcast spectrum and to regulate content.	www.ofcom.org.uk
Independent Press Standards Organisation (IPSO)	A self-regulatory body funded and controlled by the industry to take complaints from the public about newspaper and magazine content.	www.ipso.co.uk
Regulatory Funding Company	Raises money from industry to fund the IPSO.	www.regulatory-funding.co.uk
European Broadcasting Union (EBU)	An alliance of national broadcasting bodies brought together for mutual benefit.	www.ebu.ch
Defence Press and Broadcasting Advisory Committee	A body of government and media that warns editors of matters of national security. It has no power to censor, but it issues warnings.	https://www.gov.uk/government/organisations/DE-
Campaign for Press and Broadcasting Freedom (CPBF)	Campaign group of individuals and trade unions seeking to ensure a free media.	www.cpbf.org.uk
MediaWise	A charity representing victims of media excesses.	www.mediawise.org.uk
Scottish Newspaper Society	A representative voice for Scotland's newspaper publishers.	www.scotns.org.uk
Broadcast Journalism Training Council (BJTC)	Cross-industry body that accredits journalism training in the United Kingdom.	www.bjtc.org.uk
Professional Publishers Association	The U.K. industry body for magazine publishers.	www.ppa.co.uk
Skillset	Industry body that supports skills and training for people and businesses to ensure U.K. creative industries maintain their world-class position.	www.cratives killset.org

Table 9.1 (cont.)

Major Media Institutions in the United Kingdom

Organization	Description	Websites
National Council for the Training of Journalists (NCTJ)	Charity that accredits journalism training in the United Kingdom.	www.nctj.com
British Society of Editors	A society of more than 400 editors in newspapers, magazines, and broadcasting.	www.societyofedi tors.co.uk
News Media Association	Represents newspaper publishers in England, Wales, and Northern Ireland.	www.newsmedi auk.org

Table 9.2

Universities Offering Journalism Programs in the United Kingdom

Name of the Universities	Websites
Birmingham City University	www.bcu.ac.uk
Bournemouth University	www1.bournemouth.ac.uk
Brunel University	www.brunel.ac.uk
Canterbury Christ Church University	www.canterbury.ac.uk
Cardiff University	www.cardiff.ac.uk
City University	www.city.ac.uk
Coventry University	www.coventry.ac.uk
Cumbria University	www.cumbria.ac.uk
De Montfort University	www.dmu.ac.uk
Edge Hill University	www.edgehill.ac.uk
Glasgow Caledonian University	www.gcu.ac.uk
Glyndwr University	www.glyndwr.ac.uk
Goldsmiths College	www.gold.ac.uk
Kingston University	www.kingston.ac.uk
Leeds Trinity University College	www.leedstrinity.ac.uk
Liverpool John Moores University	www.ljmu.ac.uk
London College of Communication	www.arts.ac.uk
London Metropolitan University	www.londonmet.ac.uk
Napier University	www.napier.ac.uk
Newcastle University	www.ncl.ac.uk
Northampton University	www.northampton.ac.uk
Northumbria University	www.northumbria.ac.uk

Table 9.2 (cont.)

Universities Offering Journalism Programs in the United Kingdom

Name of the Universities	Websites
Nottingham Trent University	www.ntu.ac.uk
Robert Gordon University	www.rgu.ac.uk
Roehampton University	www.roehampton.ac.uk
Sheffield Hallam University	www.shu.ac.uk
Southampton Solent University	www.solent.ac.uk
Staffordshire University	www.staffs.ac.uk
Sunderland University	www.sunderland.ac.uk
The University of Sussex	www.sussex.ac.uk
University College Falmouth	www.falmouth.ac.uk
University of Bedfordshire	www.beds.ac.uk
University of Brighton	www.brighton.ac.uk
University of Central Lancashire	www.uclan.ac.uk
University of Chester	www.chester.ac.uk
University of Derby	www.derby.ac.uk
University of East London	www.uel.ac.uk
University of Glamorgan	www.glam.ac.uk
University of Gloucester	www.glos.ac.uk
University of Hertfordshire	www.herts.ac.uk
University of Huddersfield	www.hud.ac.uk
University of Kent	www.kent.ac.uk
University of Leeds	www.leeds.ac.uk
University of Lincoln	www.lincoln.ac.uk
University of Salford	www.salford.ac.uk
University of Sheffield	www.sheffield.ac.uk
University of Stirling	www.stir.ac.uk
University of Strathclyde	www.strath.ac.uk
University of the West of Scotland	www.uws.ac.uk
University of Ulster	www.ulster.ac.uk
University of West London	www.uwl.ac.uk
University of West of England	www.uwe.ac.uk
University of Westminster	www.westminster.ac.uk
University of Winchester	www.winchester.ac.uk
University of Worcester	www.worcester.ac.uk

10

The Curious Case of U.S. Journalism Education: Shrinking Newsrooms, Expanding Classrooms

Donica Mensing

From its founding as a republic, the United States has aspired to protect the rights of its citizens—including journalists—to express themselves freely. This freedom was outlined in 1791 in the First Amendment to the U.S. Constitution, which includes language to limit the "dangers uniquely associated with government interference in the development and expression of ideas" (Ambro & Safier, 2012, p. 400). Americans have celebrated, tested, and contested the rights to a free press and to free speech ever since. Journalism students are taught to revere the First Amendment. At the same time, they face an environment in which journalists are subject to increasingly broad governmental efforts to protect secrets and to extraordinary corporate efforts to promote private interests. The globalized communications network both enables and complicates commitments to free expression. Journalists, although thrust into the role of democratic protagonists in international conflicts, are compromised by dependence on market forces at home. U.S. journalism educators are responding to significant technological, economic, social, and political change in increasingly diverse ways. For example, they participate in everything from undergraduate programs teaching social journalism and entrepreneurial skills for community engagement to advanced programs focusing on sophisticated data analysis for investigative projects.

Journalism in the Media Landscape

The United States aligns most closely with Hallin and Mancini's (2004) liberal model of media systems: a market-dominated system with a strongly professional, information-oriented press that operates in an increasingly polarized political environment. America's geographic diversity and large size have created a highly localized news system with few truly national print newspapers or magazines. Although major television networks have created a national news system, the single most turned-to news source for the past two decades has been local television (Pew Research Center, 2012a). Finally, even though Americans tend to have very negative views of the press, they rate the local news organizations they regularly rely on more highly than news organizations in general (Pew Research Center, 2011).

Changes to the U.S. News Media System

Between the early 1960s and 1990s, most U.S. newspapers operated as local monopolies, earning high profits and dominating the local news ecosystem (Kaplan, 2012). With the development of the Internet, the Web, and mobile digital communication, such monopolies have collapsed. In 1990 there were 1,611 daily newspapers in the United States with a circulation of 62.3 million; in 2011 that number had dropped by 229 papers and 18 million subscribers despite significant population growth (Edmonds, Guskin, & Rosenstiel, 2011). As a result, newsroom staffs have shrunk considerably: In 2000 there were 56,200 newspaper employees working for newspapers (ASNE, 2000), and by 2015 that number had dropped to 32,900 (ASNE, 2015).

The growth in digital communication has also affected television. In 2000, 851 television stations provided local news throughout the United States (Papper & Gerhard, 2001); in 2015 this number had fallen to 719 stations creating local news (Papper, 2015). Local television news still attracts the largest audiences for news, and 71% of American adults watch local TV news each month (Pew Research Center, 2014). And although the industry is still profitable, it has undergone significant consolidation in recent years (Pew Research Center, 2014). Employment has also fallen since 2000, when TV newsrooms employed 35,061 people (Papper & Gerhard, 2001) compared to 27,600 in 2015 (Papper, 2015).

On the other hand, digital news products, while still producing much smaller revenue than traditional media products, are multiplying. Approximately 468 digital-only news outlets employed 5,000 full-time professionals in 2014 (Pew Research Center, 2014). Most analog news organizations also produce digital products. And digital-only news outlets aggregate and often produce analog-similar news products. However, there are differences. For example, many digital-only organizations, such as the Huffington Post, Buzzfeed, and Quartz, are creating overseas bureaus and focusing more attention on international coverage than more traditional counterparts (Pew Research Center, 2014).

Nielsen Media (Mobile Millennials, 2014) estimates that more than 80% of Americans between the ages of 18 and 44 own mobile devices. For many major news sites 40% of all traffic is mobile, and, on evenings and weekends, mobile traffic exceeds that of desktop traffic (Benton, 2014; Pew Research Center, 2012b). A "digital first" mindset is increasingly being accepted in small and large print newsrooms, from *The New York Times* to the *Des Moines Register* (Usher, 2015). Local TV stations are increasingly adding digital video and mobile offerings to their products in hopes of attracting the large percentage of news consumers who watch digital news videos (Pew Research Center, 2014). And while radio is experiencing resurgence as podcasting and online audio provide pathways for digital expansion (Kang, 2014), magazines are betting that tablets and mobile devices will expand their readership (Sasseen, Matsa, & Mitchell, 2013).

The Search for a New Business Model

Despite the fact its business model has been upended, the U.S. news industry remains almost exclusively a commercial enterprise with very limited government, charitable, nonprofit, and subscription funding. Advertising, the U.S. news industry's primary historical source of revenue, still accounts for roughly two thirds of all news organization earnings. That said, the total amount of money spent to advertise in news products continues to sharply decline (Holcomb & Mitchell, 2014). As a result, the journalism workforce is decreasing. Since 1992 the number of employed U.S. journalists has decreased 32%, and today there are approximately only 83,000 full-time professional journalists (Willnat & Weaver, 2014). The Bureau of Labor Statistics (2014) projects that by 2022 the number of employed journalists will decline another 13%. Efforts to expand news production revenue sources are wide-ranging, including philanthropic grants, billionaire and venture capitalist investments, new advertising models, events, and digital subscriptions

(Pew Research Center, 2014). While some news organizations are finding ways to balance revenue with expenditures, many remain financially precarious.

Meanwhile, social media is now a common way for consumers to find and engage with news: About half of those using Facebook and Twitter report getting news on these sites (Holcomb, Gottfried, & Mitchell, 2013). And journalists rely heavily on social networking sites to check for breaking news, to monitor what other news organizations are doing, and to promote and distribute their news stories (Willnat & Weaver, 2014). No longer confined to single channels, most news organizations use multiple platforms to distribute their news. They also use multiple platforms to engage audiences in conversation, obtain feedback, and crowdsource information. Such changes are transforming the way journalists think about, work with, and engage sources and audiences.

Professional Characteristics

Since 1971, national studies of U.S. journalists have been conducted every few years. The most recent such survey (Willnat & Weaver, 2014) shows a college education is the norm for journalists: Nearly all (92%) of American journalists have at least a bachelor's degree and about one half of those majored in journalism or communications. While the number of female journalists is increasing, women still comprise just over one third of all journalists (about the same percentage as in the early 1980s). Survey results also show that women tend to leave the journalism workforce earlier than men and that the largest gender gap occurs among journalists working the longest. Also, on average, women are paid 17% less than men. The median income for all journalists in 2012 was $50,000. And one half of the journalists surveyed reported their political affiliation as "independent," some 18% more than in 2002 (Willnat & Weaver, 2014).

For more than 30 years, concerns over the low number of minorities in American newsrooms and its impact have persisted. In 1978, the percentage of minorities in U.S. newspaper newsrooms (black, Hispanic, Asian American, Native American, and multiracial) was only 4%. And this number has only increased to 12.76%, according to a 2015 American Society of Newspaper Editors report (ASNE, 2015).

Although such figures are similar in radio (13%), estimates show a higher percentage (22%) of journalists in television are from minority populations (Williams, 2015). Overall, these numbers show a large gap between the general U.S. population (37.9% minorities) and news-rooms, which are still largely white (Census Bureau, 2015).

Journalists retain a strong cultural identity even as the boundaries of their work continue to unravel (Ryfe, 2012). A recent survey of 10,000 journalism and communication graduates (Rosenstiel et al., 2015) found that just over 35% of respondents consider the work they do "journalistic" even if they do not work for news organizations. For example, 20% of graduates working in technology jobs consider their work journalistic, as do 26% of those working in education jobs and 19% of those working in political jobs. Of the graduates who earned a journalism degree, 42% classified their current work as journalistic and 52% as not journalistic. Approximately 35% of the sampled population reported jobs in marketing, public relations, and advertising. Similarly, 25% said they were employed in management positions and 18% outside the media sector.

Of the graduates in the Rosenstiel et al. (2015) study who considered their work journalistic, most said their own work had improved over the past five years; only 18% said it had worsened over time. However, the journalists surveyed questioned the public's ability to access accurate information and said the overall quality of journalism was getting worse.

Likewise, nearly 60% of journalists in the Willnat and Weaver (2014) study said that journalism was going in the "wrong direction," while only 23% said it was going in the "right direction" (17% said they "didn't know"). The journalists surveyed felt the most important problems facing journalism included "declining profits (mentioned by 20.4%), threats to the profession from online media (11.4%), job cuts and downsizing (11.3%), the lack of a new business model and funding structure (10.8%), and hasty reporting (9.9%)" (Willnat & Weaver, 2014, p. 3). Less than one quarter of the journalists reported they were "very satisfied" with their jobs. This high level of job dissatisfaction matches a sense of decreasing professional autonomy (Willnat & Weaver, 2014, p. 3).

The role of journalists is changing, according to the Willnat and

Weaver (2014) survey, which compared 2002 to 2013 data sets. For example, in 2013 journalists more strongly emphasized the journalists' watchdog, investigative role than they did in 2002. In 2013, 78% of journalists stressed the importance of investigating government claims (compared to 71% in 2002) and 69% the need to analyze complex problems (compared to 51% in 2002). However, also in 2013, the number of journalists who agreed strongly with the importance of getting news out quickly dropped to 47% (from 60% in 2002). Today's journalists are also less likely to approve of the use of controversial reporting techniques than in the past. For example, those endorsing the use of confidential business or government documents dropped to 58% in 2013 (from 78% in 2002; Willnat & Weaver, 2014).

Journalism Education, Professional Training, and Research

Teaching and Training Future Newsmakers

Nearly all U.S. journalists are educated in colleges and universities (Willnat & Weaver, 2014). Nonprofit organizations are the primary sources for mid-career training, while the news industry provides some internships for early career training and relatively limited mid-career development. Nearly 1,000 institutions (nonprofit, professional, and educational) provide some training in journalism and mass communication fields (ACEJMC, n.d.; see Table 10.1 for major journalism associations and related organizations). The Poynter Institute, a leading U.S. source of journalism training, found that 88% of journalists would like more training—particularly in digital skills (Finberg, 2014). However, a lack of time seems to be a significant barrier to such training.

University journalism education. Since 1987, Becker, Vlad, and Simpson (2014a) have conducted annual surveys of journalism and mass communication programs. The 2013 survey counted 480 journalism programs in universities and colleges in the United States, enrolling 198,410 students and granting nearly 52,000 undergraduate degrees in spring 2013. Another 5,465 students earned master's degrees. Journalism students are predominantly female (64%) and predominantly white (65%). The median age of faculty in journalism programs has risen over time, with currently just over one third 56 years or older (Becker et al., 2014a).

Given the total workforce of 83,000 full-time editorial jobs in 2013

(Willnat & Weaver, 2014), the fact that U.S. academic journalism programs are graduating more than 50,000 students annually has been a cause for concern. No institutional body limits either the number of universities and colleges that teach journalism or the size of their programs (see Table 10.2 for a sample of accredited university journalism programs). The "oversupply," however, is lessened by the fact that many educators and students have adapted over time by developing related career paths within journalism programs. The Becker, Vlad, and Simpson (2014b) survey shows that only 11% of undergraduate journalism students are following the traditional news-editorial path. The remaining 89% are specializing in other types of journalism and strategic communication fields (see Figure 10.1).

According to the Becker et al. (2014b) survey, graduates are fairly satisfied with the education they have received:

> Two thirds of the bachelor's degree recipients reported satisfaction with their career choice, six out of 10 said they were prepared for the job market, and seven in 10 reported that their college coursework provided the skills needed in today's workplace. (p. 1)

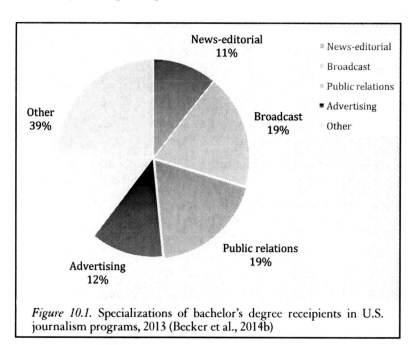

Figure 10.1. Specializations of bachelor's degree receipients in U.S. journalism programs, 2013 (Becker et al., 2014b)

In 2013, 74% of college graduates in journalism and mass communication programs reported having at least one job offer when they
graduated, and 90% had at least one in-person interview. Nearly two
thirds (64%) of recent graduates had a full-time job by Oct. 31, 2013
(the study's yearly data collection endpoint). This was up from a low
point of employment in 2009, when less than one half of recent college
graduates in journalism reported full-time employment by that date.
However, when race and ethnic group figures are considered, recovery
has been much harder for some students. In 2013, only 55% of minority
students reported a full-time job following graduation (in October),
whereas 73% of non-minority students reported full-time employment
(Becker et al., 2014a).

Accreditation. No mechanism exists for regulating the number of university journalism and mass communication programs.
However, there is one accrediting body that evaluates the quality of
professional programs offering degrees in journalism and related
fields: the Accrediting Council on Education in Journalism and Mass
Communications (ACEJMC). In 2014, ACEJMC listed 114 fully accredited programs on its website, about one quarter of the total number of
university programs that offer education in journalism. Accreditation
is voluntary, and accredited schools include small, private colleges as
well as large public universities.

ACEJMC, which has existed in some form since 1945, has the
authority to set standards, make policy, and grant accreditation. It
includes representatives of 11 industry organizations and six educational organizations, along with three public members. The accreditation review consists of a rigorous self-assessment and a multi-day site
visit by an accrediting team, which evaluates programs based on nine
standards (ACEJMC, 2012):

- ❏ mission, governance, and administration;
- ❏ curriculum and instruction;
- ❏ diversity and inclusiveness;
- ❏ full-time and part-time faculty;
- ❏ scholarship: research, creative, and professional activity;
- ❏ student services;
- ❏ resources, facilities, and equipment;

❏   professional and public service; and
❏   assessment of learning outcomes.

A comparison of research on accredited and non-accredited journalism programs has found no significant evidence that accredited
programs are clearly, let alone significantly, superior to non-accredited
programs (Seamon, 2010). The most cited reason among journalism
program directors for pursuing accreditation is reputation enhancement. The most cited reason for not pursuing accreditation is the
cap put on the number of journalism credits students can earn while
obtaining their degrees. This cap is intended to ensure students have
wide exposure to liberal arts courses (Blom, Davenport, & Bowe, 2012).
Although some studies have found evidence that accreditation hampers innovation in curriculum, accreditation does seem to help programs increase diversity to some degree (Seamon, 2010). Based on these
studies, it appears that the relatively low percentage of accredited programs does not mean accredited schools are best. Instead, accredited
schools are those successfully meeting the accrediting body's criteria,
which deal with curriculum structure, assessment methods, diversity
goals, etc. Non-accredited programs may provide greater or lesser professional quality than their accredited counterparts.

Foundations. Philanthropic organizations are having an increasingly significant influence on U.S. journalism education. They grant
millions of dollars every year to universities and related organizations
to support educational initiatives that align with foundation priorities. Henry-Sanchez and Koob (2013) documented foundation gifts of
$146.4 million in grants for journalism education between 2009 and
2011. Overall, charitable giving for journalism, news, and information
projects totaled $527.3 million between 2009 and 2011 (Henry-Sanchez
& Koob, 2013).

One highly publicized effort to address the quality of university
journalism education was the Carnegie-Knight Initiative on the Future
of Journalism Education. The Carnegie Corporation and the John S.
and James L. Knight Foundation launched the initiative in collaboration with deans at four top research universities. The two foundations gave nearly $20 million between 2005 and 2011 to develop a vision

for 21st century journalism education. The effort, eventually including programs at 12 universities, focused on curriculum enrichment, a mentoring/internship program called News21, and Carnegie-Knight Task Force work (King, 2010; Knight Foundation, 2011). The News21 program continues as a Knight Foundation project, which has also launched a $1 million Challenge Fund for Innovation in Journalism Education in partnership with the Online News Association (ONA). The challenge fund's goal is "to hack the journalism curriculum using customized versions of the teaching hospital model" (ONA, 2015). Journalism education's "teaching hospital model," a Carnegie Knight programs' cornerstone, is the primary organizing principle for the Knight Foundation's grant giving to journalism programs. In a 2012 letter to university presidents, six large grant-giving organizations strongly advocated the teaching hospital model as an ideal form of journalism education. They cautioned presidents that "schools that do not update their curriculum and upgrade their faculties to reflect the profoundly different digital age of communication will find it difficult to raise money from foundations interested in the future of news" (Knight Foundation, 2012). As government funding for higher education is reduced, along with industry-specific funding for journalism education, financial support from grants and contracts is increasingly important. Universities have a strong financial incentive to adopt approaches advocated by funders. Thus, examining foundations' interests is important when considering the overall direction of journalism education in the United States (Mensing & Ryfe, 2013; Reese, 1999).

Journalism Research

Journalism research in the United States grew from both the humanities and social science traditions. The social science emphasis on empirical and quantitative research, often with an underlying normative perspective drawn from the humanities, has characterized much research in journalism in the last half of the 20th century (Kamhawi & Weaver, 2003; Singer, 2008). As journalism and communication research has become more diverse and more specialized, the breadth of theories and methods used in research has considerably increased (Bryant & Mirron, 2004; Steensen & Ahva, 2014). Similarly, the number of scholarly journals has significantly increased, from 36 in 1997 to 74 in 2015 (Parry-Giles, 2014).

One of the oldest and most wide-ranging U.S.-based journals focused on journalism and mass communication research is *Journalism and Mass Communication Quarterly (JMCQ)*. This peer-reviewed journal is published by the Association for Education in Journalism and Mass Communication (AEJMC), the primary professional journalism educators' organization in the United States. *JMCQ*, established in 1924, is ranked 40 out of 74 communication journals (ISI Web of Knowledge, 2014). A 2005 analysis of citations and co-citations in *JMCQ* showed that most references are cited only once, which "may suggest only piecemeal contributions to the generation of theory or knowledge-building" (Chang & Tai, 2005, p. 687). The field as a whole relies on relatively older sources and does not exhibit much "cognitive competition" to explain the same phenomenon (Chang & Tai, 2005, p. 688). DeFleur (1998) noted that while a number of "milestone" studies in mass communication research were published between the 1930s and 1980s, he could not think of a single significant, seminal study published between the early 1980s and late 1990s. As Singer noted in 2008, "the paradigms that emerged for studying journalism in the 1920s, '30s and '40s remain dominant in the United States today" (p. 145).

A number of trends, however, suggest that this period of stability (or stagnation) may be ending. Singer (2008) notes that "journalism studies' first real paradigm shift may be under way" (p. 145). A number of factors seem to be important catalysts for this transformation, particularly globalization, social change, and digital technologies. A large body of journalism research has focused on the United States, with relatively few comparative studies to provide perspective and context. The increasingly international scope of academic conferences, and more international contributions to U.S.-focused publications (Riffe & Abdenour, 2014), is opening up academic journalism research to more perspectives, theories, and methods.

Historically, professional practitioners have used journalism scholarship to a very small extent. Over the years AEJMC, other professional organizations, and various industry-sponsored efforts have attempted to bridge this gap. One recent example is the Journalist's Resource, a project of the Shorenstein Center on Media, Politics and Public Policy, at the Harvard Kennedy School (funded by the Carnegie-Knight Initiative on the Future of Journalism Education). Rather than focusing on journalism research per se, the site curates research on a wide variety of news topics and highlights recent academic studies that are useful for journalists and the public (Journalist's Resource, n.d.). Other forms of professional/academic collaboration have developed more informally, as individual faculty or programs make ad hoc arrangements to focus on news organizations' particular problems or issues. For example, graduate programs at Northwestern University's Medill School and New York University's Studio 20 establish such arrangements to provide students experience addressing real-world problems. However, despite such individual efforts, there has been relatively little systematic research collaboration between the U.S. news industry and higher education in journalism.

Funding for large-scale research projects in journalism and communication is miniscule compared with funding provided for other subjects, especially science and technology. In 2011/2012 higher education institutions spent a total of $153 million on journalism, communication, and library research, which constituted .06% of university research that year (Britt, 2013). While many foundations have historically avoided funding scholarly communication research in favor of supporting capital improvements, scholarships, and reporting projects, a limited amount of research funding is available. For example, Columbia University's Tow Center for Digital Journalism (http://towcenter.org) has begun providing grants for innovative research and is publishing reports well received by journalism educators and professionals alike.

Professional Connections in Journalism Education

U.S. journalism education maintains strong connections with the profession by encouraging, and often requiring, professional internships, inviting professionals to classrooms, and hiring experienced journalists to teach courses. Many schools even encourage multiple internships to provide the contacts and experience necessary to be successful in the job market. And experienced journalists teach in many institutions as either temporary instructional faculty or permanent professors.

In past years, organizations connected to the news industry, including the Dow Jones News Fund, the American Society of News Editors, and the Gannett Foundation, have provided funding for educators to return to newsrooms to re-tool their skills. Some such programs have been reduced or phased out, while others have cropped up. One such relatively new program is the International Center for Journalists, which is supporting five professors each year from historically black educational institutions to spend summers in a newsroom (Lichterman, 2014).

While professional/academic ties have historically been strong in local settings, they are strained at regional and national levels. Much of this tension is due to professionals' tendency to devalue journalism degrees. For example, in a 2013 Poynter Institute survey, while 96% of educators said a journalism degree was "very important" to understand journalism, only 57% of professionals said the degree was "important" (Finberg, 2013).

Journalism Education's Professional Impact

Nearly one half of all U.S. journalists have college degrees in journalism or a related field, which shapes the professional orientation of news organizations. Courses in law and ethics are common and often required. They create a powerful frame for understanding and defining journalistic norms and practices while the field is in flux (Vos, 2012).

The political economy of American universities also influences dynamics within the journalistic field. The tuition-driven business model for higher education puts pressure on journalism programs to grow student enrollment. This requires attracting students and demonstrating the value of a degree for obtaining post-graduation jobs. Thus, journalism programs are diversifying their offerings into areas with better job prospects, and, accordingly, higher student demand. Emerging coursework in entrepreneurship, data journalism, social media, and related fields are preparing students to bring new skills and talents to the workplace. Therefore, journalism education may be impacting the journalism profession by diversifying what is included in "journalism." This trend contributes to the increasingly blurred lines between journalism, visual design, programming, data analysis, public relations, and strategic communications.

Future Possibilities

Journalism educators are adapting to significant changes in their field in the context of an increasingly complex communication system. In the process, as mentioned above, programs are diversifying. As some programs choose to stress student proficiency in content production, others focus on teaching new competencies in data journalism, mobile design, and data visualization. And still others focus on the community aspects of journalism—teaching the art of sharing, creating, building, and persuading—further blurring the line between journalism and strategic communications.

What does this mean for the future? First, given the impossibility of continuing general programs for a widening set of possible careers, journalism schools may increasingly specialize in particular areas. Second, some universities will probably build large media-related programs with journalism included as one specialization among many. And third, journalism may become a subject primarily for graduate-level study, with undergraduate programs providing more general media-related studies.

What might not continue? Journalism education in its current form: the university equivalent of the metro newspaper. In other words, undergraduate programs may stop training students as they have for decades: adapting at the edges but lacking a strategic response to significant changes taking place in how societies and publics communicate.

Journalism Education Issues, Challenges, and Innovations

The biggest challenge for journalism educators is developing a strategy to respond to the disruptive changes universities and the news industry face. This strategy has to address U.S. peculiarities in institutions of higher education and the news industry. Within the higher education context, tenure rules, hiring practices, and curriculum policies make change within journalism programs particularly difficult. It is also difficult for journalism educators to decide what to emphasize in curricula due to shifting understandings of what constitutes journalism (Lewis & Carlson, 2015) and rapidly changing industry standards and practices.

Given such challenges, plans for change might include the following: developing strategies to better align scholarship and classroom teaching, investing in the professional development of faculty, developing more effective pedagogical practices, and promoting more flexible academic policies in regards to hiring, curriculum development, and faculty evaluation.

Aligning scholarship and teaching. Providing more theoretically driven teaching would help accelerate the transformation of journalism instruction. The most relevant journalistic, psychological, and sociological scholarship needs to be applied to practical journalism problems in real time. The many journalistic experiments taking place across the country—within news organizations, public interest groups, and journalism schools—create living laboratories for analyzing and learning. Innovations found in trending subfields now commonly taught, such as social journalism, data journalism, and nonlinear storytelling, are ripe for examination. Such new practices are providing new opportunities to test and debate core ideals while conceptions of journalism continue evolving. More applied scholarship could catalyze change in promising new directions that might not be evident without systematic study and observation.

Professional development. New proficiencies are needed in classrooms much faster than new faculty can be hired. Consequently, current faculty need opportunities to reconceptualize their understanding of how journalism functions in a changing society and to develop new skills they can teach. Partnering with professionals and facilitating student learning with online resources will be necessary. Developing partnerships to assist faculty development in an era of shrinking budgets will be critical.

Pedagogy. Educators need to be increasingly sophisticated when designing learning modules, courses, and assignments due to rapid changes in how students respond to different teaching methods. Project-based and experiential learning have helped strengthen journalism curricula. That said, the main challenge now is designing and developing coursework with opportunities for critical self-reflection and independent learning that encourages innovation and creativity.

Academic policies. Finally, the difficulties in changing academic policies are formidable. However, revising tenure policies to recognize engagement with diverse partners and experimental and innovative teaching and scholarship will infuse programs with new energy and approaches. In addition, strategic efforts to hire faculty with more diverse experiences and backgrounds will help foster cultural change within programs. And creating flexible course units on focused topics will create a more responsive and adaptable curriculum. Lastly, rewarding faculty who develop alternative forms of scholarship, new learning opportunities, and beneficial community partnerships will help programs adjust to the challenges journalism and journalism education will face in years to come.

Conclusion: Educating Tomorrow's Journalists — The Big Picture

As described in this chapter, disruptions in the news industry and mass media and the development of a networked communication system are leading to fundamental changes in journalism and education. The big picture is that educators have recognized and are responding to these changes. They are experimenting, building, revising, and raising important questions about the future. Some of these questions include the following:

❑ What are the core concepts educators should be teaching to prepare students for an uncertain economy and fluid careers? How can educators best prepare themselves to meet these obligations to students?

❑ What obligations, if any, do journalism educators have to students who do not intend to practice journalism professionally? Given the pressing public needs in society and the value of exercising thoughtful speech, what obligations do educators have to other students, and to the wider public, in a media-saturated environment?

❑ What obligations do journalism educators have to their communities? Do they have a responsibility to fill gaps in the local news ecosystem? What is their obligation to existing local news and media entities?

❑ What obligations do journalism educators have to the news industry in general? What obligations do they have to the emerging civic/information ecosystem outside mainstream media? What type of scholarly research has the most value in this environment, and who will help fund it?

❑ What obligations do journalism educators have to their own universities and higher education in general? Do journalism faculty have any special obligation to be proactive in the face of impeding changes in education, which echo some of the changes in journalism?

These are not easy questions to address. Yet, the fact that journalistic boundaries and roles are rapidly changing (Lewis & Carlson, 2015) means the need to experiment with, study, and teach journalistic practices that are powerful and engaging has never been more important. Journalism that facilitates civil discourse, strengthens public mechanisms for accountability and verification, empowers citizens to act, and protects the right of all to speak is powerful and greatly needed. Journalism educators and students have a vital role to play in helping journalism evolve and diversify while still honoring its long-standing effort to serve its many publics.

References

Accrediting Council on Education in Journalism and Mass Communications. (n.d). Frequently asked questions concerning accreditation. Retrieved from http://www2.ku.edu/~acejmc/FAQS.SHTML

Accrediting Council on Education in Journalism and Mass Communications. (2012). ACEJMC accrediting standards. Retrieved from http://www2.ku.edu/~acejmc/PROGRAM/STANDARDS.SHTML

Accrediting Council on Education in Journalism and Mass Communications. (2014). List of accredited programs. Retrieved from http://www2.ku.edu/~acejmc/STUDENT/PROGLIST.SHTML

Ambro, T. L., & Safier, P. J. (2012). The First Amendment, the courts, and "picking winners," 87 Wash. L. Rev. 397.

ASNE. (2000). 2000 Census. Retrieved from http://asne.org/content.asp?pl=121&sl=15&contentid=172

ASNE. (2015). 2015 Census. Retrieved from http://asne.org/content.asp?pl=121&sl=15&contentid=415

Becker, L., Vlad, T., & Simpson, H. A. (2013). 2013 Annual survey of journalism mass communication enrollments: Enrollments decline for third consecutive year. *Journalism & Mass Communication Educator*, 69(4), 349–365. Retrieved from http://www.grady.uga.edu/annualsurveys/Enrollment_Survey/Enrollment_2013/EnrollmentReport2013J&MCE_Combined-

Full.pdf

Becker, L., Vlad, T., & Simpson, H. A. (2014a). 2013 Annual survey of journalism & mass communication enrollments. Retrieved from http://
www.grady.uga.edu/annualsurveys/Enrollment_Survey/Enroll-
ment_2013/2013EnrollCombined.pdf

Becker, L., Vlad, T., & Simpson, H. A. (2014b). 2013 Annual survey of journalism & mass communication graduates. Retrieved from http://www.
grady.uga.edu/annualsurveys/Graduate_Survey/Graduate_2013/Grad_
Report_2013_Combined.pdf

Benton, J. (2014). The mobile majority: Engaging people on smartphones is
the next big challenge to the news. *Nieman Reports*. Retrieved from http://
www.niemanlab.org/2014/06/the-mobile-majority-engaging-people-on-
smartphones-is-the-next-big-challenge-to-the-news/

Blom, R., Davenport, L., & Bowe, B. (2012). Reputation cycles: The value of
accreditation for undergraduate journalism programs. Retrieved from
http://scholarworks.gvsu.edu/com_articles/4

Britt, R. (2013). Higher education R&D expenditures remain flat in FY 2012.
Retrieved from http://www.nsf.gov/statistics/infbrief/nsf14303/

Bryant, J., & Mirron, D. (2004). Theory and research in mass communication.
Journal of Communication, 54(4), 662-704.

Bureau of Labor Statistics (2014). Reporters, correspondents, and broadcast
news analysts. Retrieved from http://www.bls.gov/ooh/media-and-com-
munication/reporters-correspondents-and-broadcast-news-analysts.htm

Census Bureau, United States (2015). Quick facts. Retrieved from http://www.
census.gov/quickfacts/table/PST045214/00

Chang, T. K., & Tai, Z. (2005). Mass communication research and the invisible
college revisited: The changing landscape and emerging fronts in journalism-related studies. *Journalism & Mass Communication Quarterly*, 82(3),
672-694.

DeFleur, M. L. (1998). Where have all the milestones gone? The decline of
significant research on the process and effects of mass communication.
Mass Communication & Society, 1(1-2), 85-98.

Edmonds, R., Guskin, E., & Rosenstiel, T. (2011). Newspapers: By the numbers. *Project for Excellence in Journalism*. Retrieved from http://www.sta-
teofthemedia.org/2011/newspapers-essay/data-page-6/

Finberg, H. (2013). Journalism schools need to adapt or risk becoming irrelevant. *Poynter Institute*. Retrieved from http://www.poynter.org/how-tos/
journalism-education/220410/scary-future-journalism-education/

Finberg, H. (2014). New newsroom training report shows gaps, some progress. Retrieved from http://www.poynter.org/how-tos/journalism-educa-
tion/281763/newsroom-training-report-shows-gaps/

Hallin, D., & Mancini, P. (2004). *Comparing media systems: Three models of media and politics*. New York, NY: Cambridge University Press.

Henry-Sanchez, B., & Koob, A. (2013). Growth in foundation support for media in the United States. Retrieved from http://foundationcenter.org/gainknowledge/research/pdf/mediafunding_report_2013.pdf

Holcomb, J., Gottfried, J., & Mitchell, J. (2013). News use across social media platforms. Retrieved from http://www.journalism.org/2013/11/14/news-use-across-social-media-platforms/

Holcomb, J., & Mitchell, A. (2014). The revenue picture for American journalism and how it is changing. Retrieved from http://www.journalism.org/2014/03/26/the-revenue-picture-for-american-journalism-and-how-it-is-changing/

ISI Web of Knowledge. (2014). JCR Social Science edition, journal citation reports for communication. Retrieved from http://wokinfo.com/media/pdf/qrc/jcrqrc.pdf

Journalist's Resource, (n.d.). About journalist's resource. Retrieved from http://journalistsresource.org/about

Kamhawi, R., & Weaver, D. (2003). Mass communication research trends from 1980 to 1999. *Journalism and Mass Communication Quarterly, 80*(1), 7-27.

Kang, C. (2014, September 30) Podcasting industry starts to fulfill its financial potential. *The Guardian*. Retrieved from http://www.theguardian.com/media/2014/sep/30/podcast-revival-profits-business-listeners

Kaplan, R. (2012). Journalism history. *The International Encyclopedia of Media Studies, 1*(2), 9.

King, S. (2010). The Carnegie-Knight initiative on the future of journalism education: Improving how journalists are educated & how their audiences are informed. Daedalus, *139*(2), 126-137.

Knight Foundation. (2011). Journalism education reform growing. Retrieved from http://www.knightfo undation.org/press-room/press-release/journalism-education-reform-growing/

Knight Foundation (2012). An open letter to America's university presidents. Retrieved from http://www.knightfoundation.org/press-room/other/open-letter-americas-university-presidents/

Lewis, S., & Carlson, M. (Ed.), (2015). *Boundaries of journalism: Professionalism, practices and participation*. New York, NY: Routledge.

Lichterman, J. (2014). Back to the newsroom: A new program lets professors go back to the thick of today's news work. Retrieved from http://www.niemanlab.org/2014/03/back-to-the-newsroom-a-new-program-lets-professors-go-back-to-the-thick-of-todays-news-work/

Mensing, D., & Ryfe, D. (2013). Blueprint for change: From the teaching hospital to the entrepreneurial model of journalism education. *#ISOJ Journal*, *3*(2), 26-44.

Mobile Millennials. (2014). Over 85% of generation Y owns smartphones.

Retrieved from http://www.nielsen.com/us/en/insights/news/2014/mobile-millennials-over-85-percent-of-generation-y-owns-smartphones.html

Online News Association (ONA). (n.d.). Challenge fund. Retrieved from http://journalists.org/next-gen/challenge-fund/

Papper, B. (2015). Update: TV and newspaper staffing, RTNDA. Retrieved from http://www.rtdna.org/article/update_tv_and_newspaper_staffing

Papper, B., & Gerhard, M. (2001). News, staff and making money. Retrieved from http://www.bobpapper.com/attachments/File/RTDNA_reports/staff2001.pdf

Parry-Giles, T. (2014). Journal impact factors and communication journals: A report from the National Communication Association. *AEJMC News, 47*(3), 8-9.

Pew Research Center. (2011). Press widely criticized, but trusted more than other information sources. Retrieved from http://www.people-press.org/2011/09/22/press-widely-criticized-but-trusted-more-than-other-institutions/

Pew Research Center. (2012a). In changing news landscape, even television is vulnerable. Retrieved from http://www.people-press.org/2012/09/27/in-changing-news-landscape-even-television-is-vulnerable/

Pew Research Center (2012b). Future of mobile news. Retrieved from http://www.journalism.org/2012/10/01/future-mobile-news/

Pew Research Center (2014). State of the news media report. Retrieved from http://www.journalism.org/packages/state-of-the-news-media-2014/

Poynter Institute. (n.d.). A brief history of the Poynter Institute. Retrieved from http://about.poynter.org/about-us/mission-history

Reese, S. D. (1999). The progressive potential of journalism education: Recasting the academic versus professional debate. *The Harvard International Journal of Press/Politics 4*(4), 70–94.

Riffe, D., & Abdenour, J. (2014). Editorial commentary. *Journalism & Mass Communication Quarterly, 91*(4).

Rosenstiel, T., Ivancin, M., Loker, K., Lacy, S., Sonderman, J., & Yaeger, K. (2015). *Facing change: The needs, attitudes and experiences of people in media*. Retrieved from http://www.americanpressinstitute.org/publications/reports/survey-research/api-journalists-survey/

Ryfe, D. (2012). *Can journalism survive? A look inside American newsrooms*. Cambridge: Polity.

Sasseen, J., Matsa, K., & Mitchell, A. (2013). News magazines: Embracing their digital future. The State of the News Media 2013. Retrieved from http://www.stateofthemedia.org/2013/news-magazines-embracing-their-digital-future/

Seamon, M. (2010). The value of accreditation: An overview of three decades of research comparing accredited and unaccredited journalism and mass communication programs. *Journalism & Mass Communication Educator,* 65(1), 10-20.

Singer, J. B. (2008). Journalism research in the United States of America. In M. Loffelholz & D. Weaver. (Eds.), *Global journalism research: theories, methods, findings, future* (pp. 145-157). Oxford: Blackwell.

Steensen, S., & Ahva, L. (2015). Theories of journalism in a digital age. *Digital Journalism* 3(1), 1–18.

Usher, N. (2015, February 23). Will the new Page One meetings finally make the *Times* digital first? *Columbia Journalism Review*. Retrieved from http://www.cjr.org/behind_the_news/page_one_meetings_symbolism_re.php

Vos, T. P. (2012). 'Homo Journalisticus': Journalism education's role in articulating the objectivity norm. *Journalism* 13(4), 435-449.

Williams, A. (2015, July 22). Why aren't there more minority journalists? *Columbia Journalism Review*. Retrieved from: http://www.cjr.org/analysis/in_the_span_of_two.php

Willnat, L., & Weaver, D. H. (2014). *The American journalist in the digital age: Key findings*. Bloomington, IN: Indiana University. Retrieved from http://www.news.indiana.edu/releases/iu/2014/05/2013-american-journalist-key-findings.pdf

Table 10.1

Major Journalism Associations and Related Organizations in the United States

Organization	Description	Websites
Accrediting Council for Education in Journalism and Mass Communication (ACEJMC)	Accrediting body for university and college journalism programs.	http://acejmc.org
Asian American Journalists' Association (AAJA)	Offers educational and skills training, professional development programs, and guidance on coverage of AAPI issues for the journalism industry.	http://www.aaja.org
Association for Education in Journalism and Mass Communication (AEJMC)	Primary academic association for journalism educators. Publishes a number of scholarly journals, including *Journalism and Mass Communication Quarterly*.	http://aejmc.org
Association of Alternative Newsmedia	Represents 113 alternative news media organizations in North America. It serves members and strengthens alternative journalism through advocacy and education.	http://www.altweeklies.com
Broadcast Educator's Association (BEA)	Provides juried production competitions and presentation of scholarly research related to electronic media. Publishes the *Journal of Broadcasting & Electronic Media* and the *Journal of Radio & Audio Media*.	http://www.beaweb.org/wp
International Center for Journalism (ICFJ)	Uses the latest digital technology to increase the flow of quality news and serves as a catalyst for change, leaving partners stronger and officials more accountable.	http://www.icfj.org
International Communication Association (ICA)	Academic association for scholars interested in the study, teaching, and application of all aspects of human and mediated communication.	https://www.icahdq.org
Investigative Reporters and Editors (IRE)	Grassroots nonprofit organization dedicated to improving the quality of investigative reporting.	https://www.ire.org
Knight Foundation	Funds projects of all sizes that advance the goal of promoting informed and engaged communities to support a healthy democracy.	http://www.knightfoundation.org
Local Independent Online News Publishers	Fosters the viability and excellence of locally focused independent online news organizations.	http://www.lionpublishers.com

Table 10.1 (cont.)

Major Journalism Associations and Related Organizations in the United States

Organization	Description	Websites
National Association of Black Journalists (NABJ)	Provides quality programs and services to and advocates on behalf of black journalists worldwide.	http://www.nabj.org
National Communication Association (NCA)	Advances communication as a discipline that studies all forms, modes, media, and consequences of communication through humanistic, social scientific, and aesthetic inquiry.	https://www.natcom.org
Native American Journalists Association (NAJA)	Serves and empowers Native journalists through programs and actions designed to enrich journalism and promote Native cultures.	http://www.naja.com
Online News Association	Inspires innovation and excellence among digital journalists to better serve the public.	http://journalists.org
Poynter Institute	Instructor, innovator, convener, and resource for anyone who aspires to engage and inform citizens in 21st century democracies.	http://www.poynter.org
Society for News Design (SND)	Enhances communication around the world through excellence in visual journalism.	http://www.snd.org
Society of American Business Editors and Writers (SABEW)	Promotes superior coverage of business and economic events and issues.	http://sabew.org
Society of Professional Journalists (SPJ)	Improving and protecting journalism since 1909.	http://www.spj.org

Table 10.2

A Sample of Accredited University Journalism Programs in the United States (Becker, Vlad, & Simpson, 2013)

Name of School	Name of Unit	Undergrad degrees 2013	Websites
Pennsylvania State University	College of Communications	878	http://comm.psu.edu/departments/department-of-journalism
Michigan State University	College of Communication Arts and Sciences	878	http://cas.msu.edu/places/departments/school-of-journalism
University of Florida	College of Journalism and Communications	645	http://www.jou.ufl.edu
University of Georgia	Grady College of Journalism and Mass Communication	599	http://www.grady.uga.edu
University of Alabama	College of Communication and Information Sciences	561	http://jn.ua.edu
Middle Tennessee State University	College of Mass Communication	535	http://www.mtsu.edu/programs/journalism
University of Missouri	School of Journalism	504	http://journalism.missouri.edu
University of Oregon	School of Journalism and Communication	465	http://journalism.uoregon.edu
University of Washington	College of Arts and Sciences	450	http://www.com.washington.edu/journalism
Syracuse University	S.I. Newhouse School of Public Communications	409	http://newhouse.syr.edu
University of North Carolina at Chapel Hill	School of Journalism and Mass Communication	359	http://www.jomc.unc.edu
Arizona State University	Walter Cronkite School of Journalism and Mass Communication	333	http://cronkite.asu.edu
Ball State University	College of Communication, Information, and Media	260	http://cms.bsu.edu/Academics/CollegesandDepartments/Journalism.aspx
University of Kansas	William Allen White School of Journalism and Mass Communications	242	http://www.journalism.ku.edu
Temple University	School of Media and Communication	125	http://smc.temple.edu/journalism
San Diego State University	College of Professional Studies and Fine Arts	123	http://jms.sdsu.edu

PART 2:

Contextualizing
Global Journalism Education

11

Taking Stock of Contemporary Journalism Education: The End of the Classroom as We Know It

Guy Berger and Joe Foote

Worldwide, a wide variety of non-academic training organizations are joining "traditional" journalism schools based within higher learning institutions to supply journalism education. This, among other reasons, is cause for the "traditional" providers to re-think their context, community, and role. This chapter describes key developments in new education efforts (a broad concept that in this chapter generally includes "training" efforts) over the past 20 years. The emerging scenario is one in which the supply of journalism education is becoming distributed across a range of providers globally. Moreover, there is a greater specialization of services as well as a trend toward the internationalization of many programs and learners.

Context

Journalism education at the university level has never been the "last stop" for professional education. Although in much of the world university-level journalism education continues to constitute the largest provider of journalism education, especially at the entry-level. At the same time, the question of who provides journalism education and who is a journalism teacher continues to change. For example, in 2006 the UNESCO (United Nations Educational, Scientific and Cultural Organization) search for "potential centers of excellence" in African journalism education resulted in a list of finalists including not only journalism schools based at universities, but also several based at vocational and technical-training colleges that are involved primarily in vocational training. In addition, one finalist was a commercial business and another, now defunct, was a non-government organization (NGO) with a core focus on training (Berger, 2007).

Such changes illustrate what Deuze (2008, p. 270) has called a global move toward a system of journalism education provided more by universities and stand-alone institutes than either self-education or purely on-the-job training. The current increase in university-based programs also exists within systems that are increasingly transcending national boundaries. And when one includes the providers of online courses, this profile becomes even more diverse. As journalism education clients learn and experiment with changing forms of journalism, they are increasingly being served by an array of providers and dispersed opportunities.

Developments are moving beyond scholar Jan Servaes' call for journalism education to "break out of its national carcass and 'internationalise'" (2009, p. 530). UNESCO's model curriculum (adapted in more than 60 countries and available in nine languages) is an indicator of the widening globalization of journalism education (UNESCO, 2007, 2013). A key question that merits further study and arises from these developments concerns the models of journalism education that are internationalizing, the cultural and language issues involved, and the evolution of courses that deal explicitly with globalization and journalism (Josephi, 2010; Bromley, 2009; Holm, 2002).

For the first half of the 20th century, journalism education and training worldwide was largely confined to on-the-job learning, often in an apprenticeship style. But as mass communications grew as an industry in the second part of the century, so did the need for hiring more people and requiring more high-end skills for this industry. Public institutions of higher education evolved to meet this need. Many countries accordingly introduced diploma and degree programs preparing entry-level practitioners for the job market. While this was partially a response to media industry demands to supply graduates ready for a career in industry, such programs also suited universities' institutional ambitions to swell student numbers in an area of high visibility with career-promising courses that attracted additional enrollments.

By 1950, formal journalism education at the university level was widely accepted in the United States. It did not spread widely in Europe until the privatization of media in Western Europe and the fall of communism in Eastern Europe. But it has flourished since then—both in the number of programs and the number of women enrolled in them (Nordenstreng, 2009). In the 1980s, the Asian media boom and its corresponding increase in private media created an increased demand for formal journalism education in many countries in the region. In the 1990s, there was considerable journalism education growth in higher education institutions in the Middle East and Africa. And by 2000, university-level journalism education courses were nearly universal (Hume, 2007). In China and India, journalism education programs continue to proliferate at a mind-numbing rate. The World Journalism Education Council's worldwide journalism education census has registered nearly 3,000 global programs on its database. By 2007, the bulk of these programs were spread fairly evenly between North America, Europe, and Asia (World Journalism Education Congress, 2007). In areas in which university-level education was slow to gain traction, some media organizations set up autonomous "journalism schools," mimicking some features of those within higher education. The United Kingdom, Germany, and Denmark have media organizations that follow this model.

This explosive growth of global journalism education has also attracted private sector involvement. In many regions worldwide, and especially in developing countries, commercial entities have entered the fray. However, this emerging type of journalism education has sometimes been susceptible to criticism based on quality issues and the possible exploitation of students.

At the same time, the foundation laid in the late 1900s persists in that most countries' journalism education systems appear to be grounded in established universities, and to a lesser extent technical colleges, registered by their national educational departments. In this model, journalism schools are anchored within a wider academic institutional framework.

Over time, the resulting "pipeline" of university journalism graduates has affected the media. For example, in the early 1990s, an estimated 71% of journalists in the United States had some tertiary-level media education (Medsger, 1996, p. 7). Their education often either replaced or complemented in-house or on-the-job training practices. At the same time, industry has frequently criticized not only these graduates' skills, but also the value of university journalism education at large.

Still, many university programs have established close ties with professional news organizations. Internships have developed as a key experiential learning component in curricula, which often favor professional skills. Industry professionals visit classrooms, and some teach as adjuncts. Because the media sector is known for its low investment in training, university-sponsored programs have ultimately been a blessing for media operations by increasingly supplying their labor needs.

In much of Latin America, higher education qualifications in journalism used to be regulatory pre-requisites for working in the media (International Federation of Journalists, 2010). This was in part due to union support, which had an inherent interest in limiting labor-market competition for media positions. But such requirements are no longer practiced due to the decline of unions in Latin America (as has been the case worldwide) and influential international opinions that position against any compulsory membership or qualifications to practice as a journalist (ARTICLE 19, 2012).

However, even with massive enrollment and output in university journalism education programs worldwide, there continues to be a significant number of journalists who have not taken these or other foundational programs. However, these same journalists often become interested in academic and other courses when it comes to updating their skills, or learning new ones, in areas such as investigative journalism, data-based journalism, enhanced newsroom technology, and digital security. This need has helped feed a market for "further" or "continuing" education. For example, some universities have targeted certain specialized programs toward working journalists, thereby expanding their scope of activity.

Simultaneously, industry associations, a number of individual media companies, and NGOs have also responded to mid-career training needs by elevating and formalizing ad hoc or casual training initiatives and creating institutional academies for both continuing and new employees. Thus, some in the media industry have relied on well-funded internal programs to help train their journalists. Examples include Germany's Springer Group, the U.K.'s British Broadcast

Corporation (BBC), All-India Radio, and China Television. In 2013, the three major print media companies in South Africa were all operating dedicated training programs, mainly aimed at filling gaps between tertiary education and the newsroom and providing higher-level education to existing employees. In 2014, however, one of these print companies, Independent Newspapers, shuttered its program. Examples of independent providers, linked to industry rather than universities, include the U.S.' American Press Institute and Poynter Institute and South Africa's Institute for the Advancement of Journalism. In addition, the African Woman and Child Feature Service (www.awcfs.org), a Kenyan-based NGO, provides short courses and training material for journalism students and working journalists in East Africa. Subjects covered include the reporting of parliament, economics, climate change, gender, HIV/AIDS, reproductive health, children and development issues, and newsroom management. UNESCO has responded to the need for short specialist course modules with publishing a series titled *A Compendium of New Syllabi* (2013, 2015), covering topics such as global journalism, gender and journalism, media viability, reporting human trafficking, and reporting sustainable development.

The very developments that call for upgrading the knowledge and skill levels of working journalists have also put pressure on entry-level journalists. Ten years ago, it was not essential for journalism students to know much about entrepreneurship, intellectual property, managing social networks, curating content, or digital security. And although it has become important for students to learn about such topics, many higher education sector journalism schools do not have the curricular flexibility to teach them in depth. On the other hand, several U.S. journalism programs have taken a step beyond the traditional use of books to teach such content by using software-learning exercises offered by online companies like Lynda.com and w3schools.com.

Furthermore, there has been the development of instruction linked to the rise of what may be called the "development aid industry." This "industry" evolved during the Cold War era and intensified with Western attempts to foster democratic capitalist systems in place of the failed political systems in Eastern Europe, Africa, and elsewhere. As a result, a sub-industry of short-course providers emerged to supply training to mainly working journalists (along with the promise of equipment, capital, and support for legal reform) (Hume, 2004; Nelson, 2010). Numerous cases of cross-border journalism education also occurred. For example, students from emerging democracies were funded to study in the United States, while "parachute professors" have historically often deployed to work abroad (Ognianova, 1995). In addition, British providers, including the Thomson Foundation and the Reuters Foundation (merged in 2008 into the Thomson Reuters Foundation), were prominent exporters of journalism education. American provider counterparts included Internews and the International Research & Exchanges Board (IREX). Large foundations, such as the Soros-funded "Open Society" institutes, supported journalism education and training activities in many countries. German foundations, such as the Konrad Adenauer Stiftung and Inwent, provided journalism education to thousands of people in, or from, developing countries. In many world regions, major broadcasters have also set up facilities, such as the Radio Netherlands Training Foundation, which provide, among other things, a range of courses to an international constituency. The German international broadcaster's Deutsche Welle Akademie provides extensive training as part of its general media development work.

In addition, some NGOs are providing a range of specialty courses usually relating to their particular causes, such as AIDS prevention, conflict resolution (for example the NGO "Search for Common Ground"), and transparent and fair elections. The World Bank Institute also provides courses in reporting on finances and corruption.

In the wider landscape of multiple providers of journalism education, institutions, such as the U.S.-based, nonprofit Poynter Institute, have included university faculty as clients in the hopes of updating and/or improving journalism education within the academy.

Partnerships between industry and universities are also beginning to appear. For example, the Deutsche Welle German broadcasting system has partnered with the University of Dortmund, the University of Bonn, and the Bonn Rhein-Sieg University of Applied Sciences in innovative master's degree programs. In 2010, *The New York Times*, as a part of its new business model, partnered for a short time with Ball State University to sell certified online journalism education services.

And in Australia, one public broadcaster asked university journalism schools to produce online editorial training modules for its internal use (Chadwick, 2009).

Online Initiatives

Online options in journalism education have helped make the increasingly crowded online field more universally accessible. The rise of the Internet has created a platform in which journalism education can be provided almost seamlessly across borders. The International Center for Journalists' website (www.anywhere.icfj.org) says it provides instructors who can teach journalism classes in local languages and that the site will translate comments among different-language speakers. For its part, the U.K.-based Commonwealth Broadcast Association, serving former British colonies, has set up a "Media Trust" that provides online courses in media leadership and management. And CNN announced an online learning opportunity for university students in September 2010.

And after operating in-person journalism training programs at its headquarters in St. Petersburg, Florida, for more than 30 years, the Poynter Institute established, in 2005, an online "university," News University. News University now offers more than 400 online short courses for journalists and journalism students and has more than 390,000 users (www.newsu.org/about). It also provides programs ranging from sequenced courses to one-time webinars, which are available to anyone anywhere as long as they (students, bloggers, working journalists, etc.) have an Internet connection, and, in some cases, a few dollars to spare. In 2009, the Poynter Institute demonstrated a strong interest in taking its free offerings global, and in 2010 its News University announced it would serve as a clearing house for journalism education-related global curriculum exchanges.

In 2011, UNESCO began to roll out a platform of "Open Educational Resources" based on adaptations of its model curriculum (www.unesco/webworld/en/oer). And in 2005, when a British controversy led to the resignation of the BBC's top leadership, the organization created a BBC academy and put considerable resources into it. In 2009, after four years of developing training material for in-house use, the BBC decided to make many of these materials available to the public through a third-party online vendor and Oxford University Press. Such material was "delivered" through paid online access at the BBC College of Journalism (http://bbcjournalism.oup.com). Yet in July 2014, the BBC College of Journalism suspended its paywall for a year and announced that it was making hundreds of training modules available free online. Perhaps the paid subscription model for educational materials was not as robust as the BBC originally thought (Looney, 2014). Its video and print resources, already available in 11 languages, are being translated into some 16 more to supply all 27 languages in which the BBC World Service broadcasts (Looney, 2014).

Many journalism teachers around the world are also making their course outlines and resources freely available online. One of the most prominent of such figures is Rosental Alves and his Knight Center for Journalism in the Americas based at the University of Texas, Austin. His service provides thousands of Spanish-language online courses in journalism, and his pioneering use of Massive Open Online Courses (MOOCs) for mass delivery of journalism programs has proven to be especially effective. Other well-known journalism education offerings include information provided by Alves' colleague, American journalist/journalism educator Mindy McAdams (http://mindymcadams. com/), the U.S.-based Association for Education in Journalism and Mass Communication (AEJMC, www.aejmc.org), and J Source, the Canadian Journalism Project (www.J-Source.ca). Even YouTube has a channel called "Reporters' Center" (youtube.com/reporterscenter), which hosts video tutorials on subjects such as investigative journalism, citizen journalism, journalism ethics, and how to conduct an interview. In addition, there are countless websites emanating from a wide range of sources worldwide that offer journalism instruction in various forms and/or engage in sharing knowledge—through debate, discussion, or demonstration—about the "hows" and "whys" of practicing journalism today.

Another emerging player in the journalism education online marketplace is iTunesU, sponsored by Apple. iTunesU is a free repository that encourages university faculty in a variety of fields to share their courses and tutorials online. Initially, iTunesU had few offerings in journalism and mass communication, but as of 2015 several courses have been added.

Beginning in 2012, several companies (e.g., Coursera, Udacity, edX) were formed to offer MOOCs to global audiences. Most of these courses are free, but some are proprietary and can be taken for university credit. The presence of journalism and mass communication courses will most likely follow the surge in courses in computer science and business.

In short, the range of actors providing journalism education continues to greatly expand over time, and the relationships among different constituents continue to evolve. In addition, transnational cyberspace initiatives continue to increase. This new reality has a bearing on the value of a traditional academic journalism education, the former bastion of supply, as well as on the range of media practitioners' opportunities for empowerment.

Issues

All these developments in journalism education and media training have exponentially expanded choice across universities and providers. Besides the formal courses offered, today's range of informal and indirect educational opportunities in journalism is vast.

One result of such developments has been an accelerated blurring between journalism training and journalism education (the "hows," "whats," and "whys"). Another has been an evolution of mutual respect between media professionals and educators. For example, formerly in the United States the distrust between practitioners and academics was palpable. However, the last two decades have seen a virtual love fest between the two. One reason that the Poynter Institute has been so successful in the United States is this relatively new, strong sense of interdependence between professionals and educators that allows the two to be blended easily into the Institute's training offerings. Its staff seem to recognize the value of time spent with academics as much as they do with journalists. Yet, tensions still exist. A vigorous debate has occurred over how extensively a "teaching hospital" model should be applied to journalism education. Several prominent American foundations involved in journalism education have advocated the hiring of more professionals, regardless of academic credentials. While most American universities have adhered to this approach, several academics have criticized extensive use of it.

In much of the developing world, journalism professionals' lack of respect for university journalism education remains a formidable challenge and impedes a closer relationship between professionals and the academy. Only when these barriers begin to crumble in more countries will increased connections among professionals, universities, and other training organizations blossom. In addition, in many developing countries, university-educated graduates are able to command higher salaries in communications work outside of news media organizations. Such higher salaries contribute to a relative disconnect between academy and industry in many developing countries.

In recent years, universities have felt a need to nurture connections among themselves. In 2002, a group of communication associations interested in journalism education began planning for a World Journalism Education Congress to be held in Singapore in 2007. This first meeting, and related conference, emphasized the commonality of issues facing university programs in this burgeoning field. The momentum gained from this meeting attracted 28 member organizations, which became known as the World Journalism Education Council (wjec.net) (Foote, 2008). During its formative days, the Council's member organizations decided to exclude training institutions, focusing only on problems/issues confronting university-level programs specializing in journalism education (Berger, 2010). Now that this informal group has defined itself as a coalition of specialized academic organizations, it is much more comfortable interacting with organizations devoted exclusively to journalism training. When the second WJEC convened in South Africa in 2010 (wjec.ru.ac.za), the relationship between the two types of providers received considerable discussion.

While training groups and university institutions continue to sort out their relationships, the proliferation of new players continues. In part this reflects the widening universe of actors who generate journalism outside of formal news media, and particularly those using social media platforms for text, audio-visual, graphic journalism, etc. The knowledge and skills to publish or broadcast online are necessary, but not sufficient, to do journalistic work online. But the relationship between the two domains of knowledge and skill has opened up a hybrid of capacity building that emulates aspects of journalism education and training. There are today innumerable tutorials on the Internet offering a range of learning outcomes that are relevant to practicing journalism (as well as other forms of communication). The upshot of all this is that journalism education's crowded marketplace is now demonstrating the need for traditional university-based journalism education suppliers to specialize in order to differentiate themselves better and remain competitive.

Overall, both online and off-line forms of dedicated, and often formal, journalism education have thrived. Journalism education has become one of the fastest growing academic fields in the world, even though enrollments often outnumber job opportunities within the formal media sector. As a partial result, most university journalism programs are over-enrolled. However, the proliferation of private media in the fastest-growing economies, combined with growing "internetization," is also presenting vast new job and, therefore, educational opportunities. Although the crisis facing newspapers in many developed economies has created a different set of challenges and possibilities, the thirst for structured journalism education seems undaunted—even when journalism education itself needs to be reimagined.

The traditional and newer suppliers of journalism education are not only competitors, but also potential allies. Some of these partnerships have been noted above. There seems to be a common interest among providers to promote journalism education in general and to build upon shared public domain knowledge to enhance what is offered. However, much university-based journalism education risks being out-flanked by providers in areas such as distance learning and in the creation of high-end multimedia instruction modules that transcend national and public/private boundaries.

Implications and Future Directions

Because media industries have been changing so rapidly, it is imperative that all journalism education organizations become especially nimble. Journalism education at universities has been under considerable pressure to change and update itself, especially in the area of converged media. This reality presents a good opportunity to assess the unique value that institutions in higher education bring to the cause of better-educated, empowered journalists. Higher education assets that are not easily replaceable include experience in the business side of education, the accreditation of systems, and the generation of research. Universities are particularly good at setting standards, providing consistency and continuity, presenting conceptual frameworks, and exposing students to broader academic studies.

University research requirements ensure the continuous examination of a broad range of topics in ways that the media industry and many NGOs do not. However, higher education can be painfully slow to change, and it often takes stray paths and finds itself at dead ends. That said, its competitive edge lies in its knowledge-based focus, which helps update important ideas and skills. Even university-based journalism educators who are not also journalism researchers have unique access to resources of scholarly colleagues engaged in the study of journalism and the changing global communications environment. Journalism educators can also draw upon research skills and activities from like-minded academics in cognate disciplines within their broader institutions. In addition, in theory at least, university-based journalism education practitioners are less likely to be vulnerable to "silo-ization" than journalism training providers based outside of higher education. This is due to university collegiate activities, such as research conferences and peer review practices, that can stir the intellectual pot. The significance of this aspect of universities as institutions has been highlighted recently by research stressing the need for journalism education programs to acknowledge the role of dominant ideologies, such as those based on class, race, gender, and nationality. Such ideologies work to benefit the status quo by leaning professional practice of journalism in favor of power, such as in coverage of international conflicts or economic policies (Jensen, 2014; Patterson, 2014).

Another key university-level journalism school advantage is the ability to experiment journalistically without enormous investments. Journalism school programs, which primarily exist to educate rather than to produce media, are often more concerned with creativity and generating knowledge than financial risk. When journalism schools do generate media products—even when they make a profit and/or serve the public—they usually state their motives as educational and journal-ism-outcome based rather than profit or dissemination-based.

Nevertheless, during the last decade, it has become more common for journalism schools to partner with media organizations to produce content. At Arizona State University in the United States, the *Arizona Republic* maintains a working newsroom within the Cronkite School of Journalism and Mass Communication. This newsroom handles most of the web-based breaking news for the newspaper. At the University of Oklahoma, students at the Gaylord College of Journalism and Mass Communication produce a weekly 30-minute sports program for a regional American sports network, Fox Sports Southwest. With indus-try resources becoming scarce, more of these types of content contribu-tion partnerships are likely to emerge.

What is also important in assessing the future of university-pro-vided journalism education is the notion of higher education hav-ing a degree of autonomy from the media. As Bollinger (2002/2003) has written, "A great journalism school needs to have some distance between itself and the industry which it serves." This is a critical factor since industry itself, in some aspects, has become a self-interested, rival supplier of journalism education, and one that is often instrumental-ized for short-term needs rather than having a longer-term, broader capacity-building rationale. The very externality of university-based programs from industry could be a strength that not just stimulates independent-minded journalism education, but also allows for nec-essary criticism when media institutions miss opportunities, suffer ideological myopia, or exhibit ethical lapses. Such externality is also a relevant factor when, as with the U.S. print media, jobs are scarce, and it becomes journalism schools' onus to empower would-be journalists to start their own media enterprises.

But university-based journalism education can also be manip-ulated to promote protectionist industry tendencies. For example, in Kenya the media industry and leading journalism schools have expe-rienced a move toward creating a "closed shop" through steps toward licensing the institutions that would be permitted to offer journalism education (Berger, 2009). Similarly, the Tanzanian government also considered licensing which individuals could work as journalism teachers, although this move did not ultimately materialize (Berger, 2009). Such cartel-minded measures ignore the reality of global providers beyond national jurisdictions, and they could only be effective if citizens were banned from using journalism-related international learning resources. They also contradict the notion of journalism as a specialized exercise under the broader right of free speech. As Hartley (2008) argues, journalism should be taught primarily as a human right rather than merely a means toward an institutional career. When governments license which institutions can teach journalism, with the stated motive of upholding standards, they actually create "closed clubs" based on self-serving models of journalism and who may teach them. This is close to the situation in Rwanda in the recent past, where at one point only individuals with government-approved qualifications were allowed to practice journalism.

In contrast to such controls, genuine university training in journalism is not only a practice within the rubric of academic freedom. It should also (and often does) operate to promote freedom of expression rights and access to journalistic skills and platforms to gain such rights. Another journalism education-related freedom is the freedom to use education provided. Journalism skill sets are easily transferable to other fields. In some cases, students study journalism with no intention of entering the profession. Instead they learn high-level information and communication skills to further their liberal arts studies or to pursue a related profession. It is not unusual to find journalism graduates contributing unique journalistic values to careers in law, public service, marketing, and other information sectors. Only totalitarian-leaning practices would seek to bind journalism graduates to working in media industries, although this is a complex issue when public resources are used to subsidize young people's education. Freedom to practice journalism should be matched by the freedom to not practice it, even if the general goal remains that journalism education should contribute to journalism.

An additional issue that merits discussion is that of the ultimate goal of journalism education: Regardless of its provider, journalism education needs to empower not only students, but ultimately journalism itself. In other words, quality journalism education is supposed to have an impact on the quality of citizenship and society. Similarly, journalism education can promote what UNESCO calls media and information literacy (UNESCO, 2014), by building capacity for journalistic participation among non-media professionals, such as with community media volunteers and social media users.

Programs with such goals have become important factors in journalism education in a number of countries. For instance, South Africa's Rhodes University, with Knight Foundation support, has provided (via established higher education routes) courses in citizen journalism to local residents who, for various reasons, would make journalistic contributions without becoming part-time or full-time journalists (thenewsiscoming.ru.ac.za). Around the world, many universities now require a media literacy course for all students. Such courses are seen as a way to help students become better media consumers, and, in some cases, to help them practice citizen journalism and to promote democratic change. In the West, where journalism enrollments are starting to decline, serving a broader university community via courses such as media literacy can also provide a valuable expansion of traditional missions and combine strengths of both journalism schools and their media studies or communications counterparts within the university.

Conclusion

This chapter attempts to sensitize readers to the changing landscape of journalism education and its relationship to the production of journalism. It also serves to raise citizens' ability to generate journalism and to understand it. It casts no judgment on whether one kind of education is better than another. Instead, it acknowledges a wide range of knowledge and skill-development systems in operation, all of which can help journalists provide a better service to society. This broad approach calls to mind Deng Xiaoping's famous aphorism that a cat's color is not as important as whether it can catch mice.

The business model of journalism education influences, and is influenced by, all the above. Most legacy providers (i.e., university-based schools) have not been giving away their services free of charge. In fact, students and their parents are paying ever-increasing tuition fees, and journalism education enrollments continue to grow in most parts of the world. University providers and others able to cross borders through online space are also experiencing remarkable growth. Yet the unquestioned success of journalism education also exposes its vulnerability. Because many university programs, especially in developing countries, have more students than they can handle, there has been little incentive to maximize strengths—to update and innovate—even when facing competition.

At the same time, some educators have been constructing content that possesses nearly universal utility or at least holds such value while also being amenable to being adapted to local languages and conditions. As more content is released online for free or at attractive prices, pressure could push traditional academic providers to adjust their delivery systems and/or their fee structures. Most journalism education programs have robust co-curricular opportunities that would be difficult to replicate without students being in residence. Yet, some aspects could easily be delivered in alternative ways by alternative providers.

One response to this challenge, which also reflects academia's interest in expanding student horizons beyond national contexts, has been the "pairing up" of elite journalism schools across borders. A key example is the Erasmus Mundus master's degree, which is earned in different European countries (www.MundusJournalism.com). More recently, a partnership has been formed between the journalism schools at Columbia University and the University of the Witwatersrand in South Africa. In addition, Northwestern University's Medill School of Journalism has an offshoot program in Qatar, and Australian universities with communications programs, such as Monash University, have similar initiatives abroad. All parties can gain value from such connections. Such initiatives could be analyzed as defensive or expansionist maneuvers, indicating a kind of fortress mentality among strong programs aiming to establish a closed eco-system of bastions elsewhere. But they also have great potential to engage in open, porous interactions within a global market, enriching and transforming the "mother ship" and becoming more internationalized along the way.

One area that journalism schools have yet to adequately address is the separation between content creation and content delivery. Universities have seamlessly combined the two for centuries. The same autonomous professor who creates content for a course also delivers it. Little distinction has been made between the two functions. Any challenge to this premise would shake academia's cultural foundation. However, for-profit universities and training institutions are increasingly discovering the profound distinction between the two and are realizing the great value of doing so.

For example, by investing sizable sums in creating content, for-profits can produce inherently valuable courses and modules that can then be delivered by lesser-skilled teachers/trainers at a lower cost. This process can, at least in theory, translate into higher-quality products and wider distribution at lower costs. By investing in high-quality content—with multifaceted areas of output—organizations can leverage their expertise far and wide. After an initial investment, institutions can repeatedly deploy a course at a limited expense. An additional plus is an ongoing ability to control quality.

Some universities are realizing that they cannot match the quality of content being offered by NGOs or commercial providers in specific subject areas, especially in sub-specialties (such as multimedia or climate change reporting) that may not be economically feasible to deliver even if they could create the content. If an NGO or industry provider is doing an excellent job providing learning resources in these or other subjects, there is little reason for a school to duplicate these efforts. Partnerships with a distributed model can provide a rich and coherent journalism education service.

Universities are entering a time when hybrid solutions are demanded. They can certainly no longer operate under the assumption that they are the kings of all journalism education content and practice. Yet, there is no need for them to step aside from the majority of their domain. Instead, schools should gravitate toward areas in which they can provide high-quality content, processes, and relationships for themselves and for distribution worldwide. They should also be more open to using content originating from training organizations, educational content creators, and peer institutions. Although universities may continue to deliver most of the pedagogical process themselves, they will not necessarily create all content themselves. University journalism schools should recognize and credit excellent work completed outside the academy. They could even assist such work by offering their own expertise in areas such as pedagogy, curriculum development, research resources, and linkages. Through such relationships, journalism schools can also improve in areas they may be lagging. For example, journalism education can partner with industry to learn how to better deliver, monitor, and evaluate long-distance training. Beneficiaries would be multiple learners of journalism, which would provide a wider value to society.

The situation in journalism education today mirrors the situation that individual media consumers face with increasing amounts of content choices. Such consumers also have increasing opportunities to produce their own content, which often involves self-education on an individual or shared social basis. This type of self-education becomes one of many options for students.

This chapter is based on the premise that journalism education is primarily about journalism, not the institutions through which much of its educational practice has been historically based. The objective of journalism education should not be to focus exclusive attention on journalism courses for students within mass media courses, as has often historically been the case. A wider vision is needed of empowerment of all people who want to do journalism. This indeed means providing campus-based students with the skills of journalism, although not in isolation of other knowledge bases relevant to the practice of journalism. It also means, however, that journalism education ought not to ignore the needs of off-campus learners and the learning resources availed by off-campus providers. From a journalism-centric viewpoint, journalism education should be based on a wide range of journalism education activities and content, conceptual and practical, serving a range of actors on and off campus, and coming from many diverse quarters and channels. The result can be a richer production and consumption of journalism. And reinforcing this scenario is the reality of increased complexity in the practice of journalism (such as subject knowledge, data analysis, verification standards, etc.) and the knowledge that traditional journalism educators alone can no longer provide all the journalism education/training needed.

In conclusion, journalism education should be seen as a means to an end, not an end in itself. And the landscape of journalism education providers should be viewed as a subsidiary matter in relation to this bigger picture. The broader global context and community increasingly calls for every person interested in the future of journalism to pay attention. This is particularly relevant when one considers how the complex, multiplayer whole affects the diverse individual parts—especially when it comes to university-based journalism education.

References

ARTICLE 19. (2012) Policy brief. International standards: Regulation of media workers. Retrieved from https://www.article19.org/resources.php/resource/3021/en/international-standards:-regulation-of-media-workers#_ftn1

Berger, G. (2007). In search of journalism education excellence in Africa: Summary of the 2006 Unesco project. *Ecquid Novi, 28*(1-2), 149-155.

Berger, G. (2009). How to improve standards of journalism education. *African Communication Research, 2*(2), 271-290.

Berger, G. (2010). Journalism teachers building a global community. *Journalism & Mass Communication Educator, 65*(2), 157-167.

Bollinger, L. (2002/2003). *Communications*. Retrieved from http://www.columbia.edu/cu/president/communications%20files/journalism.htm

Bromley, M. (2009). Introduction. In G. Terzis (Ed.), *European journalism education* (pp. 25-34). Bristol: Intellect.

Chadwick, P. (2009, December). A shared challenge. Contribution to a panel discussion 'Self- regulation and the media,' Perth: Journalism Education Association Conference.

Deuze, M. (2008). Journalism education in an era of globalization. In M. Löffelholz & D. Weaver (Eds.), *Global journalism research: Theories, methods, findings, future* (pp. 267-281). Malden, MA: Blackwell Publishing.

Foote, J. (2008). World Journalism Education Congress, conference report. *Journalism Studies, 9*(1), 132-138.

Hartley, J. (2008). Journalism as a human right: The cultural approach to journalism. In M. Löffelholz & D. Weaver (Eds.), *Global journalism research: Theories, methods, findings, future* (pp. 39-51). Malden, MA: Blackwell Publishing.

Holm, H. H. (2002). The forgotten globalization of journalism education. *Journalism & Mass Communication Educator, 56*(4), 67-71.

Hume, E. (2004). *The media missionaries: American support for journalism excellence and press freedom around the globe.* Miami, FL: Knight Foundation.

Hume, E. (2007). *University journalism education: A global challenge.*

Washington, D.C.: A Report to the Center for International Media Assistance.

International Federation of Journalists. (2010). *Unions in touch with the future.* Retrieved from http://congress.ifj.org/assets/docs/131/026/f757f83-48b2e1a.pdf

Jensen, R. (2014). The ideology problem. Thomas Patterson's failed technocratic dream for journalism. Retrieved from http://dissidentvoice.org/2014/01/the-ideology-problem/

Josephi, B. (Ed.). (2010). *Journalism education in countries with limited media freedom.* New York, NY: Peter Lang.

Looney, M. (2014). *BBC makes its training resources free to the public in 11 languages.* Retrieved from http://ijnet.org/blog/bbc-makes-its-training-resources-free-public-11-languages

Medsger, B. (1996). *Winds of change. Challenges confronting journalism education.* Virginia, VA: The Freedom Forum.

Nelson, A. (2010). *U.S. universities and media development.* Washington, D.C.: Center for International Media Assistance.

Nordenstreng, K. (2009). Soul-searching at the crossroads of European journalism education. In G. Terzis (Ed.), *European journalism education* (pp. 511-518). Bristol: Intellect.

Ognianova, E. (1995). Farewell to parachute professors in East-Central Europe. *Journalism & Mass Communication Educator, 50*(1), 35-47.

Patterson, T. E. (2014). A rejoinder: The problem with Robert Jensen's "Ideology Problem." Retrieved from http://www.mediaethicsmagazine.com/index.php/browse-back-issues/187-spring-2014-vol-25-no-1/3999019-a-rejoinder-the-problem-with-the-robert-jensen-s-ideology-problem

Servaes, J. (2009). Epilogue. Back into the future? Re-inventing journalism education in the age of globalization. In G. Terzis (Ed.), *European journalism education* (pp. 519-539). Bristol: Intellect.

UNESCO. (2007). *Model curricula for journalism education for developing countries and emerging democracies.* Paris: UNESCO. Retrieved from http://unesdoc.unesco.org/images/0015/001512/151209e.pdf

UNESCO. (2013). *Model curricula for journalism education. A compendium of new syllabi.* Retrieved from http://www.unesco.org/new/en/communication-and-information/resources/publications-and-communication-materials/publications/full-list/model-curricula-for-journalism-education-a-compendium-of-new-syllabi/

UNESCO. (2014). *Media and information literacy.* Retrieved from http://www.unesco.org/new/en/communication-and-information/media-development/media-literacy/mil-as-composite-concept/

UNESCO. (2015). *Teaching Journalism for Sustainable Development. A compendium of new syllabi.* Retrieved from http://www.unesco.org/

new/en/communication-and-information/media-development/
journalism-education-and-training/

World Journalism Education Congress. (2007). *World journalism education census.* Retrieved from http://wjec.ou.edu/census

12

Going Global: Journalism Education Gets Its Act Together

Ian Richards and Charles C. Self[1]

Despite a vast literature on the subject, and although journalism today is practiced "everywhere from Tierra del Fuego to Timbuktu and accessible via everything from television to the twittersphere" (Richards, 2014, p. 5), just what "journalism" means remains an open question. This elusiveness has many implications, not least for journalism education, which has to contend with a world in which approaches to student instruction are mired in ambiguity and contradiction. This wasn't always the case. When journalism education began, it seemed simple enough. The then novel idea that journalism had a place at college has been attributed to Robert E. Lee, who led the Confederate Army of Northern Virginia during the American Civil War. In 1865, after the defeat of the South, Lee became president of what was then Washington College (later Washington and Lee University) in Lexington, Virginia, and established programs in agricultural chemistry, business, and journalism "to help rebuild a shattered South" (Washington and Lee University, 2014). Despite this promising start, it was not until the 1920s that journalism education came permanently to Washington and Lee. In the meantime, the Ecole Superieure de Journalisme in Paris commenced teaching journalism in 1899, while in the United States, with support from newspaper publisher Joseph Pulitzer, the cause was taken up by the University of Missouri (1908) and Columbia University in New York (1912).

During the 20th century, university-level journalism programs mushroomed around the globe as many others took up the idea that journalism should be taught at the college level. In India, for example, formal journalism education was first introduced in the 1920s,

---

1   Ian Richards has been a member of the World Journalism Education Council (WJEC) since 2004. Charles Self directed the WJEC worldwide census project and has been involved with WJEC since 2006.

then given a major impetus in the 1950s. According to Karan (2001), a need for formal training arose when some Indian scholars who had been trained abroad worked to establish journalism schools at a few Indian universities in the mid-1950s, offering postgraduate diploma courses in journalism. Today, many Indian universities have established journalism departments, and more than 50 have postgraduate programs, many of which offer doctoral degrees (Karan, 2001, p. 299). The drive to establish journalism schools was revived after World War II and given additional momentum toward the end of the century when communism collapsed in Eastern Europe and the Chinese and Indian economies rapidly developed. Indeed, by the turn of the 21st century, journalism education in China was estimated to be expanding at a rate of approximately 100 new programs annually and, by 2010, 650 undergraduate journalism programs existed in China with an estimated student enrollment of 160,000 (Guo, 2010, p. 9). Yet despite this expansion, there was less diversity in the forms of journalism education than might have been expected because, as Zelizer (2008) has pointed out, the U.S. model of journalism education rapidly became the "gold standard for much journalism around the world" (p. 254).

Yet there is great diversity in the social, economic, political, and cultural contexts in which journalism programs operate today. This is perhaps most strikingly illustrated in the differences between the Global North (Europe and North America), where most journalism programs are located, and the Global South (Latin America, Asia, Africa, and Oceania), where relatively few are based. The "Global South" is not simply a geographic description or a euphemism for underdevelopment but, rather, "references an entire history of colonialism, neo-imperialism and differential economic and social change through which large inequalities in living standards, life expectancy and access to resources are maintained" (Dados & Connell, 2012, p. 13). Not only are there epistemological and methodological biases that marginalize programs in the South, but there are also pressing practical problems, such as minimal access to computers, inadequate infrastructure, frequent power blackouts, physical danger, and political instability (Richards & Wasserman, 2013). Life is far from easy when (Pearce, 2006) you work in a university with a less-than-adequate library and if you are demoralised by a low salary and a lack of basic equipment such as a computer . . . with disaffected students who seem to be constantly at war with the university authorities or the state. (p. 56)

Journalism and Education

Several global trends that have emerged over the last two decades or so have further complicated this picture. Sterling (2009) has identified three such trends. The first is increasing specialization in teaching and research, which has focused on issues such as media ownership, audiences, and ethics, as well as social science-driven theoretical approaches to the study of media in general. The second is a move toward international journalism, which has challenged U.S. domination of the field, contributed to growing interest in the role of media in national development, and stimulated interest in comparative studies. And the third trend is greater emphasis on issues of gender and ethnic diversity, with implications for everything from student admissions and university staffing to course content and the demographics of newsrooms.

While these trends have gained momentum, journalism itself has also changed. Although much has been written about the challenges journalism still faces, the two most significant forces related to this chapter will be mentioned here: globalization and technological change. Marginson (1999, p. 19) has identified six "aspects of globalization": finance and trade; communication and information technologies; international movements of peoples; the formation of global societies; linguistic, cultural, and ideological convergence; and world systems of signs and images. He argues that in each of these areas, globalization has contributed to the rise of "world systems which have a life of their own distinct from local and national life, even while these world systems tend to determine the local and national" (Marginson, 1999, p. 20). As these systems have evolved, the rise of the Internet and social media have begun to undermine journalism's traditional economic base and its historic watchdog role. The result has been a fundamental challenge to our understanding of what constitutes journalism and widespread soul-searching over "the kind of global information environment that would best preserve and even expand the accountability, oversight, and transparency that have historically been the function of independent media" (Simon, 2014). The net result is that "scholars, publics, journalists and thus journalism educators [have had] to reconsider their approaches, definitions and function in society" (Deuze, 2000, p. 137).

For the purposes of this chapter, it is useful to recall the four broad roles of journalism delineated by Christians, Glasser, McQuail, Nordenstreng, and White (2009). The first is the monitorial role—journalism's traditional "vigilant informer" pursuit of collecting and publishing information of audience interest and distributing information on behalf of sources and clients, which includes providing advance intelligence, advice, and warning. Second is the facilitative role, promoting dialogue among readers and viewers. This is achieved through communication that engages and actively involves readers and viewers, which helps support and strengthen participation in civil society (outside state institutions and the market). In so doing, the cultural conditions for pluralism and democratic life are facilitated. Third is the radical role, providing a platform for views that are critical of authority and the established order and support for drastic change and reform. Finally, there is the collaborative role, the development of close relationships between the media and politically and economically powerful sources, primarily the state and its agencies. There is considerable overlap between the different roles since they all have common threads, such as providing information.

While all four roles have relevance to journalism education in various parts of the world, the first two—monitorial and facilitative—have been most influential. And as a consensus developed on the nature and purpose of journalism, so too has a consensus on standards in journalism education (Fröhlich & Holtz-Bacha, 2003). This helps explain why UNESCO has suggested that today's journalism programs tend to be organized around three curricular axes or lines of development even though journalism education is "offered in many different ways by many different organizations with different educational traditions and resources, in many different settings, circumstances and cultures, and in many different political conditions (UNESCO, 2007, p. 6). UNESCO

(2007) has summarized the three curricular axes as follows:

- ❏ an axis comprising the norms, values, tools, standards, and practices of journalism;
- ❏ an axis emphasizing the social, cultural, political, economic, legal, and ethical aspects of journalism practice both within and outside national borders; and
- ❏ an axis comprising knowledge of the world and journalism's intellectual challenges.

Common Concerns, Common Goals

As university-level education gradually became the dominant mode for training journalists, an extended debate arose over the role of university programs in journalism. The relationship between practice and theory was a central part of this discussion and lead, for example, to disagreement about the extent to which journalism programs should teach industry skills and to which they should provide a broader education. The particular needs and demands of media systems differ from country to country around the globe, but balancing practical and contextual knowledge remains center stage. Over time, other points of contention also emerged. These included whether journalism is a craft or a profession, whether curricula should have a strict disciplinary focus or be more diverse, and whether journalism as an academic discipline is suited to the academy. At the same time, most programs have had to contend with wider pressures affecting the college sector, from inadequate funding and resourcing to externally imposed measures designed to ensure accountability and quality.

From time to time such discussions have attained an intensity many have perceived to be counter-productive. In Australia, for example, the 1990s were marked by "the media wars," in which many of those teaching journalism at the university level were pitted against those teaching media and cultural studies. Less localized was the response in 2003 to then Columbia University President Lee Bollinger. Bollinger argued that it was vital for universities to play a role in engendering journalism as a profession with "stronger standards and values that will provide its members with some innate resistance to other competing values that have the potential of undermining the public responsibilities of the press" (Bollinger, 2003).

Many took up Bollinger's views, leading to a trend for universities to play an increasingly central role in contributing to journalistic professionalism and "to act as an important check on some of the more deleterious effects engendered by the increased commercialization and deregulation of the media sector that has occurred in recent times" (Nolan, 2008, p. 747). Thus, while it has long been assumed that education provides a solid foundation for the attitudes and knowledge of future journalists, college journalism education has increasingly been regarded as a corrective to some of the dramatic pressures on journalism in recent years (Nolan, 2008; Josephi, 2009; Richards & Josephi, 2013).

Such discussions tended to polarize scholars about best approaches to teaching journalism. However, it did not take long for those involved in journalism education to realize they had much in common with others working in the same field, provided they were located in the same region or country. As long ago as 1912, a small group decided to set up the American Association of Teachers of Journalism (AATJ) with the expressed aim of holding "an annual conference of those interested in the teaching of journalism, and to collect statistics relating to schools, courses and teaching in journalism" (AEJMC History, 2014). Two years later, the National Communication Association (NCA) was founded as an association of teachers of public speaking and rhetoric. The AATJ subsequently evolved into the Association for Education in Journalism and Mass Communication (AEJMC), with a focus on journalism and mass communication teaching and research. Since 1965, AEJMC has had an international communication division devoted to studies of communication outside the United States. The International Communication Association (ICA) emerged from the NCA in 1950 as the National Society for the Study of Communication. It became an independent association in 1967, taking its current name in 1969, and its international identity has since been a key issue (ICA History, 2014). In subsequent years, ICA established five regional at-large seats on its board for international representatives, moved its headquarters to Washington, D.C., and established a tiered dues and conference registration charge structure using the World Bank ranking of national economies. ICA has also worked to increase representation of international scholars on its publication boards. Finally, it holds its annual convention every other year outside the United States and co-sponsors regional meetings around the world.

Although initially much of the debate around common concerns took place within individual organizations, countries, and regions, this began to change as those involved began to realize that they faced similar conflicts and dilemmas as colleagues worldwide. As journalism programs began setting up worldwide, similar associations began to follow in many such countries. This was a gradual process, and, in many places, it was not until much later in the century that journalism educator associations were established. In 1975 in Australia, for example, the Journalism Education Association (forerunner of the Journalism Education and Research Association of Australia) was established. Such associations initially tended to have a somewhat inward focus, a situation that contributed to journalism educators worldwide being regarded for many years as somewhat parochial. This pattern has broken down in recent years as journalism education has become an established part of the post-secondary education scene in most countries. Still, calls for journalism education to "break out of its national carcass and internationalise" (Servaes, 2009) were still being made in the first decade of the 21st century.

All of these factors help contextualize AEJMC's 2001 decision to set up a task force on internationalization "that aspired to interact with other like-minded organizations around the world" (Foote, 2008, p. 132). Initially led by Dennis Davis (Penn State, U.S.) and Kazumi Hasegawa (University of Maryland, Baltimore County, U.S.), and later by Joe Foote (University of Oklahoma, U.S.), the task force's deliberations led to a proposal for a serious international conference dedicated specifically to journalism education. Underlying this was a desire to convene representatives of journalism education associations worldwide to discuss the many issues affecting them. Remarkably, such a meeting would be a global "first"; journalism education had often been included as a strand at a range of conferences but had never been the sole focus. In the words of task force chair Foote, from this "germ of an idea" came a full-scale planning effort designed "to bring together all of the existing professional organizations [worldwide] that represented journalism education" (Foote, 2007, p. 132). A group consisting of representatives of journalism education organizations worldwide began planning the conventions, including representatives from the United Kingdom, South Africa, Canada, China, Australia, Finland, Saudi Arabia, Israel, and the United States. The objective of the event would be to explore areas of common interest and concern for journalism educators globally, to examine basic approaches to teaching journalism around the world, and, if possible, to reach some consensus on common principles that could form the basis of a Declaration of Principles—upon which all journalism education organizations could agree (Foote, 2008). The committee decided to meet for its first conference in Singapore.

World Journalism Education Congress

This first conference, named the World Journalism Education Congress (WJEC), did indeed convene in Singapore in June 2007 and was hosted by the Asian Media Information Centre (AMIC) in conjunction with its annual conference. By the time this first conference took place, the number of journalism education organizations involved with the WJEC had grown from eight to 28, with nearly 500 first-conference delegates (Foote, 2008, p. 132). WJEC Singapore launched UNESCO's "Model curriculum for journalism education" (UNESCO, 2007), which outlined a range of undergraduate course curriculums that could be applied around the globe. On the day preceding the first WJEC's opening session, representatives met and agreed on a "Declaration of Principles for Journalism Education" (http://wjec. net/declaration-of-principles/). Among its provisions was acknowledgement that journalism is a global endeavour and that journalism students should learn that, despite political and cultural differences, they share important values and professional goals with peers in other nations. The WJEC also voted to continue to operate as a group to be known as the World Journalism Education Council, which would be informal, voluntary, and self-supporting, without a central bureaucracy or central administration.

WJEC conferences were established as three-day events with a three-level program consisting of plenary and simultaneous sessions, workshops, and syndicates, small group discussion and analysis of timely, important topics related to journalism education. The syndicates proved to be a highly successful means of facilitating communal feedback (Goodman, 2007). Overall, the formal and informal aspects of the Singapore program combined to produce an event that is "widely regarded as a milestone in international journalism education in terms of sharing knowledge, experience, resources and skills, as well as facilitating countless new relationships and networks" (Berger, 2010).

On the basis of the WJEC's Singapore success, despite the original decision to hold this conference only once, the council decided to hold another WJEC in 2010. In July 2010 the WJEC-2 was hosted by Rhodes University in Grahamstown, South Africa. Close to 300 educators from 54 countries attended this event, which gave an especially strong voice to journalism educators from Africa. WJEC South Africa was also notable because Nobel Laureate Archbishop Emeritus Desmond Tutu addressed attendees. Tutu formally closed the WJEC's final session by signing the Declaration of Table Mountain on African Press Freedom, which called for a strong, free, and independent African Press. It was no surprise when the WJEC decided to hold another congress in 2013, this time in Mechelen, Belgium. The WJEC-3 was hosted by The European Journalism Training Association (EJTA) and the Flemish/Dutch Network of Journalism Institutes (VNOJ). With a theme of "Renewing Journalism Through Education," the Belgian congress drew a capacity attendance of 400 delegates. Its success was a clear demonstration not only of the momentum that the WJEC has built since its inception, but also that WJEC is genuinely valued and needed by those involved in journalism education. For this reason, the council decided to maintain a three-year tradition of WJEC meetings.

The result was that almost 250 delegates attended WJEC-4 at Auckland University of Technology in Auckland, New Zealand, in July, 2016. The organizing committee, led by Verica Rupar, presented a program that incorporated an emphasis on journalism education in the South Pacific and included 16 panels, 10 syndicates, 46 paper sessions, two workshops, and a number of special events. The council meeting, held in conjunction with the event, determined that the next

WJEC conference will be held in Paris in 2019. WJEC-5 will be hosted by Paris-Dauphine University with the support of the Theophraste Network, the international French-speaking journalism school network founded in 1994. The theme will be "Teaching Journalism in a Disruptive Age," and attendance is likely to be boosted by the decision of the French journalism school network (CEJ) and EJTA to hold their annual conferences immediately prior to the event.

In between congresses, the WJEC executive board meets regularly via teleconferencing and, once a year, face-to-face. Apart from planning and organizing the WJEC, the council has initiated a number of projects, including a global census of journalism education. Supported by a grant from the Knight Foundation, and led by Foote and Charles Self from the Institute for Research and Training (IRT) at the University of Oklahoma, the three-year project aimed at locating and mapping academic programs teaching journalism and mass communication worldwide. The goals of the project have been to identify as many journalism programs as possible, to find contact information for these programs and additional information to make possible comparative analysis of journalism education internationally, to assess information about international cooperation and exchange agreements among journalism programs, and to disseminate information about these programs as widely as possible (Self, 2007). The results of the census not only confirmed the dramatic expansion in the number of journalism programs around the world, but it also pinpointed key concerns facing many of them. These concerns ranged from how journalism education should be defined to finding resourcing and ways of responding to rapid technological change.

Conclusion

It seems clear that the four WJEC gatherings have been a resounding success (Foote, 2007). In addition, journalism educators around the globe seem to have much in common. For example, many contend with similar pressures and have come up with creative responses to address such challenges. The WJEC has provided a specialized forum in which programs can share their challenges and responses. Topics arousing the greatest interest include balancing the conflicting demands of industry and the academy; course content, graduate competencies, and graduate employment; issues of diversity; responding to technological change and globalization; journalism's position in the academy; and the case for journalism education to be considered as a distinct field of study.

At a more fundamental level, there have also been intense discussions about the nature and values of journalism and journalism education, the Global North-South divide, and the future direction of the field. Zelizer (2008) has drawn attention to the inability of journalism scholars, educators, and practitioners to hear what one another is saying. The WJEC has provided a framework for breaking down this lack of communication via a format that "allows big-picture, high-impact sessions and very intimate syndicate sessions and personal interaction" (Foote quoted in Bishop, 2010).

The WJEC appears to have made a significant contribution to eroding the insularity and ethnocentrism that has in the past marred progress in the field. While such attitudes have not been eliminated, many journalism educators' perspectives appear to be more genuinely international because of their WJEC experiences. Indeed, some WJEC initiatives have had a multiplier effect in a number of countries. In the United States, for example, the WJEC's census, which demonstrated the recent rapid growth of academic journalism education worldwide (Self & Schroeder, 2011), has encouraged AEJMC to launch several initiatives to better respond to the growth of journalism education around the world. Its recent "Task Force on AEJMC in the Global Century" produced a series of recommendations to encourage members to engage in greater dialogue with their colleagues in other parts of the world (Self, 2014). In the Fall of 2015, AEJMC partnered with Pontifica Universidad Católica de Chile to host a successful regional conference in Santiago, Chile, which brought scholars and students from across the Americas to hear more than 30 presentation sessions in English and Spanish from more than 100 researchers and media professionals (aejmcsantiago.cl). More regional meetings are being planned. AEJMC also began a new "South Asia Initiative," bringing together scholars from across the South Asia diaspora. This initiative resulted in a day-long set of presentations at its 2016 annual conference (http://aejmc.org/events/mpls16/wp-content/uploads/sites/4/2016/07/South-Asia-Initiative.pdf). And similar WJEC-inspired developments have occurred elsewhere.

The WJEC's progress has not been painless. Resourcing is an ongoing source of concern, as is the political context in which some delegates and member organizations operate, especially in relation to issues such as freedom of speech and freedom of the press. Regrettably, there are some parts of the world where understandings of "journalism" and "journalism education" are simply not compatible with the values reflected in the WJEC "Declaration of Principles for Journalism Education." Tensions between the academy and industry, too, have not gone away.

However, it would be difficult to argue that WJEC has not been a positive development for journalism education globally. It has provided a unique forum for discussing common issues and for developing links across cultures and national borders. It has facilitated high-level thinking and personal contact in an atmosphere characterized by what Foote has described as "the magic of all these people from so many countries" (Bishop, 2010). The WJEC has also demonstrated that journalism educators from diverse cultural, political, economic, and ethnic backgrounds are capable of working together cooperatively and collegially to tackle common issues they face. This has all been achieved on a voluntary basis, with no central administration, bureaucracy, or source of funding. Clearly, the momentum for journalism educators to "get their international act together" (Berger, 2010) is up and running. With WJEC now an established feature of the global journalism education landscape, journalism educators have a strong base from which to keep the momentum going.

References

Adam, G. S. (2004). The events at Columbia, the design of journalism programs and the sources and nature of professional knowledge. *Australian Journalism Review, 26*(1), 5-18.

Association for Education in Journalism and Mass Communication. (2014). AEJMC History. Retrieved from http://www.aejmc.org/home/about/aejmc-history/

Berger, G. (2010). Journalism teachers building a global community. *Journalism and Mass Communication Educator, 65*(2), 157-167.

Bishop, K. (2010). *WJEC 2 is a smashing success. WJEC Report: Journalism edu-*

cation in an age of radical change. School of Journalism and Media Studies, Rhodes University, South Africa. Retrieved from http://wjec.ru.ac.za/index.php?option=com_k2&view=item&id=55:wjec-2-is-a-smashing-success

Bollinger, L. (2003). Statement on the future of journalism education. Retrieved from http://www.columbia.edu/node/8316.html

Christians, C., Glasser, T., McQuail, D., Nordenstreng, K., & White R. (2009). *Normative theories of the media: journalism in democratic societies.* Urbana, IL: University of Illinois Press.

Dados, N., & Connell, R. (2012). The Global South: Understanding people in their social worlds. *Contexts, 11*(1), 12-13.

Deuze, M. (2000). Re-directing education: considering theory and changes in contemporary journalism. *Ecquid Novi, 21*(1), 137-152.

Foote, J. (2007). World Journalism Education Congress: Its importance to ASJMC administrators. *ASJMC Insights,* 4-8.

Foote, J. (2008). World Journalism Education Congress. *Journalism Studies, 9*(1), 132-138.

Fröhlich, R., & Holtz-Bacha, C. (2003). *Journalism education in Europe and North America: An international comparison.* New Jersey, NJ: Hampton Press.

Goodman, R. (2007). Eight approaches to improving journalism education worldwide. *ASJMC Insights,* 11-18.

Guo, K. (2010, July). Chinese journalism education and Chinese curricula. Proceedings. World Journalism Education Congress, Rhodes University, South Africa .

International Communication Association. (2014). ICA History. Retrieved from http://www.icahdq.org/about_ica/history.asp

Josephi, B. (2009). Journalism education. In K. Wahl-Jorgensen & T. Hanitzsch (Eds.), *Handbook of journalism studies* (pp. 42-56). New York, NY: Routledge.

Karan, K. (2001). Journalism education in India. *Journalism Studies, 2*(2), 294-295.

Marginson, S. (1999). After globalization: emerging policies of globalisation. *Journal of Education Policy, 14*(1), 19-31.

Nolan, D. (2008). Journalism, education and the formation of 'public subjects.' *Journalism, 9*(6), 733–749.

Pearce, C. (2006). Editing an African scholarly journal. *Learned Publishing, 16*(1), 54-60.

Richards, I. (2014). Differences over difference: journalism beyond the metropolis. *Australian Journalism Review, 36*(1), 5-14.

Richards, I., & Josephi, B. (2013). Investigative journalism on campus: the Australian experience. *Journalism Practice, 7*(2), 199-211.

Richards, I., & Wasserman, H. (2013). The heart of the matter: journal editors and journals. *Journalism: Theory, Practice and Criticism, 14*(6), 623-636.

Self, C., & Schroeder, J. (2011). WJEC census of international journalism education provides powerful tool for researchers. *International Communication Research Journal, 46*(1-2), 68-77.

Self, C. (2007). Conducting an international census of journalism education. *ASJMC Insights,* 7-10.

Self, C. (2014). Report and recommendations of the Task Force on AEJMC in the global century. Columbia, S.C.: Association for Education in Journalism and Mass Communication.

Servaes, J. (2009). Back to the future? Re-inventing journalism education in the age of globalization. In G. Terzis (Ed.), *European journalism education* (pp. 519–39). Bristol, Intellect.

Simon, J. (2014). What's the difference between activism and journalism? Retrieved from http://niemanreports.org/articles/whats-the-difference-between-activism-and-journalism/

Sterling, C. (2009). Education, journalism. *Encyclopedia of Journalism.* Retrieved from http://sage-ereference.com/view/journalism/n129.xml

Unesco. (2007). Model curricula for journalism education for developing countries and emerging democracies. Paris, Unesco.

Washington and Lee University. (2014). About W & L. Retrieved from http://www.wlu.edu/journalism-and-mass-communications/journalism-at-wandl/history

Zelizer, B. (2008). Going beyond disciplinary boundaries in the future of journalism research. In M. Loffelholz & D. Weaver (Eds.), *Global journalism research: theories, methods, findings, future.* (pp. 253-266). Malden, Blackwell.

13

How Good Are We?: Toward a Global Refinement of Learning Outcomes Assessment in Journalism Education

Joe Foote and Felix Wao

As higher education in developed countries faces unprecedented scrutiny concerning its quality, access, and affordability, journalism education faces increased pressure to demonstrate its educational quality and value. In developing countries, journalism education's growth is so rapid that consumers have difficulty ascertaining quality in such a dynamic higher education environment. All of this has produced an increasing demand for accountability and proof of educational value. While the tools of learning outcome assessment remain crude, the vigor in pursuing quality assurance goals remains strong. This has led to the following key questions: To what extent is the higher education curriculum in journalism equipping students with essential skills that the industry currently demands? And how can the fast-growing gap between journalism education and practice be significantly reduced and, hopefully, eventually closed? The answers seem to point, in part, to the need to drastically improve processes aimed at continuously improving student learning.

Most higher education authorities in countries worldwide have a system in place to measure the outcomes of instruction and research. While each country's efforts embrace its own national and cultural identity, the methods are frequently similar. Some systems employ accreditation while others compile databases featuring various types of output. In some cases, programs are ranked or graded beyond just meeting a quality threshold. Finally, there are systems that tend to combine two or more approaches in an attempt to maximize their measure of educational quality. The broader environment of national systems is so diverse and idiosyncratic that no attempt has been made here to categorize the multitude of systems that span all disciplines.

In light of the above, the purpose of this chapter is twofold: to explore the most high- profile instances where journalism education has carved out a unique identity and responsibility in quality assurance systems, and to assess the structures of various quality assurance systems and the extent to which various approaches may lead to systematic documentation of important skills graduates of journalism schools are expected to demonstrate.

Evaluation of Journalism Education

The first part of this chapter focuses on efforts that deal specifically with journalism education, examining the following four environments in which journalism education is evaluated (Table 13.1, at the end of this section, summarizes these four environments):

- ❑ industry-based accreditation,
- ❑ peer accreditation,
- ❑ voluntary standards and model curricula, and
- ❑ government-based accreditation.

Industry-Based Accreditation

The earliest type of quality control evaluation came through trade unions. Journalism was not considered a profession, but a craft where apprentices worked their way into the system. When vocational colleges began to offer journalism courses, professionals in the field set standards for qualifying as a journalist. Journalism guilds in several European countries continue to employ this type of professional oversight.

U.K. Origins. The National Council for the Training of Journalists (NCTJ) was founded in 1951 as an NGO in the United Kingdom to oversee the training of journalists. From the NCTJ grew oversight of university diplomas in journalism (NCTJ, 2015). NCTJ celebrated its 60th anniversary in 2013. The National Union of Journalists endorses the NCTJ, the Broadcast Journalism Training Council (BJTC), and the Periodicals Training Council (PTC). NCTJ's goals are as follows (NCTJ, 2015):

❏ to focus on the vital skills of finding and telling stories accurately and on deadline,

❏ to reflect that most journalists work in a multimedia environment and that "new" and "traditional" skills should be fully integrated and embedded in training and assessment, and

❏ to ensure that essential core skills are covered and assessed to a national standard but with flexibility to specialize.

The NCTJ accreditation period for British journalism courses is a maximum of two years. A site visit is required. To gain a Diploma in Journalism, all candidates must complete five mandatory subjects that represent the core skills for all journalists—plus at least two of the specialist options. Classes representing core skills are: Reporting, Essential Public Affairs, Essential Media Law, Portfolio, and Shorthand. The inclusion of shorthand in the core courses has been controversial among journalism educators and has led to several universities not pursuing accreditation. Opponents argue that shorthand is a skill not relevant to a university-level course and is outmoded in the digital age. The NCTJ, however, remains reluctant to drop this requirement.

Once students have fulfilled the core classes, they can pick from the following specialist options: broadcast journalism, the business of magazines, sports journalism, media law, court reporting, online video journalism, and production journalism (editing).

The NCTJ boasts that university academic programs with NCTJ accreditation gives students the best chance of getting a job in journalism. It also provides awards of excellence for students and recent graduates who outshine others. Presumably, such awards also serve as markers of quality for universities.

The NCTJ presents one of the most transparent accreditation schemes in the world. It publishes all the tables it compiles to allow prospective students to make informed choices about which individual university programs are most appropriate for them. Each table shows the following:

❏ name of the accredited course;

❏ dates and duration of the accredited course;

❏ number of students completing the accredited course;

❑ number/percentage of students gaining A to E grades in each exam and, in the case of shorthand, the number/percentage of students passing at a minimum speed of 60 words per minute (wpm);

❑ number/percentage of students gaining A to C grades in each exam and, in the case of shorthand, the number/percentage of students passing at a minimum speed of 100 wpm; and

❑ name of the center where the testing took place.

A New Zealand example. New Zealand has a system similar to the United Kingdom's. The New Zealand Journalists Training Organization (NZJTO) recognizes 10 journalism programs in the country as "industry approved" programs. NZJTO declares that (NZJTO, 2014):

❑ We supervise the training offered at registered journalism schools.

❑ We operate an accredited workplace training scheme.

❑ We promote journalism as a career.

NZJTO oversees the creation of unit standards connected with the National Diploma in Journalism, the approved entry-level requirement to work in a newsroom in New Zealand (NZJTO, 2014). Thus, an industry-backed training organization has been able to prescribe the standards for the national body that governs higher education. Presumably, only graduates from NZJTO programs can enter the profession, a powerful incentive to complete a university journalism degree.

Originally these standards applied to seven polytechnics (technical colleges) and three universities, but the universities no longer participate in this scheme. Frank Sligo of New Zealand's Massey University bristled at the thought of competence-based training (CBT) standards that have a lot of "what" and very little "why" (Sligo, 2004):

> The philosophical basis of CBT and unit standards appears to be the notion that what a trainee needs to absorb, sponge-like, can be encapsulated in a collection of pre-packaged edicts, which, once ticked off, represent that appropriate knowledge has been acquired. In fact, this is a flawed model of data-transfer, not a theory of education. (p. 193)

While industry-mandated standards for journalism education lost much of their currency when universities established full academic journalism programs, the standards served as an important marker of quality when journalism migrated from being an apprentice trade to a respectable university discipline. One could argue that these standards accelerated the field's ascent during the '80s and '90s, when journalism programs blossomed in the academy. Now that journalism education is more firmly entrenched within university structures, there is less tolerance for industry-mandated standards.

Peer Accreditation. Peer accreditation in journalism education at the discipline level was pioneered in the United States in 1945 through the Accrediting Council on Education in Journalism and Mass Communications (ACEJMC, 2013). Today, ACEJMC accredits 110 academic programs in the United States and Puerto Rico. And, there are more than six ACEJMC-accredited programs outside the United States, the first being Catholic University in Santiago, Chile. ACEJMC recently modified its standards to make them less U.S.-centric and more applicable worldwide.

ACEJMC is one of the few quality assurance programs based on voluntary peer review. Academic programs approach the council to apply for accreditation. After a self-study and site visits, the council votes on accreditation, which is for a six-year period. However, there can be a provisional accreditation for two years while the unit works on problems cited, or accreditation can be denied. ACEJMC is an NGO not affiliated with the U.S. government. Its membership is split equally between educators and professionals.

ACEJMC accreditation is a "threshold" method of accreditation, setting standards that have to be met. However, it does not rank or designate programs that might display particular excellence, although it mentions superior qualities in site team report narratives. Council members (academics and professionals) have developed the following nine standards (ACEJMC, 2013):

- ❑ Standard 1. Mission, Governance, and Administration;
- ❑ Standard 2. Curriculum and Instruction;
- ❑ Standard 3. Diversity and Inclusiveness;
- ❑ Standard 4. Full-Time and Part-Time Faculty;

❏ Standard 5. Scholarship: Research, Creative, and Professional Activity;

❏ Standard 6. Student Services;

❏ Standard 7. Resources, Facilities, and Equipment;

❏ Standard 8. Professional and Public Service; and

❏ Standard 9. Assessment of Learning Outcomes.

Integrated into the standards are 12 values and competencies that the council adopted in 2000, which follow (ACEJMC, 2013):

❏ Understand and apply the principles and laws of freedom of speech and press, for the country in which the institution that invites ACEJMC is located, as well as receive instruction in and understand the range of systems of freedom of expression around the world, including the right to dissent, to monitor and criticize power, and to assemble and petition for redress of grievances.

❏ Demonstrate an understanding of the history and role of professionals and institutions in shaping communications.

❏ Demonstrate an understanding of gender, race, ethnicity, sexual orientation, and, as appropriate, other forms of diversity in domestic society in relation to mass communications.

❏ Demonstrate an understanding of the diversity of peoples and cultures and of the significance and impact of mass communications in a global society.

❏ Understand concepts and apply theories in the use and presentation of images and information.

❏ Demonstrate an understanding of professional ethical principles and work ethically in pursuit of truth, accuracy, fairness, and diversity.

❏ Think critically, creatively, and independently.

❏ Conduct research and evaluate information by methods appropriate to the communications professions in which they work.

❏ Write correctly and clearly in forms and styles appropriate for the communications professions, audiences, and purposes they serve.

❏ Critically evaluate their own work and that of others for accuracy and fairness, clarity, appropriate style, and grammatical correctness.

❑ Apply basic numerical and statistical concepts.

❑ Apply tools and technologies appropriate for the communications professions in which they work.

An interesting dimension of American peer-review accreditation is its process of self-regulation. The U.S.-based Council for Higher Education Accreditation (CHEA), a non-government organization founded by university administrators, accredits ACEJMC and 59 other U.S.-based accrediting organizations (CHEA, 2013). Most of the board members are academics. There is no representation from the U.S. government, although CHEA works closely with the Department of Education. An accreditor of accreditors is important because in the United States any organization can become an accreditor. Yet, only those that carry the stamp of a self-regulatory organization, like CHEA, are taken seriously.

Recently, the American Communication Association (2013), a small academic body founded in 1993, began an accreditation initiative (ACA, 2013). It is similar to ACEJMC's process in that it has criteria for accreditation, a self-study, site visit, and adjudication. It is not, however, part of CHEA or any other oversight organization. Time will tell how this initiative fares and which programs apply to it for accreditation.

Voluntary standards and model curricula. In addition to establishing official accreditation bodies, there has also been initiatives to set voluntary standards in hopes that organizations will adopt and practice them. Among the first taking that approach was the European Journalism Training Association (EJTA). In June 1997, it adopted the Tartu Declaration, which established a framework for assessing quality in journalism education (EJTA Tartu-declaration, 2013). In the declaration, the educators said that journalists should serve the public by

❑ providing insight into political, economic, socio-cultural conditions;

❑ stimulating and strengthening democracy at all levels;

❑ stimulating and strengthening personal and institutional accountability; and

❏ strengthening the possibilities for citizens to make choices in societal and personal contexts while feeling responsible for freedom of expression, respecting the integrity of individuals, and being critical of sources and independent of vested interests using customary ethical standards.

The heart of the declaration is 10 competencies for journalism education. In taking this initiative, EJTA became one of the first organizations in the world to focus on outcomes-based assessment of programs. The 10 competencies outlined in the Tartu Declaration follow (EJTA, 2013):

❏ Reflect on the societal role of and developments within journalism.
❏ Find relevant issues and angles, given the public and production aims of a certain medium or different media.
❏ Organize and plan journalistic work.
❏ Gather information swiftly, using customary newsgathering techniques and methods of research.
❏ Select the essential information.
❏ Structure information in a journalistic manner.
❏ Present information in appropriate language and an effective journalistic form.
❏ Evaluate and account for journalistic work.
❏ Cooperate in a team or an editorial setting.
❏ Work in a professional media-organization or as a freelancer.

For each of these 10 competencies, EJTA established a list of indicators that would help programs understand whether or not they were meeting their goals. For example, the following indicators amplify the fairly vague competency of "select the essential information" (EJTA, 2013):

❏ Be able to distinguish between main and side issues.
❏ Be able to select information on the basis of correctness, accuracy, reliability, and completeness.
❏ Be able to interpret the selected information and analyze it within a relevant (historical) framework.
❏ Be able to select information in accordance with the requirements of the product and medium.

❑ Be aware of the impact of your information on sources, the public, and public debate.

Another pioneering effort occurred in 2007 when the United Nations Educational, Scientific and Cultural Organization (UNESCO) unveiled a model curriculum for journalism education in Africa at the first World Journalism Education Congress (WJEC) in Singapore (UNESCO, n.d.). It also named what it termed the Potential Centers of Excellence in Journalism Training in Africa (UNESCO, n.d.). After thorough research, 12 journalism and media training institutions were named on the list. UNESCO hoped that these 12 institutions in Africa would be a beacon for others and supplied a curriculum that would help programs achieve excellence.

The UNESCO model curriculum is built on four foundational competencies (UNESCO, 2013):

❑ an ability to think critically, incorporating skill in comprehension, analysis, synthesis, and evaluation of unfamiliar material, and a basic understanding of evidence and research methods;

❑ an ability to write clearly and coherently using narrative, descriptive, and analytical methods;

❑ a knowledge of national and international political, economic, cultural, religious, and social institutions; and

❑ a knowledge of current affairs and issues, and a general knowledge of history and geography.

The model curriculum included specific plans for each year of an undergraduate degree and a professional master's degree for students who have had no exposure to journalism. Syllabi were included for each class with specific lecture topics, readings, and assignments. The model curriculum was heavily weighted toward skills courses, but emphasized that conceptual courses were an important part of the curriculum that should not be excluded.

One of the virtues of the model curriculum was it was generic enough to be adopted by areas around the world. Less than four years after UNESCO issued its model curriculum for Africa, it encouraged a similar effort in Latin America. A meeting in Quito, Ecuador, in 2011 discussed how the curriculum could be modified for journalism education in the region. UNESCO promotes the model curriculum as (UNESCO, 2013) follows:

> a generic model that can be adapted according to each country's specific needs. It takes full cognizance of social, economic, political and cultural contexts of developing countries and emerging democracies, highlighting the connection between democracy and journalism, and arguing for a more cross-disciplinary approach within journalism-training organizations.

The latest region seeking to employ the UNESCO model curriculum is the Maghreb in North Africa. The Maghreb initiative was launched in Rabat, Morocco, in 2011. The effort, in partnership with several NGOs in the region, focuses on promoting gender-sensitive media content in journalism education. The major objective of this program is to "raise awareness of media professionals, decision makers, managers of training institutions and civil society groups about the representation of women in Maghreb media, and to advance gender equality in Maghreb countries" (UNESCO, 2013).

In 2005, the Carnegie and Knight Foundations in the United States announced an initiative to "advance the U.S. news business by helping revitalize schools of journalism." The Carnegie-Knight initiative's three distinct efforts follow (The Future of Journalism Education, 2013):

❑ Curriculum Enrichment: A process aimed at offering students a deep and multi-layered exploration of such complex subjects as history, politics, the classics, and philosophy to undergird their journalistic skills while raising the profile of journalism education within the university.

❑ News 21: National reporting projects incubated and organized on an annual basis and overseen by campus-based professors for distribution through traditional and innovative media.

❑ The Carnegie-Knight Task Force: Provides journalism deans with an opportunity to speak out on issues affecting journalism education and the field of journalism.

Five universities were included in the original initiative. Seven additional universities have been added. Conversations with deans and journalism professionals became the intellectual foundation for the Carnegie-Knight Initiative on the Future of Journalism Education. In some ways, the 12 universities designated as Carnegie-Knight participants have become a *de facto* list of model programs in the United States. They are as follows:

- ❑ Arizona State University;
- ❑ Columbia University;
- ❑ Harvard University;
- ❑ University of California, Berkeley;
- ❑ University of Maryland;
- ❑ University of Missouri;
- ❑ University of Nebraska;
- ❑ University of North Carolina, Chapel Hill;
- ❑ Northwestern University;
- ❑ University of Southern California, Los Angeles;
- ❑ Syracuse University; and
- ❑ University of Texas at Austin.

Another informal factor affecting quality control in journalism education has been a proliferation of surveys of top programs and student satisfaction. Australia has a ranking based on student satisfaction ratings over four years—a system the government uses to announce a rank-ordered list of programs. New Zealand's NZJTO has published a list of the country's journalism schools recognized by the industry.

Some magazines and newspapers have occasionally announced ratings of journalism programs, although popular professional fields like business, law, and medicine take priority when it comes to annual rankings. These rankings have had a significant effect on how the public and the academy perceive programs in some fields. The Internet has provided incentive for individuals to create their own subjective rankings of programs. It is usually not clear what criteria are used for websites that promote the "top 10 programs in journalism" or the "top 10 programs in advertising." Presumably, they are quite subjective. Anyone with a computer can proclaim to be an arbiter of quality in a particular field.

Government-based accreditation. In most developing countries quality control of higher education is under the jurisdiction of the government. While specific areas and extent of government oversight may vary from one country to another, such governments usually verify and/or make decisions about fundamental policies and practices in critical areas concerning colleges and universities, including, but not limited to, the following:

- ❑ number and location,
- ❑ mission,
- ❑ enrollment size,
- ❑ student access to instructional programs and degree requirements,
- ❑ quality standards expected in student performance,
- ❑ quality of research,
- ❑ academic freedom,
- ❑ appointment and promotion of staff and faculty,
- ❑ internal organizational structure, and
- ❑ allocation of resources—including financial support.

Oversight by various governments is not only applicable to public universities and post-secondary institutions, but also private universities—especially in light of policy guidelines regarding their establishment, operation, and licensing processes. In most developing countries, this model of government control is largely aimed at ensuring quality outcomes while, at the same time, promoting development and diversity in academic program offerings that match countries' job market needs.

Government-based accreditation is the norm in most of the developing world, where higher education is centralized. The following case study illustrates the structure many countries employ.

A Kenyan Case Study

In Kenya, the Commission for University Education (CUE) is responsible for ensuring quality education in all universities and post-secondary institutions. CUE is the sole regulatory agency for planning and coordinating the growth and expansion of university education in Kenya. The commission is a specialized government agency in the Ministry of Higher Education, Science & Technology, and its functions can be summarized as follows:

- ❏ accreditation and regular re-inspection of universities;
- ❏ planning for the establishment and development of higher education and training;
- ❏ mobilization of resources for higher education and training; and
- ❏ documentation, information service, and public relations for higher education and training.

The CUE's academic program standards, which include various expectations and indicators of quality focused on assessment of student learning, are intended for all academic programs in any Kenyan university. While CUE applies the standards at the institutional level, each discipline must meet them in the context of broad educational goals and specific student learning outcomes. For instance, any institution offering a baccalaureate degree in any area of journalism and media studies must demonstrate how its program achieves the following (CUE, 2014):

- ❏ creating a broad knowledge base within a discipline involving critical and analytical understanding of the major theories, principles, and concepts in the discipline;
- ❏ teaching a comprehensive range of cognitive and analytical skills and their application to various situations;
- ❏ demonstrating adequate problem-solving skills; and
- ❏ enhancing society's awareness and contributing to its general development.

Journalism and Media Education in Kenya

Journalism and media education in Kenya was built upon, and continues to mirror, colonizers' interests. As a result, journalism training designed with a curriculum that centers on African culture has experienced a very slow development. Even though the first journalism education curriculum was established at the University of Nairobi more than four decades ago, it was built on Western-style curricula. While the past two decades have seen a rapid increase in public and private institutions of higher learning offering journalism education

(Media Council of Kenya, 2015), curricula are still largely Western oriented and focused on genres such as advocacy, broadcast, database, and investigative journalism.

Review and Accreditation of Journalism Education in Kenya

While the number of higher institutions of learning offering journalism and media studies in Kenya has been growing steadily, the extent to which graduates of these programs are able to demonstrate journalistic knowledge and skills remains highly questionable. As such, a key question regarding journalism education in Kenya is whether or not institutions should be required to articulate common broad knowledge and a set of skills/abilities journalism graduates should be expected to demonstrate irrespective of their alma mater. This would not only lead to a systematic review and formal accreditation of journalism education (which does not currently exist), but would also raise the overall quality of journalism education.

The Media Council of Kenya (MCK), established in 2013, is developing a set of standards that will define specific competencies for all diplomas (somewhat similar to associate degrees in the United States) and certificate-training institutions. Since the new standards will certainly be embedded in the journalism curriculum across all journalism schools in the country, it is expected that a national, standardized examination will be developed to assess competencies reflected in the new standards.

There is wide expectation that the new standards will lead to the introduction of industry-heavy courses aimed at closing the huge gap between the current curriculum and those competencies needed in the industry. While this is a positive move, it could tilt the balance too heavily toward industry needs. Further, faculty will certainly feel left out of the equation if they are not involved in the development, implementation, and/or assessment of the new curriculum. It is unclear how MCK, which was initially formed to regulate the conduct of journalists, will assume the role of accrediting academic institutions.

Table 13.1

Analysis of Assessment-Related Deficiencies in Quality Assurance Approaches

Quality Assurance Approach	Brief Definition	Examples	Impact	Faculty Involvement	Deficiencies (Assessment-Related)
Industry-based Accreditation	Earliest type of quality control evaluation of journalism training. Industry professionals set standards for qualifying as a journalist.	New Zealand Journalists Training Organization (NZ-JTO); National Council for the Training of Journalists (NCTJ).	Industry professionals play a significant role in making decisions.	Low	Faculty are less involved in setting standards and making assessments, which leads to a disconnect between curriculum and learning outcomes.
Peer Accreditation	A peer-review board, consisting of faculty and industry professionals, sets accreditation standards for evaluating academic quality of journalism schools.	Accrediting Council on Education in Journalism and Mass Communications (ACEJMC); American Communication Association (ACA).	Industry professionals and faculty in the discipline give considerable input.	High	Inconsistencies among accreditation policies, interpretation of accreditation standards, and outcome of accreditation visits.
Voluntary Standards & Model Curricula	Organizations (national, continental, and/or international) set standards for evaluating the quality of journalism training programs and develop model curriculum.	The European Journalism Training Association (EJTA); The United Nations Educational, Scientific and Cultural Organization (UNESCO).	Various institutions appoint or invite industry professionals and faculty to jointly develop standards and curriculum models.	Medium	Although this model focuses on outcome-based assessment, faculty involvement in developing the standards and/or curriculum models is still minimal.
Government-based Accreditation	Government sets standards of evaluating academic quality of higher educational institutions via government appointees from universities, ministry of education, and businesses.	Kenya's Commission for University Education (CUE).	Government-appointed officials set standards for all universities and post-secondary institutions.	Low	Since the government appoints all accreditors, the process of quality assurance is not viewed as promoting quality improvement based on institutions' self-reflection for continuous improvement. Rather, this is a more regulatory, accountability-based approach.

Evaluation of Journalism Education

This chapter section lists deficiencies in each of the four environments in which journalism education is evaluated. It also shows how the structure of the quality assurance processes may hamper a systematic inclusion and/or implementation of authentic assessment of student learning in journalism curricula, leading to potential gaps between curricula and graduates' ability to apply acquired knowledge and skills to real-world situations. The authors provide practical recommendations focusing specifically on practical assessment strategies. These strategies can be used in a variety of environments to measure students' ability to demonstrate knowledge and skills acquired in their journalism training.

Industry-based Accreditation

As stated above, this model of evaluating educational quality is characterized by industry professionals setting standards for how the curriculum should be structured (often to mimic industry's needs) and designing examinations journalism graduates must pass after completing their formal journalism education. Accordingly, industry professionals have control of journalism curriculum and its review. Faculty, for the most part, are expected to implement the curriculum through teaching and learning processes developed in each institution.

Industry-based accreditation reflects low faculty involvement in the standards-setting process, thereby leading to obvious gaps between the intended curriculum, its execution, and learning outcomes journalism graduates are expected to demonstrate.

Faculty may be actively involved in conducting various forms of *formative assessments,* which characterize most of the non-credit strategies used to gauge student understanding during class meetings (such as frequent tests, quizzes, etc.). However, they are rarely involved in preparation or design of some of the *summative assessm*ents (especially discipline-specific, national-type exams) meant, in some countries, for journalism graduates to earn some kind of licensure for industry jobs. Such assessments would be similar to law students' bar examination, which they must pass before practicing law.

The main challenge with the above approach is the low involvement of faculty in the articulation of standards.

Recommendations for possible solutions follow:

❑ Promote a high level of faculty involvement: Boosting faculty involvement in setting accreditation standards and designing field-specific journalism examinations, usually tied to the journalism curriculum, is critical in ensuring journalism graduates' overall success.

❑ Developing internship programs: The evaluation of students during their practicums or internships should be a partnership between industry professionals and faculty. Standards for evaluating the success of students during their internships should be designed jointly by faculty and industry professionals. This will not only lead to greater partnership between journalism schools and industry professionals, but also contribute to an increased quality of journalism school graduates.

Peer Accreditation

While industry-based accreditation relies heavily on professionals in the field to set accreditation standards, some peer accreditation systems can be totally divorced from the professional environment. This is the case in the regional system of accreditation in the United States. At the discipline level, the situation is better. In ACEJMC journalism accreditation, for example, professionals comprise nearly one half of its policy body and every site team contains a professional. In ACEJMC, it could be argued that the professional focus sometimes dominates the academic. Although journalism accreditation in the United States has benefitted from a shared ownership of the process, to be effective, peer accreditation must develop a mechanism within the accreditation process that creates a balance between the classroom and industry. Accordingly, it would be important to include *professional experience* as an accreditation requirement. This would ensure that all students are provided with opportunities to apply knowledge and skills to real professional environments, and a significant reduction of the constantly growing gap between curriculum and practice would result.

Another dimension of peer accreditation is the adjudication of site-team recommendations at various levels. A voluntary peer accreditation system cannot succeed without establishing a high level of confidence in the administration of the system and its fairness to all constituencies.

Recommendations for possible solutions follow:

- ❏ develop a peer accreditation structure that provides for both academic and professional representation,
- ❏ establish a well-defined structure that clearly elaborates the standards for accreditation and its administration,
- ❏ include a strong adjudication system that addresses the needs of stakeholders in the process, and
- ❏ establish a cost structure that makes accreditation accessible for most public and private institutions.

Voluntary Standards and Model Curricula

This approach characterizes an informal, voluntary adherence to a set of standards, often expressed in terms of expected learning outcomes and/or competencies journalism graduates are expected to be able to demonstrate, as well as curricular models defining course structures to be adopted by interested institutions.

The main deficiency in the above approach is its informal nature. This can easily lead to a lack of accountability, including, but not limited to, the likelihood of not having appropriate assessments (or not having any assessments at all) to address goals and learning outcomes or competencies.

Recommendations for possible solutions follow:

- ❏ recommend a list of appropriate assessment approaches for each of the standards/goals, which may be quite helpful to faculty in institutions and regions that may be willing to adopt the standards but do not have strategies for assessing them; and
- ❏ develop a process of assessment that ensures continuous improvement of student learning.

Government-based Accreditation

This approach to accreditation is characterized by strict adherence to government-set standards and guidelines. A key feature is its heavy focus on compliance with regulations instead of concentrating on student achievement evidence for continuous improvement purposes. As a result, instruction in most institutions is centered on a heavily prescribed set of government standards. This not only limits the instructors' ability to implement authentic, real-life assessment strategies, but also inhibits creativity on the part of students who may be talented enough to think outside the box. This further leads to the inability of graduates to demonstrate what they have learned. As Wolff (2005) notes:

> When accreditation is seen primarily as a compliance-driven exercise to demonstrate the achievement of minimum standards and no more, it becomes like a trip to the dentist: a necessary task but one that should take as little time and cause as little pain as possible. (p. 87)

A potential solution to the above challenge is for governments to allow and approve formation of independent agencies consisting of university professors and professionals in various journalism fields to jointly develop concrete standards of educational quality, which would serve as a foundation for the peer accreditation process. This move would not only boost the standards and quality of journalism education, but also contribute to quality assurance of graduates and journalism programs.

Bridging the Drift Between Journalism Education, Learning Outcomes, and Practice

The well-known bridge between journalism education and practice is less well constructed and less effective than it could be. As members of a professional discipline, it is important for journalism academics, the practitioner community, and journalism professional organizations (including accrediting bodies) to reflect on how relevant learning outcomes are to current industry demands. In sum, a sound, practical assessment mechanism involving educators and practitioners may need to be intentionally and systematically embedded in the curriculum to begin to close the gap between education and practice.

As depicted in Figure 13.1, the interrelationships between journalism teaching, learning outcomes, and practice can be represented as a triangle with bi-directional connections to each of the triangle's nodes.

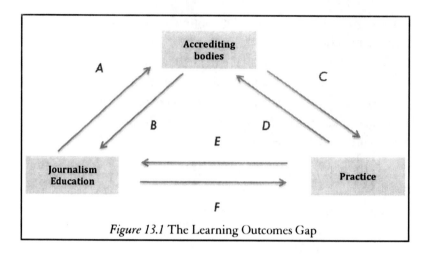

Figure 13.1 The Learning Outcomes Gap

To the extent that journalism academics, accrediting organizations, and practitioners lack alignment in their functions (including communication to enhance these links), there is a learning outcomes gap. The existence of this gap, in journalism and other disciplines, has been the subject of much research (Du & Lo, 2014).

Research on assessment with a specific focus on learning outcomes, their current practical relevance, and, most importantly, graduates' ability to clearly demonstrate knowledge and skills indicate the gap between intended curriculum (what instructors prepare or plan to teach) and learning outcomes (what students can demonstrate upon completion of a learning experience). This has led to the emergence of two different assessment communities with very different values and ideologies. While one believes in concentrating on *what* the curriculum should focus on, the other believes in the importance of graduates' ability to demonstrate knowledge and skills acquired through a set curriculum and *alignment* of learning outcomes with professional demands.

The learning outcomes gap is due to the lack of involvement of professional practitioners in identifying current knowledge and skills needed by the industry and the failure of the accrediting agencies to restructure their assessment-related standards to address the current practical industry demands in terms of knowledge and skills. The following recommendations may help significantly reduce the learning outcomes gap. Those assessing journalism education should as follows:

- ❑ Match skills and abilities required in the industry, which calls for improved and constant communication between journalism instructors and industry professionals.
- ❑ Implement authentic assessment tools, which can measure the extent to which students are achieving knowledge and skills.
- ❑ Require professional experiences for each major—the best opportunity for students in any professional field is exposure to a real workplace. This usually becomes students' first test of the extent to which they can actually demonstrate acquired knowledge and skills. To maximize students' ability to demonstrate outcomes, it is important to organize multiple opportunities for professional exposure and assess students' practical experiences.
- ❑ Communicate the learning outcomes to students, which will greatly boost their understanding of the profession and promote their self-assessment in light of the curriculum.
- ❑ Align each learning outcome with the current, practical needs of the industry. For example, accreditation standards should require evidence of a clear link between learning outcomes and industry needs, and site teams should include both journalism educators and practitioners.

Conclusion

This chapter explored journalism education's unique identity in the quality assurance process, using the three main forms of program assessment being employed around the world. While quality assurance in journalism education takes a variety of forms in different countries, measuring the educational quality and value of journalism education remains a great challenge across all continents. Yet, it is a challenge that must be fully confronted for journalism education to address the current demands of the industry and the requirements of its own academic institutions. Key among the deficiencies are the lack of faculty involvement in development of standards for quality assurance and the lack of assessment systems to ensure articulation of concrete, measurable learning outcomes and corresponding direct measures.

Journalism programs must challenge students intellectually and prepare them for careers in the industry. They must develop innovative instructional processes to equip students with critical-thinking and analytical skills. More importantly, faculty in journalism institutions should develop and implement innovative assessment practices, communicate learning outcomes and expectations to students, and deliberately align learning outcomes with authentic, valid, and reliable assessment tools. These practices will not only ensure general effectiveness of journalism courses, but also provide assurance that graduates of journalism education are able to demonstrate knowledge and skills acquired in the course of their studies to real-life situations.

References

Accrediting Council on Education in Journalism and Mass Communications (ACEJMC). (2013). Standards. Retrieved from https://www2. ku.edu/~acejmc/PROGRAM/STANDARDS.SHTML

Accrediting Council on Education in Journalism and Mass Communications (ACEJMC). (2013). Policies. Retrieved from https://www2.ku.edu/~acejmc/PROGRAM/POLICIES.SHTML

American Communication Association (ACA). (2013). Accreditation. Retrieved from www.americancomm.org/accreditation/

Carnegie Corporation of New York. (2013). The future of journalism education. Retrieved from http://carnegie.org/programs/past-commissions-councils-and-task-forces/future-of-journalism-education

Commission for University Education (CUE). (2014). Accreditation Standards. Retrieved from http://www.cue.or.ke/services/accreditation/introduction-to-accreditation

Council for Higher Education Accreditation (CHEA). (2013). Retrieved from www.chea.org

Du, R. Y., & Lo, S. C. (2014). The gap between online journalism education and practice: A Hong Kong study. *Journalism & Mass Communication Educator, 69*(4), 415-434. Retrieved from http://jmc.sagepub.com/content/69/4/415

European Journalism Training Association (EJTA). (2013). Projects. Retrieved from http://ejta.eu/projects/

European Journalism Training Association (EJTA). (2013). Tartu-declaration. Retrieved from http://ejta.eu/projects/

European Journalism Training Association (EJTA). (2013). Competence-Goals. Retrieved from http://ejta.eu/projects/

Media Council of Kenya. (2015). Colleges offering media and journalism studies in Kenya. Retrieved from http://www.mediacouncil.or.ke/en/mck/index.php/programs/mck-accreditation/colleges-offering-communication-in-kenya-2

National Council for the Training of Journalists. (2013). Want to be a journalist? Retrieved from http://www.nctj.com/want-to-be-a-journalist

National Council for the Training of Journalists. (2012). Results Tables. Retrieved from http://www.nctj.com/want-to-be-a-journalist/Accreditedcourses/Resultstables

National Council for the Training of Journalists. (2015). About us. Retrieved from http://www.nctj.com/about-us

New Zealand Journalists Training Organization (NZJTO). (2014). Combined expertise secures future for on-the-job training in print, packaging, journalism and sign-making. Retrieved from http://www.competenz.org.nz/news/competenz-cmito-announce-merger-2014

Sligo, F. (2004). NZ journalism unit standards: Are they still needed? *Pacific Journalism Review, 10*(1), 191.

UNESCO. (2007). Model curricula for journalism education. Retrieved from http://unesdoc.unesco.org/images/0015/001512/151209E.pdf

UNESCO. (2013). *Centers of excellence in journalism education: Nurturing excellence in journalism education in Africa*. Retrieved from http://www.unesco.org/new/en/communication-and-information/intergovernmental-programmes/ipdc/special-initiatives/centres-of-excellence-in-journalism-education

Wolff, R. A. (2005). Accountability and accreditation: Can reforms match increasing demands? In J. C. Burke & Associates (Eds.), Achieving accountability in higher education (pp. 78-103). San Francisco, CA: Jossey-Bass.

Part 3:

Global Innovations in Journalism Education

14

On Media and Entrepreneurship as Ways of Being in the World: A Challenge to Journalism Education[1]

Mark Deuze

We live in media. Media are to us as water is to fish. The ubiquitous and pervasive nature of contemporary media does not mean people's lives are determined by technology, but it certainly should suggest that our understanding of society and the role of journalism (and journalism education) in it must start with an appreciation of the profound mediatization of everyday life and the lifeworld (the world we experience) (Deuze, 2014). This is all the more important as the ubiquitous and pervasive nature of media in everyday life is a direct function of their disappearance from our active awareness of them. As Meyrowitz (1998) remarked, "Ironically, then, the environment of a medium is most invisible when its influence is most pervasive" (p. 106). His observations about the way people use media (e.g., media as activities) can be extended to considerations about media as artifacts. Meyer (2011), on the basis of fieldwork in Ghana, concluded that "media tend to 'disappear' when they are accepted as devices that, naturally as it were, 'vanish' into the substance that they mediate" (p. 32). Fellow anthropologist Miller (2005) suggested that media, as objects, are important because we do not "see" them:

> The less we are aware of them, the more powerfully they can determine our expectations by setting the scene and ensuring normative behavior, without being open to challenge. They determine what takes place to the extent that we are unconscious of their capacity to do so. (p. 5)

1   An earlier version of this chapter was published as Deuze, M. (2014). Journalism, media life, and the entrepreneurial society. *Australian Journalism Review, 36*(2), 119-130. The current version has been edited for content and focus. Published with permission.

The invisibility of media, coupled with their connectivity and persistency, forms the human condition of experiencing and acting in the world.

Media and life are mutually implicated physical and emotional infrastructures, in that people's lived experience with media has become so intertwined, ritualistic and natural, to draw distinctions between "us" and "them" seems fruitless. Every aspect of everyday life gets structured by (and in) media, whereas the media in people's lives are shaped by the way they fit into their environment. In the process, our relationships with media become profoundly personal. In a story reviewing a decade's worth of reports covering new technologies for the *New York Times* (November 24, 2010), Pogue (2010) considers as one of the most important insights about the role of technology in people's lives the fact, that "[t]oday's gadgets are intensely personal." We do not just abundantly use media; we really love (and hate) our media too. This puts media on the same level as emotion, the psyche, and the human body: running in the background, increasingly invisible, and generally taken for granted. Fortunati combined this infrastructural approach with Kittler's (2009) appeal for an ontology of media and argued that media both amplify and sacrifice affect in human interaction, as emotions "must submit themselves to the technological limits and languages of a machine" (p. 13). Referring specifically to today's technologies—the mobile phone and Internet—Fortunati works through the various ways in which media *give life* to the global socio-technical system that is our communicative environment. She argues that at the same time as this significant contextualization of our understanding of work, life, and play in contemporary society directs us toward the materiality of the media we care about so much, it asks us to consider its immateriality. In turn, if we acknowledge media's disappearance and reemergence as practices and feelings, it becomes imperative to observe and take seriously the lived experience and agency of people in their use of media and their ways of making sense of everyday life.

With this introduction I am neither saying our lives are completely determined by media, nor that people are necessarily empowered because of the "communication power" (Castells, 2009) they wield while using smartphones, tablet PCs, and the Internet. Rather, I would like to argue that whether we like it or not, every aspect of our lives plays out in media (in one way or another). During this process, media become part of all our playing, learning, working, and loving. In other words, media constitute individuals' lived experience. In this chapter I explore this "media life" (Deuze, 2012) within the way media industries work, focusing specifically on the currently emerging practices of journalists in the increasingly precarious context of newswork. In the end, the challenges of articulating contemporary journalism with media life are explored vis-á-vis journalism education.

Martini Media, Polymedia, Media Life

Outlining the future of the British Broadcasting Corporation (BBC) in May 2005, Director of New Media & Technology Ashley Highfield argued that the company's approach would be based on the assumption that people want to access media "on their terms—anytime, any place, any how—Martini Media. We'll see what programmes appeal in this new world and how people search, sort, snack and savour our content" (BBC, 2005). The Martini concept refers to a series of 1970s European television and radio commercials for Martini, a popular brand of Italian vermouth. The advertisements featured a jingle with the memorable words: "capture a moment—that Martini moment—any time, any place, anywhere—there is a wonderful place you can share—and the right one, the right one—that's Martini."

Highfield echoed BBC Director-General Mark Thompson (2006), who predicted in the near future media and society would be based on the "Martini media" principle, "meaning media that's available when and where you want it with content moving freely between different devices and platforms."

Highfield and Thompson argue in their speeches and policies that future media professionals would need to do more than publish and publicize their work across many different media platforms—they would also need to recognize their new audience: people who participate and collaborate in finding, producing, sharing, curating, and even remixing content.

This early vision of the BBC seems supported by research on how people use media, consistently showing not only that people worldwide spend more time with media now than ever before, but they are also concurrently exposed to multiple media (Papper, Holmes, & Popovich, 2004). Simultaneously, people's media use is increasingly "productive" in that most of what we do with media involves making media—varying from liking, sharing, uploading, or forwarding materials online to creating our own media from scratch (such as fan fiction). This mixing and matching between media consumption and production in the context of media exposure occurring across multiple devices is what Henry Jenkins (2006) considers convergence culture. Audiences seeking news—just like people who love watching television on all their devices and advertisers trying to reach everyone everywhere—use media in ways that are anything but stable and seem to flow and spill over between and across media. The best way to describe what people do and experience when using media for news is by their own vocabulary: "reading, watching, viewing, listening, checking, snacking, monitoring, scanning, searching, clicking, linking, sharing, liking, recommending, commenting and voting" (Meijer & Kormelink, 2014, p. 3). Similarly, the Reuters Institute for the Study of Journalism's annual online surveys (in France, Germany, Denmark, Finland, Spain, Italy, Japan, Brazil, the United Kingdom, and the United States, 2016), and the U.S.-based Pew Research Center's annual State of the News Media (Mitchell, 2014) report that people worldwide use multiple devices to access and share news, each year folding new devices (most notably tablets and smartphones), and new platforms (specifically social media), into their omnivorous news routines.

In the process of using news, people deploy and exchange multiple devices, interfaces, and platforms as they move through their day. This behavior is not random, it has become quite patterned, and it does not change much when new, shiny toys get introduced. Interestingly, the aforementioned surveys suggest most people get news through their online and mobile social networks "even though they did not go there looking for it [news]" (Mitchell, 2014). The challenge for journalism is to become (and stay) part of this routinized round of clicks on computer mouse buttons, touchpads, touchscreens, remote controls, keyboards (and sometimes the turning of printed pages), and therein find a balance between telling people what they need to know and letting the "people formerly known as the audience" (Rosen, 2006) play a part in the newsgathering and storytelling process.

The media, in the eyes and experiences of users, have always been an ensemble (Bausinger, 1984), as different devices and their uses mix and match in everyday routines. That experience, the feeling of more or less integrated (if not always seamless) media, is typical of media life. In recent years, Bausinger's observation is being echoed in Nick Couldry's work (2011, p. 220), who advocates the need to be aware of people's various ways of using the media, their "media manifold," and how this influences the way they do things and make sense of the everyday world. Couldry (2004) proposes a definition of media as practice, as ways of acting in the world that are always social. Couldry provides a theoretical foundation for Meikle and Young's (2012) suggestion, that "For many people, the media are no longer just what they watch, read or listen to or read—the media are now what people *do*" (p. 10).

Miller and Madianou (2012) take this notion of media as practice one important step further, suggesting that we treat the media environment "as an integrated structure of affordances" (p. 4). They introduce a theory of polymedia to both articulate the enveloping media ecosystem in everyday life and to consider "additional layers of meaning, functions and consequences" (Miller & Madianou, 2012, p. 5) when looking at what people are doing with media. This work in turn is informed by the recent convergence of mediation and mediatization studies, emphasizing the ways in which communication media transform social processes while being socially shaped themselves (Hepp & Krotz, 2014).

What all these industry and scholarly approaches have in common (Martini media, convergence culture, media as ensemble, polymedia, manifold and practices, and mediation and mediatization) is a growing awareness that understanding everyday life cannot be separated from an appreciation of the formative role media play, while at the same time recognizing that, in media, people create as much as consume the world.

Our media use is not just a series of individual activities or a set of distinct practices, but rather a social phenomenon specific to media life. Immersed in media we wield all kinds of tools interchangeably to communicate with ourselves and the world around us to make the world we live in fit and feel comfortable (or, at the very least, to make reality something we can handle). Media practices are neither new nor exclusive to the forms of our media manifold. Instead, the ways we use media, express ourselves in and through media, and give meaning to media should be seen as signaling (and shaping) broader social, economic, and technological trends.

Selfies and Mass Self-Communication

As our media are anytime, anyplace, and anywhere, so are we. In media, we witness crucially intimate occurrences in people's lives from around the world. Whether it is a wedding video of a friend who lives overseas or the beheading of a journalist somewhere in Syria, a series of tweets about a great concert we chose not to attend, or a Facebook status update with shocking news about the suicide of a celebrity we follow, we get confronted by intense emotional life experiences on a minute-to-minute basis. Our media use turns us—at times—from people who listen to and watch stories about people's lives to people who witness other people's lives (and deaths). A mundane media diet is anything but stable in terms of what it exposes us to. We are navigating an ocean of stories that inform, shock, and entertain, contributing ourselves along the way in the form of personal data we directly or indirectly share when using digital media services with media that seem to multiply all the time. Life in media is an emotional rollercoaster, one most people try to control one way or another.

At the heart of understanding people's immersive engagement in media is the reconstruction of the "self as source" (Sundar, 2008). Based on his experimental work on people's media use, Sundar highlighted the importance of ourselves in the co-evolution of technology and psychology, showing that the most seductive part of media is not what they have to offer (in terms of professionally produced content or carefully prepared and neatly packaged experiences), but their potential for customization and individual agency. We can make something of and in media, and media to some extent seem to put us into the driver's seat when navigating the world around us.

A powerful expression of the self as source is the meteoric rise of social media as the major "place" to be in media. This trend prompted

Time magazine to make "YOU" its "Person of the Year" in 2006, featuring a front cover with a *YouTube* screen functioning as a mirror (Grossman, 2006). According to the editors of the American magazine, social media put people in control of the information age, effectively turning the Web into "a massive social experiment, and like any experiment worth trying, it could fail" (Grossman, 2006). This supposed control primarily manifests itself in individual self-expression and what some would call oversharing our private lives. The media that connect people also stimulate us to look more or less exclusively at ourselves. Instead of this making us feel in control of the information age, it seems to inspire incessant self-searching and exuberant self-exhibition. Therefore, it is no surprise that seven years later, in 2013, "Selfie" became "Word of the Year" according to the Oxford Dictionary Online (2013) and a host of national associations worldwide. Rather than the selfie being the product of an increasingly narcissistic generation of young people, selfies have become the default operation in media life propagated by people as varied as U.S. President Barack Obama (during a remembrance ceremony for former South African President Nelson Mandela), Pope Francis (regularly during formal visits and informal street meetings), Ellen DeGeneres (during the 2013 Oscars live television show), and everyone else during the "Selfie Olympics," the 2014 Winter Olympics in Sochi, Russia. In fact, selfies have become so banal that they are finally boring enough to warrant serious interest (such as special issues of academic journals and chapters in learned volumes).

Rather than serving a strict function of self-documentation, the selfie's core purpose is to be shared with others *in media*. Castells terms this at once self-centered yet instantly connected social behavior in media as "mass self-communication" (Castells, 2007):

> It is mass communication because it reaches potentially a global audience through the p2p networks and Internet connection .... *And it is self-generated in content, self-directed in emission, and self-selected in reception by many that [sic] communicate with many.* (p. 248, emphasis in original)

As numerous observers note, while people using media are at once and instantaneously connected with large and multiple dynamic groups and networks, they also seem to be ascribed with a deeply individualized and seemingly self-centered value system. Our media certainly seem to single us out, giving us endless customization options—both in terms of technological affordances and content choices—in their embrace of the Martini concept. In doing so, the shared selfie as an act of mass self-communication can be seen as an instance of what Sloterdijk considers our "modern individuality [that is] supported by a complex media environment that enables multiple and permanent auto-references" (2004, p. 235), enabling the individual to form a couple with himself. This "connected self" is at once endlessly archived (in media) as well as impermanent—it is constantly torn between being in the *nowhere* of media and the *somewhere* of life. Indeed, the connection between self-formation and shared locale (Thompson, 1996, p. 207) has become comprehensively mediated. However, this does not necessarily mean that we are not in touch with one another and the world anymore. As Wellman (2002) suggests: "The shift to a personalized, wireless world affords networked individualism, with each person switching between ties and networks. People remain connected, but as individuals rather than being rooted" (p. 16).

What people do with Martini media is not only partake in increasingly complex and at times quite sophisticated media usage patterns, from "binging" on television shows to "snacking" on byte-sized news headlines. They are also producing themselves and their stories online. It would be a mistake to see the emergence of mass self-communication alongside professional Martini media production solely as a consequence of a widespread diffusion of ubiquitous and easy-to-use new information and communication technologies. Using data from social values surveys in 43 countries, Inglehart (1997) observed a global shift of people in their roles as citizens away from nation-based politics and institutional elites toward a distinctly skeptical, globally linked yet deeply personal type of self-centered civic engagement. This shift occurred in the context of a trend, particularly among Western democratic countries' overdeveloped populations, toward post-materialist values and ideals. This development, which emerged in the early 1970s, is indicated by a shift in emphasis from economic and physical security toward personal goals that emphasize self-expression and quality-of-life issues. Similarly, during the 1990s authors such as Putnam (2000) and Norris (1998) detailed broad societal trends toward distinctly individualized and often outright anti-authoritarian attitudes, leading Beck (2000) to conclude: "We are undoubtedly living in an anti-hierarchical age" (p. 150). This does not preclude political engagement, as Papacharissi (2014) notes. She outlines the emergence of a fluid, issue-driven politics by "affective publics" that coalesce around emotions and feelings of engagement facilitated through social media. In the same way as social movements mixed with current events (such as police killings) become hashtags on Twitter, outrage online fueled the street demonstrations during the Arab Spring. It is clear that people deeply care about the world they live in, and today's personal (and social) media amplify and accelerate that emotion.

The current media culture is one where people expect media exactly when and how they want it, engaging in mass self-communication next to (and often mixed with) passive consumption and handling media in intimate and affective ways primarily to explore matters of personal significance. It must be clear that media are central to any understanding of the world. Surely, all of this must be great news to media industries and professionals, and particularly to the practitioners in journalism: their stories fuel what gets shared online, their work flows across all media, and their professional roles and identities set them apart from colleagues in advertising, games, music, and film.

The Entrepreneurial Society

People spend more time with media today than at any previous point in history. The number of media channels, forms, genres, devices, applications, and formats is multiplying. More media are produced every year, and we spend more of our time concurrently exposed to these Martini media. At the same time, the news about work in the media in general, and journalism in particular, is less than optimistic. Reports about continuing layoffs across all media industries are paramount, most notably film and television entertainment, journalism, digital game development, and advertising. This suggests a paradox:

as people engage with media in an increasingly immersive, always-on, almost instantaneous, and interconnected way, the very people whose livelihood and sense of professional identity depend on delivering media content and experiences seem to be at a loss on how to come up with survival strategies. For example, they struggle to discover effective business models and regulatory practices, such as those regarding copyrights and universal access provisions. And perhaps, most specifically, they search for entrepreneurial working conditions that would support and sustain the creative process needed to meet the demands of media life.

In the context of Martini media and people's affective mass self-communication, the ecosystem for media professions in general, and journalism in particular, has been evolving toward what some call a "post-industrial" news model (Anderson, Bell, & Shirky, 2013). Anderson et al. (2013) suggest that for journalism to adapt to the new media environment (with its social, economic, technological, and cultural implications), the profession needs new tactics, a new self-conception, and new organizational structures. They allude to a trend benchmarked by the creative industries: a gradual shift from centralized and hierarchical modes of industrial production to what Castells (2010) coins a network enterprise form of production. Castells argues that the relationships among capital and labor in our at once global and local network society are increasingly individualized (rather than more or less exclusively institutional). This type of post-industrial mode of production integrates the work process globally through digital telecommunications, transportation, and client-customer networks. Workers find themselves collaborating or coordinating their activities with team members in different parts of the company, sometimes located in different parts of the world, working from places that are more often than not like the formally sanctioned office environments of the past (coffee shops, libraries, bare-bones renovated factory spaces, on the road, or simply at home).

In the current digital and network media ecosystem the roles played by different professional disciplines in the production of culture—media makers, financial executives, advertising creatives, and communication managers, including marketing and sales practitioners—are increasingly intertwined. This network characteristic also reveals the often translocalized nature of the media production process, as media industries offshore subcontract and outsource various elements in the production process to reduce cost and redistribute risk. In journalism this practice is called "remote control journalism," in which news organizations move certain divisions or departments to another part of the world (Deuze, 2006c). The International Federation of Journalists and the International Labour Organization found adverse effects of the network enterprise at work in journalism in a 2006 survey among journalism unions and associations in 38 countries from all continents. The study signaled the rapid rise of so-called "atypical" work in the media, documenting that close to a third of journalists worldwide work in anything but secure, permanent positions with contracts. It found freelance journalism, independent news entrepreneurship, and uncontracted labor paramount, particularly among young reporters and newcomers in the field.

In recent years, such work trends have continued. For example, in The Netherlands a national survey of journalists found that those under contract and in permanent positions dropped from 77% to 50% from 2000 to 2010 (Hermans, Vergeer, & Pleijter, 2011, p. 15). Also, less than 25% of journalists younger than 35 were "typically" employed. The Dutch national association of journalists, traditionally organized around departments representing different media—newspaper, magazine, broadcast and online journalists—today counts as its largest group "independent" journalists, 2,128 of its 7,400 members. In 2013, several organizations representing journalists in The Netherlands collaborated in a survey of their freelance or otherwise independently working members (some 7,087 reporters, editors, videographers, and photographers). Two thirds of these independently working journalists preferred this kind of arrangement over a permanent, full-time job in a newsroom. They attributed this preference to freedom, flexibility, passion, and opportunity. Although most of these freelance journalists work on average with four different clients from home or within editorial collectives and news startups, many of these independent reporters work within legacy media newsrooms. After all, the legacy media increasingly depends on flexible, part-time, and temporary or uncontracted arrangements to run their departments.

Even though we can find some optimism among the atypically employed, studies in Germany (Ertel, Pech, Ullsperger, Von dem Knesebeck, & Siegrist, 2005); Australia (Gregg, 2011); the United Kingdom (Hesmondhalgh & Baker, 2010); and the United States (Neff, Wissinger, & Zukin, 2005) consistently show adverse psychosocial effects, rising levels of stress, and overall poor health among freelance media workers. Reports based on interviews with entrepreneurs in various cities across the United States in 2015 suggest that the "high-stress, hyper competitive and demanding lifestyle" of striking out on your own often links to depression (*The Business Journals*, 2015; Twitter hashtag #startupdepression).

The real or perceived freedom of entrepreneurship clearly comes at a cost to many, if not most, media professionals. This picture of increasingly flexible and precarious working conditions for journalists and media workers corresponds with trends in the Dutch labor market as a whole, as 2013 data from the Dutch Central Statistical Agency (Centraal Bureau voor de Statistiek) show a continuous growth of independent businesses and freelance entrepreneurship despite (or inspired by) the ongoing economic crisis. This trend clearly is not unique to The Netherlands or journalism. It seems to be a feature of all media work (Deuze, 2007) and a structural condition of labor. We therefore need to take a step back and consider entrepreneurship not just as a subset of individual activities necessary to secure survival (and opportunity) in a globally networked economy, but also as *lived experience* increasingly particular to the contemporary arrangement of society as a whole.

As Landström and Johannisson (2001) wrote, "entrepreneurship [is] a phenomenon that lies beyond individual attributes and abilities. Entrepreneurship encompasses, to our mind, the organizing of resources and collaborators in new patterns according to perceived opportunities" (p. 228). Considering the theory of entrepreneurship as a social phenomenon put forward by Landström and Johannisson, it does not seem to be a stretch to argue that navigating access to society for anyone demands an increasingly entrepreneurial skillset. This includes gathering and organizing information, verifying and curating resources, and interacting with many (potential) collaborators. It also involves finding one's way despite constantly changing systems, networks, and people. This is true whether one is trying to figure out a country's nebulous tax system, securing a contract with competing service providers (from home insurance policies to telecommunications access), developing a strategy for one's professional "portfolio career" (Platman, 2004), or navigating the frothy waters of our romantic life in a turbulent "post-dating" world (Deuze, 2012, p. 212).

Additionally, entrepreneurship as a social phenomenon cannot be separated from a ubiquitous and pervasive media environment, necessitating an advanced (and critical) multimedia literacy for all. As Hartley (2007) suggested, "Popular self-publication can however now be contemplated because the era of one-way 'read-only' media of mass and broadcast communication is transforming into the interactive era of 'read-write' multimedia" (p. 137). A fundamental issue for developing some kind of consistent and functional literacy model for media life is our rapidly changing media environment. Briggs and Burke (2009) concluded, after comprehensively reviewing the social history of media from the early days of the printing press up to today's "high-definition, inter-drive, mutually convergent technologies of communication" (p. 12), that the entire media system can best be understood as being in continuous flux. In other words, today's media are really complex and difficult to master. And once we have gained some sort of read-write literacy, a new version, device, or system comes along that requires a costly process of deskilling and reskilling. Most of us neither have the time nor the inclination to engage in this process. At the same time, our involvement with media becomes increasingly encompassing and intimate.

As life plays out in media, we have no choice but to engage with the media environment—no one is outside anymore. Society's near-complete mediatization goes hand-in-hand with its increasing complexity. I would argue that the entrepreneurial mindset and its corresponding skill-set are necessary, required for anyone navigating our "hypercomplex" (Qvortrup, 2003) society. Qvortrup suggests that contemporary society is not a permanently unstable network, constantly veering out of control. To account for society's surprisingly stable state given current disruptive social, economical, and technological developments, it is perhaps better to see world society as a global social system that self-organizes through communication (Luhmann, 1990). The advantage of this approach is that it explains how the stability and coherence of world society is maintained through communication (rather than through the acts or actions of any individual human being or range of technologies), which is particularly poignant to consider in the current context of media life. Seen from this perspective, people's affective mass self-communication contributes to the maintenance of social order even though it seems—in terms of the endless status updates, tweets, posts, and messages sent and published on any given day—to exemplify social chaos.

In this Luhmann-inspired conceptualization of society, no one person or institutional entity (or paradigm, such as capitalism, communism, or Sharia law) is effectively in control as society adapts itself and self-organizes through communication to deal with increasing internal and external complexity. Connecting the pressure and risk of managing hyper-complexity with media life makes entrepreneurs of us all. The organization of resources and collaborators in new patterns to address challenges and opportunities is a way to manage complexity (in society) by complexity (in media), and vice versa.

Discussion and Conclusion: A Challenge to Education

The key to thinking about entrepreneurial journalism as an answer to (or the consequence of) precarity in media work is to recognize how it is tied to broader trends in contemporary society. Society self-organizes itself through communication, and within it people live their lives in media, where media professions both contribute to the experience of complexity and provide the tools (devices and content) to manage complexity. Entrepreneurship is not a set of skills and activities that are somehow exceptional or unique to a particular kind of individual. It is rather a mundane aspect of everyday life, work, and play.

Understanding entrepreneurialism in the context of broader trends in society, technology, and media can be the key for journalism educators to understand not only what's going on in the field but to help their students navigate it. The social, technological, and industrial trends outlined in this chapter all point toward greater *complexity, precarity,* and *affect* (as in emotional engagement) marking the way people are in the world (as citizens, consumers, producers, and professionals). Entrepreneurialism, rather than *just* a category particular to the culture of contemporary capitalism (Sennett, 2006), can also be seen as a way to navigate core components of today's social and media system. As I see it, schools and programs of journalism have a specific role to play here.

But first, the paradigm of journalism education needs to be decided (Deuze, 2006a, p. 24): Should a program or curriculum prepare journalists for future employment or serve to educate "super citizens"? A focus on future employment reduces teaching and training to helping students internalize the occupational ideology and practices of journalism *as is*. Shifting the paradigm to educating super citizens, the industry, and its social and technological context, should continuously be looked at with a critical eye. Journalism, in this sense, should be considered to be the heart of what it takes to perform successfully in the information age. Going beyond the motivations that inspire individual students to choose an education in journalism, one should note that a critical-reflective skillset, toolkit, and outlook of a journalist would benefit all in the global economy.

Second, since media life and entrepreneurialism are integral parts of journalism, they should be recognized in all program decisions (Deuze, 2006a, pp. 26-27). After all, journalism cannot be separated from the community in which it exists: the intimate, pervasive, and unstable ways in which people (and professionals) navigate their "oceans of media." In terms of the professional ethos of journalism, journalism educators need to decide once and for all whether the journalist is a neutral observer, an outsider to the inner-workings of community life, or a participant— someone who works with elements of the community (while always being mindful of their agendas, biases, and often conflicting interests). A journalist in media life is inevitably drawn into the living archive of (nearly) everything that is the Internet, prompting news organizations worldwide to hastily come up with social media guidelines. Since journalists must participate in the community they cover in order to understand their beats and contemporary media culture, journalism education should teach them how to do so (Deuze, 2006b).

Third, a word on entrepreneurialism as a popular direction for many schools of journalism around the world (Baines & Kennedy, 2010; Briggs, 2011; Claussen, 2011). The common wisdom seems to be to include business skills and knowledge into the curriculum and to add coursework on entrepreneurship. Although I am not contesting these decisions, entrepreneurship classes should not just focus on journalists setting up their own enterprises in a precarious marketplace. As Storey, Salaman, and Platman (2005) note (referring to Rosen's work):

> A significant feature of the concept of enterprise is precisely that it operates at a number of levels—economy/political, organization/institutional, and the individual self. Enterprise thus acts as a fundamental principle of integration among polity, organization, and individual. (p. 1034)

Therefore, any class or curricular entrepreneurial intervention should come with a mode of instruction and pedagogical materials that would inspire critical engagement with a way of being in the world beyond *just* a way of setting up shop.

Finally, in terms of curriculum, media life and the Martini media context open up possibilities and opportunities for what Jenkins calls "transmedia" storytelling (Jenkins, 2003). Jenkins defines transmedia as "a process where integral elements . . . get dispersed systematically across multiple delivery channels for the purpose of creating a unified and coordinated . . . experience" (Jenkins, 2007). In 2009 Jenkins created a list of seven principles of transmedia storytelling, emphasizing how the contemporary professional should consider spreadability, continuity, immersion, seriality, subjectivity, performativity, and world-building when producing media content or experiences. In 2011 Moloney (2011) graduated from the University of Denver with a thesis on transmedia journalism, outlining on his blog how Jenkins' principles might be applied to journalistic storytelling. Where transmedia journalism differs from multimedia journalism (Deuze, 2004) or convergent journalism (Quinn, 2005) is in its use of the audience in all aspects of the creative process: from generating story ideas to gathering information, from contributing parts of the narrative and research to assisting in its funding and distribution, and from marketing the content to following it up with comments and additional story lines. It is my contention that the distinction between crossmedia journalism (also known as multimedia or convergent journalism) and transmedia journalism should be the basis on which journalism schools and programs acknowledge media life in the future. This should replace the traditional organization into medium-specific sequences (of newspaper, magazine, radio, television, and online journalism).

A teaching curriculum that embraces the implications of entrepreneurialism, super-citizens, media life, a Martini mode of thinking about media, and transmedia journalism would in some ways look quite differently from the traditionally siloed ways of working in schools and programs of journalism. It advocates the following:

- ❑ integration of coursework (for example, combining case studies of the business side of the industry with insights from marketing and advertising);
- ❑ cross-sectional modules (for example, integrating different media sequences in lab-type courses);
- ❑ centralization of ethics and critical reflection on journalism and the role of individual journalists in society as the benchmark for all coursework; and
- ❑ a recognition of journalism as a form of atypical and affective labor: It is work that tends not to be defined anymore by clear career trajectories (including benefits and support offered by stable employer-employee relationships), as well as it is work journalists profoundly care about.

In all of this I hope and trust we stay mindful about the affective engagement of publics with their communities, and of journalists with their field—for it is that emotional connection that most intensely determines the way these constituencies experience and give meaning to their roles as citizens, consumers, and journalists.

References

Anderson, C. W., Bell, E., & Shirky, C. (2013). *Post-industrial journalism: Adapting to the present*. New York, NY: Columbia Journalism School, Tow Center for Digital Journalism.

Baines, D., & Kennedy, C. (2010). An education for independence. *Journalism Practice*, 4(1), 1-17.

Bausinger, H. (1984). Media, technology and daily life. *Media, Culture & Society*, 6, 343-351.

BBC. (2005). BBC announced iMP content trial. Retrieved from http://www.

bbc.co.uk/pressoffice/pressreleases/stories/2005/05_may/16/imp.shtml

Beck, U. (2000). *The brave new world of work*. Cambridge: Polity.

Botton, A. de (2014). *The news: A user's manual*. London: Hamish Hamilton.

Briggs, M. (2011). *Entrepreneurial journalism*. New York, NY: CQ Press.

Briggs, A., & Burke, P. (2009). *A social history of the media*. Cambridge: Polity.

Castells, M. (2007). Power and counter-power in the network society. *International Journal of Communication, 1*, 238-266.

Castells, M. (2009). *Communication power*. Oxford: OUP.

Castells, M. (2010). *The rise of the network society*. Malden: Blackwell.

Claussen, D. (2011). CUNY's Entrepreneurial journalism: partially old wine in a new bottle, and not quite thirst-quenching, but still a good drink. *Journalism & Mass Communication Educator, 66*(3), 3-6.

Couldry, N. (2004). Theorising media as practice. *Social Semiotics* 14(2), 115-132.

Couldry, N. (2011). The necessary future of the audience . . . and how to research it. In V. Nightingale, (Ed.), *Handbook of media audiences* (pp. 213-229). Chichester: Wiley-Blackwell.

Deuze, M. (2004). What is multimedia journalism? *Journalism Studies, 5*(2), 139-152.

Deuze, M. (2006a). Global journalism education: A conceptual approach. *Journalism Studies, 7*(1), 19-34.

Deuze, M. (2006b). Participation, remediation, bricolage: Considering principal components of a digital culture. *The Information Society, 22*(2), 63-75.

Deuze, M. (2006c). Remote-control journalism. Retrieved from http://deuze.blogspot.com/2006/11/remote-control-journalism.html

Deuze, M. (2007). *Media work*. Cambridge: Polity Press.

Deuze, M. (2012). *Media life*. Cambridge: Polity Press.

Deuze, M. (2014). Media life and the mediatization of the lifeworld. In A. Hepp & F. Krotz, F. (Eds.), *Mediatized world: Culture and society in a media age* (pp. 207-220). New York, NY: Palgrave.

Ertel, M., Pech, E., Ullsperger, P., Von dem Knesebeck, O., & Siegrist, J. (2005). Adverse psychosocial working conditions and subjective health in freelance media workers. *Work & Stress: An international Journal of Work, 19*(3), 293-299.

Gregg, M. (2011). *Work's intimacy*. Cambridge: Polity.

Grossman, L. (2016, December 25). You—yes, you—are Time's person of the year. *Time*. Retrieved from http://content.time.com/time/magazine/article/0,9171,1570810,00.html

Hartley, J. (2007). There are other ways of being in the truth: The uses of multimedia literacy. *International Journal of Cultural Studies, 10*(1), 135-144.

Hepp, A., & Krotz, F. (2014). (Eds.), *Mediatized world: Culture and society in a media age*. New York, NY: Palgrave.

Hermans, L., Vergeer, M., & Pleijter, A. (2011). *Nederlandse journalisten in*

2010. Nijmegen: Radboud University.

Hesmondhalgh, D., & Baker, S. (2010). *Creative labour: Media work in three cultural industries*. New York, NY: Routledge.

Inglehart, R. (1997). *Consuming the romantic utopia: Love and the cultural contradictions of capitalism*. Berkeley, CA: University of California Press.

Jenkins, H. (2003, January 15). Transmedia storytelling. *MIT Technology Review*. Retrieved from http://www.technologyreview.com/news/401760/transmedia-storytelling

Jenkins, H. (2006). *Convergence culture*. New York: NYU Press.

Jenkins, H. (2007, March 22). Transmedia storytelling 101. (Web log comment). Retrieved from http://henryjenkins.org/2007/03/transmedia_storytelling_101.html

Kittler, F. (2009). Towards an ontology of media. *Theory, Culture & Society*, 26(2-3), 23-31.

Landström, H., & Johanisson, B. (2001). Theoretical foundation of Swedish entrepreneurship and small-business research. *Scandinavian Journal of Management*, 17, 225-248.

Luhmann, N. (1990). The autopoiesis of social systems. In N. Luhmann. *Essays on self-reference* (pp. 1-20). New York, NY: Columbia University Press.

Meijer, I. C., & Kormelink, T. G. (2014). Checking, sharing, clicking and liking: Changing patterns of news use between 2004 and 2014. *Digital Journalism*, DOI: 10.1080/21670811.2014.937149

Meikle, G., & Young, S. (2012). *Media convergence: Networked digital media in everyday life*. Basingstoke: Palgrave.

Meyer, B. (2011). Mediation and immediacy: Sensational forms, semiotic ideologies and the question of the medium. *Social Anthropology*, 19(1), 23-39.

Meyrowitz, J. (1998). Multiple media literacies. *Journal of Communication*, 48, 96-108.

Miller, D. (Ed.), (2005). *Materiality*. Durham: Duke University Press.

Miller, D. & Madianou, M. (2012). *Technologies of love*. London: Routledge.

Mitchell, A. (2014). State of the news media 2014. *Pew Research Journalism Project*. Retrieved from http://www.journalism.org/2014/03/26/state-of-the-news-media-2014-overview

Moloney, K. (2011). Transmedia journalism principles. (Web log comment). Retrieved from http://transmediajournalism.org/contexts/transmedia-journalism-principles

Neff, G., Wissinger, E., & Zukin, S. (2005). Entrepreneurial labor among cultural producers: "Cool" jobs in "hot" industries. *Social Semiotics*, 15(3), 307-334.

Norris, P. (1998). *Critical citizens: Global support for democratic governance*. Oxford: Oxford University Press.

Oxford Dictionary Online. (2013). The Oxford Dictionaries Word of the Year

2013. Retrieved from http://blog.oxforddictionaries.com/press-releases/oxford-dictionaries-word-of-the-year-2013

Papacharissi, Z. (2014). *Affective publics: Sentiment, technology, and politics*. Oxford: Oxford University Press.

Papper, R., Holmes, M., & Popovich, M. (2004). Middletown media studies. *The International Digital Media and Digital Arts Association Journal, 1*(1), 1-56.

Platman, K. (2004). "Portfolio careers" and the search for flexibility in later life. *Work, Employment and Society, 18*(3), 573-599.

Pogue, D. (2010, November 24). The lessons of 10 years of talking tech. *The New York Times*. Retrieved from http://www.nytimes.com/2010/11/25/technology/personaltech/25pogue.html

Putnam, R. (Ed.), (2000). *Democracies in flux: The evolution of social capital in contemporary society*. Oxford: Oxford University Press.

Quinn, S. (2005). *Convergence journalism*. New York, NY: Peter Lang.

Qvortrup, L. (2003). *The hypercomplex society*. New York, NY: Peter Lang.

Reuters Institute for the Study of Journalism. (2016). Digital News Report 2016. Retrieved from http://www.digitalnewsreport.org

Rosen, J. (2006). The people formerly known as the audience. Retrieved from http://archive.pressthink.org/2006/06/27/ppl_frmr.html

Sennett, R. (2006). *The culture of the new capitalism*. New Haven, CT: Yale University Press.

Sloterdijk, P. (2004). *Sphären*. Berlin: Suhrkamp Verlag, 2004.

Storey, J., Salaman, G., & Platman, K. (2005). Living with enterprise in an enterprise economy: Freelance and contract workers in the media. *Human Relations, 58*(8), 1033-1054.

Sundar, S. (2008). Self as source: Agency and customization in interactive media. In E. Konijn, S. Utz, M. Tanis, & S. Barnes, S. (Eds.), *Mediated interpersonal communication* (pp. 58-74). New York, NY: Routledge.

The Business Journals. (2015, March 23). Full coverage: Depression, entrepreneurs and startups. Retrieved from http://www.bizjournals.com/bizjournals/news/2015/03/22/full-coverage-entrepreneurs-and-depression.html

Thompson, J. (1996). *The media and modernity: A social theory of the media*. Palo Alto, CA: Stanford University Press.

Thompson, M. (2006, April 25). BBC creative future: Mark Thompson's speech in full. *The Guardian*. Retrieved from http://www.theguardian.com/media/2006/apr/25/bbc.broadcasting

Wellman, B. (2002). Little boxes, glocalization and networked individualism. In M. Tanabe, P. Besselaar, & T. Ishida. *Digital cities II* (pp. 10-25). Berlin: Springer.

15

Pop-Up Newsroom: Liquid Journalism for the Next Generation

Melissa Wall

I nstability in the journalism industries of Western democracies has become an increasing concern as observers and journalists themselves call it a "crisis," implying that the field is withering toward an eventual demise. Or, as a popular book on the state of the American news industry asked, "Will the last reporter please turn out the lights?" (McChesney & Pickard, 2011). Yet others suggest that we are actually seeing not the death but a vital transformation of journalism that will enable innovation and creativity to flourish (Gillmor, 2013).

These concerns and conflicting points of view have played out in journalism education programs around the world. Voices from the professional journalism world have often viewed journalism education as overly theoretical and impractical, if not an outright waste of time. The current crisis merely confirms to them that the educational realm does not understand the needs of industry. Eric Newton, a leading critic of journalism education and former head of the Knight Foundation, has repeatedly chastised journalism programs for failing future journalists (2013). A survey of professional journalists in the United States came to a similar conclusion with almost one half of respondents believing American journalism education was keeping up with the dramatic changes in the field only "a little" or "not at all" (Sivek, 2013). Studies of journalism education from within the academy suggest changes are being made. Indeed, in their national survey of journalism programs, Becker, Vlad, and Simpson (2013) found that while an overwhelming majority of administrators reported that their programs had updated their curricula, more than one half reported obstacles to change, including faculty resistance and bureaucratic holdups.

Many still believe that journalism education continues to be not only valuable, but even more necessary than ever due to rapid changes in the media industry as a whole (Scruggs, 2012). In fact, many journalism educators have taken up the call to envision new educational models and practices for their programs (Baines & Kennedy, 2010; Berger, 2011; Deuze, 2006; Robinson, 2013). These forward-thinking journalism educators suggest that their peers need to be more willing to "experiment with new types of information creation, distribution and organization" (Mensing, 2011, p. 25), and some argue that journalism educators must make wholesale changes to "revolutionize curricula to prepare students for the digital age" (Robinson, 2013, p. 2). As Jarvis (2012) argues, industry disruptions should be seen as opportunities to rethink journalism education, including reconsidering the importance of classroom spaces for learning and the actual forms of news itself. He notes that journalism educators ought to consider not "what the industry *is* [demanding] but what it *should be* demanding" (Bennett, 2014, para. 5). Thus, the pessimists and the optimists appear to agree that journalism education must continue to dramatically evolve to remain relevant.

This chapter examines an effort to rethink how journalism is taught through an exploration of a university-based initiative, the Pop-Up Newsroom. Many of the most highly touted projects said to reimagine journalism education urge educators to have their students take on professional journalism responsibilities, filling the gaps of the shrinking professional world in what has been called the "hospital model" (Newton, 2012). Yet tying journalism education to the news industry's needs and values is precisely what critics such as Mensing (2011) believe holds journalism education back from developing truly different visions of what the discipline could be. The Pop-Up Newsroom offers a different possible direction. This model emphasizes the following:

❑ Creating a **temporary** news operation that seeks only to cover an event or topic for a short period of time (often less than a day), rather than establishing a permanent newsroom.[1] The Pop-Up Newsroom thus mimics the velocity of the digital

---

1   Students have covered live events such as the LA Marathon, the 2012 U.S. Presidential Elections, and the Oscars (a hometown story in Los Angeles). They also employed the same live reporting techniques to cover topical stories such as long-distance bus riders in Los Angeles. Partial archives of this work can be viewed at popupnewsroom.net. The Pop-Up Newsroom does not operate with the same goals each time it opens. For example, for the presidential elections, the students both produced their own stories and recruited ordinary citizens to produce coverage.

start-up world, where the quick birth and collapse of even the most innovative ideas are common.

❏   Using **personal** media devices as opposed to expensive professional equipment. This provides a model of how to run independent solo news operations such as Tim Pool's coverage of the U.S. Occupy movement (De Rosa, 2012). Using personal media devices, fledgling journalists can gain insights into the practices and challenges of both citizen journalism and independent mojos (mobile journalists).

❏   Relying on **social media tools** such as Twitter and RebelMouse. Students learn the benefits and challenges of reporting with existing tools and resources, rather than the prevailing journalism educational model encouraged by the Knight Foundation and others that emphasizes building original websites, mobile apps, etc.

❏   **Developing networks** for their content by connecting with other students along with communities of interest related to the topic, while also tapping into their own **personal social networks.**

This type of model/operation often produces hybrid news content—more developed than what ordinary citizen witnesses might produce—but less polished than the work of a professional or quasi-professional news outlet. Ideally, students develop an ability to work as Castells' (2007) mass self-communicators, who can see news as a fluid fragment of reporting that begins to circulate immediately upon collection within a media sphere open to all. The lack of a permanent newsroom encourages students to rely more on sources and actors at the sites where they are reporting from (Wall, 2014), which may contribute to the greater community connections Mensing (2011) calls for.

Dramatically rethinking student news media operations is important because traditional newsrooms have been identified as places of socialization for journalists and also as a means of controlling them (Tuchman, 1973), practices the Pop-Up Newsroom seeks to avoid. Furthermore, creating student versions of professional news outlets means journalism students adopt the values of professional journalism. When this happens, they potentially limit themselves to a narrow interpretation of what journalism can be.

Liquid Journalism

This project employs the concept of liquid journalism as the theoretical scaffolding for analyzing the Pop-Up Newsroom. Bauman (2000/2012) argues that liquid modernity characterizes our society, which is so marked by change and flux that it remains permanently unstable, constantly shifting shape and reforming itself. He describes this as "forever 'becoming,' avoiding completion, staying under defined," as the "quest" to become solid, ironically, keeps society in constant motion (p. x). Adapting that concept to today's new media ecology, Deuze (2009) argues journalism too can be characterized by those same qualities; he suggests that we are seeing the rise of liquid journalism, which is also in a constant state of change that can never again solidify into the expected. Deuze (2009) connects such journalism with the pop-up concept, which has appeared widely around the world (pop-up cafes, bookstores, art galleries, etc.). Indeed, Deuze's connection of journalism and the pop-up concept inspired the Pop-Up Newsroom described in this chapter. Deuze (2009) describes the pop-up phenomenon as being "intrinsically temporary, transitory, a moment in time that cannot be relived" (p. 16).

Bauman further notes that the idea of cyclical time— for example, annual farming events such as planting crops—no longer applies to much of our lives (Deuze, 2007). Time is neither cyclical nor linear, and organizational progress requires thinking differently about time in a society marked by "short term projects" (Deuze, 2007, p. 673) within a "high speed society" (Rosa & Scheuerman, 2009). Bauman uses the term "pointillist," a painting style, to characterize modernity's disconnected qualities. Working from this idea, Deuze reasons that "reporting of news is 'pointillist without configuration'" (p. 674). That is, news is fragmented and thus weak at providing the big contextual picture; unlike the painting genre, it is rarely able to come together to provide a coherent larger tableau. The disconnected qualities of news have become even more evident in a liquid society. Indeed, Rosa and Scheuerman (2009) argue that today we engage in such rapid, constant movement that there is no time for the big picture to even form.

Unsurprisingly, such ideas particularly appeal to those seeking to explain digital journalism, leading some journalism researchers to join Deuze in seeing applications of liquid modernity to journalism. However, it should be noted that Bauman is quite negative about the possibilities of the Internet, arguing that its connective possibilities are illusory. Widespread claims that the Internet enhances democracy are, in Bauman's view, practically delusional (Deuze, 2007). Instead, Bauman sees many small communities of interest groups that briefly come together and then rapidly disperse; he suggests that such formations cannot create real, sustained change in society.

In terms of journalism, Kantola (2013) suggests that while daily newspapers and national television news operations from the "solid" age still exist, many newer media organizations reflect a liquid ethos in terms of their temporary, ever-changing natures (p. 608). She writes that "[w]herever possible, teams and projects, decomposable and flexible to change, have replaced organizational pyramids" (p. 609). This applies not just to organizational structures but, importantly, also to the professionals who are the key actors in modernist organizations. Hierarchical career ladders are disappearing as are full-time permanent positions. Temporary and/or contract workers are increasingly getting work. In the case of news, this means traditional modernist professions, such as journalism, are also in a state of dramatic upheaval. Initially, many of these changes were viewed as occurring at the periphery of professional journalism in the form of blogs and other types of "black market" or "postmodern" journalism. These were often temporary side projects for professional journalists or even the work of non-professionals (Wall, 2005). But today, dramatic changes have seeped across the profession, particularly via the rise of digital media, leading to the absorption of what once were fringe practices into mainstream news practices. In sum, we have seen the widespread appearance of liquid news, "an erratic, continuous, participatory, multi-modal and interconnected process that is producing content according to journalistic principles" (Karlsson, 2012, p. 388).

Indeed, Karlsson and Strömbäck (2010) argue that liquid news is produced by the qualities commonly identified as key to online journalism: immediacy, interactivity, and convergence. For these researchers, immediacy within the liquid journalism framework means there is no longer a permanent news story. Constant updates change a single story many times throughout its reporting over the course of days, hours, or even minutes. Interactivity also means that a range of actors can contribute to its production, potentially leading to more versions of the story. Convergence is the blurring of forms (print, video, etc.) online. They further argue that studying the "liquidity" of news is quite difficult because online news is constantly morphing through the processes of immediacy and interactivity and often in a non-linear fashion. Karlsson (2012) concludes that this way of creating news can be radically different from traditional modes of news production, in which the

> publishing rhythm has been pre-planned and is predictable, consumers have played a small, if any, part in news production, newspapers have been limited to tell stories in text and photos and news stories have had clearly defined beginnings and endings with a linear progression between them. (p. 388)

Further developing the concept, Kantola (2013) characterizes journalists by categories of liquidity based on how they are adapting to these changes: the "solid moderns (born 1939-1955)," the "liquefying moderns (born 1956-1969)," and the "liquid moderns (born after 1970)" (p. 614). The first category, solid modern journalists, are believers in the objectivity model, which ties them closely to elite sources. They view themselves as providing a public service. The second group, liquefying moderns, is more oriented toward the media organizations they work for. They view themselves as career professionals. They continue to prize objectivity but are less concerned with public service; their work is guided by other professional journalists' work. Kantola (2013) describes the third group, liquid moderns, as "anti-institutional" and oriented instead toward "projects and teams" with no expectations that they will remain in one position or organization for very long (p. 614). They reject objectivity and over-reliance on permanent, professional sources and see the "man on the street's" view as just as legitimate: "The liquid journalists oppose journalistic routines and the ready-made conventions for what makes an important piece of news. Instead, their aim is to look at the 'everyman' and 'everywoman'" (Kantola, 2013, p. 618).

The concept of liquid journalism is not without its critics. Rebillard and Touboul (2010) ask if liquid journalism is in fact "an empirically solid theory" (p. 326). They suggest it is too optimistic about levels of independent citizen participation in news processes. Thus, they argue that we should be skeptical of the term to avoid suggesting that liquid journalism somehow eradicates power structures. This is similar to McDevitt and Sindorf's (2012) broader warning about the dangers of "digital sublime" tendencies to reconfigure journalism education by glorifying digital skills while ignoring more abstract critical theory approaches (p. 114).

While this chapter deploys liquid journalism as its analytical framework, it does not celebrate this phenomenon. Rather, it views this concept as a potentially effective lens for examining new journalism configurations. As Bauman himself notes, while liquid modernity as a concept is not without its flaws, it can help us consider processes taking place around us. He also mentions that such concepts are intended to "focus the searchlights and the spotlights in a way that would assist orientation and help us find the way" (Gane, 2004, p. 17). In other words, while liquid modernity can serve as a helpful means of viewing phenomena such as journalism, it is not a complete explanation.

Creating A Liquid Newsroom

A new type of student media operation, the Pop-Up Newsroom, was created at California State University, Northridge in 2012. As explained above, it intended to respond to the instability of the news profession, drawing on the power of social media, personal communication devices, and fluid communication networks enabled by such tools. Examining this project can both help us consider new ways of teaching journalism and, more broadly, contribute to the growing body of research concerning liquid journalism. While Karlsson (2012) and Karlsson and Strömbäck (2010) have sought to define liquid news and Kantola (2013) has examined issues surrounding the liquidity of journalists' identities, these researchers focused on existing news operations and professional journalists. The Pop-Up Newsroom project explores a non-permanent newsroom and a seemingly less stable category of reporters: student journalists. The rest of this chapter will examine the Pop-Up Newsroom through the lens of liquid news as applied to student journalism.

The two iterations of Pop-Up Newsroom being considered here took place during the Fall 2013 semester with a group of 15 graduate students in a mass communication research class. Early in the semester, the Pop-Up Newsroom sprang to life as the students covered CicLAvia, an event inspired by the Colombian *ciclovía*, or bikeway, in which public streets are regularly closed to vehicles to make way for cyclists.

CicLAvia is a large, one-day outdoor event in downtown Los Angeles in which the streets also are closed to motorized traffic as pedestrians and bicyclists take over. A month later, they joined with students from three other universities across the world to report a topic—poverty—for 24 hours of rolling coverage.[2]

The first question this researcher asked was: In what ways is the Pop-Up Newsroom liquid? In answering this question, she drew on the definitions produced by both Karlsson and Strömbäck (2010), who suggest that liquid news is immediate, interactive, and convergent, as well as Karlsson's (2012, p. 388) additional definition of liquid news as "erratic, continuous, participatory, multi-modal and interconnected." She also assessed the practices of the Pop-Up Newsroom through analysis of her notes taken both during observations of the newsroom in action and during informal follow-up discussions with its reporters.

The second question asked was: How did the students respond to reporting for a temporary newsroom? This researcher focused in particular on what benefits and obstacles, if any, students perceived while working without a physical newsroom and how they related to liquid journalism. She also analyzed notes taken while observing the students as they reported and as they curated content. At the same time, she analyzed documents, including field notes students wrote while they were reporting and student reflection papers written after the Pop-Up

---

2   The Asian College of Journalism in India, Newcastle University in the United Kingdom, and National Chung Cheng University in Taiwan joined the California students. Each university independently generated its own content about poverty, reporting from its specific location by producing digital content with tools such as Twitter, YouTube, and Facebook. For designated portions of the day, each school's students curated the content being produced. To do so, they used the Twitter account @PopUpNewsroom. Some universities used other additional Twitter accounts specific to their coverage. All of the programs used a shared hashtag to connect content: #LivePoverty.

Newsroom ceased operating.

"Disembedding" the Newsroom

One of the most important characteristics of the Pop-Up Newsroom is that it has no permanent news space. Instead, students, equipped with their personal cellphones or tablets, collect information and disseminate it from wherever they are reporting. For example, at CicLAvia, students reported from five different official event hubs spread across the city (Chinatown, MacArthur Park [a low-income immigrant neighborhood], etc.). For reporting on issues of poverty, they positioned themselves at locations such as homeless shelters, or other volunteer agencies, or at events related to the topic (such as a job fair for homeless people or a soccer match in which girls from low-income communities play). With both iterations of the Pop-Up Newsroom, there was no expectation that they would return to a newsroom to "finish" or otherwise update or polish their reports. Thus, the reporting process was stripped of some of the usual educational scaffolding. Some students commented that the lack of a permanent newsroom heightened their "mobility," which "allowed (them) to thoroughly cover the event." Interestingly, in light of the conceptual framework being employed in this paper, other students suggested that a physical newsroom would have been more "stable" (the term liquid news was never discussed with the class.)

In addition to reporting, students also paused at designated times to monitor the Twittersphere for content related to what they had been working on, including content from fellow students. They sometimes would selectively re-share this content through the Twitter account@ PopUpNewsroom. At CicLAvia, monitoring was carried out wherever students chose—most often a space with a wireless connection where they could work from their laptops, which most preferred over their phones for monitoring and re-sharing content. One student picked a Starbucks from which to curate content, while another used her phone, working from her parked car. Yet another student explained, "I found a little coffee shop called Tava Primera, which provided the wifi I needed." This temporary, unstable mode of news production embodies a key quality of liquid modernity, in which "individuals must conjure up the locations as they go" due to an "era of disembedding" (Gane, 2004, p. 36). For some students, this fluid arrangement did not seem unusual or difficult to manage. One noted, "When we want to meet up, we can meet at a Starbucks or anywhere and we can exchange comments and charge our equipment." Once they have completed their tasks or merely interacted, they could move on to their next stop.

That said, some students faced problems curating content. At various points during the day, they were unable to log in to the @PopUpNewsroom Twitter account, as an error message would notify them that they had reached their daily maximum number of posts. (Twitter limits accounts to 1,000 tweets in a 24-hour period and will shut off at regular intervals before then.) In part, the clogging of the account took place because students were logging in and posting without letting others know exactly when they were doing so. This upped the number of repeat posts and of tweets being posted at the same time. Some students suggested that the lack of a physical newsroom heightened this problem, with one concluding, "it was hard to function without an actual newsroom" when such problems arose. Another added that a lack of permanent space combined with technical difficulties meant some students were "confused with no central location to refer to." Thus, for some students, the Pop-Up Newsroom itself was "erratic," a quality Karlsson (2012) identifies as a key aspect of liquid news content. However, here it applies to the actual news operation.

In contrast to CicLAvia, for the topical project on poverty, students curated content from a seminar room at the university to which they brought their laptops either before or after field reporting. This space existed only as long as students were working. This was neither a typical news space, campus media center, nor even a computer lab. Therefore, it maintained some sense of impromptu appropriation. While establishing predictability for problem solving seemed necessary to some students (as noted above), Bauman argues that "learning [routines] may disempower in the long run" (Gane, 2004, p. 22). More broadly, this raises the following question: If routines have been considered crucial to establishing and maintaining journalism practices and identities (Zelizer, 2004), what happens when journalism becomes liquid? The answer may lie in what some students did when left without a solid space or permanent routine: "[I] had to think on my feet, solve unforeseen problems, improvise." They did what observers of liquid modernity propose is a potentially effective response: constantly experiment with whatever resources are available at that moment (Gane, 2004).

Fragments of Multimodal News

Stories reported through social media, particularly Twitter, often included not just text but also photos and short-form video. One student suggested that it "takes some effort to jump between looking for people/things to cover, photographing and writing tweets and also retweeting classmate [sic] coverage. Each is a different skill." While this fits with Karlsson's (2012) definition of liquid news as multimodal, he envisioned liquid news stories constantly evolving from basically a headline to a more fully developed, multi-media piece over the course of minutes or hours. While Pop-Up Newsroom content was occasionally developed further when students chose to Storify their reports, this was the exception. Instead, their reporting was posted as quickly as possible and then forgotten as the reporters moved on. As one student noted, "there was no opportunity to tell the full story in a long form" as she would have for a traditional news outlet because she herself was in constant motion—interviewing, posting, moving to the next interview, etc. This changed the form of her stories: "[H]ashtags and photos were used to tell stories that I would normally write [using text]." Others also said they changed their reporting routines to first focus on images and then on writing the tweet's text to the photo or video. The end result of such reporting would seem to be journalism as pointillism—media fragments of the moment that never coalesce into an entirely complete account.

In Karlsson's (2012) model, the reporter makes additional judgments as the liquid news item develops. Here, students make snap judgments rather than continuing to collect and incorporate more material. As one explained, "With live tweeting, you have to go with your 'gut feeling' as to what is important – and you don't have much time to reflect on it." In contrast, Karlsson's (2012) liquid news content would potentially pass from reporter to editor or others on a news desk where the additional context and reporting would be provided. Pop-Up Newsroom reporters observed that "there is no editor to show [anything] before tweeting." In this way, the student's liquid journalism seems to come closer to citizen journalism, or as one student said, "I saw it more as an individual newsroom when it came to reporting your own tweets on your Twitter account." The students become mass self-communicators. The lack of gatekeeping or vetting empowered some—"we can post what we want" and "a physical newsroom would slow the reporting down"—while others believed that a more solid process would have potentially improved their reporting. "An actual physical newsroom environment is filled with people that you can run your ideas by." However, this again suggests that students (like some of their professors) may be envisioning a well-staffed newsroom with plenty of experienced hands ready to help the story along, a vision that does not necessarily match the dramatic loss of reporters, particularly in the print news media industries. Moreover, on a conceptual level, Bauman (2001, p. 126) has argued that for most of us going about our lives today "disembeddedness is now an experience which is likely to be repeated an unknown number of times." We will be constantly experiencing change as opposed to finding permanent stopping points.

"Integrated into the Story"

The importance of ordinary people or others who are not professional journalists participating in the news process has been well documented by journalism researchers (Andén-Papadopoulos & Pantti, 2011; Domingo, 2011; Thurman, 2008; Williams, Wardle, & Wahl-Jorgensen, 2011). Indeed, Karlsson (2012) identified participation along with interconnectedness as specific indicators for liquid news. With the Pop-Up Newsroom, reporters' awareness that they were sharing Twittersphere space with others was evident as they retweeted fellow classmates, citizens, and organizations also on social media. One said, "It definitely makes you more aware of the people reading your reporting as they can reply directly to you." Another noted that "I surfed around Twitter . . . to see what others were tweeting," and then she tweeted at ordinary citizens who were also producing content on her topic. This brought her retweets, favorites, and replies. When a Twitter user from Norway replied to a photo she posted, she said, "I felt the power of global community on Twitter."

An additional aspect to participation and interconnectedness beyond what takes place online became evident through the Pop-Up Newsroom: Some students appeared to become less concerned with maintaining boundaries between themselves, their sources, and their coverage topics. One said the temporary news space format meant they were not just interviewing people. He responded at the time, "We are interacting with the people . . . [because] we are not stuck in a room." In fact, Kantola (2013) finds that liquid journalists do not subscribe to traditional expectations that reporting should rely on permanent, elite sources; instead, opinions from "the man on the street" are just as legitimate. Thus, they tend to concentrate on the voices of ordinary people. Here, some students explained that the Pop-Up Newsroom provided the "freedom . . . to truly experience the event which helped us convey the event to own [sic] followers."

Likewise, Kantola (2103) argues that liquid journalists reject objectivity. This appears to describe what happened with at least some of the students observed here. Students repeatedly emphasized how they became connected at least temporarily to the people and events involved in the stories they were reporting. As one student said, "The lack of a physical newsroom made us [the reporters] more integrated into the story . . . personally I had moments where I got so caught up in my surroundings that I forgot I had to report." For example, several students reporting during the CicLAvia event joined a Zumba lesson on the streets, while other students reporting on an event for homeless veterans (as part of the poverty project) became "sources" themselves when interviewed for Skid Row Radio about their perceptions of the issue. In traditional journalism, students learn to create networks of sources and maintain relationships with them while still aiming for professional distance from those they report on. Here, the students were not building source networks but interacting with people instead. The difference reflects Bauman's argument that in liquid modernity relationships are unstable, and it is the processes of relating that matters most.

Conclusion

The Pop-Up Newsroom model embodies suggestions for how journalism education might respond to the contingent, unstable environment through which we all must now navigate. If, as the explication of liquid modernity suggests, establishing long-standing routines and set responses is considered ineffective, journalism educators must consider new ways of preparing students in a never-ending process. By focusing on short-term projects that spring rapidly to life and then end, the Pop-Up Newsroom offers one approach. The temporary newsroom does not seek to provide an on-going permanent delivery of information, an action that, however carried out, seems difficult to untether from traditional understandings of news.

Instead, the Pop-Up Newsroom provides its denizens a fluid framework for reporting, leaving much of the creation and enactment up to the students themselves as they carry out their individual acts of journalism. In this way, they are its creators, working briefly in sporadic moments of production and connection. The temporary newsroom allows—indeed encourages—them to experiment, to both continually use new forms of content production while potentially forgetting what they learn as soon as they are finished: a key recommendation for adapting to liquid modernity. Bauman argues that routines never gel, and thus zealously working to internalize them does not prepare a student reporter for the future. Rather, this approach represents a sort of nostalgia for a permanence that is constantly beyond reach. However uncomfortable such a response might be to traditional journalism, which relies on agreed-upon practices for its authority, the status quo cannot be maintained in the current news environment. As Bauman says, "not contemplating change is no longer an option" (Gane, 2004, p. 36).

References

Andén-Papadopoulos, K., & Pantti, M. (Eds.), (2011). *Amateur images and global news*. Chicago, IL: University of Chicago Press.

Baines, D., & Kennedy, C. (2010). An education for independence: Should entrepreneurial skills be an essential part of the journalist's toolbox? *Journalism Practice*, 4(1), 97–113.

Bauman, Z. (2000/2012). *Liquid modernity*. Malden, MA: Polity.

Bauman, Z. (2001). Identity in the globalizing world. *Social anthropology*, 9(2), 121–129.

Becker, L. B., Vlad, T., & Simpson, H. A. (2013). 2012 Annual survey of journalism and mass communication: Enrollments decline for second year in a row. *Journalism & Mass Communication Educator*, *68*(4), 305-334.

Bennett, E. (2104, July 17). How do journalism schools measure up as a training ground for newsroom innovators. Retrieved from http://blog. wan-ifra.org/2014/07/17/how-do-journalism-schools-measure-up-as-a-training-ground-for-newsroom-innovators

Berger, G. (2011). Empowering the youth as citizen journalists: A South African experience. *Journalism*, *12*(6), 708-726.

Castells, M. (2007). Communication, power and counter-power in the network society. *International Journal of Communication*, *1*(1), 238–266.

De Rosa, A. (2012). Tim Pool: Occupy Wall Street's mobile journalist. *Tech Tonic*. Retrieved from http://blogs.reuters.com/anthony-derosa/2012/02/25/tim-pool-occupy-wall-streets-mobile-journalist-tech-tonic/

Deuze, M. (2006). Global journalism education: A conceptual approach. *Journalism Studies*, *7*(1), 19-34.

Deuze, M. (2009). Journalism, citizenship and digital culture. In Z. Papacharissi (Ed.), *Journalism and citizenship: new agendas in communication* (pp. 15-28). New York, NY: Routledge.

Deuze, M. (2007). Journalism in liquid modern times: An interview with Zygmunt Bauman. *Journalism Studies*, *8*(4), 671-679.

Domingo, D. (2011). Managing audience participation practices, workflows and strategies. In J. B. Singer, A. Hermida, D. Domingo, A. Heinonen, S. Paulussen, T. Quandt, Z. Reich, & M. Vujnovic (Eds.), *Participatory journalism: Guarding open gates at online newspapers* (pp. 76-95). New York, NY: Blackwell Publishing.

Gane, N. (2004). Zygmunt Bauman: liquid sociality. In N. Gane (Ed.), *The future of social theory* (pp. 17-46). New York, NY: Continuum.

Gillmor, D. (2013, December 27). Call me an optimist, but the future of journalism isn't bleak. *The Guardian*. Retrieved from http://www.theguardian.com/commentisfree/2013/dec/27/journalism-future-not-bleak-advertising

Jarvis, J. (2012, September 18). Here's a blueprint for radical innovation in journalism education. *Nieman Labs*. Retrieved from http://www.niemanlab.org/2012/09/jeff-jarvis-heres-a-blueprint-for-radical-innovation-in-journalism-education/

Kantola, A. (2013). From gardeners to revolutionaries: The rise of the liquid ethos in political journalism. *Journalism*, *14*(5), 606-626.

Karlsson, M. (2012). Charting the liquidity of online news. Moving towards a method for content analysis of online news. *International Communication Gazette*, *74*(4), 385-402.

Karlsson, M., & Strömbäck, J. (2010). Freezing the flow of online news: Exploring approaches to the study of the liquidity of online news. *Journalism Studies*, *11*(1), 2-19.

McChesney, R. W., & Pickard, V. (2011). *Will the last reporter please turn out the lights: The collapse of journalism and what can be done to fix it.* New York: The New Press.

McDevitt, M., & Sindorf, S. (2012). How to kill a journalism school: The digital sublime in the discourse of discontinuance. *Journalism & Mass Communication Educator, 67*(2), 109-118.

Mensing, D. (2011). Realigning journalism education. In B. Franklin & D. Mensing (Eds.), *Journalism education, training and employment* (pp. 15-32). New York, NY: Routledge.

Newton, E. (2013, March 17). How does your school measure up? *Knight Foundation Blog. Retrieved from* http://www.knightfoundation.org/blogs/ knightblog/2013/3/17/do-universities-hear-critics-journalism-education/

Newton, E. (2012). Reply to Francisco, Lenhoff, Schudson: Promise, peril of "teaching hospitals." *International Journal of Communication, 6,* 4.

Robinson, S. (2013). Teaching "journalism as process": A proposed paradigm for J-School curricula in the digital age. *Teaching Journalism and Mass Communication, 3*(1), 1-12.

Rosa, H., & Scheuerman, W. E. (Eds.), (2009). *High-speed society: Social acceleration, power, and modernity.* University Park, PA: Pennsylvania State University Press.

Scruggs, A. O. (2012, October 11). In defense of journalism education: The 3 essentials it teaches. *Poynter.* Retrieved from http://www.poynter.org/ how-tos/journalism-education/190429/in-defense-of-journalism-education-the-3-essentials-it-teaches/

Sivek, S. (2013, August 12). Do journalists need a journalism degree? Educators, practitioners disagree. *MediaShift.* Retrieved from http://www.pbs.org/mediashift/2013/08/do-journalists-need-a-journalism-degree-educators-practitioners-disagree/

Thurman, N. (2008). Forums for citizen journalists? Adoption of user generated content initiatives by online news media. *New Media & Society, 10*(1), 139-157.

Tuchman, G. (1973). Making news by doing work: Routinizing the unexpected. *American Journal of Sociology, 79*(1), 110-131.

Wall, M. (2005). 'Blogs of war'; weblogs as news. *Journalism, 6*(2), 153-172.

Wall, M. (2014). Change the space, change the practice? Re-imagining journalism education with the Pop-Up Newsroom. *Journalism Practice,* 1-15.

Williams, A., Wardle, C., & Wahl-Jorgensen, K. (2011). "Have they got news for us?" Audience revolution or business as usual at the BBC? *Journalism Practice, 5*(1), 85-99.

Zelizer, B. (2004). *Taking journalism seriously: News and the academy.* Thousand Oaks, CA: Sage Publications.

16

Going Mojo: Students Covering Severe Weather, Sports, and Racial Conflict

Julie Jones

Mobile reporting, as with the terms "convergence" and "Web 2.0" before it, has become a buzzword in the news industry (Barthel, 2015; Buttry, 2011). From mobile-centric conferences to the growing number of mobile-first initiatives, it is apparent both on the professional and the journalism educational side of news that mobile has gained notable attention (Aimonetti, 2011; Herndon, 2014). What is less clear, though, is whether mobile is merely a trend, a new distribution channel, or an entirely different way to approach news reporting (Westlund, 2012). Even those adopting a mobile-first mindset conceptualize mobile journalism somewhat differently and, thus, take different approaches to the notion of mobile journalism. This uncertainty at the professional and scholarly level can cause confusion for journalism educators. On one hand, being able to report professionally via one's smartphone appears to be a skill that differentiates a program's journalism students from others in the job market or in the newsroom (Wenger, Owens, & Thompson, 2014). On the other hand, exactly how to adopt mobile technology into classrooms, for what purposes, and for what learning outcomes is less obvious.

Over the last four years, the Gaylord College's Mobile Reporting course at the University of Oklahoma (OU) has experimented with different classroom structures, professional partnerships, and kinds of news coverage to find the inherent value in having students pick up mobile devices to report news. This chapter examines the four different iterations of the mobile journalism class to better understand *what* mobile reporting has provided these students beyond other skills-based journalism courses and *how* these experiences translated into the professional world. In short, this study asked what is mobile *good for* within a journalism curriculum and how educators can structure a course for particular learning outcomes. To answer these questions, former mobile students, many of whom are now working in professional newsrooms, were interviewed about their experiences in the class and what they learned from it. Because a different approach was applied each year of the Mobile Reporting course, the students' reflections offer a unique window by which to compare different configurations of one mobile reporting class across time to flesh out the advantages each version provided students. First, though, the literature review addresses *why* many consider mobile to be salient in the current media environment.

The Case for Going Mobile

A common argument for an organization to "go mobile" is based simply on the rapid adoption and worldwide reliance on mobile devices. Currently, there are about as many mobile phones (cell and smartphones) in the world as there are people (Kemp, 2015; Fernholz, 2014). Of course, this was not the case when the first Internet-connected cell phone, the Nokia Communicator, was introduced in 1996 (Baguley, 2013). According to The World Bank (2015), three years after the Communicator's release, cell phone subscriptions in Finland (Nokia's home base) and neighboring Norway and Sweden were the highest in the world—hovering at around 60% of each country's population. Cell phone subscription rates 20 years later are quite different. China, Hong Kong, and Kuwait, respectively, are now the top three cellular regions in the world. As with cellular subscriptions, mobile access to online content is also increasing quickly and now accounts for one third of the page views on the World Wide Web (We are social, 2015). Accessing content via mobile devices is more salient in some regions of the world and for certain ethnic cohorts. In Nigeria, for example, mobile accounts for three quarters of the country's Web traffic, a rate three times greater than that of the United States or United Kingdom (We are social, 2015). Google data (2015) indicates that most users in South Africa and Malaysia prefer smartphone over all other devices (desktop, tablet, etc.) to access online content and, again, at rates that are nearly twice as much as in the United States or United Kingdom. The perceived value of news delivered on a mobile device also varies nationally and culturally. For example, Westlund (2010) found that Japanese users consider mobile news more favorably than Swedish users even though they are also more likely to consider it too costly. In the United States, mobile is more central to the lives of Hispanic, African-American, and Asian cohorts than their Caucasian counterparts, and this saliency also translates into greater rates of seeking and sharing news (Smith, 2015).

There is also a growing interest in *mobile-only* consumption. Mobile-only users have either dropped traditional modes of accessing online content (via Internet providers) or never adopted them in the first place. In the United States, mobile-only users surpassed desktop-only users for the first time in 2015 (Lella, 2015). Although they are increasing, the mobile-only users account for about 10% of the overall U.S. online population. Because they tend to belong to lower socio-economic classes, this cohort is completely dependent on mobile for online access (Smith, 2015). Mobile-only is also a term that refers to traffic measured at a site itself. For example, Facebook recently announced that users who *only* use mobile devices to access its platform surpassed desktop-only and desktop/mobile users in late 2015 (Rosoff, 2015; Weber, 2015).

News sites are also finding similar mobile-only patterns in their traffic. The BBC acknowledged that 65% of its web traffic is mobile-only, and 36 of the 50 top U.S. news sites were mainly accessed in 2014 through mobile devices (Lee, 2015; Mitchell, 2015). Those who anchor their argument for mobile solely on consumption patterns tend to discuss the need to develop apps, create mobile-responsive sites, and intensify news cycles throughout the day (Bell, 2015; Reilley, 2015). However, others consider the power of mobile reporting not so much by the sheer numbers and patterns of use but rather in the connections mobile devices afford between journalists and the public (Mabweazara, 2011; Marymont, 2007; Wei, 2013).

Mobile in Terms of Citizens, Crowds, and Communication

Another way to conceptualize mobile journalism is to focus less on the end product and more on the front-end reporting process. Even then, the arguments for going mobile vary from ones centered on how citizen journalists add value during breaking news events to the advantages of crowdsourcing to arguments that mobile is the perfect communication tool for news work. Taken as a whole, though, the reasons for adopting a mobile strategy can be summarized in one simple notion: sourcing.

As Twitter executives recently stressed with their stockholders, significant news events—from the Michael Brown shooting in Ferguson, Missouri, to the capture of Osama Bin Laden in Abbottabad, Pakistan—are now being first reported by citizens with smartphones, not journalists (Allan, 2007, 2014; Robinson & Robison, 2006; Sheller, 2014). From the journalism side, these random moments of "citizen-journalism" step on the core function of news operations: to report and witness from the scene (Snowden, 2012). Journalists further worry that citizen journalism loosens professional standards of verification and ethical principles and, given the number of recent newsroom layoffs, threatens the most personal side of being a professional journalist—being (and staying) employed (Deuze, 2009). Citizens, though, talk about the excitement of witnessing events and are more inclined to see their actions as a form of sharing rather than an act of, or a threat to, journalism (Cheesman, 2015; Snowden, 2012). The citizen witness, then, is first acting upon a natural impulse to share a key moment in time with family and friends (Allan, 2014; Berger, 2011). When their phones flood with text messages and their social media exposure grows exponentially, the idea of how their content is valued *beyond* their social circles dawns on them (Zdanowicz, 2014).

Another way to conceptualize the advantage of mobile devices for the news industry is to consider it a tool for collaboration rather than competition. The crowd-mapping, open-sourced software Ushahidi, "testimony" in Swahili, is an example of how mobile tools can leverage crowd-sourced information for news purposes. Ushahidi was first used to track cases of violence after the 2008 Kenyan elections. Since then, news organizations, nongovernmental organizations, community groups, and individuals have used Ushahidi during crisis events. For example, within 30 minutes after the first terrorist bomb went off in 2011 in Mumbai, India, a vacationing software engineer created an Ushahidi map to gather reports and tweets from those close to the subsequent explosions (A.A.K., 2011). Because Twitter hashtags were coded into the programming, the map quickly filled with reports and information that identified *what* was happening *where*. For those caught in the event, this map provided crucial information on what parts of the city to avoid. In this way, Mumbai residents had access to the hyper-local information they needed in-the-moment, much the same way New Orleans' citizens relied on bloggers to give them block-by-block information in the days following Hurricane Katrina (Norris, 2006).

The last way to look at how mobile devices are changing news routines is so basic it often goes unmentioned. Mobile phones are, quite literally, phones *that go with you*. Mobile phones keep journalists connected to their sources, communities, and the newsroom on a 24/7 basis (Mabweazara, 2011). Constant access is both a blessing and a curse. On the positive side, sources can quickly offer reporters tips to newsworthy information with a call, text, or direct message through social media. Similarly, journalists no longer need to work through a system of assistants, interns, or receptionists before getting to the person they need to reach. Community ties are also strengthened when reporters stay in the field to write and edit their stories rather than heading back to the newsroom (Marymont, 2007). On the negative side, the line between the world of work and one's personal life is rapidly disappearing.

Expanding Boundaries:
Benefits for Going Mobile in the Classroom

The benefit for adopting mobile media into journalism programs goes beyond simply following industry trends. Cochrane, Mulrennan, Sissons, Pamatatau, and Barnes (2013) contend that mobile journalism courses create experiential opportunities by shifting the locus of learning from the instructor to the students. In this way, the classroom becomes more like an apprenticeship than a formal classroom environment. Moreover, social media platforms can provide the opportunity for journalism students to monitor professional reporters. In adopting Twitter into his classroom, Hewett (2013) found that students not only began to follow professional journalists but, at the end of the semester, ranked the professional journalists' posts more valuable than journalism professors' Twitter feeds.

Ambient Journalism

Adopting mobile also provides instructors and students an opportunity to engage in Hermida's (2010) ambient journalism. Hermida contends that social media platforms, like Twitter, are functioning as an "always-on, always around you" awareness system where quick "digital fragments of news and information from official and unofficial sources . . . are enabling citizens to maintain a mental model of news and events around them" (Hermida, 2010, p. 2). As the quote suggests, much of Hermida's definition centers on individuals' collective role in contributing, communicating, and sharing content that creates for users a mental touchstone of what is happening. For journalists, the ambient environment provides a means to discover potential news stories and find sources throughout the news process. Burns (2010) argues that Hermida's definition gives too much credence to the participatory side of the paradigm and ignores the core values journalists provide, such as multiple sourcing and verification. Burns adds that in this fluid, dynamic environment rumors can be taken as facts and users' strategic motives may be unclear or purposefully obscure.

Journalism programs should use both Hermida's notion of ambient journalism and Burns' concerns to experiment with mobile reporting within social media environments. By doing so, students can learn how to best use mobile devices to gather news content and publish their stories on social media platforms like Twitter. Students also need to be taught how to monitor emerging trends, find and vet potential sources, verify information, and collaboratively engage with users while maintaining professional standards. The question becomes how to best structure a course to provide this kind of learning experience. This study sought to help answer this question.

Cross-Case Study: Four Years of Mobile Journalism

The mobile journalism course at OU presents a unique opportunity to examine the inherent value of "going mobile" for journalism educators. The author and a colleague began to conceptualize the Mobile Reporting class in the Fall of 2011. The goal was to have students report news events in real-time with as close to "in-your-pocket" devices as possible while maintaining journalism standards and professional media quality (Jones, 2013). At the time, creating a mobile reporting class was a novel concept with scant literature to help guide it (Hernandez & Rue, 2012; Väätäjä, Männistö, Vainio, & Jokela, 2009). Every Fall, the instructors considered the weaknesses of the last class as they designed the next iteration. These trial-and-error alterations to the course were far from simple readjustments. Instead, the four iterations of the Mobile Reporting class each had their own pedagogical strategies, classroom structures, and professional partnerships (see Table 16.1). These four different approaches to one class provide a window by which to examine the unique pedagogical value(s) a mobile reporting course offers journalism students and how certain course structures can either support or hinder these outcomes. Cross-case analysis is appropriate for this work because of the comparative nature of the study, the small numbers involved (four classes with a handful of journalism students in each), and the author's personal connection as the main instructor of the class (Minnis, 1985).

Reflections from former mobile journalism students on the value of their particular mobile reporting class are presented, along with the author's description of that year's classroom structure. Mobile Reporting is offered only in the Spring semester. This study examined the semesters spanning from 2012 to 2015 (previously referred to as years one through four respectively). Although 43 students have taken the course since Spring 2012, not all have been journalism majors, and not all journalism majors were working as journalists or media producers at the time of the study. Because the purpose of this work was anchored in journalism education, only those working as professional journalists or media producers in a closely related field (professional sports, broadcast weather, etc.) or those who were currently enrolled as journalism students were interviewed. These parameters narrowed the subject pool down to 17 potential participants: 10 working professionals (journalists, media producers, or broadcast meteorologists), six journalism students still in school, and a recent graduate just finishing a national journalism internship. Of these, two did not participate—one did not wish to participate, and one was unreachable. The 15 subjects who did participate represented the four different class cohorts fairly

Table 16.1

Comparison of Class Structure, Partnerships, and Key Moments Across Four Iterations of Mobile Reporting Class

Year / Class website name	Partnerships	Video posting	Social media	Class size	Weekly expectations	News focus	Key news moments
Year 1: StormCrowd	Weather technology company	Ushahidi, YouTube	Facebook, Twitter	16 students 2 editors	On-call shifts created	Severe weather	EF-1 tornado on campus and surrounding area
Year 2: StormCrowd	Small town community weekly	StormCrowd website	Twitter, Vine	14 students 2 editors	On-call shifts and sports schedule created	High school sports Severe weather	Severe weather and tornado headed toward campus 48-hour video feature on small-town life
Year 3: Not applicable	Local community newspapers	At the organization's discretion	Twitter	3 students 1 editor	Organizations set weekly expectations	Local papers determined coverage	Car/train collision near campus, possible shooter on campus
Year 4: NewsCrowd	No formal partnerships	NewsCrowd website	Twitter	7 students 2 editors	At least four stories a week	Racial issues SAE story/fallout Severe weather	Video of SAE fraternity members chanting racist song

Note. The total enrollment in year three was six students: three journalism students, two public relations, and one broadcast. The public relations and broadcast students were embedded in a nonprofit, disaster recovery organization. They are not included in the study because a) they are not journalism students, and b) they had different duties than the journalism students.

evenly: five were from year one, five from year two, two from year three, and four from year four. Among the participants were the six student editors for the course. Except for the first year, all editors had taken the class twice—once as a student and then as an editor. In the interviews, they were first asked about their student experiences and then later about their editor experiences the following semester.

One parameter remained across all four years: The class is a one credit-hour practicum, and the emphasis is on *practice* rather than lectures and grades. Student editors, all of whom volunteered for this role, serve as mid-level managers by maintaining communication with the group via text messaging, directing students during breaking news, sending out alerts when news is developing (e.g., approaching bad weather), mentoring students, verifying sources, and editing stories either before they are published on a class website or, in the case of Twitter, correcting students' posts when content is incorrect or unclear. In return, editors receive independent study credit. Students in the class were required to respond to the editors' text message requests immediately (if only to say they are in class and cannot report), to be ready to report at any moment, to stay aware of story possibilities around them as they went about their lives, and to post a minimum number of stories each week. All students were required to create and use a professional Twitter account.

All participants were interviewed on the phone, and their responses were recorded for data collection only. The interviews took between 20 to 42 minutes to complete. To help jog memories, participants were asked to rate their agreement with 11 statements on a five-point Likert scale, with 1 indicating strong disagreement and 5 indicating strong agreement with the statements. At the time of the study, the participants who were still students had completed at least one internship either during or after their semester in Mobile Reporting. Thus, when interviewing current undergraduate student participants, the word "job" was changed to "internship" to match their experiences. One of the Likert statements addressed whether the participants believed they had experienced ambient journalism during their semester; a definition of ambient journalism was read to them beforehand to clarify the construct. The Likert items were used to prime participants' memories and as a gauge for subtle differences in the extent of agreement across class cohorts.

Year One: The Experiment Year

The first year can best be described as the experimental year. Through the support of an AEJMC/Knight Bridge grant, a mobile-responsive site was built upon the Ushahidi platform that was branded as OU StormCrowd. Weather Decision Technologies (WDT), a weather data and technology company located on the OU Norman campus, adapted the Ushahidi platform and hosted the website on its servers. Severe weather coverage was the focus of the class, and a number of speakers helped to teach the students how to report on and from severe weather events (Jones, 2013). The most salient moment during the semester was an EF-1 tornado that passed through Norman and the OU campus (see Figure 16.1 for an example of tornado coverage from mobile reporters). According to the U.S. National Weather Service, this specific tornado had winds ranging from 90-100 mph that left moderate damage to homes, trees, businesses, and churches. Although 20 people were injured in Norman, there were no fatalities. It was one of a dozen tornados that struck central Oklahoma that day (National Weather Service Weather Forecast Office, 2012).

The first-year mobile students still remember their role as the initial "beta" run of the Mobile Reporting class. They talked about being "gung-ho" and excited about "living the experiment."

One student said the class was the first to give him a glance into where the industry "was going . . . and pushed me to continue into what I wanted to do and still do to this day."

Another talked about how the experience changed the direction of his subsequent career. "I didn't even like Twitter before that class," he responded. However, since graduation he has maintained the social media platforms for a major sports organization and is a regular Twitter contributor.

Though the opportunities to cover spot news were slim during the semester, all mentioned having the chance to cover breaking news as something "no other class" taught them.

"I was never forced to sit down and pound out a story," said one student, who now reports for a mid-sized Northeastern newspaper.

In their current work lives, only two talked about using what they learned from the mobile class on a daily basis. Others talked about a

Figure 16.1. Screen grab of StormCrowd coverage of an EF-1 tornado that landed in Norman, Oklahoma, on Friday, April 1, 2012. StormCrowd site was based on Ushahidi structure and hosted on Weather Decision Technologies (WDT) servers.

mobile mindset helping them with the social media aspects of their jobs, such as monitoring Facebook or Twitter for content. Although students felt the class gave them journalism experience, this cohort had the lowest agreement with the following statement: "During my semester of mobile reporting, I experienced the notion of ambient journalism." All responded with a neutral 3 on the five-point Likert scale.

Year Two: The Local Newspaper Partnership Year

The main lesson from the first year of mobile reporting was simply this: waiting around for weather to happen was not conducive to practicing mobile reporting skills. To address this problem, we partnered with a local weekly newspaper serving a small community close to the OU campus. While weather and breaking news were still priorities, the weekly practice for students became covering high school sports for the newspaper's Twitter feed and posting content to a newly designed StormCrowd website. Other new tools were also adopted: a GroupMe account helped the class, editors, and instructors keep in communication throughout the week; an editor encouraged students to use Vine, a newly released app for capturing seven-second video clips; and live tweeting became a new component of the class. Key moments during the semester included a tornado that threatened the campus (Gibson, 2013) and a weekend challenge to produce a day-in-the-life type video feature that was shot and edited entirely from the field. As with the first-year group, the second-year students talked about learning techniques for covering breaking news as the main value the class provided them.

"The majority of your work was hands-on," said one editor now working at a large metro newspaper. "There were other [journalism] skills classes but it [mobile] was a more specific skill. I loved that it was very focused."

"The field, the mobile aspect of it, gave me more of an experience of [reporting] as it happens than other classes," said one former student now working as a broadcast meteorologist. The live-tweeting before, during, and after high school sports was "cool … that gave you some social media experience as opposed to [going] live."

Another now meteorologist, whose small market station serves a region of the country often inundated with weather severe enough to make national news, said the mobile class helped to distinguish her work from other newsroom reporters and weather anchors.

"I can easily notice a difference," she said. "Some don't tweet, they don't Facebook, and they don't get much interaction from the viewers. You have to do it all . . . use Facebook, Twitter, Periscope, Instagram. You have to cover all your bases."

Some believed mobile reporting for a small-town paper had value. Both second-year editors noted how visiting newsrooms and having professional editors set expectations was helpful for the class. Also, working for a local paper via mobile tools meant the reporters *stayed* in the community longer than they would have for other class assignments or student media organizations.

"We were enjoying it," said one, who compared the mobile assignment of editing in the field to the broadcast approach of bringing the video back to the student newsroom to finish a story. "We were able to connect more with the people."

"It was the first time I connected with a community itself," said the individual who called live-tweeting sports "cool."

Unlike the first-year cohort, the second-year cohort strongly agreed that it had experienced some kind of ambient journalism.

Year Three: The Embedded Year

Although we did not realize it at the time, the third year of mobile reporting drifted the furthest away from the original challenge to report as close to the pocket and moment as possible. Because the pressure of working for a "real" newspaper editor was helpful in year two, we decided to see if more local papers could use mobile students assigned to their publications. With only three journalism students enrolled this semester, one student went to a mid-size daily, another to a small-town weekly located about an hour from campus, and the last student worked with the weekly partnered with in year two. Of the three former mobile students, two agreed to be interviewed for the study. They reported that, despite the newspapers' initial interest in experimenting with mobile and social platforms, the editors used the students in traditional ways.

"It hurt me that [the] paper was very small and had a staff of five," said the student embedded at the newspaper farthest from campus. "They had a Twitter [account] that they might have used twice and a Facebook page. But they used me the way they always used people . . . I had all this knowledge but I did not have an application for it."

Things were no better at the other paper. This student was assigned to write text stories and to make sense of the paper's in-house video system. He recalled that the editors eventually told him "we are not really big on video so we will put you on the copy desk."

Still, both students said that the mobile class gave them a unique learning experience.

Year Four: The Big News Year

Taking a lesson from the mistakes of year three, the instructors took back editorial control for the Spring 2015 mobile class. From the start of the semester, racial issues were the top news across campus. *Unheard*, a newly formed African-American student advocacy group, brought

Figure 16.2. Screen grab of NewsCrowd story. One of the "person-on-the-street" responses to the question "Do you feel heard?" posed to African-American and Muslim students on campus.

a list of grievances to the university president in January. As its name suggests, *Unheard* contended that black student voices at OU have been "unheard" for quite some time. The class was directed to cover news and events salient to marginalized cohorts on campus. Person-on-the-street type interviews that focused on diversity issues were assigned during slow news or weather weeks. The first of these assignments was to ask African-American and Muslim students if they felt heard on campus (see Figure 16.2). Purposefully, the semester focused on building connections to communities of color on campus. A new mobile-responsive site, named NewsCrowd, was created through donations to the college and was operational from the start of the semester. The student editors brought new ideas and skills. One pushed mobile reporters to incorporate the Twitter handles of any person they interviewed or photographed into the 140-character posts. The other editor stressed using apps like Ban.jo to find stories and people close by. In previous years, students used mobile kits with Apple iPod Touches equipped with frames that held Sennheiser shotgun microphones. The kits also included external batteries for charging in the field. However, fourth-year students preferred to use their phones over the mobile kits.

The key event that semester was a story that broke over social media and, within hours, became national news. Rumors of a video showing Sigma Alpha Epsilon (SAE) fraternity members chanting a racist song began to spread across campus on Sunday, March 8, 2015. The NewsCrowd editors—independently of each other—began to see Twitter chatter about the SAE video early that evening. From there, events progressed rapidly. The on-call editor alerted the mobile students and monitored key Twitter accounts (*Unheard,* SAE, the university, etc.). Students were assigned tasks for the night and following morning. Both the editors and one student from the class covered a midnight gathering; another student in the class dug into SAE's history of controversial moments; and two others prepared to cover *Unheard*'s early morning protest march the next day. This hectic pace continued throughout the week as other protests, marches, vigils, and press conferences occurred with little or no warning.

The fourth year came the closest to our original goals: to report real-time and with a device that can fit in one's pocket. Students mentioned learning to report during breaking news as a valuable skill. This time, though, they talked about "report[ing] in the moment," "reporting exactly where you are," and having "a sense of urgency" that they did not find in other journalism classes. One student compared the speed of the class' reporting to other student media on campus.

"We were quick," she recalled. "Really quick. . . . Everyone else does not get it out as quick[ly] as we do, and I thought that was cool and interesting."

By using their own phones, class students were first to actually report from the devices they normally carried in their pockets (or purses or student backpacks). Two students said having their phones on them helped at their internships. One recalled covering a midnight event where tripods and flashes were not allowed. Although the professional journalists struggled to handle the low light situation with their cameras, the phone photos she took were "a bit fuzzy but got the point across."

"It is learning you can do a lot more with less," another student explained. "You can do something in a short amount of time, and you don't always need the [big] equipment. You are more independent."

Twitter, in particular, gave the students a number of ways to experience ambient journalism during the SAE week. Through their Twitter accounts they monitored official and unofficial sources, followed their classmates' and other student media's coverage, and watched their own number of followers quickly grow as others started to follow them and shared their posts. By using the Twitter handles of people they interviewed or photographed, their own brand seemed to grow during the coverage. Requests to use their images and/or video came directly to them almost immediately via Twitter messaging from college, national, and international news organizations. Furthermore, the NewsCrowd brand gained credibility as it began to show up—unprompted by the students or editors—in other users' posts during the week. Whether it was due to the students' SAE work, the Twitter attention that followed, or the students' focus on under-represented groups, this cohort had the strongest sense that others were watching their work and that news and sources are always around them.

"Mobile is real," said a sophomore. "We are doing real news out there that people are going to see and feel that their story is being told."

The Take-Away: Lessons From a Mobile Reporting Class

This study asked a basic question: What are mobile devices good for within a journalism course? Learning to report breaking news was the main benefit across all semesters—even in years when breaking news events were slim. Mobile, then, is first and foremost an *in-the-field tool* that keeps students in the field and working on evolving stories. Covering unfolding events, even the potential of snowstorms or thunderstorms, are perfect opportunities to practice quick responses, nimble thinking, and focused reporting while maintaining core journalistic values of sourcing and verification. However, mobile assignments do not need breaking news to gain pedagogical benefits. Students tasked with producing a video story on a small-town community within a 48-hour window still talked about the experience as being significantly different than assignments in other journalism courses. Mobile assignments keep students working in the field and connected to the story environment past the moment when they usually would have returned to campus to finish up stories.

This observation leads to the second take-away: Mobile is *social*. Feeling a connection to others was especially true for the students who reported for the community paper or on the SAE video. Instructors should define a community to serve from the start and allow students to form their own connections as they work through the semester. Students reporting from their own Twitter accounts, using the Twitter handles of the people they are reporting on, and mentioning the course's Twitter handle help forge their own connections while growing both their and the course's credibility during key news moments.

Finally, mobile is a *communication tool*. Since the second year, classes were able to maintain a virtual newsroom throughout the week through their phones. More than just a "check status" tool for the editors, the GroupMe thread gave students a way to compliment one another, check on one another's location during big events, and help troubleshoot problems.

There were also missteps along the way. In particular, the Mobile Reporting class in years one and three did not provide the students an optimal learning environment. The take-away from these semesters is simple: Do not expect technology or partnerships with professional newsrooms to deliver pedagogical value. Mobile technology is more than just a new tool students can experiment with while reporting, and professional newsrooms, in our experience, are not ready to fully embrace new ways of working. Even though all three newspapers were open to the notion of having mobile reporting students in their newsrooms, daily demands eroded the organizations' original commitment to let them use such skills. In the end, newsroom editors asked the students to report in conventional ways with conventional deadlines. Similarly, thinking of a mobile class as a way to experiment with "cool" gadgets—much like how we approached the first year of Mobile Reporting—is not helpful. Instructors should focus on delivering opportunities for students to sharpen their mobile *mindset* and to learn what works best for their own classrooms and learning outcomes.

The learning objective for this course was to teach students how to report from mobile devices during unfolding events with quick information and media in a professional—and Westernized—manner. Other pedagogical objectives may be more centered on serving communities in a particular context. For example, students could use an Ushahidi platform to find information and media posted by citizens as a means to covering a specific environmental issue that is salient to a particular geographic community. In this manner, they may learn how to work with communities, vet citizen-contributed information, and discover how geo-located data can be used in news reporting. While such goals are different than teaching students how to report from their phones during breaking news events, the main take-away is similar: mobile devices combined with social media *connect* students to people in a quick and personal way. These social connections deliver a new, profound learning experience via the device that is always on and always with you.

References

A.A.K. (2011, July 25). Online crisis management: A web of support. *The Economist*. Retrieved from http://goo.gl/ECcoRL

Aimonetti, J. (2011, December 22). Gannett outfits newsroom with iphones, ipads. *CNET*. Retrieved from http://goo.gl/kVXD2L

Allan, S. (2007). Citizen journalism and the rise of "mass self-communication": reporting the London bombings. *Global Media Journal, Austrialian Edition* 1(1), 1-20.

Allan, S. (2014). Witnessing in crisis: Photo-reportage of terror attacks in Boston and London. *Media, War & Conflict*, 7(2), 133-51.

Baguley, R. (2013, August 1). The gadget we miss: The Nokia 9000 Communicator. *Medium*. Retrieved from https://goo.gl/hC9xBX

Barthel, M. (2015, April 29) 5 key takeaways from *State of the News Media 2015*. Retrieved from http://goo.gl/S3cMfX

Bell, E. (2015). *The rise of mobile and social news—and what it means for journalism*. Retrieved from http://goo.gl/KN29rZ

Berger, G. (2011). Empowering the youth as citizen journalists: A South African experience. *Journalism*, *12*(6), 708-726.

Burns, A. (2010). Oblique strategies for ambient journalism. Retrieved from http://journal.media-culture.org.au/index.php/mcjournal/article/viewArticle/230

Buttry, S. (2011, December 10). How news organizations can create a mobile-first strategy. Retrieved from http://goo.gl/YTXFXM

Cheesman, C. (2015, February 17). Are citizen journalists killing reportage? *Amateur Photographer*. Retrieved from http://goo.gl/07V6kx

Cochrane, T., Mulrennan, D., Sissons, H., Pamatatau, R., & Barnes, L. (2013). *Mobilizing journalism education*. Paper presented at the International Conference on Information Communication Technologies in Education

(ICICTE 2013), Crete, Greece.

Deuze, M. (2009). The people formerly known as the employers. *Journalism, 10*(3), 315-318.

Fernholz, T. (2014, February 25). More people around the world have cell phones than ever had land-lines. *Quartz.* Retrieved from http://goo.gl/1jK3Jy

Gibson, T. (2013). Covering Oklahoma weather one tweet at a time. *NewsOK.* Retrieved from http://goo.gl/Gtjtze

Google (2015). *Consumer Barometer with Google.* Retrieved from https://goo.gl/4a14mc

Hermida, A. (2010). Twittering the news: The emergence of ambient journalism. *Journalism Practice,* 4(3), 297-308.

Hernandez, R. K., & Rue, J. (2012). *Mobile reporting field guide.* Berkeley, CA.: UC Berkeley Graduate School of Journalism.

Herndon, K. (2014). UGA's Grady College pilots mobile news lab. Retrieved from http://news.uga.edu/releases/article/mobile-news-lab-launched-uga/

Hewett, J. (2013). Using Twitter to integrate practice and learning in journalism education: Could social media help to meet the twin challenge of both dimensions? *Journal of Applied Journalism & Media Studies* 2(2), 333-346.

Jones, J. (2013, January 22). How Oklahoma students beat the press with mobile coverage of a tornado. *MediaShift.* Retrieved from http://goo.gl/92rzaS

Kemp, S. (2015, January 21). Digital, social & mobile worldwide in 2015. Retrieved from http://wearesocial.net/blog/2015/01/digital-social-mobile-worldwide-2015/

Lee, D. (2015, March). BBC News switches PC users to responsive site. *BBC News.* Retrieved from http://goo.gl/U9pcw8

Lella, A. (2015). *Number of mobile-only Internet users now exceed desktop-only in U.S.* Retrieved from http://goo.gl/cBzMq8

Mabweazara, H. M. (2011). Between the newsroom and the pub: The mobile phone in the dynamics of everyday mainstream journalism practice in Zimbabwe. *Journalism,* 12(6), 692-707.

Marymont, K. (2007). MoJo a Go-Go. *Quill, Supplement Journalist,* 18-21.

Minnis, J. R. (1985). Ethnography, case study, grounded theory, and distance education research. *Distance Education* 6(2), 189-98.

Mitchell, A. (2015). *State of the news media 2015.* Retrieved from httpthat://goo.gl/oBd3Sf

National Weather Service Weather Forecast Office. (2012). Information about the April 13-14, 2012 severe weather event in Oklahoma. Retrieved from http://www.srh.noaa.gov/oun/?n=events-20120413

Norris, M. S. (2006). The journalistic response to Hurricane Katrina. *Midday.* Retrieved from http://goo.gl/Qao0Kp

Reilley, M. (2015, July 21). 7 tips for building a mobile-first, multi-platform newsroom. *MediaShift*. Retrieved from http://goo.gl/YjBvsc

Robinson, W. & Robison, D. (2006). Tsunami mobilizations: Considering the role of mobile and digital communication devices, citizen journalism, and the mass media. In A. Kovoori & N. Arceneaux (Eds.), *The cell phone reader: Essays in social transformation* (pp. 85-104). New York, NY: Peter Lang.

Rosoff, M. (2015, November 5). Facebook is officially a mobile-first company. *Business Insider*. Retrieved from http://goo.gl/Q3f3wJ

Sheller, M. (2014). News now. *Journalism Studies, 16*(1), 12-26.

Smith, A. (2015). *U.S. smartphone use in 2015*. Retrieved from http://goo.gl/iAtyVV

Snowden, C. (2012). As it happens: Mobile communications technology, journalists and breaking news. In N. Arceneaux & A. Kovoori, (Eds.), *The mobile media reader* (pp. 20-34). New York, NY: Peter Lang.

Väätäjä, H., Männistö, A., Vainio, T., & Jokela, T. (2009). Understanding user experience to support learning for mobile journalist's work. In R. Guy (Ed.), *The evolution of mobile teaching and learning* (pp. 177-210). Santa Rosa, CA: Informing Science Press.

We are social (2014). Social, digital & mobile in 2015. Retrieved from http://goo.gl/CijJOp

Weber, H. (2015, June). Nearly half of Facebook's users only access the service on mobile. *VentureBeat*. Retrieved from http://goo.gl/HAzgGt

Wei, R. (2013). Mobile media: Coming of age with a big splash. *Mobile Media & Communication, 1*(1), 50-56.

Wenger, D., Owens, L., & Thompson, P. (2014). Help wanted: Mobile journalism skills required by top U.S. news companies. *Electronic News, 8*(2), 138-149.

Westlund, O. (2010). New(s) functions for the mobile: A cross-cultural study. *New Media & Society 12*(1), 91-108.

Westlund, O. (2012). Mobile news. *Digital Journalism, 1*(1), 6-26.

World Bank. (2015). Mobile cellular subscriptions (per 100 people). Retrieved from http://goo.gl/bR2iiX

Zdanowicz, C. (2014, January 14). "Miracle on the Hudson" twitpic changed his life. *CNN*. Retrieved from http://goo.gl/rBIwQF

17

When Alternate Reality and Real Reality Collide: From Playing Games to Covering Real-World Events

Wajeehah Aayeshah

J ournalism education is going through an interesting phase following advances in digital technology, changed business models, and the increasingly interactive nature of the industry. This chapter provides a discussion on Alternate Reality Games (ARGs) as an innovative journalism educational resource and their use in journalism education. It reviews ARGs strengths and weaknesses in the classroom. It presents and discusses an ARG named *The Seed* as a case study developed and tested in a journalism classroom. And finally it offers a rationale and suggestions for using ARGs in journalism education.

Alternate Reality Games (ARGs)

McGonigal (2008) defines an ARG as follows:

> An interactive drama played out online and in real world spaces, taking place over several weeks or months, in which dozens, hundreds, thousands of players come together online, form collaborative social networks, and work together to solve a mystery or problem that would be absolutely impossible to solve alone.

ARGs are gradually gaining attention from academics all around the world. Mostly used as a marketing and promotional tool, ARGs are games that combine digital game mechanics with real-world locations, blending the digital and the physical. The game, as denoted by its name, takes place in an alternate reality; participants are required to play a character in a real-time situation that exists in real life. This chapter reviews some of the ARGs that academics have tested and considered and identifies the challenges and benefits academics have experienced after incorporating ARGs as a pedagogical tool.

Unlike traditional digital games, ARGs do not make a player sit for hours to complete a mission. In contrast, players have to search for clues in real life. To solve a mystery they must talk to strangers, travel, read books, watch the news, search the Internet, and more. In most cases, easily accessible media platforms like the Internet, text messages, pamphlets, and newspapers provide the information required for the game. Although initiated individually, players usually end up collaborating to complete the game within a specific time frame. According to the International Game Developers' Association, "alternate reality games take the substance of everyday life and weave it into narratives that layer additional meaning, depth, and interaction upon the real world" (Martin, Thompson, & Chatfield, 2006, p. 6).

Educational Benefits of ARGs

The effectiveness of ARGs has generated interest from several academics, who are exploring their potential as an educational resource. Tsvetkova et al. (2009, p. 1) advocate that "ARGs are especially suited to the needs of teaching and learning." An ARG mainly requires players to solve problems and challenges. As these problems are positioned in the real world, the players may find them more realistic than digital games. There will always be a gap between a course taught in a classroom environment and experiences faced at work. Scholars agree that it is quite difficult to replicate real-life scenarios in a classroom (Gossman, Stewart, Jaspers, & Chapman, 2007). However, the puppet master model used in ARGs has uncovered a new digital realism: "a kind of psychological realism that perfectly complements the 'immersed in reality' framework of real-world, mission-based gaming" (McGonigal, 2008).

Thus, ARGs can allow academics to incorporate real-life environments into a curriculum, aligning the game narrative with course goals. A "puppet master," the actual term used to describe the person running an ARG, works in a similar fashion as a project manager. Teachers also run academic courses in a similar manner, handling the curriculum within a particular time frame. Hence, the idea of a puppet master running an ARG works quite well in an academic setting, especially when the ARG is based in a realistic game narrative. It is not that ARGs are more engaging than digital games, but that their existence outside the gaming console or digital setting adds to the realism of the experience.

Designing an ARG takes time. It requires extensive planning and arrangement of settings, the amount of time depending on the complexity of its game design. However, it can also be quite cheap to develop. Phillips and Martin (2006, p. 53) strongly suggest that cheap ARGs do not have to mean low quality. An ARG hardly requires any heavy software or time spent on programming. The Alternate Reality Games for Orientation, Socialisation and Induction (ARGOSI) report argues that ARGs "offer a low-fidelity solution, using established Web technologies to create cost-effective and accessible content, with an ongoing narrative and visual theme to link the challenges into a coherent game" (Whitton, 2009, p. 5). Greater resources can make an ARG more interesting and engaging. However, a basic ARG can run on a small budget. ARGs' cost-efficiency is one of a list of very strong attributes, a reason why academia should be interested in using them as educational tools.

Alternate reality games can easily be customized according to the needs of students and their educational level. They have the flexibility to inculcate diverse game narratives to varied populations. As Whitton suggests, "they can be easily modified or changed to accommodate a different overarching storyline that may be more appropriate for different age groups, locations or subject disciplines" (2008, p. 4). ARGs' simple technology can be used in various geographical locations, they can easily be incorporated into different social, cultural, and/or economic requirements. *Half the Sky Movement: The Game* 2012 (see Figure 17.1) is a good example of the spatially flexible gameplay of ARGs and their cultural adaptability.

Half The Sky (2012) has gained international recognition from human rights activists and the general public. Initiated by Pulitzer Prize-winning journalists Nicholas Kristof and Sheryl WuDunn, this ARG is part of a broader movement aimed at empowering women around the world. Participants play as an Indian-looking female avatar, Radhika, runs different errands to improve her life. She has to take care of the children, work for community development, and deal with her husband without breaking traditional customs in a patriarchal society.

Figure 17.1. Half The Sky Movement: The Game.
Source: Games for Change, 2016. (http://www.gamesforchange.org/play/half-the-sky-movement-the-game/)

There are mini-games, such as harvesting crops and collecting books, which have tangible results. For example, as one plays, Radhika's financial situation gradually improves.

Furthermore, throughout the game players can contribute to real nonprofit organizations like the Fistula Foundation, GEMS, Heifer International, Room to Read, and World Vision. For instance, players can "unlock" a free book while playing a game about collecting books, and this free book will be delivered to a real person. Similarly, players can donate money to *Half The Sky* to be used for purposes relevant to the context of the game. For instance, when Radhika buys a goat for community development, players are asked if they would like to pay U.S. $10 to donate a goat to a real community. The player goes from becoming a common villager to an advocate, an activist to a leader, etc. As each player performs more tasks, his level in the game and the community improve. The United Nations Foundation, Rockfeller Foundation, and Intel support the game. *Half The Sky* incorporates social media to raise awareness of women's issues and money to support women. According to halftheskymovement.org, by 2013 some 1.1 million players around the world had played the game. *Half The Sky* is accessed through Facebook. Since this means that players do not need a particular gaming console and it is free to play, the game incorporates a strategy that encompasses a new breed of casual gamer.

Half The Sky demonstrates the transmedia story-telling attribute of ARGs. This technique allows the narrator to tell a story through a range of media. According to Jenkins (2006, p. 96), transmedia story-telling enables each medium to use its strengths, "so that a story might be introduced in a film, expanded through television, novels, and comics; its world might be explored through game play or experienced as an amusement park attraction." This transmedia narrative offers diversity in experience and stimulates audience engagement. This strength of ARGs can be harvested for educational purposes and enables academics to engage with 21st century digital native students, who are used to ubiquitous information flow (Adam & Perales, 2015; Bonsignore, Hansen, Kraus, & Ruppel, 2012).

A number of academics has stated that our educational system needs to move into the 21st century and use innovative technologies in education (Liu, 2011; Koelher & Mishra, 2005; Oliver & Herrington, 2003). Gene Foreman, a journalist and journalism academic, strongly supports the use of modern educational technologies for teaching students (Foreman, 2004):

> It is amazing to me that in the modern age, when we have technologies like the Internet and the hand-helds and the computers and the computer games, we are still teaching inside four walls, where all the information is coming from within those walls. (p. 53)

Foreman might as well have been referring to ARGs, since they allow academics to use all suitable platforms to provide the best educational outcomes.

According to both active learning and transformational play theory, while students are deeply engaged in ARG gameplay, propelled by intrinsic motivation, they gain learning benefits. *The Seed* ARG, developed to train investigative journalism students, uses a number of intrinsic motivators, including:

- ❑ competition (a reward point system gives the impression of competition even though teams are not actually competing with one another),
- ❑ narrative (a story-based scenario surrounding genetically modified crops),
- ❑ community (group work and collaboration through Facebook),
- ❑ creativity (writing a news feature), and
- ❑ completion (filing a news report).

Furthermore, diverse platforms are incorporated into the ARG, including mobile phones, email, class-based activities, and fieldwork. Players can benefit from multimodal learning.

Most of the educational ARGs have to be developed from scratch. No current template exists for ARG design. Educational ARGs are developed according to available resources and are planned for a suitable time frame. These existing games provide us with significant insight into the utility of ARGs in education. This sort of constructive learning experience not only enhances learning by "doing," it also boosts students' confidence and motivation. Important attributes like flexible narrative and context-based learning design were identified in these games. This formed part of the rationale to incorporate *The Seed* ARG into an investigative journalism class.

ARGs and Journalism Pedagogy

Due to rapidly changing trends in the industry, journalism academics are finding it difficult to prepare students for the field. There are a number of experimental projects worldwide attempting to make educational experiences as realistic as possible and provide hands-on investigative experience for journalism students. Other skills that are hard to teach in a classroom include the art of building trust and developing sources and networks. Compounding these issues is the fact that journalism courses must teach students according to a rigid timeline, with some semesters being as short as 12 weeks. This is especially problematic for investigative journalism, which requires an investment in time often far in excess of a normal semester.

Alternate reality games have been identified as a more suitable genre of digital games to teach investigative journalism due to their real-life traits. Indeed, realism is one of the most important ARG attributes often not offered in traditional teaching approaches. This chapter author uses the term "traditional teaching" in the context of linear, one-way teaching in a classroom, with a book and both teacher and student physically present. Journalism students already go through hypothetical scenarios in class exercises (D. Bossio, personal communication, July 18, 2011; J. Hollings, personal communication, November 16, 2011). They also take part in activities like conducting interviews and covering events. But alternate reality games can place students in real-life scenarios while reporting real-life events. An ARG allows journalism students to gain field experience through the realistic nature of its gameplay. Consequently, this allows a practice-based style of upgrading journalistic skills, which are required for quality journalistic work. As Sereda (2013) has stated:

> Reality games encourage players to see ordinary world in a new light and change it. This may include actions, not widely accepted per se. For example, changing the street lights' color, making a sweater for a statue, changing the look of a building. Participants do not imagine or recreate another world within reality or parallel to it. They operate in reality. (p. 9)

Hence, an ARG allows students to experience what journalists experience in daily routines. This ability to blend gameplay with reality is the key factor for their usability in journalism education. The ARG discussed later in this paper, designed to train journalism students, is based on a real-world context with actual problems—such as those related to genetically modified crops sown in Australia.

An ARG game design develops and modifies as the gameplay ensues. Therefore, for a journalism subject that requires uncovering events in real time, each iteration of an ARG will be better than the previous version. The game design can be continuously tweaked according to recent occurrences. An ARG also allows organized curriculum design and assessment evaluation for academics as it provides sound groundwork for a more traditional-length semester. It also allows the flexibility of scheduling when student journalistic work is due. In real-life journalism, interviews get postponed, breaking news takes up space allocation, and the timing of news stories is constantly reprioritized. An ARG is flexible enough to incorporate these changes and use these real-life routine occurrences when needed for student projects.

An ARG is based on collaborative work. It ensures collaborative learning through peer cooperation among students and enhances skills required for teamwork, a mandatory soft skill required in journalism (K. Moore, personal communication, November 1, 2011). It can also allow interaction with students outside class as well. Anyone can immediately send text messages about important information. This makes an ARG closer to real-life journalistic experience than purely class-based exercises. Alternate reality games can also last longer, spanning several weeks, whereas classroom exercises tend to last only one class. An ARG can allow investigation on stories that need more time and can even be distributed over several semesters.

Although an ARG can include role-play in its game narrative, it is different from typical classroom exercises or role-play exercises that journalism academics often use. The temporal and spatial flexibility of ARGs means they are not restricted to the classroom, unlike a typical role-play exercise. In addition, the continuous game narrative does not end when the class finishes. It can also incorporate a reality-based context. Both of these attributes make ARGs more suitable to the needs of a journalism unit than role-playing. Finally, ARGs include emergent gameplay, supported and shaped by players' participation (Fujimoto, 2010). The end of a reality-based ARG can have a different outcome than intended, which is not unlike journalistic stories.

Since most of the activities in an ARG are problem-based, students learn by "doing." This important tenet of constructivism, along with situated learning and active learning theories, advocates that "learning is not a spectator sport" (Chickering & Gamson, 1987, p. 4) and argues that "students learn better through activity rather than through instruction and memorisation" (Cameron, 2004, p. 25). Also, many activities undertaken in an ARG require prior knowledge, which is also a proponent of both constructivism and situated learning.

In the literature, one successful example of an ARG used for real-life journalism is "Investigate Your MP's Expenses," run by *The Guardian*. The newspaper had received around 558,832 documents about the expense accounts of members of parliament in the United Kingdom, and it invited the public to analyze these documents. According to McGonigal (2011), the public studied 170,000 documents in the first three days of the ARG. By the ARG's conclusion, the stories covered resulted in resignations, penalties, and changes in rules and laws.

Another example of an ARG designed and tested for an investigative journalism course is *Birds of Paradise* (2005-2006), developed by Stephen Tanner from the University of Wollongong, Australia. The ARG uses a fictional scenario based on a real-life issue: a bird-smuggling ring in West Papua. Students from this region, in Port Moresby and Madang, initially played the game. The first iteration was simple and involved development of traditional research skills and competency in Microsoft Access and Excel. The participants were required to think about how they would tackle the investigation. This approach was similar to most in-class scenarios academics use to teach journalism (B. Birnbauer, personal communication, July 20, 2011; J. Hollings, personal communication, November 16, 2011).

The second iteration of the game was much more developed and included real-life contacts and interviews with relevant experts to get facts (Tanner, 2005). The participating students were required to track down a smuggler by solving puzzles, using clues provided every week, and feeding the information to a website to advance in the game. These students were also required to conduct out-of-class activities, requiring both individual and collaborative investigation styles. They also had to make a judgment call on whether to submit their report every week (to their instructors) or to wait and potentially add late information. And they needed a cultural understanding of West Papua so they could investigate the issue appropriately. Discussion about ethical, legal, moral, and economic consequences of submissions was an important part of the learning requirements. The instructor provided relevant material on the Wollongong website so other academics could also play this game with their students. The fact that *Birds of Paradise* was repeatable is considered one of its biggest strengths. Although this ARG was very well structured, it took much time and effort in planning, designing, and implementing. Also, it was fictional. In the words of its developer, Stephen Tanner (S. Tanner, personal communication, December 4, 2012),

> although I was quite happy with the achievement of students, the time and effort invested in this project was more than I could offer conveniently. Therefore, I won't be working on developing such a project again, unless there is a way to make it easier to develop.

Based on an effort to make such games more accessible, the author developed an ARG in a real-life context for doctoral study at Swinburne University of Technology, Australia. The author used insights from the literature, interviews with journalism academics and journalists, and feedback from conference presentations.

The Seed ARG

This chapter's author developed *The Seed* ARG for an undergraduate class called Journalism Practice IV in the journalism program at Swinburne University of Technology (Swinburne), Hawthorn campus, Melbourne. The first class of a three-year bachelor's of arts program in journalism graduated in 2012. This class was organized by Dr. Saba Bebawi and assisted by tutor Dr. Denis Muller. *The Seed* ARG part of this course represents the program's first attempt to teach investigative journalism in this class. This ARG's teaching goals directly supported the course's investigative journalism unit's goals. Swinburne's Higher Education Research Ethics Committee approved ethics clearance for testing this ARG. As it was a part of doctoral study, both Dr. Mark Finn (supervisor) and Dr. Andrew Dodd (assistant supervisor) provided continuous support through discussions and feedback. The ARG contained two tutorials: tutorial A with 18 students and tutorial B with 16—a total of 34 students in the class.

ARG Design and Game Narrative

There are a few design challenges when effectively integrating an ARG into a journalism context. These include the following:

❑ How does one develop a game narrative that incorporates real-life experience?

❑ What platforms would be most suitable for student engagement?

❑ How would the instructors include elements of gamification in the game design?

❑ How would the instructors/developers ensure that the game design reflects an ARG and not just any other journalism project?

As discussed earlier, an ARG narrative developed for an investigative journalism unit would ideally be placed in a real-world context. This would allow students a realistic experience while researching and writing their news stories, perhaps even with the potential to publish them in a media outlet. Figure 17.2 illustrates *The Seed* ARG design, which was used for this project.

The Seed ARG's game narrative was based on genetically modified (GM) wheat in Australia. The instructors chose this topic because of its current recognition and importance in Australia. Before the game's start, in week one, the instructors informed students about the ARG. Participants received consent information and signed consent forms. The game narrative was based on controversy surrounding GM seeds, and, in particular, a farmer concerned about contamination of his non-GM crops. The game started when students received an anonymous text message, a tip, before the start of their class from a fictional farmer worried about cross-pollination with GM crops (see Figure 17.2). Although the farmer was fictional, the issue raised was close to reality. Within this overarching story, students had the flexibility to choose their own angles and researched them accordingly. Furthermore, they were required to use Facebook groups, developed for this experiment, for online interaction.

In addition to text messages, the instructors provided students with actual government press releases from The Australian Department of Health and Ageing, which regulates gene technology. The first press

Figure 17.2. The Seed ARG

release provided information about issuing licenses for controlled testing of GM wheat and barley in the Australian Capital Territory (ACT). This mix of real and fake resources was intended to engage students with the ARG by obscuring the reality-game boundary. Alternate reality games provide the opportunity to develop characters in the game narrative suited for a particular purpose. It is important to have characters with realistic personalities who are suited to the game narrative so that the students can engage with them. The characters can be anonymous. This means that even if they do not exist, their story can be realistic. In *The Seed* ARG, two fabricated characters—a farmer and an agricultural company employee—sent text messages to students to steer them along the game narrative.

By week two, the instructors had converted the class into a newsroom. The tutors encouraged students to find out about their issue in detail. Students were required to come up with one topic to investigate regarding GM crops. Subsequent tutorials included more press releases, more text messages from the anonymous farmer, and newsroom discussions. The instructors revealed a real-life company, Monsanto, selling GM seeds via a real news item. They also provided students with leads during tutorial discussions. These leads directed them to environmental, financial, and health issues relevant to GM technology. Those who followed up on the first text message were directed to two real-life Canadian farmers, Matt Gehl and Peter Eggers, who were conducting seminars against GM technology and visiting Australia at the time. The students also attended a seminar about gene technology and its effects on the environment. The instructors planned and organized this while working on the game design. Students also had to find scientific evidence and locate scientists expressing concern over their subject matter. Based on their research findings, students were allowed to develop their own conclusion, which was "filed" as a news report.

By nature, ARGs are comprised of task-oriented activities. Thus, ARGs lend themselves well to a problem-based learning approach. This type of learning advocates that there is no one right answer to a problem (Chamberlin & Moon, 2008, p. 7), which complements the teaching of journalism. After all, there can be several angles to one issue, and several ways of reporting one angle. Additionally, researchers (e.g., Moseley, 2008) have proposed a number of ARG features for educational contexts, some of which were incorporated into *The Seed* ARG. These include problem-solving elements, the use of rewards, and narrative devices (see Table 17.1).

Table 17.1

Moseley's (2008) Features Integrated Into The Seed ARG

General ARG features	Features of *The Seed*
Narrative devices (e.g., characters, plot, story)	There were characters, a loose narrative, and a leading real-life story the students developed.
Influence on outcomes	The news stories and the particular angles that the students covered were influenced by *The Seed* ARG.
Regular delivery of new problems/events	Regular updates were happening in real-time as it was a real-life ARG.
Potential for large, active community	*The Seed* ARG could also be played by a bigger group.
Based on simple, existing technologies and media	*The Seed* ARG included simple technologies like text messages and Facebook as an online platform.

Evaluation of *The Seed* ARG

The instructors collected student feedback on *The Seed* ARG through surveys and focus groups. They also collected interview feedback from the academics involved. Through *The Seed* ARG, the instructors provided students with clues and a basic narrative framework. However, students then investigated the topic themselves, delving into their choice of story angles. By adopting the role of an investigator, students not only gained a new perspective about the topic but were also transformed from a learner into an investigative journalist.

According to the feedback collected from survey and focus groups, the students approached this project with an assessment-oriented focus. Their main purpose seemed to be to get a good grade. Although they did not necessarily "believe" they were actual journalists, the instructors still consider this ARG's reality-based content as one of its main strengths.

Students may not have approached the investigation in exactly the same manner as a journalist, and academics continuously monitored and reviewed their progress. Regardless, these students operated in the real world, reporting on a real topic and interacting with real contacts. In this regard, they did actually experience elements of real-world journalism. Furthermore, many students stated that it did not feel like they were playing a game. And the fact that they could not separate the game from the unit suggests that the game was closely assimilated with the course curriculum.

One of the major hypotheses of this chapter was that the use of games in education could improve student motivation, interest, and engagement. One of the transparent gamification elements used in *The Seed* ARG was a reward point system based on the actions students posted on Facebook. Interestingly, the point system motivated many students even though their scores were not tied to their overall grades. Only group members could see one another's scores. Although students did appear to be more engaged by elements they perceived to be part of the game (although everything was part of the game), they were not as enthusiastic about the anonymous tips they received. The developers used Facebook to assist with group communication, to add to the multimodality of the ARG, and to also "play to the strengths" of current students' knowledge and interest (M. Bachelard, personal communication, July 26, 2011).

From an academic perspective, Facebook allowed monitoring of individual effort and group progress. An added benefit of this was that students felt more compelled to participate on Facebook because they knew teachers were monitoring them. There were a few issues with Facebook, however, including confusion caused by conversation thread updates, the academic workload of the monitoring, and ethical considerations regarding teachers being Facebook "friends" with students. Nevertheless, the students appeared to engage quite strongly with this mode of communication, especially with the added gamification technique of the point system.

Ultimately, the instructors concluded the use of Facebook as an online platform was successful as a facilitator of group communication and as a motivator for student participation. Facebook could also provide an appropriate online platform for student learning in other contexts and warrants further research to better understand the ways in which it could be adopted in teaching.

The skills students needed to submit an investigative news feature included the following:

❑ interview techniques (W. Bacon, personal communication, December 10, 2011; K. Moore, personal communication, November 1,

2011; D. Bossio, personal communication, July 18, 2011),

❑ contacting relevant people (R. Moynihan, personal communication, November 7, 2011), and

❑ deciding which information was most relevant and which leads to follow (J. Hollings, personal communication, November 16, 2011).

Since all of the above technical skills and attributes are important for investigative journalism, they were included in the game design. Student feedback stated that the ARG helped them become more confident speakers in class and in interviews. And many students repeatedly approached certain contacts, via online and telephone, until they managed to interview them. This demonstrated considerable persistence, an extremely important journalistic attribute (M. Bachelard, personal communication, July 26, 2011; R. Baker, personal communication, July 26, 2011; J. Tucker, personal communication, December 1, 2011; J. Tully, personal communication, December 2, 2011). In addition, the quality of the submissions, the story themselves, was quite high. Such student actions and other tangible results help to establish the effectiveness of this ARG in regards to educational outcomes.

Overall, the students found *The Seed* ARG to be a unique and interactive learning experience. Many thought Facebook was a good way of collaborating and sharing information with others. Several thought it was a creative way to investigate an issue and compile a news report. This is quite useful, as investigative journalism is mainly about exploring the unknown and discovering the truth. Overall, the academics thought that *The Seed* ARG was a good method of running a unit on investigative journalism. It helped in regular monitoring of student work and allowed editorial interference from the tutors. It also helped in arranging groups and encouraging collaboration, an important part of journalism.

Limitations of ARGs as an Artifact

The Seed ARG had a limited scope since it was an external project tested by the author, who was not the course unit's teacher. The school's research committee also raised ethical concerns that the author had to abide by while planning and developing the ARG. There is also a lack of guidelines available on the topic of presenting an ARG as a research artifact. And although the literature review provided in-depth analysis and studies on some ARGs, it did not cover presentation as an artifact.

An ARG is transient in nature. Hence, once played, it is gone—there is no physical proof it existed. Consalvo (2013) suggested a similar problem with online games, many of which no longer exist. She encourages archiving online games through snapshots and keeping a record of related discussion boards. However, it is complicated to archive an ARG. On one hand, the online or virtual element can be archived, as done in this case, by taking snapshots of Facebook group activities, developing sketches of classroom activities, and taking snapshots of text messages sent to students. On the other hand, classroom and group discussions and actual activities and tasks students performed while finding/approaching people to interview could not be archived because of ethical restrictions and practical limitations. One suggestion for documenting an ARG for a course would be to collect images of all the activities carried out. These would include images taken in class and during fieldwork, but they would require extensive and potentially difficult ethical clearance.

Also, there were limitations regarding the types and quantities of digital technologies the instructors could use. There was a gap between the author's level of knowledge about digital technologies and that of the tutors who handled the unit. And it was considered impractical to train the tutors before the teaching began. Therefore, the developers had to take the tutors' digital expertise into consideration while developing the game design. Both such limitations could be easily removed if the course conveners or the tutors themselves design ARGs or if the developer provides more training.

Conclusion

This chapter investigated the possibility of using ARGs for teaching an investigative journalism unit. An ARG has a flexible design module, the potential to engage students, and can provide them with a real-life experience, which is what journalism students need. Therefore, it was considered practical to design an ARG. An ARG has the potential to make a unit in investigative journalism more practical, real, interactive and engaging, while teaching journalism students the skills they require to operate as media professionals.

The Seed ARG developed and tested for the journalism class allowed students to complete an investigative report by working within a series of parameters. Most of the students did not feel that they were playing a game, perhaps a credit to the careful blending of game elements with the curriculum. The real-life investigation enabled students to gain experience and practice their journalistic skills, including interviewing, researching, and writing. The academics credited the ARG for supporting the course design in a structured manner. As a prototype, *The Seed* ARG was found to be a useful and successful tool for the investigative journalism course it was designed for.

The field of investigative journalism is rapidly changing. Journalism academics are trying to respond to these changes by adjusting their teaching methods. Harnessing the power of games by amalgamating game elements into the curriculum (Annetta, 2008), as this chapter has attempted, may be one way of addressing such changes. In addition to incorporating digital technology into journalism education to mirror changes in the industry and prepare students for it, games can provide a semi-realistic environment in which students are motivated to practice journalistic skills. ARGs are a relatively new development that might become a part of mainstream education in the years to come. In particular, ARGs could be useful for teaching journalism as they allow students to explore and develop a news story, each different from the next. While there are still many issues to resolve, the author hopes this case study can offer a practical starting point for such innovative educational tools and a positive contribution to the field of investigative journalism pedagogy.

References

Adam, F., & Perales, V. (2015). Experimenting with locative media games and storytelling in fine arts. In C. Holden, S. Dikkers, J. Martin, & B. Litts (Eds.), *Mobile media learning* (pp. 123-135). Pittsburgh: ETC Press.

Annetta, L. A. (2008). Video games in education: Why they should be used and how they are being used. *Theory Into Practice, 47*(3), 229-239.

Bonsignore, E., Hansen, D., Kraus, K., & Ruppel, M. (2012). Alternate reality games as platforms for practicing 21st century literacies. *International Journal of Learning, 4*(1), 25-54.

Cameron, D. (2004). *Giving games a day job: developing a digital game-based resource for journalism training.* (M.A. Hons. Thesis). University of Wollongong, Wollongong.

Chamberlin, S. A. & Moon, S. M. (2008). How does the problem-based learning approach compare to the model-eliciting activity approach in mathematics instruction? Retrieved from http://www.cimt.plymouth.ac.uk/journal/chamberlin.pdf

Chickering, A. W., & Gamson, Z. F. (1987). Seven principles for good practice in undergraduate education. *AAHE Bulletin, 39*(7), 3-7.

Consalvo, M. "Being Social in Online Games—Five Research Elements to Consider." Public lecture, Melbourne, Australia, July 8, 2013.

Foreman, J. (2004). Game-based learning: How to delight and instruct in the 21st century. *Educause Review, 39*(5), 50-66. Retrieved from http://net.educause.edu/ir/library/pdf/ERM0454.pdf

Fujimoto, R., & Solutions, S. L. (2010). Designing an educational Alternate Reality Game. Retrieved from http://www.shoyu.com/education/Research_DesigningAnEducationalARG.pdf

Games for Change. (2016). *Half the Sky Movement: The Game.* Retrieved from http://www.gamesforchange.org/play/half-the-sky-movement-the-game/

Gossman, P., Stewart, T., Jaspers, M., & Chapman, B. (2007). Integrating web-delivered problem-based learning scenarios to the curriculum. *Active Learning in Higher Education, 8*(2), 139-153.

Jenkins, H. (2006). Convergence culture: *Where old and new media collide.* New York, NY: New York University Press.

Koehler, M. J., & Mishra, P. (2005). What happens when teachers design educational technology? The development of technological pedagogical content knowledge. *Journal of Educational Computing Research, 32*(2), 131-152.

Liu, C. J. (2011). Research on professional development of PE teachers from the view of modern educational technology. *Advanced Materials Research, 187,* 122-126.

Martin, A., Thompson, B., & Chatfield, T. (2006). Alternate Reality Games White Paper, IGDA ARG SIG. Retrieved from http://archives.igda.org/arg/resources/IGDA-AlternateRealityGames-Whitepaper-2006.pdf

McGonigal, J. (2008). Saving the world through game design: Stories from the near future. New Yorker Conference. Retrieved from http://www.newyorker.com/online/video/conference/2008/mcgonigal

Moseley, A. "An alternative reality for higher education? Lessons to be learned from online reality games." Presentation at the ALT-C, Leeds,

UK, September 9-11 2008. Retrieved from http://moerg.files.wordpress. com/2008/10/moseley2008a.pdf>

Oliver, R., & Herrington, J. (2003). Exploring technology-mediated learning from a pedagogical perspective. *Interactive Learning Environments, 11*(2), 111–126.

Phillips, A., & Martin, A. (2006). Business models. In A. Martin, B. Thompson, & T. Chatfield. (Eds.), *Alternate Reality Games White Paper, IGDA ARG SIG.* Retrieved from http://www.christydena.com/wp-content/ uploads/2007/11/igda-alternaterealitygames-whitepaper-2006.pdf

Sereda, A. (2013). *Designing a context-aware campus area gaming environment for mobile platforms,* MSc thesis, Technical University of Denmark, Kongens Lyngby.

Tanner, S. (2005). Investigating the hypothetical: Building journalism skills via online challenges. *Asia Pacific Media Educator, 1*(16), 89-102. Retrieved from http://ro.uow.edu.au/cgi/viewcontent.cgi?article=1035&context=apme

Tsvetkova, N., Stoimenova, B., Tsvetanova, S., Connolly, T., Stansfield, M., Hainey, T., Cousins, L., Josephson, J., O'Donovan, A., & Ortiz, C. R. (2009). "Arguing for multilingual motivation in Web 2.0: The teacher training perspective." Presentation at the 3rd European Conference on Games-Based Learning (ECGBL), Graz, Austria, October 12-13, 2009.

Whitton, N. (2008). "Alternate reality games for developing student autonomy and peer learning." Presentation at the Learners in the Co-creation of Knowledge (LICK) Conference, Edinburgh, U.K., October 30, 2008.

Whitton, N. (2009). Alternate Reality Games for Orientation, Socialisation and Induction (ARGOSI). Retrieved from http://www.jisc.ac.uk/media/ documents/programmes/usersandinnovation/argosifinalreport.pdf

18

Coding the Curriculum: Journalism Education for the Digital Age

Cindy Royal

Computer programming, or what is commonly referred to as "coding," has been a much-heralded skill set in recent years and is quickly becoming an expected 21st century literacy. Since 2013, celebrities and technologists, like Facebook CEO Mark Zuckerberg, Microsoft's Bill Gates, actor Ashton Kutcher, and popular musician Shakira, have promoted an Hour of Code (Hour of Code, 2015), a campaign to encourage people to experiment with coding skills. Since the start of this campaign, more than 91 million people have participated.

Politicians and icons have amplified the importance of programming. During Computer Science Week in 2013, President Barack Obama said, "Learning these skills isn't just important for your future. It's important for our country's future" (The White House, 2013). And as far back as 1995, tech visionary Steve Jobs said, "Everybody in this country should learn how to program a computer, should learn a computer language, because it teaches you how to think" (Code.org, 2013).

But coding is no longer limited to the realms of computer and information sciences. Technology may be used to solve problems across a range of fields, but only if those disciplines have people who understand how to apply and teach the skills associated with it. This is particularly relevant in journalism and mass communication, where the usage, application, and presentation of data are reflected in recent, high-profile topics in the news. Visual skills have long supported journalism, but have been coopted from the fields of art and design. For example, photojournalism is an offshoot of photography produced in art programs, and video journalism is a specific application of the skills offered in film schools. Coding skills should be understood in much the same manner, an important skill set with unique applications to communicators. Making sense of data and presenting it is becoming one of journalism's unique propositions, which should be taught as such in J-Schools.

This chapter examines the reasons for journalists, journalism students, and educators to learn to code. It also explores how coding skills can be integrated into curricula.

Literature Review

The teaching of technology skills in journalism programs has become an important topic as online content delivery has evolved. Researchers have long assessed the role of digital communication in journalism education (Thompson, 1995). Early efforts to teach students a range of technology skills were given the title "convergence" and included the teaching of multimedia skills, like video and audio editing, along with more traditional writing and editing skills. Convergence was often thought of as a merging of print and broadcast curricula. Several studies outlined the successes and failures of such approaches in the late 1990s and early 2000s (Thelen, 2002; Dailey, Demo, & Spillman, 2005). Difficulties were identified in teaching print and broadcast skills, and early professional convergence projects were considered unsuccessful (Kraeplin & Criado, 2005; Castaneda, Murphy, & Hether, 2005; Thornton & Keith, 2009; Sarachan, 2011; Kolodzy, Grant, DeMars, & Wilkinson, 2014).

Along with teaching multimedia editing skills, some programs began adding online journalism and Web concepts to their curricula (Friedland & Webb, 1996; Sutherland & Stewart, 1999; Huesca, 2000; Royal, 2005; Daniels, 2006). Such curricula included skills in Hypertext Markup Language (HTML), Cascading Stylesheets (CSS), and the use of programs like Adobe Dreamweaver and Flash. Later programs added social media and networking components (Bor, 2014; Berkeley, 2009) to include blogging and the use of sites like Twitter and Facebook. It became apparent that the digital media landscape was more than the merging of text and video, and students needed a broader appreciation of Internet, Web, and mobile concepts.

In the late 2000s, Web development techniques became more sophisticated. Technologies that allowed for user interaction and access to databases were emerging, making websites dynamic and interactive.

Web browsers were able to support the JavaScript language, and other languages, like PHP, Ruby, and Python, were growing in usage. Open source content management systems, like Wordpress, were widely available, and websites were gaining advanced functionality through programming libraries, such as JQuery and grid-based frameworks, like Bootstrap. Mobile development for devices, like smartphones and tablets, introduced different languages unique to their platforms.

At the same time, data was becoming a frequently discussed topic. With news investigations involving government information leaks and "big data," understanding the role of data in our lives has become more relevant than ever. The phrase "data journalism" began being used in place of the more traditional "computer-assisted reporting" in the mid-2000s (Gray, Bounegru, & Chambers, 2012). News organizations began publishing data-driven interactives on their websites, such as *The New York Times'* "Is It Better to Rent or Buy?" (Bostock, Carter, & Tse, 2014); "New York State Test Scores" (Evans, Gebeloff, & Scheinkman, 2015); "Toxic Waters" (Duhigg, Ericson, Evans, Hamman, & Willis, 2012); and projects dealing with the Olympic Games and Academy Award coverage. *The New York Times'* interactive dialect quiz "How Ya'll, Youse and You Guys Talk" (Katz, Andrews, & Buth, 2013) was the most visited story in 2013 on its website (nytimes.com, and it was developed by an intern). NPR, *Texas Tribune*, WNYC, *ProPublica*, Vox Media, and the *Washington Post* publish similar data-driven projects. Royal (2012) and Parisie and Dagiral (2013) have studied this emerging professional role at *The New York Times* and the *Chicago Tribune* respectively.

Many organizations that collect social media and search-related data are using data visualization as a means to tell stories. These include traditional media organizations, online upstarts, like *ProPublica* and *Texas Tribune*, and technology companies, like Google and Twitter. In addition to the projects mentioned above, other notable projects include the following:

❑ *ProPublica*'s Dollars for Docs (Ornstein, Groeger, Tigas, & Grochowski Jones, 2015), which allows users to search for doctors to see what types of financial contributions they have received from pharmaceutical companies for speaking engagements, research, and consulting;

❑ *Texas Tribune* Public Schools Explorer (Murphy, Daniel, & Hutson, 2016*)*, which allows Texans to research and compare information about school districts;

❑ Google Research's Music Timeline (Google, n.d.), which charts the rise and fall of music genres over time with links to relevant artists and albums; and

❑ The #Oscars Race on Twitter (Twitter, n.d.), Twitter's interactive chart portraying conversations during the 2015 Academy Awards.

While these organizations are at the forefront of the data trend, others are seeking to recruit those with the skills to participate in this type of storytelling. This is an opportunity for students, as demand for people with such skills currently exceeds supply.

Wenger and Owens (2012) reviewed job descriptions to identify the skills the media profession requires. They found that "Web/multimedia skills" were the third most popular skill set listed in job descriptions, after "previous professional experience" and "strong writing." Job descriptions for hybrid coder-communicators have started to emerge. In 2014, the online news site BuzzFeed sought investigative reporters "proficient in at least one modern programming language," and Quartz looked for reporters "to help us commit acts of journalism with code." These are just two examples of the new kinds of skills in demand for communicators at media companies. While few journalism programs are equipped to provide this level of coding education, some are pursuing collaborations with computer science and engineering programs (Columbia University, 2015), recruiting computer science graduates for journalism master's degrees (Northwestern University, 2013), and/or developing new concentrations and degrees to merge these topics. Some journalism schools are also introducing a related area of media entrepreneurship (Ferrier, 2013). These courses expose students to important concepts in business, design, and programming to encourage them to create their own media projects, applications, and organizations.

Why Learn Computer Programming?

In its most general application, coding supports algorithmic thinking and problem solving and is the basis for creativity and innovation.

Since problem solving and creativity have always been characteristics of journalism, this common foundation provides a bridge between the disciplines. The journalism field must now adapt to new tools that support these activities. With computers being a part of any media career and most other careers, it will be important for more people to understand the languages and culture of technology. At the most basic level, journalists may be required to customize code in a content management system or set up a website for a special project. Understanding programming skills will allow students to have the most flexibility in their media careers.

The role of the media platform is increasingly what defines a media organization's business (Royal, 2014). It specifies who can publish, participate, and share. The platform dictates what types of stories media professionals can tell and provides important analytics for decision-making. To understand media businesses, one has to understand media platforms, and that means understanding something about how they are developed. The distribution platforms of social media now often belong to other companies. The field therefore needs graduates who understand how these important dynamics relate to media organizations.

Storytelling has become interactive. Many projects visualize data and allow users to interact with it, and more are being developed every day. Coding provides ways to make a story more meaningful to a user by

- ❏ allowing user engagement with the story;
- ❏ finding, using, and presenting data;
- ❏ visualizing the story;
- ❏ creating tools to help users; and
- ❏ educating users.

Another aspect of programming relating to journalism has to do with retrieving data. With some programming skill, an individual can open a world of data that can inform a story's direction or be used as a source. One can grab data from websites and access data via application programming interfaces (APIs) provided by various services, including Twitter, Facebook, and Spotify. By using a little code to retrieve data, inserting it into a spreadsheet, and creating a visualization, one can share powerful, visual stories.

Perhaps the most exciting opportunity associated with programming in journalism and mass communication is associated with the high percentage of females in these academic programs. Computer science departments and the technology industry have a dearth of women (Henn, 2014). However, young women can be introduced to coding skills in journalism programs when they are taught in a communication context and with a supportive environment.

Most importantly, jobs exist in media and journalism for those with coding skills. These are not back-office jobs running computer networks, but journalism and reporting jobs that require advanced technology skills. Since these are skills relevant to storytelling and information dissemination, they are skills that should be integrated in J-School curricula.

Finally, it is helpful to understand programming to comprehend the possibilities it has for the media industry. Media professionals will have to work on collaborative teams or supervise technology resources. They will be asked to contribute to strategy and to envision new products and services. In some cases, students will wish to create their own endeavors and explore the world of media startups.

What is Computer Programming?

So, what is computer programming, and what specifically do communication educators need to understand to teach these skills? Simply stated, computer programming is the process of developing and implementing various sets of instructions to enable a computer to perform tasks (BusinessDictionary.com, 2015). There is a range of computer languages that perform different functions, some more relevant to communication disciplines than others. (See Table 18.1 for a description of the different types of programming languages most relevant to communication disciplines.) It is important to understand these different types of languages in order to determine what students should learn and what educators should teach them.

Coding in the Curriculum

There are several ways coding can be conceived as part of a mass communication curriculum. Many journalism programs introduce

Table 18.1

Description of Programming and Related Languages

Markup languages	Hypertext Markup Language (HTML) and Cascading Stylesheets (CSS) provide the foundation for the Web. These are languages that are interpreted by a Web browser that displays the structure, design, and content of a Web page. HTML is used to structure the content in a Web site, while CSS provides a central location to control the design.
Interpreted languages	Languages like JavaScript, Python, Ruby, and PHP (pre-hypertext processor) work well with markup languages to add logic-based features like form processing and advanced interactivity. The ability to store information and apply logic comes with these logic-based languages that introduce variables, statements, loops, and functions. These are common elements of all programming languages, although the exact syntax may be different. They also work with data-oriented languages to provide a backend for content management systems. JavaScript is generally considered a client-side language, with operations occurring in the browser on a user's computers, and it integrates well with HTML and CSS. Node.js, however, has been introduced to add server-side functionality to JavaScript. Python, Ruby, and PHP are all server-side languages with processing of instructions occurring on the server in which the site is hosted.
Data-oriented languages	Structured Query Language (SQL) is an example of a data-oriented language. These languages provide methods for inserting, modifying, and querying elements of a database. MySQL is a popular open source installation of the SQL database.
Visual languages	Some languages, like Scratch, which is a visual programming application for children, can provide an introduction to the logic associated with computer programming.
Web development frameworks	Django and Rails are examples of frameworks that provide a "head start" on application development. With a few lines of code, the coder develops a basic framework that provides the foundation for an application that one can then customize. Wordpress and Bootstrap could also be considered Web development frameworks in that they provide quick access to certain features that are much more difficult to achieve from scratch. These frameworks all work within the concept of rapid application development, the ability to quickly achieve a working project. This category also includes lightweight, static-site generators like Flask and Middleman, which provide the development capabilities of a framework while building static sites that can be run without server-side technologies.
Libraries	Furthering the understanding of rapid application development are libraries associated with various languages. JQuery is an example of a JavaScript library that provides ready-made code to achieve certain features in fewer steps.
Compiler languages	Languages like Java, C, and C++ are primarily used for large system development and are not often used in a communication context. However, their features and concepts are similar to those of the interpreted languages.

Web design concepts in a course or series of courses (Royal, 2005). This provides a good foundation for programming skills, which can be added to these courses to introduce interactivity and engagement features. However, an individual Web design course can quickly become overwhelming when it is too ambitious. A follow-up course that introduces programming concepts can be a valuable elective for students. Some programs have begun to offer courses in data journalism that integrate data and programming skills (Rogers, 2015).

Other programs have encouraged students to take computer science courses or have developed courses that involve computer science students and/or faculty. And, as mentioned above, some schools have developed majors as collaborative efforts between computer science and mass communication.

Case Study

The graduate program at Texas State University (TXST) has, over the past several years, introduced a coding course called Advanced Online Media (advanced.cindyroyal.net). Recently, TXST has offered a similar coding course, Coding and Data Skills for Communicators (coding.cindyroyal.net) at the undergraduate level. This course was developed through the support of a Challenge Fund Grant provided by the Online News Association, the John S. and James L. Knight Foundation, the Excellence and Ethics in Journalism Foundation, the Robert R. McCormick Foundation, the Democracy Fund, and the Rita Allen Foundation.

Course Description and Assignments

Each semester since 2014 that Coding and Data Skills for Communicators has been taught, 10 to 12 students have enrolled in it. However, it can accommodate as many as 20 students, based on the capacity of the computer lab. In both graduate and undergraduate curricula, the coding courses are a follow-up to a more basic Web design course that serves as a prerequisite. This basic course teaches HTML, CSS, graphic design, video editing, Bootstrap, and Wordpress. Additionally, in the undergraduate program, a required course, The Fundamentals of Digital/Online Media (FDOM), offers a basic introduction to HTML and CSS. Since having a foundation in Web design is fundamental to coding, programming concepts can be taught in a Web development context. This context also allows for quicker application to areas relevant to communicators, in which the primary goal is to present information for online user interaction.

The purpose of this case study is to share lessons learned in teaching this course and through student observations. At the end of the semester, students completed a special evaluation to assess their attitudes toward the course's topics and their own performance. Comments from these evaluations are provided below.

The course is offered in three main sections: coding, data analysis, and charting tools. The coding section introduces the basics of programming that can be applied across any language, and it then focuses on using JavaScript in conjunction with HTML/CSS skills in designing Web and mobile experiences. Students in the Web design course have already been exposed to responsive design techniques and the Bootstrap framework. Accordingly, these topics are used in conjunction with more advanced programming understanding to introduce logic and interactivity to projects – things like dropdown menus, form processing, and data retrieval. Student projects in this section included interactive quizzes and calculators (Larson, 2015b, see Figure 18.1a; Brown, 2015, see Figure 18.1b).

In the data module, students are introduced to a range of data skills. This starts with basic spreadsheet analysis, the use of tools for Web scraping (extracting data from Web page content), like the Chrome Scraper extension, and more advanced scraping using Scraperwiki. Students are also shown how to use the Python language to create and modify scripts to retrieve data via the Twitter API. The assignment in this section is to modify the API scripts with their own search terms— using terms associated with local festivals, favorite musicians, or recent news items—to begin identifying final project topics.

During the charting module, students are introduced to various visualization tools that use different levels of coding to make and customize data presentations—such as Chart.js, HighCharts, Google Chart API, Fusion Tables, and Google Maps. In this segment's assignment, students are encouraged to experiment with their own data,

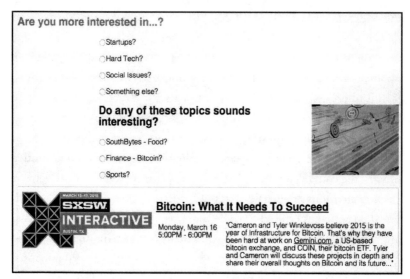

Figure 18.1a. Interactive student project at SXSW Interactive 2015.
Source: Rebecca Larson (http://beckslarson.com/sxtxapp/)

Figure 18.1b. Interactive student project on Tolkien Fan Quiz.
Source: Jordon Brown (http://jordonmbrown.com/tolkien/quiz.html)

associated with their final project topic, using each of the charting platforms introduced.

Throughout the semester, students complete readings and are
introduced to professional projects that tell stories with data. Students
also provide insights via required blog posts that allow them to gain

Figure 18.2a. Loud music complaints recorded in Austin.
Source: Rebecca Larson (http://loudaustin.beckslarson.com)

an understanding of the professional environment of data journalism.

The course's final project is a complete multimedia package using the data tools and programming techniques covered throughout the semester. The grant for this course was written for telling stories about Texas music communities. Thus, students were instructed to find data and select topics that would support this theme. Students covered issues including loud music complaints recorded in Austin and global presence at music festivals (Larson, 2015a, see Figure 18.2a; Slade, 2015, see Figure 18.2b). The projects were visual and interactive, and they demonstrated new ways to explore these types of issues.

In a recent iteration, the course had a co-instructor from the computer science department. This instructor provided specific coaching for using more advanced coding applications for scraping and application programming interfaces. The collaboration worked well, but it required good communication between instructors. The co-instructor was identified after many months of discussions and emails with various members of the computer science department to find exactly the right fit and interest. The lead instructor also sought professionals to assist with instruction some semesters, including guest speakers from media companies who demonstrated their process for developing news applications.

The course used a "flipped-classroom" model, in which lessons

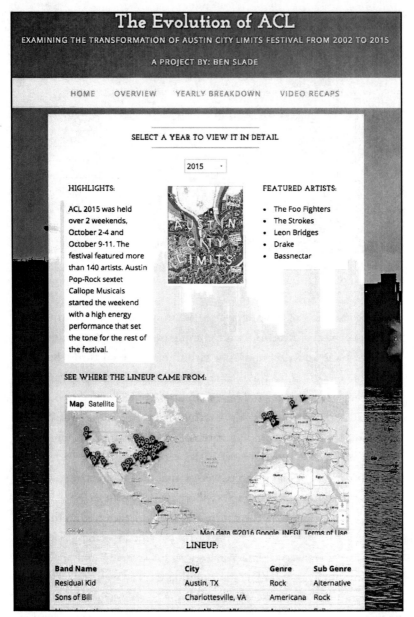

Figure 18.2b. Global presence at music festivals.
Source: Ben Slade (http://bengslade.com/acl/)

were recorded for students to watch in advance, with class time used for the review of material and lab work. In the sections that met twice per week for 75 minutes, it was difficult to work in the amount of time needed to lecture and provide lab assistance. This was made easier in sections that were taught once per week for longer time periods, but this format still did not allow ample time for work and assistance. Although the course was taught in a computer lab, many students wanted to work on their own laptops so they could use the same coding environment all the time. A benefit of this type of instruction is that the majority of data and programming tools are free and open source, not requiring students to invest in expensive software. Students could do the bulk of the work in a text editor like TextWrangler, using a browser like Chrome or Firefox, and working with freely available charting packages.

The class encouraged students to seek out their own solutions to problems and to push themselves beyond the basic instruction of the course. This approach can be difficult for many students who are used to being specifically told how to do certain tasks or projects. In many cases, the instructor was also learning and sharing new techniques. Accordingly, students needed to be prepared for an environment of experimentation and, sometimes, failure.

One approach the instructors introduced in the course was the concept of agile development (Agile Manifesto, 2015). This is a method of problem solving in software projects that encourages smaller increments toward innovation instead of traditional waterfall or rigid step-by-step methods to developing a completed product. In this manner, the instructors introduced the agile concepts of scrum—short, standup meetings to update one another on our progress and challenges. And sprints—project stretches of two-to-three weeks to work on individual modules. We found that some aspects of agile methodology worked well in the academic setting, given the finite timeframe of a semester. But the limited time with students in class made it difficult to practice agile methodology beyond familiarity with the terms and processes.

During some semesters the instructors also instituted pair programming, encouraging students to work on their projects in groups of two. Professional organizations use this process to assist in training and to encourage innovation across teams. Some groups were more successful than others in finding the time to work together. In most cases, the teams simply split up the work and completed it individually due to busy, end-of-semester activity. But the teams who used pair programming as their primary method of work performed better. Finding more opportunities to build pair programming into the semester will be a goal for future classes.

Guest speakers were also critical to the learning environment, demonstrating to students how technology skills could be beneficial to their careers. The Challenge Fund Grant allowed speakers from Google News, Vox Media, and NPR Visuals to join the class in-person. One class took a field trip to Austin radio station KUT-Austin to learn about its Web development activities. Additionally, the instructors scheduled Skype visits with personnel from Twitter and *The Guardian*.

Students seemed to respond well to this environment. They were excited about what they were learning and did not seem to have a problem with the ambiguous and experimental nature of their projects. However, limited time at the end of the semester did not allow many students to perform as well as they could have with final projects. As a result, the instructors have decided in future classes to start earlier with providing specifics for final projects.

Student Feedback

In their course evaluations, students expressed an appreciation for the course and how they might use their new skills in the future. Their comments included the following:

- ❑ "I can see myself using these skills a lot, if not every day. These skills I learned are so helpful when it comes to marketing myself in so many new ways now."
- ❑ "I will use the skills I learned in this course for my profession; I want to eventually become an investigative reporter. As a reporter, I will use these skills in my articles that incorporate data. In the far future, I will also use these skills in building the website for my production company."
- ❑ "I will be able to communicate better with professional coders on how I want things to be displayed or the functionality of a website."
- ❑ "I think I will use the skills in any job I have. As the world becomes more and more digital, I think that having these skills

will make me more valuable in the job market. Also, I will use them for my own fun. I think looking at the Twitter API example is very interesting, and I may do it just to see what I can find out about the topics I enjoy."

Finding the exact emphasis for a programming course can be a challenge. Students indicated various interests and frustrations across the curriculum in comments such as the following:

❏ "The entire course was interesting and beneficial, but if I had to pick one element that stood out to me it was working with APIs, specifically the Twitter API. Learning how to use Python seems to be one of the aspects of the class that was very beneficial for the future."

❏ "I would've focused more on one subject. I think the way the class was setup . . . was very rushed. Every time I would start getting slightly comfortable with a topic we would switch over to something completely different and that was a bit frustrating because I never felt like I fully learned any of the topics. I did feel introduced to them, which I think was the goal of the course."

❏ "I really enjoyed the Twitter API project and the Web scraping exercises. I think it would have been more beneficial to drop the Form and Form Processing assignment and spend more time on the API, maybe add something to do with Spotify's API."

❏ "I think all of the JavaScript that we learned was the most beneficial tool to know."

In most cases, students gained confidence in their abilities with these tools in creative and meaningful ways, as is suggested by the following comments:

❏ "Every assignment pushed our creativity and work skills. I feel like every student really took in something new from each assignment."

❏ "The class was a great experience, and I hope it continues to grow as part of our program."

❑ "I could definitely see myself doing online work from a PR perspective, and I think everything I have learned in this class will only help. I would also feel pretty comfortable about applying for a digital journalism position, where before I would not have."

The most important lesson instructors learned in teaching coding skills is that introducing them as electives in one or two courses is not sufficient to providing students the exposure and experience they need to practice them professionally. To achieve this goal, journalism educators will have to make programming a part of an integrated curriculum that focuses on digital media immersion. This may mean introducing new modules in existing courses, creating additional courses, or even introducing new majors that emphasize these areas throughout curricula. It may also mean collaborations with computer science or other technology-based departments or with community resources. Universities will need to take inventory of faculty programming and technology competencies that will allow them to move rapidly in this direction.

Challenges to Include Coding in the Curriculum

While some mass communication programs have pursued collaboration with computer science departments, this approach has challenges. Computer science departments do not necessarily view coding education as their primary mission. Computer scientists proudly proclaim that the main goal of their curricula is not to teach tools. They see their role as introducing algorithmic thinking and problem solving with less regard for any specific technology. While this is a reasonable stance in theory, learning to solve problems in practice requires one to apply the technologies at hand. It is true that one must exercise judgment in selecting and applying proper technologies and continue to develop and learn over time. But it is ultimately what one does with technology that demonstrates competency. While there is merit to this theoretical approach, its pure application seems less relevant to the specific needs of communication disciplines.

Computer science is also primarily concerned with the development of large systems and machine and compiler languages. Web and mobile development, which can be applied to a range of problems that require creative approaches to interactive and collaborative engagement, require a different set of knowledge and tools.

Other lessons learned include working with professional partners, working across disciplines, collaborating, coding across spectrums, accommodating different levels of coder expertise, coding schools filling educational gaps, changing curricula, and coding skills in every discipline.

Working With Professional Partners Provides its Own Challenges

Having local guest lecturers is a wonderful way to get professional insight into the classroom. But professionals are busy and have their own priorities. They can demonstrate a concept or process in class, but, once they leave, the instructor has to support the material they introduced and assist students with their implementation of it. Finding professional partners who understand the nuances of teaching and learning can also be a challenge.

Different Disciplines Require Specialized Context and Support in Delivering Coding Education

While everyone who codes needs to understand the basics—data types, variables, loops, functions, and algorithms—the ways in which these features are applied vary across disciplines like communication, the arts, humanities, and science. Different professions might use coding to develop a customizable data visualization, design an interactive work of fiction, or develop an immersive museum experience. Instructors can also use coding to create simulated learning environments or to explain difficult concepts. Coding can seamlessly navigate the virtual and the physical, using cues from surroundings, past experiences, and social media. To take advantage of these opportunities, journalism educators will have to teach coding in the contexts that support these applications and more.

But students (and faculty) in these disciplines may feel they do not have the background nor the mindset to code. Specialized support in the form of small lab environments, personalized instruction, and discipline-specific learning communities will be necessary to meet such

broad-ranging needs. (Refer to this chapter's appendix directly following references for information about training, programming language,
and web scraping resources, as well as lists of charting tools, organizations and events, notable projects, and relevant articles.)

Collaborations are Hard

Cross-discipline efforts do not come easily in the university environment. Different missions and goals prevent natural integrations
across departments. Moreover, expecting one discipline to teach another
its specialized coding context is unreasonable and untenable. However,
just because collaborations are hard, does not mean they are not worth
pursuing. Departments will need proper communication between
them to understand roles and expectations and forge productive partnerships. Collaborations in the professional community are another
avenue to seeking support for programming curricula. However, these
also require proper communication, clear expectations, and acquiring
the right resources.

Coding Knowledge will be Perceived on a Spectrum, Not Something You Either Can or Cannot Do

Based on this approach, there will be a range of coders: those who
understand enough to know what is possible, those who are increasingly able to solve their own problems with technology, and the
uber-coders—those who can craft new solutions with technology. But
it is a reasonable expectation that all media workers will need to participate in some manner on collaborative, technology-oriented teams.

Code Schools are Filling the Gaps that the Academy has Left Wide Open

For-profit entities—like General Assembly, MakerSquare, and
The Iron Yard—have popped up around the country over the past few
years, charging students in excess of U.S. $10,000 to learn to code in a
few weeks. They have jumped at a market opportunity. While no single
university department could or should take up the exact model of these
code schools, such departments might be able to close the gap by defining

the coding knowledge relevant to graduates entering specific professions.

Curricula Will Need to Change

Whether it means new course modules, new majors, or new collaborations, the integration of coding across the curriculum will require educators to rethink the ways a university education is delivered. The Hasso Plattner Institute of Design at Stanford (known as the "d.School") has generated ideas for reimagining higher education that have included extending the undergraduate experience throughout one's career, redefining a "major" as a "mission," and redesigning the academic transcript (Hayward, 2014). Programming is simply a part of a larger disruptive trend in education, and educators need to recognize and treat it as such.

Universities Will Need Educators in Every Discipline Who Can Teach Coding

These trends do not mean educational institutions need completely new people. It means they need faculty and staff who recognize the opportunities that coding skills represent and are curious about learning new approaches. Departments need people who are comfortable with what they do not know and who are willing to gain skills on an as-needed basis. However, they also need people who are committed to giving students the best possible introduction to coding skills that are relevant and meaningful in their field. It means continuous learning, not always having all the answers, and modeling the ways in which we craft solutions. It means redefining what it means to be an educator.

Conclusion

In the future, coders will not be hired to support journalism, storytelling, art, or science. They will be the journalists, storytellers, artists, and scientists. As media and technology further meld, programming will be part of what the leaders and innovators in the communication fields can perform.

J-Schools need to reflect upon what they are doing to introduce, and more importantly immerse, students in the technology-driven fields they will enter. Problem-solving techniques and innovative approaches, like data analysis and agile methodology, have broad and relevant applicability to our students' futures. This is an exciting time to be studying media, and media faculty must convey enthusiasm, passion, and opportunity to their students. Students will respond accordingly. Media faculty need to give students the skills and perspectives they need to not just work, but to lead, disrupt, and innovate.

References

Agile Manifesto. (2015). Manifesto for Agile software development. Retrieved from http://www.agilemanifesto.org/

Berkeley, L. (2009). Media education and new technology: a case study of major curriculum change within a university media degree. *Journal of Media Practice, 10*(2-3), 185-197.

Bor, S. E. (2014). Teaching social media journalism challenges and opportunities for future curriculum design. *Journalism & Mass Communication Educator, 69*(3), 243-255.

Bostock, M., Carter, S., & Tse, A. 2014. "Is it better to rent or buy?" *The New York Times*. Retrieved from http://www.nytimes.com/interactive/2014/upshot/buy-rent-calculator.html

Brown, J. (2015). What Type of Tolkien Fan Are You? Retrieved from http://jordonmbrown.com/tolkien/quiz.html

BusinessDictionary.com (2015). Computer programming definition. Retrieved from http://www.businessdictionary.com/definition/computer-programming.html

Castaneda, L., Murphy, S., & Hether, H. J. (2005). Teaching print, broadcast, and online journalism concurrently: A case study assessing a convergence curriculum. *Journalism & Mass Communication Educator, 60*(1), 57-70.

Columbia University. (2015). Dual degree: Journalism and computer science. Retrieved from http://www.journalism.columbia.edu/page/276-dualdegree-journalism-computer-science/279

Code.org. (2013, October 22). Steve Jobs on Computer Science [Video file]. Retrieved from https://www.youtube.com/watch?v=1Y7EsTnUSxY

Dailey, L., Demo, L., & Spillman, M. (2005). The convergence continuum: A model for studying collaboration between media newsrooms. *Atlantic Journal of Communication, 13*(3), 150-168.

Daniels, G. L. (2006). Flash journalism: How to create multimedia news packages/convergence journalism: Writing and reporting across the news media. *Journalism & Mass Communication Educator, 61*(3), 333.

Duhigg, C., Ericson, M., Evans, T., Hamman, B., & Willis, D. (2012, May 16). Toxic waters. *The New York Times*. Retrieved from http://projects.

nytimes.com/toxic-waters/contaminants

Evans, T., Gebeloff, R., & Scheinkman, A. (2015, July 13). New York school test scores. *The New York Times*. Retrieved from http://projects.nytimes. com/new-york-schools-test-scores

Ferrier, M. B. (2013). Media entrepreneurship curriculum development and faculty perceptions of what students should know. *Journalism & Mass Communication Educator*, 68(3), 222-241.

Friedland, L. A., & Webb, S. (1996). Incorporating online publishing into the curriculum. *Journalism and Mass Communication Educator*, 51(3), 54-65.

Google. (n.d.) Music timeline. Retrieved from http://research.google.com/big-picture/music/

Gray, J., Bounegru, L., & Chambers, L. (2012). *The data journalism handbook: How journalists can use data to improve the news*. Sebastopol, CA: O'Reilly Media.

Hayward, B. (2014). Exploring provocative ideas for undergraduate education at Stanford. *Stanford Report*, May 5, 2014. Retrieved from http://news. stanford.edu/news/2014/may/dschool-undergrad-reimagined-050514. html

Henn, G. (2014). When women stopped coding. Retrieved from http://www. npr.org/blogs/money/2014/10/21/357629765/when-women-stopped-coding

Hour of Code (2015). Retrieved from http://hourofcode.com/us

Huesca, R. (2000). Reinventing journalism curricula for the electronic environment. *Journalism and Mass Communication Educator*, 55(2), 4-15.

Katz, J., Andrews, W. & Buth, E. (2013, December 21). How y'all, youse and you guys talk. *The New York Times*. Retrieved from http://www.nytimes. com/interactive/2013/12/20/sunday-review/dialect-quiz-map.html

Kolodzy, J., Grant, A. E., DeMars, T. R., & Wilkinson, J. S. (2014). The convergence years. *Journalism & Mass Communication Educator*, 69(2), 197-205.

Kraeplin, C., & Criado, C. A. (2005). Building a case for convergence journalism curriculum. *Journalism & Mass Communication Educator,* 60(1), 47-56.

Larson, R. (2015a). Loud Austin: The Live Music Capital with a Loud Music Problem. Retrieved from http://loudaustin.beckslarson.com

Larson, R. (2015b). SXSW Interactive Panel Advisor. Retrieved from http:// beckslarson.com/sxtxapp/

Murphy, R, Daniel, A & Hutson, M. (2016) *The Texas Tribune*. (n.d.) Public schools explorer. *The Texas Tribune*. Retrieved from http://www.texastribune.org/public-ed/explore/

Northwestern University. (2013). Knight Foundation scholarship. Retrieved from http://www.medill.northwestern.edu/admissions/financial-aid/knight-foundation-scholarship.html

Ornstein, C., Groeger, L., Tigas, M., & Grochowski Jones, R. (2015, July 1). Dollars for docs. How industry dollars reach your doctors. *ProPublica*.

Retrieved from https://projects.propublica.org/docdollars/

Parasie, S., & Dagiral, E. (2013). Data-driven journalism and the public good: "Computer-assisted-reporters" and "programmer-journalists" in Chicago. *New Media & Society, 15*(6), 853-871.

Rogers, S. (2015). Data journalism at Berkeley: course syllabus. J298 Advanced data journalism, Berkeley J-school. Retrieved from http://simonrogers. github.io/datajournalism/

Royal, C. (2005). Teaching web design in journalism and mass communications programs: Integration, judgment, and perspective. *Journalism and Mass Communication Educator, 59*(4), 400-414.

Royal, C. (2012). The journalist as programmer: A case study of *The New York Times* interactive news technology department, *ISOJ Journal, 2*(1), 5-24.

Royal, C. (2014). Are journalism schools teaching their students the right skills? Retrieved from http://www.niemanlab.org/2014/04/cindy-royal-are-journalism-schools-teaching-their-students-the-right-skills

Sarachan, J. (2011). The path already taken: Technological and pedagogical practices in convergence education. *Journalism & Mass Communication Educator, 66*(2), 160-174.

Slade, B. (2015). The Evolution of ACL: Examining the Transformation of Austin City Limits Festival From 2002 to 2015. Retrieved from http://bengslade.com/acl/breakdown.html

Sutherland, P. J., & Stewart, R. K. (1999). How accredited programs use the World Wide Web. *Journalism and Mass Communication Educator, 54*(1), 16-22.

Thelen, G. (2002). Convergence is coming. *The Quill, 90*(6), 16.

The White House. (2013, December 8). Computer Science Education Week 2013 [Video file]. Retrieved from https://www.youtube.com/watch?v=yE-6IfCrqg3s

Thompson, D. R. (1995). Digital communications: A modular approach to curriculum. *Journalism and Mass Communication Educator, 50*(3), 35-40.

Thornton, L. J., & Keith, S. M. (2009). From convergence to webvergence: Tracking the evolution of broadcast-print partnerships through the lens of change theory. *Journalism & Mass Communication Quarterly, 86*(2), 257-276.

Twitter. (n.d.) The #Oscars race on Twitter. Retrieved from https://interactive. twitter.com/oscars2015race/

Wenger, D. H., & Owens, L. C. (2012). Help wanted 2010: An examination of new media skills required by top U.S. news companies. *Journalism & Mass Communication Educator, 67*(1), 9-25.

Appendix	
Coding Resources for Educators	
Training Resources	▪ Codecademy.com ▪ Lynda.com ▪ CodeSchool.com ▪ CodeActually.com ▪ For Journalism - github.com/forjournalism ▪ Data Journalism Handbook - datajournalismhandbook.org
Programming Language Resources	▪ JQuery - jquery.com ▪ Ruby - www.ruby-lang.org ▪ Ruby on Rails jquery.com ▪ Python - www.python.org ▪ Django - www.djangoproject.com ▪ Wordpress - wordpress.org ▪ Bootstrap - getbootstrap.com ▪ PHP - php.net ▪ MySQL - www.mysql.com ▪ Flask - flask.pocoo.org ▪ Middleman - middlemanapp.com ▪ Static Site Generators - www.staticgen.com ▪ Stack Overflow - stackoverflow.com ▪ GitHub - GitHub.com
Web Scraping Resources	▪ Scraperwiki.com ▪ Import.io ▪ Scraper Chrome Extension - chrome.google.com/webstore/detail/scraper/mbigbapnjcgaffohmbkdlecaccepngjd ▪ OutWitHub - www.outwit.com
Charting Tools	▪ Chart.js - www.chartjs.org ▪ HighCharts - www.highcharts.com ▪ GoogleCharts - developers.google.com/chart ▪ Google Docs - www.google.com/docs ▪ Google Fusion Tables - tables. googlelabs.com ▪ Google MyMaps - www.google.com/mymaps ▪ Tableau Software - www.tableau.com
Organizations and Events	▪ National Institute for Computer-Assisted Reporting (NICAR) ire.org/conferences/nicar2015 ▪ Online News Association (ONA) - journalists.org ▪ Investigative Reporters and Editors (IRE) - www.ire.org ▪ International Symposium on Online Journalism (ISOJ) - online.journalism.utexas.edu/

Appendix (cont.)

Coding Resources for Educators

Notable Data Visualization Projects	■ Is it better to rent or buy?, *The New York Times* - www.nytimes.com/interactive/2014/upshot/buy-rent-calculator.html
	■ New York state test scores, *The New York Times* - projects.nytimes.com/new-york-schools-test-scores
	■ Toxic waters, *The New York Times* - http://projects.nytimes.com/toxic-waters/contaminants
	■ Where were you on September 11, 2001, *The New York Times* - www.nytimes.com/interactive/2011/09/08/us/sept-11-reckoning/where-were-you-september-11-map.html
	■ How ya'll, youse and you guys talk, *The New York Times* - www.nytimes.com/interactive/2013/12/20/sunday-review/dialect-quiz-map.html
	■ Dollars for docs, *Propublica* - projects.propublica.org/docdollars
	■ *Texas Tribune* public schools explorer - www.texastribune.org/public-ed/explore
	■ Google music genre timeline - http://research.google.com/bigpicture/music
	■ Twitter's #Oscar 2015 race - interactive.twitter.com/oscars2015race
	■ Pinterest board of data visualization projects - www.pinterest.com/cindyroyalatx/data-visualizations

Appendix (cont.)
Coding Resources for Educators

Articles on Coding in the Curriculum	▪ Cook, L. (2015, May 7). Why journalism students don't learn CS. *Source*. source.opennews.org/en-US/learning/journalism-students-and-cs/
	▪ Krueger, K. (2014, October 9) How journalism schools can address the gender gap. *MediaShift*. www.pbs.org/mediashift/2014/10/how-journalism-schools-can-address-the-gender-gap/
	▪ Krueger, K. (2014, July 7). How j-schools are tackling the demand for data journalism skills. *MediaShift*. www.pbs.org/mediashift/2014/07/how-j-schools-are-tackling-the-demand-for-data-journalism-skills/
	▪ Royal, C. (2014, April 28). Are journalism skills teaching their students the right skills. Nieman Journalism Lab. www.niemanlab.org/2014/04/cindy-royal-are-journalism-schools-teaching-their-students-the-right-skills/
	▪ Royal, C. (2012, October 9). Journalism schools need to get better at teaching tech where the girls are. Nieman Journalism Lab. www.niemanlab.org/2012/10/cindy-royal-journalism-schools-need-to-get-better-at-teaching-tech-where-the-girls-are/
	▪ Royal, C. & Blasingame, D. (2015). Data journalism: An explication. *#ISOJ Journal*. isojjournal.wordpress.com/2015/04/15/data-journalism-an-explication/
	▪ Royal, C. (2013, August 26). We need a digital-first curriculum to teach modern journalism. *MediaShift*. www.pbs.org/mediashift/2013/08/we-need-a-digital-first-curriculum-to-teach-modern-journalism/

19

Reconsidering News Production: How Understanding the Interplay of Actors, Actants, and Audiences Can Improve Journalism Education

Oscar Westlund and Seth C. Lewis

News has long been an important part of how people make sense of the world. Yet, the ways in which news is produced, distributed, and consumed have transformed significantly in recent decades (Anderson, Bell, & Shirky, 2012), even though some aspects of professional reporting remain stubbornly consistent (Reich, 2013). The rise of digital media—including the diffusion of mobile devices and social media affordances—is a key engine of change among news institutions. So is the shifting character of industry competition, as legacy news organizations struggle against an ocean of online competitors to claim sustained audience engagement and related revenue opportunities (Picard, 2014; Westlund, 2011). Important questions must be asked, such as: What is the future of institutional forms of news production and circulation in democratic societies? (Peters & Broersma, 2013; Ryfe, 2012). And the fate of news institutions raises key questions for journalism education and training. For example, what processes of thinking and doing should be taught when the news landscape seems so liquid and uncertain? (Mensing, 2010; Robinson, 2013).

Rather than rushing into normative conclusions about the evolving news production process' impact on journalism education worldwide, it is important to step back and size up the current news production process. This chapter outlines a perspective on news production that moves beyond taken-for-granted notions about "human" journalists and their centrality in such *processes*. Instead, it focuses on the potential interplay of social *actors*, technological *actants*, and *audiences*—how they are interconnected in news work and their impact on journalism education.

Westlund and Lewis (2014, p. 13) define actors, actants, and audiences as follows:

❑ *Actors* refer to humans working within media organizations (e.g., journalists, technologists, and businesspeople), though they may also include social actors wielding influence from beyond the organization (e.g., citizens contributing to news production).

❑ *Actants* include all nonhuman technologies such as algorithms, applications, networks, interfaces, content management systems, and other material objects enrolled in media work, whether programmed to work from inside, outside, or across organizational boundaries.

❑ *Audiences* refer to the publics (of different kinds, represented on different platforms, assembled via different techniques) who are situated on the receiving end of media production and distribution, but who also contribute to media work by virtue of the data created about their engagement with content. The full range of dynamics among actors, actants, and audiences are interconnected through the *activities* of news organizations: from day-to-day processes to high-level strategies that define an organization's *raison d'etre*.

To date, a growing body of journalism studies has examined the role of technology (including actants) in journalistic activities (Domingo & Paterson, 2011; Mitchelstein & Boczkowski, 2013; Steensen, 2011). Such research generally has developed consistent findings about how individual journalists or news media organizations have appropriated or often resisted emerging technologies. It also outlines reconfigured relationships with audiences and other stakeholders, which are entangled in that process (Anderson, 2013; Boczkowski, 2004; Lewis, 2012; Ryfe, 2012; Singer et al., 2011). Such research has also focused on journalists and their routines, role conceptions, norms, cultures, and other professional milieu. However, it has given little if any attention to other social actors involved in news organizations—most notably businesspeople and technologists (exceptions include Ananny, 2013; Nielsen, 2012; Westlund, 2011, 2012). Few scholars have acknowledged and analyzed the distinct role of digital media technologies and tensions that arise between technology and humans (exceptions include Anderson, 2013; Boczkowski, 2004; Westlund, 2011, 2012). This calls for conceptualizations that take a more holistic approach to the people, digital technologies, and processes associated with news organizations. Journalism educators and their students alike can use such conceptualizations to make sense of the continuously transforming mediascape, in which journalism is embedded. They can also use them to determine the expertise and ethical approaches needed for media professionals to properly do their jobs and to prioritize what belongs in course curricula.

Regarding the human/technology tension mentioned above, Latour's (2005) actor-network theory helps to reveal actants and the roles they play. This theory has recently served as a guiding framework for a number of ethnographic investigations of journalism (Anderson, 2013; Micó, Masip, & Domingo, 2013; Plesner, 2009; Schmitz Weiss & Domingo, 2010). It has become increasingly obvious that different kinds of technologies—including algorithms, content management systems, robots, and sensors—are capable of replacing human journalists' activities (Clerwall, 2014; Van Dalen, 2012; Westlund, 2011, 2013). As Latour (1988) argues, we can only begin to account for nonhuman actants when we start imagining what would happen if they were not present. Importantly, journalists, technologists, and businesspeople have negotiated and inscribed specific affordances into editorially oriented services such as mobile news applications (Westlund, 2012) and news blogs (Nielsen, 2012). Therefore, journalism studies should better account for the roles such technologies play in both the production and distribution of news. In working to address this gap, as part of much larger efforts to rethink theory for journalism in a digital era (Steensen & Ahva, 2015), we recently laid forth conceptualizations that acknowledge the roles diverse human actors and technological actants play when seeking to comprehend routinized media work and/or media innovations (Westlund & Lewis, 2014; Lewis & Westlund, 2015) in the case of journalism.

There is a complex, transforming interplay of social actors and their "old" and "new" activities, in relation to "old" and "new" technological tools and systems being used to produce and distribute news. News production processes are becoming more deeply intertwined with—and dependent upon—digital media technologies and services (Lewis & Westlund, 2016). Contemporary journalistic content practices in news work may well include both human and technological modes of orientation, as the *model of journalism* illustrates (Westlund, 2013). This model visualizes the relative gravitational pull of technological actants opposed to human actors in, for instance, the news production process.

This chapter proposes adopting a more holistic and sociotechnical approach to how we understand, engage in, and teach about the agents involved in contemporary news production processes. More specifically, it draws upon the *Four A's (4A's) approach* (actors, actants, audiences, activities) and the *cross-media news work matrix* (a matrix combining the 4A's with five stages in the news production process)—both outlined by Lewis and Westlund (2015)—to more fully explain the agents involved in contemporary news production. Accordingly, this chapter emphasizes actors, actants, and audiences in the study of contemporary news production activities, focusing on the first four specific stages of the news production process (among the five outlined by Domingo et al., 2008). It proceeds by outlining the theoretical framework, followed by a systematic discussion of the interplay of actors, actants, and audiences in the news production process. And it concludes with a section discussing the implications of such conceptualizations for journalism education.

The News Production Process: Interconnections among Actors, Actants, and Audiences

In journalism, and in media and information work, digital information technologies are contributing to new configurations involving human actors, technological actants, distinct groups of audiences, *and* work-practice *activities* (including news production processes) through which these agents are interconnected.

The 4A's approach conceptualizes an effort to develop a non-deterministic, sociotechnical emphasis in journalism studies. It has the ambition of "helping to reveal nuances in the relationships among human actors inside the organization, human audiences beyond it and the non-human actants that cross-mediate their interplay" (Lewis & Westlund, 2015, p. 21). Researchers have emphasized three groups of social actors within news organizations (journalists, technologists, and businesspeople), technological actants (within and outside news organizations), and three audience representations (recipient, commodity, and active participant). Altogether, Lewis and Westlund (2015) designed the 4A's approach to facilitate a more thorough understanding of the relationships among agents inside and outside news organizations.

This chapter employs the 4A's approach for a discussion of the agents potentially involved in the news production process, which will conclude with implications for journalism education. To accomplish this first task, it builds upon the five stages of news production outlined by Domingo et al. (2008):

(1) access/observation,
(2) selection/filtering,
(3) processing/editing,
(4) distribution, and
(5) interpretation.

More specifically, the chapter takes its point of departure from the cross-media news work matrix (see Table 19.1), in which the authors merged and conceptualized these five stages in relation to actors, actants, and audiences (Lewis & Westlund, 2015). Since this chapter concentrates on journalism education, it focuses on the first four stages (excluding the *interpretation* stage, which would mean a transition from the actors being focused on in this chapter to a focus on audiences). However, as the JHo matrix illustrates, journalists, technologists, and actants are involved in all five stages. Moreover, because audiences are represented as active participants, they also can take part throughout the news production process.

The involvement of—and collaborations and tensions among—actors, actants, and audiences in each of the news production process stages naturally influence the ways news is customized and/or repurposed (Westlund, 2013). Considering how these three groupings of agents may interrelate, there are seven plausible combinations in each of the stages (Westlund & Lewis, 2014, p. 23). These combinations follow:

❏ actor-led,
❏ actant-led,

- ❑ audience-led,
- ❑ actor/actant-led,
- ❑ actor/audience-led,
- ❑ actant/audience-led, and
- ❑ three A-led (3A) (combining actors, actants, and audiences).

Although actors, actants, and audiences will now be referred to as separate, distinct groups, previous discussions demonstrate their respective heterogeneity and complexity.

Table 19.1							
The Cross-Media News Work Matrix							
Actors			Actants		Audiences		
Journalists	Technologists	Business people	Internal	External	Recipients	Active participants	Commodities
Yes	Yes	No	Yes	Yes	No	Yes	No
Yes	Yes	No	Yes	Yes	No	Yes	No
Yes	Yes	No	Yes	Yes	No	No	No
Yes	Yes	Yes	Yes	Yes	No	Yes	Yes
Yes	Yes	No	Yes	Yes	Yes	Yes	No
Source: Lewis & Westlund (2015)							

Note. The cross-media news work matrix displays different sets of actors, actants, and audiences along the horizontal axis, whereas the vertical axis displays the activities that constitute the five stages of news production (Domingo et al., 2008). "Yes" and "No" indicate whether specific actors, actants, and audiences are deemed likely to be involved in a specific stage of the news production process. Note that the cross-media news work matrix should be seen merely as a conceptual starting point: Further empirical research is needed to determine the respective involvement of the different actors, actants, and audiences.

Reconsidering Four Stages of News Production for Teaching Purposes

This section discusses how actors, actants, and audiences engage in and lead news production *activities*. It frames the discussion in light of the first four (and most salient) stages of the news production process (Domingo et al., 2008). Within each of these subsections below, it examines the seven plausible combinations of actors, actants, and audiences (Westlund & Lewis, 2014). With the social actors (journalists) traditionally steering the news production process, it first discusses their role in each stage. Thereafter, it explores the remaining six plausible combinations of agents in a more integrated fashion. Each of these seven plausible combinations reveals possible ways to approach the news production process. And herein lies implications for journalism educators: each stage can be practiced and taught in significantly different, non-traditional ways. As a result, journalism students could be provided more nuanced perspectives on how to approach and collaborate with technological actants and audiences.

In order to truly understand and best teach different forms of digital journalism, two important factors must be understood. First, the roles each of these agents play are often deeply intertwined. Second, unlike with traditional print journalism, where routinized processes always result in a specific, material news *product*, the rise of digital journalism has brought forth a *process* in which agents may have to move back and forth between the five different stages (Robinson, 2011; Picard, 2014). That is, a first iteration of a digital news article opens opportunities for audience participation, which in turn might lead actors and actants to revise or reposition a news article.

Access/observation. The first stage of the news production process focuses on access/observation, which includes diverse ways in which agents get information and observe phenomena. Taking charge of the actor-led approach, journalists have traditionally engaged with their community and sources to make observations and gain access to potential news stories. Journalists have also used their legal rights (in many countries) to acquire public records and other documents. Digital media technologies have strengthened these "manual" methods of observation. Journalists, in many cases, enjoy broader and faster access to online records and eyewitness accounts of events via social media, such as Twitter (Hermida, Lewis, & Zamith, 2014).

Looking beyond journalists in the actor-led approach, Lewis and Westlund (2015) describe how both technologists and technological actants may assist journalists in access/observation. Technologists can play an important role in the actor-led approach, configuring or even creating technological tools (or actants) that journalists can use in their pursuit of valuable information and better source networks (Fink, 2014). Turning to an actant-led approach, technological actants in the form of computer code and systems (e.g., audience sentiment analysis) offer important forms of access and observation (Anderson, 2011; Godbole, Srinivasaiah, & Skiena, 2007). Technological actants can be used for increasingly automated observations of diverse forms of "news." However, there are few examples of entirely audience-led approaches. This is the case even though the potential for participatory journalism has grown (Singer et al., 2011), particularly as citizens use their smart mobile devices to post text, pictures, and video about current events (Allan, 2013; Westlund, 2013). Such examples of participatory journalism may be characterized as emerging forms of actor/audience-led collaboration, especially as journalists begin to take advantage of the potential for more mutually beneficial forms of exchange with audiences (Lewis, 2015; Lewis, Holton, & Coddington 2014).

An example of an actant/audience-led approach is when algorithms are programmed to observe and detect patterns consciously or unconsciously reported by audiences. Conscious forms of reporting may include audiences corroborating algorithmically found data on an earthquake by reporting observations (Cruz, 2014).

Finally, the combined 3A-led approach occurs in instances where access/observation is the result of interplay among actors, actants, and audiences together. In the earthquake example, humans may be involved in developing algorithms with editorial-minded protocols, in manually editing algorithm-written stories, and in assessing user contributions before publication (Carlson, 2015). Another example follows: At the Swedish evening tabloid *Aftonbladet*, journalists observe events with the help of a panel of audience members who have agreed to allow a technological actant to trace their GPS position. Through a mobile app, journalists may alert users to events happening in their geographical area and ask them to report on them (Lewis & Westlund, 2015).

Turning to implications for journalism educators, the key takeaway is that journalism students must not only learn traditional manual methods for access/observation carried out by journalists—rather than automated via technological actants—but also how to effectively partner with technologists, technological actants, and audiences in this process. Journalists need to develop skills in managing and developing a broader and more advanced architecture for access/observation. Although this architecture will ease their workload in identifying relevant subjects to cover, it still requires journalists to make critical assessment of the information sources involved.

Selection/filtering. The second stage, selection/filtering, addresses how certain agents make news judgments. Professional journalists have well-established (and actor-led) routines for deciding what is news (Tuchman, 1978) and have long maintained control over this stage in the news process (Domingo et al., 2008). A symbolic wall between the editorial and business sides of news organizations has been critical to preserving the sanctity of such news judgment determinations (Coddington, 2015; Underwood, 1993). Although businesspeople and technologists have traditionally not been allowed to influence selection and filtering, this is changing. Internal news organization groups now collaborate more fully with journalists in developing editorial products such as mobile news apps (Westlund, 2011) and blogging platforms (Nielsen, 2012) and coordinating such activities via global trade associations such as WAN-IFRA (Raviola, 2012).

Turning to actant-led processes, both internally and externally placed technological actants have growing significance for the selection/filtering of news. Specialized companies such as Narrative Science, among other automated journalism operations, provide algorithm-generated news (Carlson, 2015). Other actants, such as applications and CMS technologies, are incorporated into the fabric of news judgments (Westlund, 2013). Routinized and easily quantifiable news subjects, such as sports results and quarterly financial reports, are relatively easy to manage through actant-led processes. However, practitioners and pundits have questioned whether technological actants are capable of adequately selecting and filtering news without human journalists. At the same time, actants' technical capacities are improving, and Clerwall's (2014) research indicates that audiences might not be able to tell the difference between news produced by humans or technological actants. Moreover, technological actants may be used for user-personalized selection of news material (discussed in the distribution stage section).

Audience-led approaches are noticeably absent, except in rare cases where gatekeeping has been opened to forms of "gatewatching" (Bruns, 2005). Journalists are reluctant to cede control over the selection/filtering stage of news production (Robinson, 2011). They prefer to have audiences either provide source material on the front end or online commentary on the back end (Singer et al., 2011; Lewis, 2012). Nevertheless, some legacy news media organizations, in limited instances, are experimenting with more fully active roles for audiences—giving them a certain degree of power to select and filter information. In one such case, at the Swedish newspaper *Göteborgs-Posten,* businesspeople promoted such ideas with journalists and technologists while pushing for the development of a mobile news app. The active-audience proposition, however, was rejected due to misgivings by journalists and technologists (Westlund, 2012).

The actor/actant-led approach occurs as social actors rely on information gathered via technological actants and manually decide which news to publish. Meanwhile, the actor/audience-led approach is followed, for example, when news publishers allow audiences to help cover, via crowdsourcing, the investigation of politicians' expense reports. Further, an actant/audience-led approach may entail more technologically oriented forms of user selection and filtering, without newsroom social actors' intervening. This can occur when news algorithms are programmed to detect and respond to audience interests as they are registered either consciously (via manual user input) or unconsciously (via the user's digital traces). Finally, 3A-led approaches are orchestrated when social actors rely on technological tools to filter and select news according to relevant audience data. Tandoc's (2014) research, like others in this vein (Petre, 2015), has shown how news organizations respond to online metrics as they make pre- and post-publication news judgments, thereby influencing selection and filtering processes.

Thus, journalism educators need to keep updated with developments in participatory journalism to maintain an understanding of how news media are guarding their gates. To date, few legacy news media have allowed audience engagement in selection/filtering information. This may change, however, as audiences become more active and news staffs continue to shrink. In any instance, technological actants will surely play an increasingly important role for selection and filtering of information. Journalism educators therefore have to adequately understand and explain these concepts to future media professionals.

Processing/editing. The third stage deals with the possible involvement of distinct agents in the processing and editing of news and information. Actor-led modes of (manual) editing by journalists have long dominated legacy news media routines, leading to institutionalized (and so-called path-dependent) practices (DiMaggio & Powell, 1983). Moreover, the processing patterns newspapers have developed manually editing print publications have formed behaviors that have guided how such news organizations re-mediate their journalism for digital spaces. Because journalistic editing carries the distinction of quality, legacy news organizations initially hired online-specific editors to address the rise of Internet journalism. They later recruited and trained editors specifically for mobile and social media platforms (Westlund, 2011). However, such news organizations, especially newspapers, fell into financial distress. They then started to cut back in human resources, such as editing personnel. Consequently, many news media conglomerates worldwide, including Sweden's Stampen Media and MittMedia, now have centralized editing staffs. In addition, they have reduced their need for manual editing by using other technological interfaces (discussed below).

Actant-led approaches include news publishers that process/edit in different and less time-consuming ways. They rely on semi-automated actants such as editorial content management systems (CMS) provided by external companies like Atex or Escenic. With digital journalism now routinized, such technological actants are becoming naturalized. Their capacity for developing and exercising journalism is still evolving. Nevertheless, CMS are continuously improving through efforts by social actors both within and beyond the news organizations using them. Currently, editorial CMS are facilitating the processing/editing of digital journalism through templates. In essence, journalists feed the editorial CMS news content for publishing and make or confirm settings for cross-media news publishing. Then, technological actants take care of the "editing," ensuring a technology-led publishing process in which journalistic content may be seamlessly customized and/or repurposed (Westlund, 2013). Ultimately, there is less need for human editing when technological actants can adapt headlines, pictures, videos, etc., for various platforms to suit their needs (e.g., applications for Android vs. iOS mobile ecosystems). Moreover, platform-agnostic approaches, such as responsive Web design (e.g., HTML5), have recently gained traction, further reducing the need for social actors to customize content and code for specific platforms.

Finally, as of publication, audience-led approaches to processing/editing are literally non-existent. None of the three possible representations of the audience are likely included in this stage of the news production process (Lewis & Westlund, 2015). Similarly, actor/audience-led, actant/audience-led, or 3A-led approaches are unlikely. On the contrary, the actor/actant-led approach—combining journalists' manual editing with technological actants' activities—should become more common.

What are the implications for journalism educators at this stage? Traditional forms of editing at large news organizations—often involving multiple assignment and copy editors—are simply disappearing. Future journalists should be trained to publish content through editorial CMS for diverse platforms, particularly as newspaper executives and managers deem human copy editors less and less necessary (for better or worse). Journalism educators should teach students how to develop their own ideas for innovating editorial CMS—and other technological actants—for editing and other journalism purposes. And as editing becomes an increasingly automated process facilitated by algorithms, future journalists will need to understand how certain editing choices may be inscribed into systems for news processing and publication.

Distribution. The fourth stage of the news production process focuses on distribution. In a cross-media environment, social actors need to make editorial decisions with regard to several digital media platforms and devices (not to mention possibly print, radio, and/or television). They also need to inscribe technological actants to channel their journalistic content to both proprietary platforms (controlled environments such as mobile apps) and non-proprietary platforms (non-controlled environments such as social media spaces). The representation of the audience is clearly important, ultimately influencing who accesses what news. The matter of digital distribution, and the growing sense that content that fails to "spread" is effectively dead (Jenkins, Ford, & Green, 2013), highlights the extent to which traditional publishers have lost control over news and information (Lewis, 2012). A related outcome, as audience attention fragments and gravitates to social media, is the loss of advertising revenue to competitors like Facebook and Google. Control and profits also shift with initiatives such as Facebook Instant Articles, Google News, and Snapchat's Discover. Thus, educators must teach future journalists the nature of information diffusion online: from search engine optimization (SEO) to social media optimization (SMO) to the rhythms of particular digital spaces and online communities. While journalists may not control how social algorithms redistribute their content, they can take a more active role in understanding how to publish effectively on their own platforms and promoting their content across multiple channels targeted for distinct publics.

There are concerns about the so-called echo chambers and filter bubbles that may develop in social media spaces as users are exposed to increasingly personalized news and information (Pariser, 2012). Future journalists should recognize the possible democratic consequences associated with deeply targeted creation and circulation of information (Couldry & Turow, 2014). For example, a recent article in *Science* analyzing news accessing and sharing behaviors—among 10 million Americans who had declared their political preferences—suggests that people with heterogeneous networks of Facebook friends (friends from school, work, etc.) may discover a wider variety of news topics and perspectives (Bakshy, Messing, & Adamic, 2015). However, at the same time, social media such as blogs and Twitter, in which participation is driven by specific interests, may be more likely to encourage homogeneity and less diversity in content and perspectives (Conover et al., 2011).

Actor-led approaches to distribution take place when human social actors are in charge of publishing and distributing news. The process of printing words into ink—and physically transporting printed newspapers to readers—stands out as an actor-led approach. Obviously, social actors use a number of technologies and tools in this process. The literature generally has focused on editors as the actors responsible for steering news distribution. However, considering strategic matters involved in distribution, business managers are also participating in such decisions (Lewis & Westlund, 2015). And, as news distribution becomes increasingly digitized and technically complicated (Braun, 2015), technologists are also getting involved in such issues (Westlund, 2011; Westlund & Krumsvik, 2014).

An increasingly salient characteristic of contemporary news distribution is the rise of actant-led approaches. As previously discussed, media organizations use internally situated technological actants for processing/editing, and these actants also play an important role in the distribution of digital news. Outside of the newsroom, a host of technological actants are facilitating news redistribution through aggregators such as Flipboard, Google News, Omni, Pulse, Zite, and Apple's News app, launched in 2015. Likewise, audience-led approaches to the distribution of news/information have become vital. Audiences represented as active participants engage in sharing and commenting on news in ways that make them increasingly central to how others access the news (Anderson & Caumont, 2014). Meanwhile, actor/actant-led approaches may involve technologists shaping news distribution by translating journalistic values into the algorithms and code used for directing actants (such as CMS) used for distribution. Essentially, social actors are instructing their technological actants to act like human journalists, possibly adding customization through technological affordances (Westlund, 2012). Moreover, social actors—and technological actants—are engaged in both search engine optimization (SEO) and social media optimization (SMO), tweaking headlines and wording for short-term social impact and longer-term search success. The actant/audience-led pattern is exemplified by personalized news applications (such as Omni by Schibsted) through which audiences initially register their preferences for different subjects. Thereafter, the media organization continuously synchronizes its selection and filtering of news with audience members' interests and behavioral patterns. Finally, with a 3A-led approach, actors, actants, and audiences blend together in diverse processes of distribution and redistribution, blurring the boundaries of production, distribution, and consumption (Mitchelstein & Boczkowski, 2013).

News distribution has expanded far beyond one news medium, even beyond several proprietary platforms, toward embracing a great variety of non-proprietary platforms. Journalism educators need to understand and acknowledge that technological actants and audiences have become increasingly significant for the redistribution of news, and, accordingly, train their students in SEO, SMO, and related approaches.

Conclusion: Reconsidering the Reconsiderations

Diverse digital media technologies and systems (i.e., actants) and distinct audience representations of audiences have been associated with great transformations in the global mediascape, especially in the field of journalism. Journalists and journalism educators need to step back and reflect more holistically on how they might approach the news production process, both in practice and teaching. After applying the 4A's approach and the cross-media news work matrix (Lewis & Westlund, 2015) to a more specific, systematic discussion of seven plausible combinations of actors, actants, and audiences (Westlund & Lewis, 2014) in the news production process, the authors come to the following conclusions: Each of the three agents (actors, actants, audiences) should be considered equally important in the news production process, although the significance of one relative to another may vary depending on the stages of news production in question. It is clear that technological actants are significant yet taken for granted. It is also clear that greater coordination among the agents—especially social actors and technological actants—would bring many benefits to news organizations. In the next decade this may be particularly true for newspapers, as many of them shed legacy costs of printing but need to make up for print advertising revenue losses through new efficiencies and strategies. These are likely to involve closer interactions between humans and machines, each doing what they do best.

What are the overall implications for journalism education? Above all, journalism educators will need to continuously learn about audiences and technological actants. They must also refine how they teach related theoretical and practical implications. This involves better recognizing distinct types of audiences, including how their preferences and practices unfold over time within particular media platforms. It also means better acknowledging the distinct internal and external roles— past, present, and potential—that technological actants may play in the news production process. And this remains the case even when such technological developments threaten to displace human journalists.

From the above analysis, four directions for journalism education can be charted, one for each of the news production process stages discussed. The point of departure is considering how journalists may be instructed to approach and collaborate with other agents.

First, educators can teach journalists to better collaborate with technologists to appropriate useful, user-friendly technologies (i.e., actants) to facilitate access/observation. This includes communicating with audiences and sources through platforms that may be either proprietary (e.g., CMS and website architecture) or non-proprietary (e.g., social media) in nature. Such training ideally occurs through greater collaboration with industry partners, experimenting with and learning from new approaches.

Second, educators may need to reconsider the journalistic ideals and norms they teach—particularly attitudes such as professional control, which limit the profession's capacity for innovation (Lewis, 2012). For instance, challenging the profession's reluctance to interact with audiences and making more productive use of actants may lead to improved forms of selection/filtering, ultimately leading to more widely sourced and publicly relevant news accounts.

Third, educators should question the need for manual editing in the case of contemporary "newspapers" engaging in cross-media news work. While human judgment and contextual awareness will always remain necessary, journalism educators could shift some of their focus away from actor-led processing/editing. In other words, they should consider how their students can collaborate with technological actants to produce news content customized for a plethora of platforms and audience-directed purposes.

Fourth, journalism educators need to pay more attention to distribution, as news institutions shift from focusing on their proprietary and analog platform(s) to a wider array of digital destinations. As Braun (2015) points out, distribution has been long neglected in media research. Beyond teaching students about best practices and platform-specific considerations, educators can base larger conversations around the interlocking roles of audiences and actants in the sharing and recirculating of news and information, both in closed environments (such as mobile apps) and more open platforms (such as social media).

It is clear that news media organizations need a better accounting and configuration of their human and technological resources if they hope to innovate in a turbulent media environment (Westlund & Lewis, 2014). If journalism education is to help them, it will first need to teach the next generation of journalists how to appreciate and appropriate the generative potential that resides at the intersection of actors, actants, and audiences.

References

Anderson, C. W. (2011). Deliberative, agonistic, and algorithmic audiences: Journalism's vision of its public in an age of audience transparency. *International Journal of Communication, 5*. Retrieved from http://ijoc.org/index.php/ijoc/article/view/884

Anderson, C. W., Bell, E., & Shirky, C. (2012). *Post-industrial journalism: Adapting to the present*. Retrieved from http://towcenter.org/research/post-industrial-journalism/

Anderson, C. W. (2013). *Rebuilding the news: Metropolitan journalism in the digital age*. Philadelphia, PA: Temple University Press.

Anderson, M., & Caumont, A. (2014). How social media is reshaping news. Retrieved from http://www.pewresearch.org/fact-tank/2014/09/24/how-social-media-is-reshaping-news/

Ananny, M. (2013). Press-public collaboration as infrastructure: tracing news organizations and programming publics in application programming interfaces. *American Behavioral Scientist, 57*(5), 623-642.

Bakshy, E., Messing, S., & Adamic, L. A. (2015). Exposure to ideologically diverse news and opinion on Facebook. *Science, 348*(6239), 1130-1132.

Boczkowski, P. J. (2004). *Digitizing the news: Innovation in online newspapers*. Cambridge, MA: MIT Press.

Braun, J. (2015). *A fuller spectrum: Distributing television news online*. New Haven, CT: Yale University Press.

Bruns, A. (2005). *Gatewatching: Collaborative online news production*. New York, NY: Peter Lang.

Carlson, M. (2015). The robotic reporter: Automated journalism and the redefinition of labor, compositional forms, and journalistic authority. *Digital Journalism, 3*(3), 416-431.

Clerwall, C. (2014). Enter the robot journalist: Users' perceptions of automated content. *Journalism Practice, 8*(5), 519-531.

Coddington, M. (2015). The wall becomes a curtain: Revisiting journalism's news–business boundary. In M. Carlson & S. C. Lewis (Eds.), *Boundaries of journalism: Professionalism, practices, and participation* (pp. 67-82). New York, NY: Routledge.

Conover, M. D., Ratkiewicz, J., Francisco, M., Goncalves, B., Menczer, F., & Flammini, A. (2011). Political polarization on Twitter. *Fifth International AAAI Conference on Weblogs and Social Media.*

Couldry, N., & Turow, J. (2014). Advertising, big data and the clearance of the public realm: Marketers' new approaches to the content subsidy. *International Journal of Communication, 8,* 1710-1726.

Cruz, D. (2014, March 18). Journalist uses algorithm to gather earthquake data and write reports in minutes. *Knight Center for Journalism in the Americas.* Retrieved from https://knightcenter.utexas.edu/blog/00-15305-journalist-uses-algorithm-gather-earthquake-data-and-write-reports-minutes

DiMaggio, P. J., & Powell, W. W. (1983). The iron cage revisited: institutional isomorphism and collective rationality in organizational fields. *American Sociological Review, 48*(2), 147-160.

Domingo, D., Quandt, T., Heinonen, A., Paulussen, S., Singer, J. B., & Vujnovic, M. (2008). Participatory journalism practices in the media and beyond: An international comparative study of initiatives in online newspapers. *Journalism Practice, 2*(3), 326-342.

Domingo, D., & Paterson, C. A. (Eds.), (2011). *Making online news: Newsroom ethnographies in the second decade of Internet journalism.* New York, NY: Peter Lang.

Fink, K. (2014). *Data-Driven sourcing: How journalists use digital search tools to decide what's news.* (Unpublished doctoral dissertation). Columbia University, New York.

Godbole, N., Srinivasaiah, M., & Skiena, S. (2007). Large-scale sentiment analysis for news and blogs. *ICWSM.* Boulder, CO.

Hermida, A., Lewis, S. C., & Zamith, R. (2014). Sourcing the Arab Spring: A case study of Andy Carvin's sources on Twitter during the Tunisian and Egyptian revolutions. *Journal of Computer-Mediated Communication, 19*(3), 479-499.

Jenkins, H., Ford, S., & Green, J. (2013). *Spreadable media: Creating value and meaning in a networked culture.* New York, NY: NYU Press.

Latour, B. (1988). Mixing humans and nonhumans together: The sociology of a door-closer. *Social Problems, 35*(3), 298-310.

Latour, B. (2005). *Reassembling the social: An introduction to actor-network-theory.* New York, NY: Oxford University Press.

Lewis, S. C. (2012). The tension between professional control and open participation: Journalism and its boundaries. *Information, Communication & Society, 15*(6), 836-866.

Lewis, S. C. (2015). Reciprocity as a key concept for social media and society. *Social Media + Society, 1*(1), 1-2.

Lewis, S. C., Holton, A. E., & Coddington, M. (2014). Reciprocal journalism: A concept of mutual exchange between journalists and audiences. *Journalism Practice*, 8(2), 229-241.

Lewis, S. C., & Westlund, O. (2015). Actors, actants, audiences, and activities in cross-media news work: A matrix and a research agenda. *Digital Journalism*, 3(1), 19-37.

Lewis, S. C., & Westlund, O. (2016). Mapping the Human-Machine Divide in Journalism. In T. Witschge, C. W. Anderson, D. Domingo & A. Hermida (Eds.), *The SAGE Handbook of Digital Journalism* (pp. 341-353). New York, NY: Sage.

Mensing, D. (2010). Rethinking (again) the future of journalism education. *Journalism Studies*, 11(4), 511-523.

Micó, J. L., Masip, P., & Domingo, D. (2013). To wish impossible things: Convergence as a process of diffusion of innovations in an actor-network. *International Communication Gazette*, 75(1), 118-137.

Mitchelstein, E., & Boczkowski, P. J. (2013). Tradition and transformation in online news production and consumption. In W. H. Dutton (Ed.), *Oxford Handbook of Internet Studies* (pp. 378-400). Oxford: Oxford University Press.

Nielsen, R. K. (2012). How newspapers began to blog: Recognizing the role of technologists in old media organizations' development of new media technologies. *Information, Communication & Society*, 15(6), 959-978.

Pariser, E. (2012). *The filter bubble: How the new personalized web is changing what we read and how we think.* New York, NY: Penguin Books/Penguin Press.

Peters, C., & Broersma, M. J. (Eds.), (2013). *Rethinking journalism: Trust and participation in a transformed news landscape.* London: Routledge.

Petre, C. (2015). *The traffic factories: Metrics at Chartbeat, Gawker Media, and The New York Times.* New York, NY: Columbia University. Retrieved from http://towcenter.org/research/traffic-factories/

Picard, R. G. (2014). Twilight or new dawn of journalism? Evidence from the changing news ecosystem. *Digital Journalism*, 2(3), 273-283.

Plesner, U. (2009). An actor-network perspective on changing work practices: Communication technologies as actants in newswork. *Journalism*, 10(5), 604-626.

Raviola, E. (2012). Exploring organizational framings: Journalism and business management in news organizations. *Information, Communication & Society*, 15(6), 932-958.

Reich, Z. (2013). The impact of technology on news reporting: A longitudinal perspective. *Journalism & Mass Communication Quarterly*, 90(3), 417-434.

Robinson, S. (2011). "Journalism as process": The organizational implications of participatory content in news organization. *Journalism & Communication Monographs*, 13(3), 138-210.

Robinson, S. (2013). Teaching 'journalism as process': A proposed paradigm for j-school curricula in the digital age. *Teaching Journalism and Mass Communication*, *3*(1), 1-12.

Ryfe, D. M. (2012). *Can journalism survive? An inside look at American newsrooms.* Malden, MA: Polity Press.

Schmitz Weiss, A., & Domingo, D. (2010). Innovation processes in online newsrooms as actor-networks and communities of practice. *New Media & Society*, *12*(7), 1156-1171.

Singer, J. B., Domingo, D., Heinonen, A., Hermida, A., Paulussen, S., Quandt, T., Reich, Z., & Vujnovic, M. (2011). *Participatory journalism: Guarding open gates at online newspapers.* Malden, MA: Wiley-Blackwell.

Steensen, S. (2011). Online journalism and the promises of new technology: A critical review and look ahead. *Journalism Studies*, *12*(3), 311-327.

Steensen, S., & Ahva, L. (2015). Theories of journalism in a digital age: An exploration and an introduction. *Digital Journalism*, *3*(1), 1-18.

Tandoc, E. C. (2014). Journalism is twerking? How web analytics is changing the process of gatekeeping. *New Media & Society*, *16*(4), 559-575.

Tuchman, G. (1978). *Making news: A study in the construction of reality.* New York, NY: Free Press.

Underwood D. (1993). *When MBAs rule the newsroom: How the marketers and managers are reshaping today's media.* New York, NY: Columbia University Press.

Van Dalen, A. (2012). The algorithms behind the headlines: How machine-written news redefines the core skills of human journalists. *Journalism Practice*, *6*(5-6), 648–658.

Westlund, O. (2011). *Cross-media news work: Sensemaking of the mobile media (r) evolution.* (Doctoral dissertation). University of Gothenburg, Gothenburg.

Westlund, O. (2012). Producer-centric vs. Participation-centric: On the shaping of mobile media. *Northern Lights*, *10*(1), 107-121.

Westlund, O. (2013). Mobile news: A review and model of journalism in an age of mobile media. *Digital Journalism*, *1*(1), 6–26.

Westlund, O., & Krumsvik, A. H. (2014). Perceptions of intra-organizational collaboration and media workers' interests in media innovations. *The Journal of Media Innovations*, *1*(2), 52-74.

Westlund, O., & Lewis, S. C. (2014). The agents of media innovation: Actors, actants, and audiences. *The Journal of Media Innovations*, *1*(2), 10-35.

20

Journalism Education's First Century: Markers of Progress

Joe Foote

Journalism education is barely one century old as a discipline. Yet, it has become an established part of the higher education environment in practically every country of the world. The greatest growth spurt has come during the past 30 years as a variety of transitory experiences have swept the globe.

When the United States established land-grant institutions in every state during the mid-19th century, it paved the way to a variety of professional disciplines that had never been accepted by traditional European universities. Each of these land-grant universities created for every state included a school of agriculture, which had a vested interest in reaching a larger audience with its technology and improved methods. Iowa State was the first university to receive the benefits of the Morrill Acts of 1862 and 1890 (Iowa State University, 2007). Other examples of land-grant colleges include the University of Wisconsin-Madison, Michigan State University, and the University of Missouri. Agricultural communication extension arms were needed to spread the word about agricultural innovations and best practices. In this environment, having a separate operation for communication was a logical outgrowth for getting agricultural messages to those who wanted advice. Later, departments of English felt a need to branch out into the applied area of journalism. Once the large Midwestern state universities headed in this direction, others followed. By the end of World War II, practically every state university taught journalism or some form of mass communication.

For many years European universities maintained a strong bias against applied education at the elite level of higher education. The training of journalists was seen as a craft to be learned on the job or to be studied in a polytechnic. It was not until the 1980s that a great expansion of programs occurred at the university level. When the United Kingdom elevated its polytechnics to university status in 1992, a slew of journalism programs in that country blossomed overnight. Similar trends appeared in continental Europe.

Then came the fall of communism in the 1990s, which created opportunities for higher education reform and expansion in the former Soviet Union and Eastern Europe. The training needs of new private publications and broadcast stations in a market economy with a freer flow of information led to the upgrading of journalism and mass communication as a major field of study. During this period, extensive foreign resources poured in to build a proper infrastructure for the teaching of journalism. For example, journalism education in Russia, no longer serving as an arm of the state during the Soviet period (1917-1991), expanded rapidly—aided by U.S. and European journalism educators (Morrison, 1997). Even though Russia had a well-established elite corps of universities, the compelling need for journalism education penetrated the establishment.

At about the same time, the economies of Asia were exploding, creating greater demand for media institutions. Traditional Asian universities quickly expanded their mass communication offerings, and a new system of private universities emerged. Journalism and mass communication became prime offerings alongside engineering, business, and computer science. Expanding literacy in several developing countries with growing economies created accelerated demand for more journalism outlets and professionals to staff them.

Despite growing media censorship in many world regions—such as Latin America, the Middle East, and communist countries—journalism education continues to grow (Self, 2015). For example, although China ranks low in global press freedom rankings, undergraduate journalism programs in China surged from seven university programs in 1949 (Hao & Xu, 1997) to more than 1,000 undergraduate programs in 2013 (CHESICC, 2013).

By the beginning of the 21st century, the demand for journalism education was strong throughout the world. Large countries with rapidly expanding economies like China, India, and Brazil experienced major expansions in journalism programs. Against this backdrop, in

2001, the idea for the World Journalism Education Congress (WJEC) emerged; its first global congress, in 2007, has been followed by congresses every three years. The field was maturing at a fast pace, and there was a clear need for collaboration and mutual recognition. This book is recognition of this growth and maturity at both the country and global levels.

This chapter discusses three major challenges in journalism education: striving for recognition and respect within the university, bringing the journalism and mass communication professions closer to the academy, and remaining current in a highly dynamic professional and technological environment.

A Place Within the University

Like all emerging fields, journalism and mass communication has had to fight to be recognized by established universities. Being a cross-disciplinary field with an extremely professional orientation has not necessarily been an advantage. Even today, many university colleagues look at journalism programs as "trade schools" with little redeeming academic value. Journalism administrators have had to take criticism from two polar extremes. While universities have questioned the academic legitimacy of the field, professionals have questioned the curriculum's "real world" relevance. As late as the 1990s in Britain, for example, on-the-job and apprenticeship training for journalists and editors was more respected than academic training (Herbert, 2000). With two masters demanding to be served, journalism programs have had to do battle simultaneously on two challenging fronts.

Discipline Legitimacy

Journalism education benefitted from a growth surge during the second half of the 20th century. Even in universities, size matters. With journalism and mass communication enrollments burgeoning during the 1990s, several departments became colleges with a dean. College-level status guaranteed a seat at the table among academic heavyweights and conveyed legitimacy. University administrators began to appreciate benefits to the institution from growing enrollments in programs like journalism, which were also relatively low cost. When students came to the university's door wanting to study journalism, there was every incentive to meet that demand. During this growth period, programs had an opportunity to upgrade their offerings and facilities and to enhance their position within the university.

In countries where professionals dominated journalism education, the field tended to be more academically isolated. Professional faculty who felt closer kinship with the profession than the academy had little incentive to build relationships with academic colleagues. Often, they felt uncomfortable in the academic environment. As doctoral programs became stronger and as more people with professional experience pursued advanced degrees, a more balanced faculty emerged in the 21st century—representing both professional and academic interests.

Despite the various challenges associated with developing a new field, journalism education is far more solidified into university hierarchies than it was 30 years ago. In the West, the generation of faculty repulsed by journalism being taught as a subject within the university is long gone. Today's faculty came of age when journalism was one of the most vigorous disciplines within the university. What journalism lacked in research prestige it made up for in student demand, visibility, and relevance to the marketplace of ideas. Alumni tended to be high-profile, agile communicators who had used their skills to great professional advantage.

In developing countries, there is a dichotomy between traditional programs that have eschewed professional training and those that eagerly emphasize experiential learning and close ties to the profession. Much of the professional impetus comes from private universities that want to build their reputation on the ability to place graduates in the industry.

Research Legitimacy

The cross-disciplinary nature of the field that seemed like a liability has started to become an asset. For many years after World War II, the best mass communication research came from social psychologists, sociologists, political scientists, experimental psychologists, anthropologists, linguists, and economists. While outsiders were peering into the media field, it was difficult for journalism educators to get traction. Stronger research from within is now reversing that flow. The prestige, influence and impact of mass communication journals are rising, along with their number. Researchers in both the social sciences and hard sciences often seek out mass communication scholars as collaborators and tend to value their contributions. Mass communication scholars have the luxury of having a reason to do research in nearly all of the social sciences and some of the hard sciences, especially the health communication field.

While most journalism programs split their faculty between research and professionally oriented faculty, a new generation of journalism educators with advanced graduate degrees bring both research interests and professional experience to universities. Perhaps such dual-strength faculty will increase both the quantity and quality of research. Another positive sign has been the increased juried recognition of creative activity. Faculty who produce documentaries, narrative films, persuasive videos, creative design, and several types of journalism now have a greater launching pad for recognition of their work. The Broadcast Education Association (BEA) in the United States has been a leader in this area. For example, it established a Festival of Media Arts in 2004 that has become a juried focal point for the best creative work in the nation. This kind of sustained effort has bolstered participating faculty's opportunities for advancement.

With an expanding number of doctoral programs associated with journalism education, the number of qualified researchers is expanding rapidly. Conferences in most parts of the world are now filled with aspiring scholars ready to make their mark on the field. For instance, in Asian countries like Korea the proliferation of scholars over the past 40 years, and their research output, has been astounding.

Overall, there is evidence that the quality of worldwide scholarship is improving. The number of communications journals included in Thomson Reuter's Web of Science Journal Citation Reports expanded by 64% from 2008 to 2013. More scholarship is coming from outside the United States and Europe. New journals are appearing monthly, some available only online (Antell, Foote, & Foote, 2016).

The indexes that convey journal prestige have been slow to recognize publications from outside the United States, but this is changing. New measures of scholarly impact and prestige—like the H-5 Index (tied to Google Scholar), which recognizes a scholar's recent output from a wide range of sources—are far more receptive to international publications. The number of foreign journals in the traditional index of scholarly work that computes "impact factors" is also expanding (Antell et al., 2016).

A hiccup on the road to legitimacy for newly upgraded journalism programs occurred with the implementation of national research evaluation schemes during the 1990s. When every academic unit was judged on the strength of its research publication record, often to the exclusion of more professional indices, journalism education was left in the backwater. It has been particularly challenging for programs upgraded from polytechnics to instantly compete with their older brothers, who had centuries to build their academic birthright.

Major organizations emphasizing research are helping research's flow and recognition. Organizations such as the International Association of Mass Communication Research (IAMCR), the International Communication Association (ICA), and the Asian Media Information Centre (AMIC) have been major drivers of increased exposure for— and recognition of—quality research on a global scale.

While there are many professional organizations devoted to the broad area of communication studies, there are far fewer devoted exclusively to journalism education. The Association for Education in Journalism and Mass Communication (AEJMC), begun more than 100 years ago in the United States, is the largest and strongest professional association in the field. Country-specific associations in the United Kingdom, Australia, and New Zealand, and regional organizations like AMIC in Asia, also are pioneers. The formation of the WJEC initiative in 2001 brought together other like-minded associations from every continent. By 2010, there were 32 organizations specifically focused, completely or partially, on journalism education.

A test of the field's maturity will be how journalism education organizations grow in stature—whether they hold annual meetings, produce scholarly or applied journals, have secretariats, and/or add value to the academics they represent. Currently, there is a wide spectrum of such organizations. Some are very informal groups run on a volunteer basis by peer faculty. Many times, the level of development corresponds to the experience the nations have had in the field and the economic wealth of the country. One factor that has made WJEC viable is the increasing ability of journalism educators in developing countries to travel and support professional activities.

Original Content Legitimacy

Long reliant on books and teaching materials from the West, programs in high growth areas are eager to develop their own curricular software. Because journalism education in the United States had a big head start on other nations, most journalism text books have been written by U.S. or British professors in English and promote the cultural norms of Western journalism. Even though Western books have not always fit culturally in the countries where they have been used, their quality has been generally high. While the reliance on foreign journalism materials has been a source of frustration and resentment for years, until recently educators in non-Western countries had been slow to respond in tangible ways.

Since more faculty possess terminal degrees and more developing countries are becoming stronger economically, more human and financial resources are now available. As a result, more journalism teaching materials are being locally produced in local languages using local, relevant examples. Producing content is easier when a country has a large local market, like China or Brazil, or where languages are spoken regionally, like Arabic or Spanish. But while India has the critical mass of a large market, the multiple languages spoken there present a challenge (Eapen, 2000). And it is more difficult economically in smaller nations with few journalism education programs to produce books in native languages.

Sometimes locally produced materials consist of simply English-translated books. Sometimes they are the re-telling of the same materials in a different language and different cultural context. It will be interesting to watch how new, indigenously written materials will differ from the West in their conceptual directions and normative content. For example, will we see different ways of teaching ethics based on Confucian principles? Will we see new approaches to press freedom and social responsibility based on the unique and more constrained experiences of different countries? Will we see the emergence of different norms for newsgathering, news processing, and news distribution based upon local experience? Will different economic models produce different standards for news organizations?

Regardless of the form, teaching materials untethered from the West will change the contours of journalism education and provide valuable new choices. The next decade should bring a plethora of new teaching materials to market from the far corners of the globe, distinguished by theoretical concepts and language/cultural content significantly different from all that has come before.

Quality Control Legitimacy

Another important university quality marker is the level of sophistication a field employs to assess its own quality—whether it can have input into standards set by the government or develop its own, meet the standards it sets, use feedback from its quality assurance processes to improve, and create incentive for innovation.

Increasingly, journalism education stakeholders (students, peer faculties, administrators, government, and professionals) will demand greater accountability. A mature field is prepared to assess itself and meet that demand. It also has the ability to examine itself in an objective, dispassionate way, to plan strategically, and to achieve greater quality.

Journalism education has a vested interest in developing a method of peer assessment. It is far better to be judged by people in our field than by those in governmental bodies more distant from it. Currently, the peer assessment infrastructure is nascent outside the United States, although several developing countries are expanding government-sponsored review programs to involve academic peers. We still have limited knowledge of learning outcome assessment around the world. A global audit would be helpful to ascertain the level of development in our learning outcomes assessment systems.

Societal Legitimacy

Potential for increased relevance and prestige within the university also comes from the need for a more media literate public. As media permeate human behavior, universities have an opportunity to develop content to help students responsibly and intelligently navigate the blizzard of content they are encountering. This is the new frontier of journalism education. Courses in media literacy have become an important secondary priority in journalism education, helping to transcend the field's relatively narrow professional niche. In programs where enrollment is in decline, media literacy initiatives can provide an attractive platform for generating income and demonstrating relevance to the institution.

Increasingly, students are gravitating to journalism education as an area of study even though they have no interest in pursuing it professionally. In some ways, it has become a de facto liberal arts degree. The skill sets of information gathering, information analysis, and information distribution have become highly sought-after skills in an information economy. The fact that the worth of those skills is increasing conveys added value and legitimacy to the field.

Relevance to the Profession

Since its founding, journalism education has been tied closely to the journalism profession. In the early days, publications often had a powerful say in whether a university entered into this endeavor. Surprisingly, some publications actively campaigned against opening journalism programs, fearing that better educated journalists would disrupt the status quo and unnecessarily raise the pay standard for workers.

Climate of Distrust

The track record of developing relationships with the profession has been a mixed one. In most countries, establishing credibility in the professional sphere is a major problem. Journalists and other media professionals do not believe that universities are producing the caliber of student who can be productive in the professional media world. Editors and news directors still fear hiring employees better educated than themselves and who might be more demanding and independent.

In most cases, professionals are considerably out-of-date in their assessment of journalism education's progress during the past 30 years. However, the perceived lack of professional relevance is a genuine concern in some academic programs. Today's journalism education leaders have a responsibility to build strong relationships with industry and erase any lingering doubts about the credibility of the field.

Historically, the industry has preferred its own training schemes, where publications could dictate exactly what a capable journalist should know. While most of these programs have disappeared because of cost and the emergence of credible journalism education programs, some remain. For example, Fairchild Media in Australia and New Zealand offers an in-house journalism program for a small group of trainees within the company as part of its management development scheme. And while the Axel-Springer Journalism Academy in Germany trains its own personnel, it also admits fee-paying students for a two-year program that features a year-long stint at Columbia University's Graduate School of Journalism. It is clear, however, that such boutique training schemes, which serve a small niche, cannot make a significant difference in the professional development of the profession.

There is an elite camp that believes a well-rounded liberal arts education is the best training for journalism. In the United States, Europe, and India, such journalists at the highest ranks proudly boast that they have no journalism education beyond on-the-job training and see no need for journalism schools. There is no doubt that highly capable people can pick up the rudiments of journalism without formal training and be quite successful. Yet, these elites constitute only a sliver of the industry and will never populate an entire profession that is hungry for new talent. As the industry demands that graduates have a firm grasp of professional skills before they get a job, university journalism programs are the only way to meet current demand.

The liberal arts argument ignores the very real value of journalists being socialized into the field. Journalism education programs focus much of the curriculum on ethics and societal responsibility issues that one is not likely to get without a journalism education. There have been multiple instances where people without this socialization have stumbled into journalism at their peril. Several high-profile mistakes costly to the reputations of individuals and news organizations might have been avoided if those involved had a better grounding in the ethics and social responsibility inherent in the profession.

Experiential Learning

During the past 20 years, significant progress has been made in bringing the academy closer to the profession. A majority of academic programs agree that an essential ingredient of journalism education is a strong applied component, which provides students with a realistic view of the profession and an opportunity to get real-world experience while still a student. The reasoning follows: If all students hear our lectures and never get an opportunity to practice what they learned or are never exposed firsthand to the profession, they will rarely reach a professional standard upon graduation.

Nearly all programs in the developed world and most developing countries have a laboratory component, where students apply what they learn in the classroom. Coursework with final projects involving a real-time environment helps to fill the gap between academics and professionals. Some journalism colleges in Britain use simulated newspapers or virtual newsrooms and incorporate social media and mobile technology for students to practice. Students sometimes work up to four weeks at a newspaper or broadcast station as a requirement to complete a course at their schools. Most programs in South Asia have a media laboratory with enough computers and peripherals to accommodate the most skills-intensive classes.

An increasing number of programs have equipment students can check out to produce products similar to what one finds in a professional setting. With the cost of computers and broadcasting equipment decreasing rapidly in the digital age, even programs in the poorest countries have an opportunity to provide their students with some digital learning tools.

Many programs have active student media outlets that serve a particular community on a regular basis. There are thousands of student newspapers and student radio stations globally. Some are operated directly under the control of a journalism unit, while others are controlled by another area of the university or are independent.

During the past 40 years, the concept of the "internship" has gained global traction. Time spent in a media organization under the dual supervision of a university and media outlet provides an opportunity for students to transition from student to professional environments.

While this process has become second nature in the West, it has proven to be more difficult to implement consistently in developing countries. Some media managers do not have confidence in the worth of the sponsoring academic program and cannot justify the time commitment to the student. Some academic programs are not set up to organize and supervise an initiative beyond the university's walls. And students sometimes do not have the resources or time to get to a professional workplace off campus.

In some countries, women are at a logistical and security disadvantage taking part in off-campus programs. There may be a stigma to taking public transportation or roaming throughout a city alone to cover a story. There may be sexual harassment within the newsroom. With a rapid rise in the number of women in mass communication programs, these issues are significant. Journalism educators have an opportunity through quality, well-supervised internships to establish new norms of behavior.

A successful internship has an ecosystem that must be organized, promoted, regulated, and evaluated on a regular basis. It requires the commitment of the academic program, the professional organization, and the student. Strong academic programs worldwide have made significant progress establishing these systems. And internships alone go a long way in bridging the professional/academic gap.

Technology Leveler

The diffusion of "smart" phones across a wide spectrum has enabled journalism students everywhere to become reporters and video producers. Even without additional software or hardware attachments, a student can practice digital journalism. With a few inexpensive apps, students can edit HD video and package stories.

The impressive capabilities of smartphones could be the great leveler in journalism education and an important bridge to the profession. For example, now students in Mozambique can use the same tools as students in France. And university programs without resources to fully equip media labs and studios can now leapfrog to a sophisticated digital news operation without a huge capital infusion.

The smartphone revolution also lessens the gap between university students and the profession. Students now have the tools to equal or surpass their professional counterparts. And students can become their own media brand and bypass legacy media altogether. Obviously, it is an exciting time for journalism educators and journalism students.

The lower bar to entry for such digital tools should accelerate experiential learning. Students will continue demanding more practical experience, and universities will have fewer reasons not to offer it. As a result, for example, newly minted private universities in developing countries are injecting a strong competitive influence that is pressuring established government-supported universities to take a more practical, hands-on approach.

In the United States, programs that make journalism education more experiential through student media and that welcome professionals as full-fledged professors are known to have adopted a "teaching hospital" approach. The idea is that university faculties should have a healthy mix of research faculty and clinical faculty from the profession and that every student should have the benefit of a rich student media experience. While it can be challenging to manage faculty with such different points of reference, the blend of the two has produced high student satisfaction and closer ties with the profession.

There is a danger, of course, of pandering to the profession. Being part of a university demands a robust conceptual, theoretical component. Most programs have developed a good conceptual/professional mix of courses that socialize students in areas like ethics, freedom of expression, social responsibility, and audience behavior. While publications can establish academies that cover most training needs, they are hard-pressed to match the diversity and breadth of thought found in a quality, multifaceted university.

When members of the profession are actively engaged with a journalism education program, the chances of mutual respect greatly accelerate. Success stories abound where professionals have become adjunct professors, guest speakers, advisory board members, and external evaluators. Any such activities bind academics and professionals. While there is suspicion on both sides of this divide, one feels that deeper involvement will pay dividends, especially in situations where a professional's view of journalism education is outdated or misdirected.

Historically, nearly all of the initiatives forging closer academic-professional relationships have come from the academy. Universities have tried hard to build credibility with the journalism community. With the emerging economic crisis in developed countries caused by a disrupted business model, that balance is changing. Now, it is often the professional who takes the initiative to develop closer ties with academic programs. Professionals see a talent pool valuable to their organization during tough times. Professional managers and academic leaders now work together creatively to merge their interests. Some news organizations have actually inserted part of their newsgathering operations into universities, outsourcing specific responsibilities to students. Others have recruited more actively on college campuses, upgraded their internship programs, or engaged faculty on a consulting basis. In some cases, media organizations have been critical of academics for dragging their feet or not exerting the needed energy to remain current and build partnerships.

In rapidly developing countries, the burgeoning increase in media outlets, especially broadcast, has left professionals desperately searching for qualified personnel to fill positions. This is a major problem in countries like Bangladesh, which grew from zero private television stations to more than 40 in less than a decade. Poaching from other outlets will satisfy some demand, but this behavior has a limited upside and significant risk. Enlightened managers are realizing that the quality and productivity of media education programs can directly affect their hiring prospects. While private universities have capitalized most on this market reality, government universities also enjoy a good climate for improving their relationships with media professionals.

Another area where journalism education can make a significant contribution to the profession is in workforce diversification. Universities currently attract a better gender balance than the profession and, in most places, are more hospitable to those from ethnic minorities. As pressure increases on newsrooms to better resemble the population they serve, professionals' best approach accelerating such efforts is through journalism education.

As respect has grown for journalism education within the professional community, there have been voices demanding more industry-focused research. Even practitioners who are strong supporters of journalism education question whether academics are doing enough to solve the very real problems that plaque the field. Yet academics do research a wide variety of practical issues, including those involving business and distribution models, technology innovation, and ethical concerns.

The professional/academic relationship is as dynamic today as the state of the media. Interpersonal relationships have improved, interdependence is greater, and respect is building. Although professional respect remains a huge inhibitor to the advancement of journalism education, concrete cooperative initiatives should eventually bridge this perceptual chasm.

The Premium on Currency

Both journalism and journalism education enjoyed the luxury of a static environment during much of the 20th century. The basic structures and business models that led to unprecedented levels of riches and prestige were locked in place. Scarcity abetted the insularity of the "haves." The challenge for journalism education was to teach faculty and students how to crack the code that opened this privileged environment. Journalism education found itself in an aspirational setting with clear rules. The challenge was to prepare students to climb a well-defined, highly competitive ladder of success.

Highly disruptive Internet initiatives, which largely undermined the legacy media in the West toward the end of the 20th century, affected journalism education as well. Suddenly, it was not good enough for educators to produce narrowly focused, highly proficient students with the drive to succeed. Journalism education needed to be much broader and much more agile and integrated to remain relevant. Students had to think of themselves more as self-contained brands and creators rather than "company men."

The silos dominating the profession for years were alive and well in the academy. Students in a particular course of study rarely interacted with their counterparts in others. Programs that clung to the separate courses of study with no interdependence suddenly looked odd and irrelevant. Likewise, programs that emphasized a legacy media distribution model with no experimentation in other areas seemed hopelessly out-of-date.

While smartphones and lower-priced digital gear are lowering the barriers to technology, the lack of resources to maintain a multimedia classroom environment is a major challenge in most of Africa and some parts of Asia. Many schools in these continents and others are still dependent on foreign donors to thrust them into the digital age.

Turnover in academia has been far less frequent than in the professional world during this difficult period of adjustment. Professors have traditionally trained for a 30-year career in a particular segment of media and have been rewarded for their fidelity to that professional area. Now they are being asked to become much broader in their outlook, add additional media to their repertoire, and learn a rapidly changing technology that has turned traditional media on its head.

Being current not only includes understanding technology and applying it, but being able to navigate a more complex profession with more loose ends. While newsrooms have been changing to better define their practices in a digital age, journalists in time of transition hold mixed attitudes toward new technologies and the Internet. A recent survey in Chile found that while more than 88% of journalists agreed that the Internet improved their ability to investigate news events, more than half were worried about false information being published before news could be verified (Universidad Alberto Hurtado, 2012). Because of citizen journalism pitfalls, fake photos, questionable sources, and ethical minefields, the journalists of tomorrow will have to be socialized and trained in new, more sophisticated ways than their predecessors.

Around the turn of the century, one could see that academic leaders were highly sensitive to the need for a quick pivot. The drumbeat of conferences, symposia, external reviews, and social media all pointed inexorably toward change. University administrators selected departmental/college leaders who were highly motivated by this need for reform. Faculty and administrators who could not adapt became outliers.

Administrators attacked the problem with exceptional zeal and commitment. "Convergence," "multimedia," "cross-media," and "transmedia" became impassioned rallying cries. "Being current" became a value equal to being ethical, fair, and free. A few programs rewrote their mission statements to put the currency norm front and center.

Several chapters in this volume reflect these changing values and are a testament to how change has manifested itself in the curricula. Agility, innovation, creativity, entrepreneurship, and interactivity all became prime qualities for which to strive. Professors with 21st century technology skills became the focus of a high percentage of employment searches. Graduate students, caught in the breech of this major restructuring, retooled their resumes to appear multimedia friendly.

Thus, the ability to change directions quickly, to mirror the dynamism of new media, to transcend the boundaries of traditional media, and to collaborate on a much broader front have all become benchmarks of quality for journalism education.

Future Directions

While only economists have a free pass for predicting the future with impunity, here are 10 near-term predictions for journalism education:

1. The full acceptance of journalism education as a discipline, abetted by increased interdependence with other academic units, will be universally achieved.

2. The teaching of media skills and media literacy to students from other disciplines will be a major instrument of growth and centrality within academic institutions.

3. In countries with rapid upward economic mobility, private universities with larger budgets, more up-to-date technology, and greater sensitivity to market demands will erode the dominance of public universities.

4. The number of indigenous books and teaching materials will rise significantly over the next 20 years as more doctoral students graduate, but so will the number of trans-border multimedia course packages that capitalize on the separation of content creation from content delivery.

5. Journalism educators will be held to a higher research standard within universities as the global flow of well-trained doctoral student graduates raises the standard of research. Professionals will demand research that helps the profession economically, editorially, and ethically.

6. Proof of the quality of journalism education will increase exponentially as stakeholders demand it and assessment systems grow more sophisticated.

7. More programs in more countries will have a unique opportunity to move from the "sand box" to the "main stage" as interdependence with professional media increases.

8. Cross-border interaction among scholars will greatly increase, along with more highly developed, independent professional associations representing journalism educators.

9. Journalism education's ability to produce diverse graduates will accelerate gender equality and a greater presence of ethnic minorities in the workplace.

10. Journalism educators will increasingly be expected to be a beacon of conscience as press and Internet freedom continues to be challenged.

After a century of struggling to earn a respected place in the modern university and lessen the gap between the academy and professionals, journalism education has reached a credibility high. Its initial battles have been won. Meanwhile, the turbulence in the industry, incredible pace of technological change, and threats to freedom of expression present new challenges. When the next volume of this saga is written, journalism education's first century expeditionary force will be credited for providing an auspicious launching pad for its future.

References

Antell, K., Foote, J. B., & Foote, J. S. (2016, February). *Who moved my metrics? New impact measures for journalism and communication research*. Paper presented at the 2016 AEJMC Midwinter Conference, Norman, OK.

CHESICC. (2013). Information database on undergraduate major programs in colleges in China. Retrieved from http://gaokao.chsi.com.cn/zyk/zybk/index.jsp?pageId=1050050301&type=xk

Eapen, K. E. (2000, July). *Problems of research in some third world countries*. Paper presented at the 22nd IAMCR Conference, Singapore.

Hao, X., & Xu, X. (1997). Exploring between two worlds: China's journalism education. *Journalism & Mass Communication Educator,* 35-47.

Herbert, J. (2000). The changing face of journalism education in the U.K. *Asia Pacific Media Educator, 1*(8), 113-123.

Iowa State University. (2007). History of Iowa State: Time Line, 1858-1874. Retrieved from http://www.public.iastate.edu/~isu150/history/time-line-1858.html

Morrison, J. (1997). The changing model of Russian media and journalism education. *Journalism & Mass Communication Educator, 52*(3), 26-34.

Self, C. (2015, June). Global journalism education: A missed opportunity for media development? Retrieved from http://www.cima.ned.org/wp-content/uploads/2015/06/CIMA-Global-Journalism-Education.pdf

Universidad Alberto Hurtado (UAH). (2012). *Encuesta Estado del Periodismo Nacional 2011, Informe de Resultados* [Survey on the state of national journalism 2011. Report on results]. Retrieved from http://periodismo.uahurtado.cl/wp-content/uploads/2010/10/Resultados-Encuesta-Estado-Nacional-del-Periodismo-2011.pdf

Epilogue
Global Journalism Education Moving Forward: Its State of Mind, Pursuit of Truth, and Support of Civic Life

Robyn S. Goodman

The burgeoning growth of journalism education worldwide begs for regular updates to monitor its development and to predict its future. Researchers in turn produce "state of journalism education" type progress reports and flesh out yet-to-be-fully-understood phenomena, which help guide future theory building, and conceptual models. *Global Journalism Education's* update on the field has observed the following: Journalism education worldwide, influenced in part by shared occupational needs and Western bias, tends to be growing increasingly professionalized, formalized, standardized, university-connected, and homogeneous. That said, it has also found—as Nordenstreng (2009) previously discovered in his analysis of 33 European journalism education case studies—that it is difficult to characterize even seemingly similar journalism education systems due largely to cultural differences. As he put it, "the situation of journalism education seems to be quite specific to each country" (p. 513).

Final Observations

My final *Global Journalism Education*-related observations focus on the following three topics:

- ❏ the current state of Western journalism education bias, ethnocentrism, and related provincial thinking,
- ❏ efforts to de-Westernize global journalism education and broaden journalists' understanding of the world they live in, and
- ❏ whether journalism educators worldwide are demonstrating

enough passion and ability to help their students become valuable global citizens and/or journalists.

Western Bias and its Construction of Knowledge Impact

One such area begging for additional research in the post-truth world is the state of Western bias in journalism education systems worldwide and its influence on the construction of knowledge. In *Global Journalism Education*, one cannot miss a lingering Western presence despite an increasingly networked world. For example, every case study chapter, including Australia and the United Kingdom, speaks of a significant U.S. and/or Anglo-American (hereafter "Western") influence that still persists at some level. Most such influence is based on journalism education systems founded on Western models and a prevalence of Western books, teaching materials, and English-language academic and professional journals. In addition, international scholarly interactions—both face-to-face and virtual—seem to mostly take place within Western "spaces." And while non-Western educators bring valuable, diverse viewpoints to the scholarly mix, they also become integrated into a system predominantly vetting their research and ideas—often subconsciously—via Western perspectives.

Richards and Self argue in their *Going Global: Journalism Education Gets Its Act Together* chapter that even though such biases still exist, organizations like UNESCO and the World Journalism Education Council (WJEC), especially its conferences, are helping erode the "ethnocentrism that has in the past marred progress in the field." Foote, in this text's conclusion, also acknowledges Western bias while remaining optimistic. For instance, he argues that because more non-Western faculty possess terminal degrees and "more developing countries are becoming stronger economically, more human and financial sources are available . . . and more journalism teaching materials are being locally produced in local languages using local, relevant examples." In addition, he predicts that "cross-border interaction among scholars will increase, along with more highly developed, independent professional associations representing journalism educators." Regardless of how exactly this process unfolds, it is clear that de-Westernization in journalism education has a significant yet fascinating road to travel. As

Foote continues,

> Teaching materials untethered from the West will change the contours of journalism education and provide valuable new choices. . . . The next decade should bring a plethora of new teaching materials to market from the far corners of the globe, distinguished by theoretical concepts and language/cultural content significantly different from all that has come before.

However, it is difficult to imagine how such predicted changes can gain enough traction without increased "ways of knowing" efforts and stepped-up professional and educational buy-in. In an increasingly globalized, networked world, journalists still largely operate according to old-world, pre-Internet international information flows. Information still predominately travels from developed to developing countries, and hyperlink studies indicate journalists are reluctant to tap easily accessible links to news created by different countries—especially those with divergent views (e.g., Chang, Himelboim, & Dong, 2009; Chang, Southwell, Lee, & Hong, 2012). As Chang et al. (2012) argue,

> American journalists appear to privilege U.S. hyperlinks over foreign ones, especially links to their own internal websites. They are also predominantly against linking to foreign news media that cover the same events or issues. . . . Such a consistent pattern seems to be a conscious organizational design to keep users of the news websites in-house and domestically bound [for financial reasons]. It [also] suggests an ethnocentric journalistic practice that directs audience attention to U.S. sites presumably more worthy than others located in remote settings. (p. 696)

This tendency to favor/protect one's own news turf, referred to as "jurisdictional protectionism" (Chang et al., 2012), makes it more difficult for journalists to overcome culturally biased knowledge and news narratives.

Efforts to De-Westernize Global Journalism Education and Broaden Knowledge

Western bias is so entrenched in journalism education worldwide that it is difficult to imagine its elimination. That said, educators seem to generally agree on how to start tackling the problem: through increased contact with one another and with additional stakeholders worldwide, international student exchanges, and news literacy efforts directed toward educators, journalists, and citizens alike. The common theme underlying at least the first two strategies is stepped-up interpersonal interactions. This approach seems to be in alignment with the "invisible college" tradition, which represents, according to Chang and Tai (2005, p. 673) quoting Lievrouw, "a set of informal communication relations among scientists or other scholars who share a specific common interest or goal." As Chang and Tai (2005) further explain,

> The invisible college is a 'community of scholars' that has collegial relevance and potential for its members. As such, it is closely related to the central premise of the sociology of knowledge perspective: social relationships influence modes of conceiving and doing things. . . . At the risk of oversimplification, the essence of the sociology of knowledge as a theoretical framework, according to [Karl] Mannheim, centers on the ideas of 'collective knowing' and 'a community of experience.' It seeks to uncover the devices of thinking and perceiving that individuals or groups use to 'accumulate, preserve, reformulate, and disseminate' their intellectual heritage in society and their connections to the social conditions or structures in which they occur . . . (p. 673)

In other words, interpersonal interactions among members of a worldwide community—including at conferences and meetings and during joint-projects, brainstorming sessions, and old-fashioned conversations—tap into new perspectives. Accordingly, they can help break down Western and other biases and build a more universal knowledge base. As discussed throughout this book, organizations like UNESCO and the WJEC are deeply involved in such efforts. So are additional stakeholders, such as, universities, news outlets, media advocacy groups, think tanks, and foundations, which help fund activities.

When it comes to students, social interactions, especially journalism related and on international soil, seem especially effective. A good example of student connections taking place within a global media literacy institution combating Western bias can be found at the Salzburg Academy on Media & Global Change (www.salzburg.umd.edu). The academy gathers students and scholars from around the world to investigate the intersection of media, civic agency, and global change. As they share essential human connections, they grapple with some of the most important global issues of the day and how to cover them. Along the way, they challenge cultural biases coloring their often nation-based perceptions and narratives about information, news, and the world at large. As mentioned throughout this book, journalism educators around the globe continue to push for international student experiences despite limited funding and institution-based structural support.

As for the current state of news literacy, American professor Paul Mihailidis—director of the Salzburg Academy and a prominent global news literacy professor and expert—is encouraged by what he calls a significant growth of media literacy training in the United States over the past five years (P. Mihailidis, personal communication, December 16, 2016). Mihailidis adds that global media literacy training throughout the world is limited, mostly due to a lack of funding. That said, international educators and students, including those based at the Danish School of Media and Journalism and Beirut's Media and Digital Literacy Lab (MDLab), are demonstrating a passionate interest in such endeavors. He says he is heartened by this inclination since future storytellers need to truly understand the world they live in to effectively advance civic life and critical discourse.

The Future of Global Journalism Education: Educators Leading the Way

This book, and the research that informs it, makes me optimistic about global journalism education's future and its ability to prepare future storytellers for their incredibly important societal roles during the new post-truth era. Throughout *Global Journalism Education,* the many challenges educators and students face are clear. Yet so are the many innovations, and innovators, dealing with them. Educational systems and professional bureaucracies are slow to adapt. However, innovative administrators, educators, and professionals—many featured in this book—are finding, and sharing, creative ways to teach quality journalism in a continuously changing news ecosystem.

In the introduction to this book, I posed the following question: Are journalism educators dedicated enough to their field—and do they possess enough chutzpah—to make needed changes and innovations possible? My answer: a resounding "yes." This book's top scholars/professionals alone have demonstrated the type of conceptual thinking, theory building, empirical investigations, and technical skills needed to meet global journalism education's challenges. And they have done so with palpable passion for their field. Educators have a deep commitment to teaching their students how to most effectively seek the truth and report it. They will continue to do so by inspiring their students to question the status quo, challenge cultural biases, and expose flawed/fake news infiltrating societies worldwide. And that is good news not only for journalism's vibrant future, but also for citizens of the world pursuing freedom and dignity for all. A March 2017 *Time* magazine cover story asks, "Is Truth Dead?" (Scherer, 2017). Global journalism education's answer: Not as long as educators, students, journalists, and citizens continue to passionately seek it out.

References

Chang, T. K., Himelboim, I., & Dong, D. (2009). Open global networks, closed international flows: World system and political economy of hyperlinks in cyberspace. *International Communication Gazette*, *71*(3), 137-159.

Chang, T. K., Southwell, B. G., Lee, H. M., & Hong, Y. (2012). Jurisdictional protectionism in online news: American journalists and their perceptions of hyperlinks. *New media & Society*, *14*(4), 684-700.

Chang, T. K., & Tai, Z. (2005). Mass communication research and the invisible college revisited: The changing landscape and emerging fronts in journalism-related studies. *Journalism and Mass Communication Quarterly*, *82*(3), 672-694.

Nordenstreng, K. (2009). Soul-searching at the crossroads of European journalism education. *European Journalism Education*, 511-517.

Scherer, Michael. Can President Trump Handle the Truth?" *Time*, 23 Mar. 2017. Retrieved from http://time.com/4710614/donald-trump-fbi-surveil-lance-house-intelligence-committee/?xid=homepage&pcd=hp-magmod

Contributors

Wajeehah Aayeshah is Senior Tutor (Curriculum Design) at The University of Melbourne, Australia. She earned her Ph.D. from the Swinburne University of Technology, Australia. Her thesis explores the use of games in journalism education. She also holds an M.A. in Film, TV and Media Studies from the University of Auckland, New Zealand, and an MPhil and a B.S. in Communication Studies from The University of Punjab, Pakistan. Wajeehah has been teaching media and communication studies courses for eight years. Her current research interests are in media studies, journalism studies, educational technology, educational games, practice-based education, and intercultural communication. She is a guest editor for *Asia Pacific Media Educator* (APME) and has professional experience in the media and journalism industry. Email: wajeehah@gmail.com

Rasha Allam is Affiliate Professor of Journalism and Mass Communication at the American University in Cairo. Dr. Allam is a specialist in media management with an emphasis on broadcast media regulations. She serves on the editorial advisory board of the *Journal of Social Studies* and the *Journal of Telecommunication and Information Technology*. Her research interests include Egyptian and Arab media systems and Arab press and broadcast media laws and regulations. Email: rallam@aucegypt.edu

Hussein Amin is Professor of Journalism and Mass Communication at the American University in Cairo. He earned a Ph.D. from The Ohio State University. He has been an invited lecturer to many universities around the world and has presented keynote addresses to different international media organizations and communication associations. Dr. Amin is an active contributor to an extensive list of communication journals and internationally recognized media publications. In addition to his academic work, he has been recognized for his media projects and professional work. Dr. Amin has received numerous awards to recognize his contributions to the journalism and mass communication field. His research mainly focuses on global media systems, with an emphasis on Middle Eastern media law and policies. Email: h_amin@aucegypt.edu

Guy Berger is former Head of the School of Journalism and Media Studies at Rhodes University, Grahamstown, South Africa. He led the school's hosting of the second World Journalism Education Congress (WJEC) in South Africa in July 2010. Under his leadership, the university held five colloquia on South African journalism education. Between 2006 and 2010, he worked with UNESCO to map and network African journalism schools, which led to the identification of potential centers of excellence on the continent. In 2011, he joined UNESCO as director for freedom of expression and media development. His work includes overseeing an initiative to promote international conversations about excellence in journalism education, as well as the commissioning and publishing of selected global syllabi for cutting-edge issues in journalism education. E-mail: g.berger@unesco.org

Arnold S. de Beer is Professor Extraordinary in the Department of Journalism at Stellenbosch University, South Africa, and former Head of Communication Studies at Free State University and North-West University. His research topics include journalism education and the role of media in society. In 1980 he founded *Ecquid Novi: The South African Research Journal for Journalism*, now titled *African Journalism Studies*, the first ISI-listed communication journal in Africa. He edited *Global Journalism: Topical Issues and Media Systems* (5th edition, 2005). He is a member of the executive committee and African coordinator of the Worlds of Journalism Study. He is a former member of the South African Broadcasting Corporation (SABC) Board, South African Press Council, and South African Press Ombudsman Appeal's Committee. Email: asdebeer@imasa.org

Mira K. Desai is Associate Professor and In-Charge Head at the Department of Extension Education, Shreemati Nathibai Damodar Thackersey (SNDT) Women's University, Mumbai, India. She has qualifications in commerce, development communication, distance education, women's studies, and gender and home science. She also has professional experience as a freelance journalist, television host, documentary filmmaker, and researcher. She has 25 years of experience in social/communication/media research, documentation, and communication education, including experience in curriculum design, teaching, administration, and assessment. She has published five books, including her doctoral work coauthored with Binod C. Agrawal (*Cry for cultural crisis: An analysis of transnational television in India,* 2009), and scholarly papers (e.g., *Television in India—Many faces,* 2010). Her research interests include audience reception, Indian television, research methodology, women's studies/gender and development, and the sociology of technology. Email: drmiradesai@gmail.com

Mark Deuze is Professor of Media Studies, specializing in journalism, in the University of Amsterdam's (UvA) Faculty of Humanities. From 2004 to 2013, he worked at Indiana University's Department of Telecommunications in Bloomington, United States. His work includes more than 50 articles in academic journals and eight books, including *Media Work* (Polity Press, 2007) and *Media Life* (Polity Press, 2012). As a journalist, he worked for newspapers in The Netherlands and South Africa. Email: M.J.P.Deuze@uva.nl

Joe Foote is Former Dean and Edward L. Gaylord Chair in the Gaylord College of Journalism and Mass Communication at the University of Oklahoma, United States. Previously, he headed the Walter Cronkite School of Journalism and Mass Communication at Arizona State University and the College of Mass Communication and Media Arts at Southern Illinois University. Before entering university teaching, Foote served as press secretary to House Speaker Carl Albert and administrative assistant to U.S. Rep. Dave McCurdy. He was a journalist at the Voice of America, KTOK Radio, and the Oklahoma News Network. Foote is the author of *Live from the trenches: The changing role of the television news correspondent* (1998) and *Television access and political power: The networks, the president, and the loyal opposition* (1990). E-mail: jfoote@ou.edu

Chris Frost is Emeritus Professor of Journalism at Liverpool John Moores University, United Kingdom. He has been a newspaper journalist, editor, and journalism educator for more than 40 years. He is a former Chair of the Association for Journalism Education, which represents university journalism departments in the United Kingdom and Ireland. He is also coeditor of *Journalism Education* and an editorial board member of several other journals. He is a member of the National Executive Committee of the National Union of Journalists and one of its former presidents, and he chairs its Ethics Council. He has authored several books, including *Journalism ethics and regulation* (2016) and *Reporting for journalists* (2010), as well as many book chapters and papers. He has also been a consultant or visiting professor in much of Eastern Europe, Malaysia, India, South East Asia, and Africa. Email: C.P.Frost@ljmu.ac.uk

Robyn S. Goodman is Professor, Director of the Communication Studies Program at Alfred University, New York, United States. Her teaching and research interests focus on improving journalistic coverage, especially international and minority ("other") related; global journalism education; and the social construction of knowledge. She publishes in top academic journals, serves as an editorial board member at the *International Communication Research Journal* (ICRJ), and is a former Head of AEJMC's International Communication Division (ICD). She is also a World Journalism Education Congress (WJEC) founding officer and an executive committee council member and an award-winning journalism professor and university newspaper adviser. She has reported for newspapers throughout the United States and continues to freelance. She also taught journalism at Beijing Foreign Studies University and guest-lectured at Lomonosov Moscow State University. She earned her Ph.D. in Mass Media (Journalism) at Michigan State University, her M.A. in News-Editorial at the University of Missouri—Columbia, and her B.A. in International Relations at California State University, Chico. Email: fgoodman@alfred.edu

Gang (Kevin) Han is Associate Professor at Greenlee School of Journalism and Communication, Iowa State University, United States. Han received his Ph.D. from Syracuse University and previously taught at the State University of New York and Fudan University. His research interests include framing, social networking analysis, health risk communication, and strategic communication, mainly from a comparative perspective with an emphasis on international implications. His articles have appeared in leading journals, such as *Journalism & Mass Communication Quarterly, Health Communication, Mass Communication & Society, Public Relations Review,* and *Asian Journal of Communication.* His book chapters have been published by Sage (London), Gakubunsha (Tokyo), Shanghai Jiaotong University Press, and Shanghai People's Press (China). Han's teaching areas include public relations, research methods, communication theory, health communication, social media, and public opinion. Email: ghan@iastate.edu

Imran Hasnat is an international Ph.D. student in journalism at the Gaylord College of Journalism and Mass Communication, University of Oklahoma. He earned an M.A. in International Relations at Jahangirnagar University in Bangladesh. His research focuses on the interrelationship between the media and international politics. He has presented conference papers on this topic and has published on domestic and international politics in the Bangladeshi popular press. In 2014 he launched an online journal, *Glocal,* focusing on international politics. Before enrolling at the University of Oklahoma, he worked as secretary to the High Commissioner of Canada to Bangladesh and was a UNESCO youth peace ambassador. Email: im@ou.edu

Julie Jones is Associate Professor at the Gaylord College of Journalism and Mass Communication, University of Oklahoma, where she teaches multimedia and mobile journalism. Her research focuses on how journalists, communities, and individuals engage with emerging technologies such as mobile devices. Her work has been published in journals such as *Journalism and Mass Communication Educator, New Media & Society,* and *The Journal of Social Media in Society.* Before earning her Ph.D. at the University of Minnesota, Jones was an award-winning video photojournalist in Arizona. She has won national teaching awards from the International Communication Association and Kappa

Theta Alpha. In addition, the National Press Photographers Association recognized Jones' by honoring her with the Joseph Costa Award, named for the founder of the nearly 70-year-old organization. Email: juliejones@ou.edu

Nicola Jones is Academic Leader of Research in the School of Arts, College of Humanities at the University of KwaZulu-Natal, South Africa. She has a D.Litt. from the former University of Durban-Westville, South Africa. Her research focuses on new media ethics, journalism, and social responsibility in media. She spent 10 years working as a political journalist and news editor and continues to freelance. Email: jonesn1@ukzn.ac.za

Seth C. Lewis, Ph.D., is the Shirley Papé Chair in Electronic Media in the School of Journalism and Communication at the University of Oregon, United States. He studies the digital transformation of journalism, publishing widely on topics such as big data, social media, open source, innovation, and digital audience analytics. He edited a special issue of *Digital Journalism* ("Journalism in an era of big data") in 2015, coedited *Boundaries of journalism: Professionalism, practices and participation* (Routledge, 2015), and won "Outstanding Journal Article of the Year" in *Journalism Studies* in 2013 for his piece "The tension between professional control and open participation: Journalism and its boundaries." Email: sclewis@uoregon.edu

Yehiel "Hilik" Limor is Former President of the Israel Communication Association, dean-elect of the School of Communication at Baqa College, and adjunct professor in the departments of communication at Tel-Aviv and Bar-Ilan universities, Israel. For many years he served as a senior correspondent and editor for Israeli newspapers and radio. He earned an M.A. in Communication from Hebrew University in Jerusalem and a Ph.D. in Political Science and Communication from Bar-Ilan University. His main fields of interest and research are media history, media ethics, and journalism. Among his publications are: *The in/outsiders: Mass media in Israel* (1998); *Lexicon of communication and media studies* (2007); *Pirate radio in Israel* (2007); *Journalism: reporting, writing and editing* (1997); *The mediators: Mass media in Israel 1948-1990* (1992); and

Public relations—Strategy and tactics (2014). Email: hilik43@013.net.il

Maria Lukina is Associate Professor of Journalism and Deputy Dean of Programs and Curricula at the Faculty of Journalism, Lomonosov Moscow State University, Russia. She heads the Online Media graduate program, and she teaches basic journalism and news reporting and writing courses. Her method of teaching intensive news production training has been included in the curricula of several Russian universities. She has published two texts, *Interviewing technologies* (2005) and *Internet media: Theory and practice* (2010), and she is the author of about 30 academic papers. Her current research focuses on online media, new trends in media content, and communication technologies. She is a board member at the European Journalism Training Association (EJTA) and other national and international associations. Email: lukina.maria@smi.msu.ru

Donica Mensing is Associate Dean at the Reynolds School of Journalism at the University of Nevada, Reno, United States. She earned degrees from the University of California, Berkeley; George Washington University, Washington, D.C.; and the University of Nevada, Reno. She coedited *Journalism education, training and employment* (2010) with Bob Franklin and has published a number of articles on journalism education. She teaches and conducts research on digital news, participatory journalism, and news networks. Email: dmensing@unr.edu

Penny O'Donnell is Senior Lecturer in International Media and Journalism at the University of Sydney, Australia. A national leader in media and journalism education for domestic and international students, she is responsible for core units in the undergraduate and graduate media and communications degree programs. She is past vice president for research of the Journalism Education and Research Association of Australia and a member of the International Communication Association (Journalism Studies Division) and the International Association for Media and Communication Research. She has authored the "Journalism Education" entry in the *Companion to Australian media* (2014) and numerous articles in journals such as *Australian Journalism*

Review, African Communication Research, Continuum, Ethical Space, Journalism, and *Journalism Practice.* Her current research investigates employment trends and cutbacks in the journalism industry around the world. Email: penny.odonnell@sydney.edu.au

Silvia Pellegrini is Dean for the School of Communications at Pontificia Universidad Católica de Chile. She has also served as the university's director of the School of Journalism, dean of the School of Letters, and vice-rector. She has been a consultant for curriculum development in several Latin American universities, leads a research group on journalism quality named VAP (the Spanish acronym for Added Journalism Value), and has published 47 peer-reviewed articles. She has been a member of the board and former president at Canal 13, a member of the National Television Council, founder and former vice president of CLAEP (Latin American Accreditation Council in Journalism), and a member of the Fulbright Foundation Board. She has been awarded four journalism awards, including the AEJMC Presidential Award in 2008. Email: spellegrini@uc.cl

Sandra Pitcher is a Contract Lecturer in the Department of Media & Cultural Studies at the University of KwaZulu-Natal (Pietermaritzburg), South Africa. She earned her M.A. at the University of KwaZulu-Natal and is currently completing her Ph.D. at the same institution. Her research interests are in new media, journalism, and media ethics. She has published a number of international, peer-reviewed journal articles and is frequently invited to speak about her research at both national and international conferences. She also works as a freelance technology journalist for a number of publications and is currently working with Google SA to design a journalism curriculum focused on the development of online skills. Email: pitcher@ukzn.ac.za

Ian Richards is Professor of Journalism at the University of South Australia in Adelaide, Australia. Since 2003 he has been the editor of the *Australian Journalism Review*, Australia's leading refereed journal in the academic fields of journalism and journalism studies. His publications include *Quagmires and quandaries: Exploring journalism ethics* (2005). He is an executive member of the Journalism Education and Research Association of Australia (JERAA) and has been on the executive committee of the World Journalism Education Council (WJEC) since 2004. He has been involved in all three WJEC congresses between 2007 and 2013, and he helped plan the 2016 conference in Auckland, New Zealand. A former newspaper journalist, he has worked and studied in Australia and the United Kingdom. Email: ian.richards@unisa.edu.au

Cindy Royal is Associate Professor in the School of Journalism and Mass Communication at Texas State University, United States. She teaches digital and data-driven media skills and concepts. She completed her Ph.D. in Journalism and Mass Communication at The University of Texas at Austin in 2005. Prior to her doctoral studies, she spent 10 years in the technology industry. Her research focuses on data journalism, coding education, and gender issues in technology. In 2013, Royal received Texas State University's Presidential Award for Excellence in Teaching and the AEJMC/Scripps Howard Journalism and Mass Communication Teacher of the Year Award. She was also a 2014 Knight Journalism Fellow at Stanford University. More detail about her research, education, and experience can be found at cindyroyal. com. Email: croyal@txstate.edu

Amy Schmitz Weiss is Associate Professor in the School of Journalism and Media Studies at San Diego State University, United States. She has a Ph.D. in Journalism from the University of Texas at Austin. Schmitz Weiss is a 2011 Dart Academic Fellow and a 2014-2015 recipient of the Challenge Fund for Innovation in Journalism Education by the Online News Association. She is also a 2011-2012 recipient of the AEJMC Bridge Grant with funding from the John S. and James L. Knight Foundation. She has worked at the *Chicago Tribune Online* and *Indianapolis Star News Online*. She teaches journalism courses in basic writing and editing, multimedia, web design, data journalism, and mobile journalism. Her research interests include online journalism, media sociology, news production, multimedia journalism, and international communication. Email: aschmitz@mail.sdsu.edu

Charles C. Self is President of 227 International, LLC, a Washington-area consulting firm focused on journalism, civil discourse, and media education. He is a former dean of the Gaylord College of Journalism and Mass Communication at the University of Oklahoma and director of its Institute for Research and Training. He is also a former president of the Association for Education in Journalism and Mass Communication (AEJMC) and the Association of Schools of Journalism & Mass Communication (ASJMC) and has served on the boards of regional and national journals and communication education organizations. He directed the global census of journalism programs for the World Journalism Education Council (WJEC) and the Knight Foundation. He has worked with journalists and journalism educators from many countries and is coauthor of a journalism book and scores of articles, book chapters, and papers about journalism and journalism education. Email: cself.self@gmail.com

Elanie Steyn is Associate Professor and the Head of Journalism at the Gaylord College of Journalism and Mass Communication, University of Oklahoma. She teaches and researches media management, women in media leadership, and business trends in media. She has been the co-Principal Investigator on nine U.S. Department of State/University of Oklahoma grants that involve students, entrepreneurs, and media professionals from South Asia. She has published several peer-reviewed articles, chapters for academic books, and international research projects. Steyn received an M.A. in Business Communication from the former Potchefstroom University (now North-West University), South Africa. She also received an M.A in Communication Policy Studies from City University, London, United Kingdom, and a Ph.D. in Business Management at North-West University, South Africa. Email: Elanie@ou.edu

Elena Vartanova is Professor, Dean, and Chair in Media Theory and Economics at the Faculty of Journalism, Lomonosov Moscow State University, Russia. Her research focuses on Russian media systems, media economics, media theory, and journalism in Russia. Dr. Vartanova has published more than 10 academic monographs, including *Post-Soviet* *transformations of Russian mass media and journalism* (2014). Recently she also contributed chapters to *Comparing media systems beyond the Western world*, edited by Hallin and Mancini (2012), and *Mapping BRICS media*, edited by Nordenstreng and Thussu (2015). She is a president of the National Association for Media Researchers (NAMMI) and a member of different international organizations. Dr. Vartanova is also the editor of the academic journals *Medi@lmanac*, *MediaScope*, and *Media Trends*. Email: eva@smi.msu.ru

Melissa Wall is Professor in the College of Arts, Media and Communication at California State University—Northridge, United States, where she researches and teaches participatory and mobile media. She is the editor of *Citizen journalism: Valuable, useless or dangerous?* (2012). She was a Fulbright Scholar in Lebanon and an Open Society Foundation International Scholar in Ukraine. She has also taught journalism to early career professionals in Ethiopia. Her B.A. is from the University of Virginia, and her M.A. and Ph.D. are from the University of Washington. Email: melissawall@gmail.com

Felix Wao is Director of Academic Assessment at the University of Oklahoma. He holds a B.S. in Mathematics from St. Mary's University of Minnesota and an M.A. and Ph.D. in Higher Educational Administration and Policy Studies from the Catholic University of America, Washington, D.C. His research focuses on the use of assessment and analytics to enhance student learning in higher education. He has presented at various national and regional assessment conferences, including American Educational Research Association (AERA), Association of Institutional Research (AIR), Assessment Institute, and the Higher Learning Commission (HLC). He has spent more than 11 years overseeing development and implementation of assessment in research institutions. He is a member of the HLC Peer Review Corps and a Mentor in the HLC Assessment Academy. Email: wao@ou.edu

Oscar Westlund, Ph.D., serves as Research Leader for Media Inquiry ("Medieutredningen") at the Government Offices of Sweden, Ministry of Culture. He also holds a tenured position as Associate Professor at the University of Gothenburg, Sweden. Westlund has, for a decade, researched the production, distribution, and consumption of news through various methods, focusing especially on the shifts toward digital technologies such as mobile media. He has published more than 60 book chapters and reports and articles in approximately 20 international journals. He serves on the editorial boards of *Digital Journalism, Journal of Media Business Studies, Journal of Media Innovations*, and *Mobile Media & Communication.* Email: oscarwestlund@gmail.com